Indigenous Intellectuals

Indigenous Intellectuals

Knowledge, Power,
and Colonial Culture in
Mexico and the Andes

Gabriela Ramos and
Yanna Yannakakis,
EDITORS

Duke University Press
DURHAM & LONDON 2014

Printed in the United States of America on acid-free paper ♾
Designed by Kristina Kachele
Typeset in Quadraat by Tseng Information Systems, Inc.
Library of Congress Cataloging-in-Publication Data
Indigenous intellectuals : knowledge, power, and colonial culture in Mexico
and the Andes / Gabriela Ramos and Yanna Yannakakis, editors.
pages   cm
Includes bibliographical references and index.
ISBN 978-0-8223-5647-9 (cloth : alk. paper)
ISBN 978-0-8223-5660-8 (pbk. : alk. paper)
1. Indians of Mexico—Intellectual life.   2. Indians of Mexico—Civilization.
3. Indigenous peoples—Andes—Intellectual life.   4. Indigenous peoples—Andes—
Civilization.   I. Ramos, Gabriela.   II. Yannakakis, Yanna, 1967–
F1219.3.I56I53 2014
305.80098—dc23
2013045004

For Nancy Farriss

Contents

Foreword

Elizabeth Hill Boone

Tlamatini
In tlamatini tlauilli ocutl, tomaoac ocutl apocio, tezteatl, coiaoac
tezcatl, necoc xapo, tlile, tlapale, amuxoa, amoxe, tlilli, tlapalli,
utli, teiacanqui, tlanelo, teuicani, tlauicani, tlaiacanqui

The Wise Man
The wise man [is] exemplary. He possesses writings; he owns books. [He is] the tradition,
the road; a leader of men, a rower, a companion, a bearer of responsibility, a guide.

Thus begins the description of the position of sage in the Preconquest society of the Mexica Aztecs, according to the Franciscan friar Bernardino de
Sahagún in Book 10 of his *Florentine Codex: General History of the Things of New
Spain*.[1] Sahagún included the sage among the male occupations of the indigenous people. Although tlamatini is usually translated into Spanish as "sabio"
and into English as "wise man," the Nahuatl tlamatini is gendered neutral,
and there are accounts of accomplished female poets, so we should also recognize women among the *tlamatinime*.[2] These Mexica tlamatinime were intellectuals, readers, and implicitly also writers of books using the indigenous
pictographic script, persons who had personal libraries of such books, and
likely had access to larger libraries attached to temple complexes and noble

palaces. By means of these books, the tlamatinime had cultural knowledge reaching from the deep past and extending to the then present. Their knowledge of history and traditions gained through studying their books enabled them to chart a course forward for their people. Their communities therefore looked to them to be both "the tradition," with access to the past, and "the road" that led from that past surely and clearly into the future. In these ways, the sage was a leader and guide. Often sages were of noble birth, a social distinction that carried its own sense of responsibility, but the knowledge they held brought even greater responsibilities for leadership. Sahagún qualifies this position of leadership, however, by describing the sage as "a companion, a rower," which conveys the understanding that the sage was not above the community, as a supreme ruler or *huetlatoani* (great speaker) was, but instead was one member of the community who strove alongside the others as a leader among men and women.

Sahagún's description of the sage presents us with an ideal type. The sage is not only a kind of individual but is also an occupation, one that was defined vis-á-vis a great variety of other occupations (from nobleman to singer and stonecutter). There is a conceptual purity to this characterization of the Preconquest sage, as if all sages were simply versions of a single ideal. This purity greatly belied the multiethnic, multilingual, and heterogeneous nature of central Mexican culture in the century before the Spanish conquest. The sage so described was also idealized from the perspective of people who had already undergone fifty years of Spanish occupation, who looked back on a Preconquest past that had already ceased to exist, and who viewed with eyes and minds that were inculcated in European ways of seeing and thinking. Sahagún's *General History*, including this description, was written in the late 1570s with the copious assistance of many of the sons of the Mexica and other Nahua lords who had been trained since childhood in the schools established by the Franciscans soon after the conquest. These Franciscan-trained noblemen were the ones who provided Sahagún with the knowledge and wording to characterize the ancient sages.

The Nahua men who assisted Sahagún may have also conceptualized themselves as tlamatinime, casting their present set of skills, knowledge, and social obligations optimistically as a continuation from the Preconquest past. Certainly they knew how to read and write (in the new European system as well as the old indigenous one); they had access to books (both pictographic screenfolds and bound alphabetic books); they were among the leaders of

ELIZABETH HILL BOONE

their people in the difficult decades of the middle to late sixteenth century; and they carried responsibility both for preserving knowledge of the past and for guiding their people forward through the economic and cultural tumult of the times. In all these ways, they bore the attributes and responsibilities of the tlamatinime.

The new colonial intellectuals, however, lacked the conceptual purity characteristic of the ancient sages. With the influx of Europeans, Africans, and Asians after the conquest, their world became profoundly multicultural to an extent that makes the century prior to the conquest seem culturally cohesive, and their occupation was much more challenging than that of their forerunners. The situation of indigenous intellectuals in the early colonial period was radically different from that of the Preconquest past. Their great libraries had been lost at the fall of Tenochtitlan, Texcoco, and other metropolitan centers. The administrative systems that supported the Preconquest sages had been consciously disbanded if they had not simply collapsed because of the social disruption, and the old master sages had died. The old religion was outlawed, and the traditional political system had been usurped and contorted to serve Spanish colonial ends. This was no less true in the Andes than in Mexico.

In place of the old sages, a new kind of tlamatinime was born, one trained in mendicant or Jesuit schools and educated in European ideals, practices, and forms of discourse. They were taught to speak Latin and Spanish, to write these languages as well as indigenous ones alphabetically, and to read the newly introduced European art of pictorial illusionism. They learned the literature of the European classical authors, to the extent that some became great rhetoricians, considered by the friars to be as accomplished as the great classical rhetoricians Cicero and Quintilian.[3] Moreover, they were forged in a pragmatism necessitated by the conquest, the demographic collapse, and the domination by European systems and expectations.

But these men (and the colonial intellectuals all seem to have been men) necessarily kept a foot in the colonial vestige of the world of their ancestors. Although this world had been profoundly compromised and altered following the conquest, they still retained some knowledge of the earlier times and earlier ways or could access indigenous documents that contained this knowledge. In Mexico and the Andes they participated as researchers and analysts in projects to recapture and record knowledge of the ancient ways. In Mexico they maintained pictographic competence, and in the Andes some of them retained literacy in khipus.

Their task was to make sense of both the Spanish culture as it was adapted to the Americas and the indigenous culture that had evolved under Spanish domination, all within the reality of the bicultural, multilingual world of their times. In this respect the indigenous intellectuals found themselves straddling both cultures, functioning as mediators (translators, interpreters, and social guides). They facilitated and enabled Spanish projects to understand indigenous society (such as those of Sahagún in Mexico and Francisco de Avila in Peru), and they worked as activists for their indigenous communities. They enabled indigenous individuals and polities to acquire rights and privileges and to negotiate for positions of power within the Spanish colonial system. For their indigenous communities they helped legitimize the authority of the ruling elites and helped communities retain their lands. For the Spanish, they brought access to these indigenous communities and populations because not only were they partially of these communities, they could also interpret indigenous discourses. The indigenous intellectuals were key contributors to the success of both groups in reaching a variety of goals.

This volume is the first to focus squarely on the political lives, productions, and epistemological networks of these key agents of colonial culture in Latin America—the indigenous intellectuals—and it does so through a broadly comparative lens, embracing both Mexico and the Andes. Although others have focused on some of the same individuals and the production and impact of indigenous literature, contributing importantly to an impressive corpus of scholarship on indigenous agency in the colonial period,[4] none have targeted the indigenous intellectual as squarely as a group, nor has there been much comparative analysis between Mexico and the Andes. With the recent growth of so much well theorized and deeply probing scholarship concerning indigenous people following the conquest, it is a fitting time to focus on the intellectuals who made colonial culture possible.

Containing chapters by top scholars in the field, the volume has the potential to move colonial studies forward in a significant way. It brings a richness and nuance to our perspective on early colonial Latin America because of several respects. First, it extends the definition of the intellectual more broadly than has heretofore been done, to include not solely authors of literary works, such as histories and religious texts, but also the interpreters, scribes, notaries, and legal agents who mediated importantly between indigenous and Spanish cultures, expectations, and discourses. It recognizes that some of the same scholarly issues are informed by analyzing the local scribe who controls the "paper khipus" in the Andes as well as the Nahua his-

ELIZABETH HILL BOONE

torian don Domingo de San Antón Muñón Chimalpahin Quauhtlehuanitzin writing in Mexico about the glories of his ancestors. Second, the volume considers the range of cultural contexts in which these individuals practiced and especially the networks of knowledge production and circulation in which they participated: from their formal training in Spanish religious schools (in the major centers) and their critical positions with colonial courts and indigenous communities, to the less formal networks of knowledge production within indigenous communities in rural areas. Third, the volume is purposefully attentive to the similarities and the differences between Mexico and the Andes, recognizing that their differences stem both from their distinct Preconquest cultures as well as the varied nature of the Spanish domination. The volume recognizes, and allows the reader to see, that one can best understand a particular cultural expression by studying others that differ and thus bring its own features into starker relief.

Indigenous Intellectuals participates in a very exciting and rewarding trend in colonial studies, one that is characterized by well-targeted investigation and perceptive analysis of the many varied cultural elements that composed the colonial situation. This investigative trend looks beyond and through systemic Spanish dominance to highlight the many forms of indigenous agency. This is a trend that not only recognizes that ethnic and social pluralism is more than simply the indigenous people versus the Spaniards but is also composed of a complex mosaic of individuals who themselves are culturally mixed and who pursue specific agendas according to local demands. Framed as they are in this volume by a broadly theoretical introduction and synthetic conclusion, the specific and the local are allowed to inform powerfully about the larger issues of colonialism.

Notes

1. Bernardino de Sahagún, *Florentine Codex: General History of the Things of New Spain*, Book 10, 29.

2. Elizabeth H. Boone, "In Tlamatinime: The Wise Men and Women of Aztec Mexico," 9–25.

3. Robert Ricard, *The Spiritual Conquest of Mexico*, 223; Frances Karttunen, "From Court Yard to the Seat of Government: The Career of Antonio Valeriano, Nahua Colleague of Bernardino De Sahagún."

4. See, for example, Rolena Adorno, *Guaman Poma: Writing and Resistance in Colonial Peru*; Louise Burkhart, *The Slippery Earth: Nahua-Christian Moral Dialogue in Sixteenth-Century Mexico*; Kathryn Burns, *Into the Archive: Writing and Power in Colonial Peru*; John Charles,

Allies at Odds: The Andean Church and Its Indigenous Agents, 1583–1671; Durston, *Pastoral Quechua: The History of Christian Translation in Colonial Peru, 1550–1650*; Frances Karttunen, *Between Worlds: Interpreters, Guides, and Survivors*; Susan Schroeder, *Chimalpahin and the Kingdoms of Chalco*; Camilla Townsend, *Here in This Year: Seventeenth-Century Nahuatl Annals of the Tlaxcala-Puebla Valley*; and Yanna Yannakakis, *The Art of Being In-between: Native Intermediaries, Indian Identity, and Local Rule in Colonial Oaxaca*.

ELIZABETH HILL BOONE

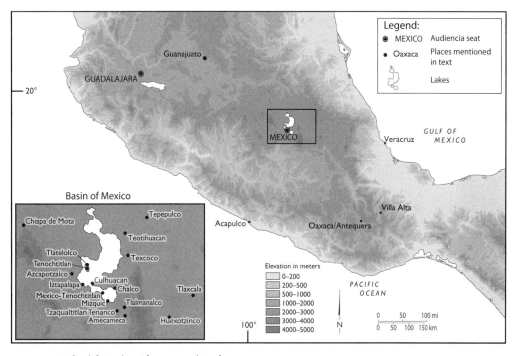

Colonial Mexico: Places mentioned.

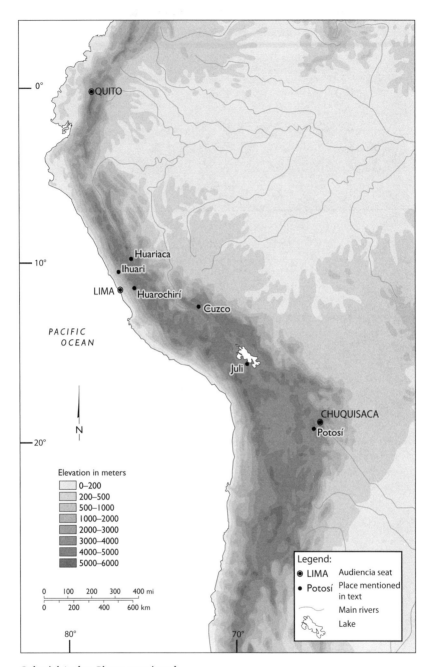

Colonial Andes: Places mentioned.

Acknowledgments

This volume originated with a panel titled "Indigenous Intellectuals in Mexico and the Andes" organized by the editors at the 2009 American Historical Association Annual Meeting and Conference on Latin American History. Our objective was to further our understanding of political culture in Latin America, particularly how indigenous people operated within bureaucracy, shaped civil and ecclesiastical institutions; and in their roles, interpreted, translated, and represented indigenous individual and collective objectives for diverse audiences. The discussion, which focused on these figures' ideological and practical actions, left us wanting more. The panel, which spanned the colonial period to the present, made clear that the scholarship on indigenous intellectuals in contemporary Latin America is much more developed than that of the colonial period. We also felt strongly that to analyze the role of indigenous intellectuals in the making of colonial culture and society, we needed to approach Mexico and the Andes, the sites of the hemisphere's two major pre-Columbian societies and colonial viceroyalties, from a comparative perspective. Few colonial studies have compared the two regions; doing so puts much that we take for granted in each field into strong relief.

With a comparative volume in mind, we organized a symposium at Cambridge University in September 2010, and invited both veteran and up-and-coming scholars from a wide range of disciplines—history, anthropology, art history, Spanish literature, and linguistics—whose research spoke directly to our concerns. We would like to thank the institutions and individuals that made the symposium a success: The Trevelyan Fund of the Faculty of History, University of Cambridge; the University of Cambridge Centre for Research in the Arts, Social Sciences, and Humanities (CRASSH), especially Michelle Maciejewska and Sam Mather; and the Centre of Latin American Studies, University of Cambridge. We would also like to thank Newnham College, Cambridge, Senior Members Research Fund who provided resources for organizing the symposium and editing this volume, and Emory University College of Arts and Sciences and the Laney Graduate School for providing a subvention for the maps and index.

When we approached Valerie Millholland and Gisela Fosado, editors at Duke University Press, about the idea for the volume, they were enthusiastic and supportive, but also told us "don't do it!" Based on extensive experience, they cautioned us that editing a volume could lead to endless headaches. We have been very lucky on that front. The professionalism of our contributors has streamlined our editing work and made it quite enjoyable. We thank all of them. We would also like to thank Valerie Millholland for taking on this project, Gisela Fosado for her meticulous guidance, and the anonymous reviewers at Duke University Press for their valuable comments. We would also like to thank Tom Cummins and Michael Swanton for their contributions to the symposium. Special thanks go to Anne Pushkal, who helped us with editing, and Daniel Giannoni and Natalia Majluf, who generously provided images, and Evelyne Mesclier, who edited the maps.

Finally, it gives us real pleasure to dedicate this book to Nancy Farriss, a distinguished scholar of colonial Latin America, whose work has significantly shaped the field. We are grateful for her mentorship, and her ideas and influence are at work in this volume.

Introduction

Gabriela Ramos and Yanna Yannakakis

This volume offers a framework for approaching and understanding indigenous intellectuals and their knowledge in the colonial context. Although we recognize that classifying knowledge into neat categories obscures historical realities it is useful for analytical purposes to conceive of it as primarily pragmatic or ideological. By pragmatic, we mean knowledge acquired and expressed through habitus and performance, which could be mobilized and put into action. By ideological, we mean knowledge in its discursive forms, more widely recognizable as intellectual production. We assume that indigenous intellectuals produced and made use of both forms simultaneously. The challenge for historians is to move beyond the assumption that intellectuals were those who wrote, an assumption reinforced by the fact that writing provides the most accessible evidence of intellectual work. We can access traces of the pragmatic work of indigenous intellectuals by paying attention to their practical action and by focusing on what they did to make colonial society viable.

To further our understanding of indigenous agency in colonial life, we must broaden our conception of intellectual work to encompass this pragmatic aspect. In this regard, we find particularly useful Antonio Gramsci's definition of an intellectual. In principle, all people are intellectuals in that anyone facing any task must make use of both knowledge and experience stored in her/his mind. However, certain people are distinguishable as intellectuals by virtue of their directive, organizational, or educative function in society. Intellectuals not only lead, but also persuade, mediate, and animate.[1] Steven Feierman's study of peasant intellectuals in colonial and postcolonial Tanzania, which expands upon Gramsci's paradigm, provides a model for the study of intellectuals in pragmatic terms.[2] Feierman examines the interface between continuity and change in the wide and complex arena of political action. Following Feierman's lead, we ask: how did indigenous intellectuals make choices and adaptations—ideological, linguistic, and performative— between new and well-established practices and beliefs as they dealt with a range of authorities and forces within colonial society? What were the different incarnations and political significances of such choices?

Our decision to call the individuals whose lives and work are discussed in this book *intellectuals* expresses our understanding of the role indigenous people played in shaping the colonial state and society in Spanish America.[3] This understanding was not encompassed by the term often used at the time to refer to what we would today call an intellectual (*letrado*). Letrado referenced the small and exclusive world of those literate in Latin, although it also extended to the larger number of (usually) university-educated Spaniards and creoles. Because of its association with the white colonial elite, the term implicitly carried racial connotations.[4] In short, the idea of letrado implied its opposite: the illiterate Indian who was simultaneously a passive recipient of European culture, someone to be acculturated, but also someone incapable of creatively engaging with Spaniards on their terms.

The story we present here is a different one. The relation between conquerors and conquered was not a one-way process. Although many historical sources suggest that the Spanish often dismissed or undermined indigenous epistemology, a closer reading reveals that Spaniards maintained an ambiguous relationship to indigenous intellectuals; they often feared indigenous knowledge, and longed to capture, control, and make it their own. For their part, native people did not cling obstinately to their traditional beliefs, means, and values for the sake of resistance, but made use of knowledge rooted in the past as a means of survival, in the widest sense of the term possible. The impulse toward survival also encouraged innovation. In an effort to make colonial life feasible, native people quickly engaged with and adapted to new media, ideas, and practices in order to advance their own interests within the often difficult circumstances of Spanish colonial rule. Coloni-

GABRIELA RAMOS AND YANNA YANNAKAKIS

zation thus involved mutual loans, thefts, struggles, and negotiations over knowledge.[5]

Forms of Knowledge and Their Value

Spanish attitudes toward indigenous knowledge were ambiguous and changed over time. In fact, much of what we know today about pre-Columbian indigenous cultures has survived thanks to detailed descriptions of a range of activities, ideas, objects, monuments, and stories usually penned by missionaries who were also committed to their destruction or transformation. Spanish interests oscillated between the ideological and the practical, and the choices of what to keep and what to repress must have been the subject of continuous debate. For example, fray Bernardino de Sahagún presided over the gathering of a marvelous collection of stories about the Nahua, stories whose contents and significance the friars most likely wanted to do away with. Alongside *pagan* myths, Sahagún also compiled an important body of indigenous medical knowledge. Numerous therapies and references to curative plants abound in his *General History of the Things of New Spain*, though removed from the rituals intrinsic to their uses and thus effectiveness.[6] A few decades later, the Augustinian friar Antonio de la Calancha wrote that Spanish doctors travelled across the Andes to learn about medicinal plants from indigenous medical specialists.[7] The Second Lima Church Council (1567) agreed to grant indigenous medics special permits to exercise their trade with the proviso that they should limit themselves to curing their patients, dispensing with any religious references or insinuations.[8] The owners of these permits not only performed their task without fear of being persecuted, but also presented themselves to their potential clients as *bachilleres* and *licenciados*, granting themselves the authority enjoyed by their Spanish colleagues who had attended medical school.[9] For all the mistrust and hatred the Spanish professed for indigenous healers—who were often local religious specialists—they had to admit that the care of the bodies and minds of a good proportion of the people lay in their hands.[10] This ambiguous attitude resulted in tense relations between Spanish priests and officials and indigenous healers and other intellectuals, and erupted from time to time in local conflicts or extirpation campaigns.

As the example of healing reveals, indigenous forms of knowledge were embedded in deep and wide-ranging contexts of ritual practice and social and cultural authority. Thus the historical traces of this knowledge—primarily in written form—lack the crucial contexts in which they were produced. To recover this lost world, we must seek out indigenous intellectuals and writers in their daily lives and social webs, in their practices and habits of mind. It is not only one voice that speaks in the texts they produced but also the voices belonging to people who never put pen to paper. Even if we cannot access these voices definitively, we must be aware of them as we consider questions of authorship and intellectual and political agency.

All knowledge had political significance, evidenced by Spanish reactions and responses to indigenous expressions of it. When indigenous intellectuals wrote and acted, they made choices. In making those choices, they innovated using the materials, discourses, and traditions available to them. Some of these intellectual resources were rooted in the past. The work of indigenous intellectuals was to transform these resources according to the circumstances of the colonial present.

Alphabetic writing marks one of the most enduring and significant innovations in the hands of indigenous intellectuals. Before we elaborate on the relationship of writing to indigenous knowledge, a cautionary note on writing is in order. The focus on writing can obscure the social contexts in which it was produced, communicated, and performed. Indigenous intellectuals wrote for a reason. What elicited their writing? What were they responding to and attempting to shape? Writing had an immensely transformative impact on indigenous society. Even the most simple document—a one-page petition written by a municipal scribe in a mountain village to a court interpreter in the district seat or in the Real Audiencia—can help us understand the transformative effect of writing on indigenous social and political life. The effort that writing entailed in a society that did not practice it fifty years earlier is difficult to fathom. The transformation of orality into the written word entailed a complex process of standardization, a system of orthography, a familiarity with genres and forms, and a deep knowledge of the Other: its institutions, authorities, and expectations. The aforementioned scribe had to imagine the halls of the Real Audiencia in which the university-trained judge made sense of the petition that he had penned. The scribe made himself heard through the marvel of pen and paper, though the petition represented the tip of an iceberg: a collective process of voicing a complaint, in which the municipal council and village notables drew upon traditional and newer forms of conflict resolution and authoritative discourse, and in some cases, indigenous forms of inscription. Writing was therefore not only the most visible and readily comprehensible form of knowledge; it was also em-

GABRIELA RAMOS AND YANNA YANNAKAKIS

bedded in other complexes of knowledge and action. At its foundation, then, writing was a collective enterprise.

Over the course of the sixteenth century and afterward, alphabetic writing became the dominant means by which many indigenous intellectuals encoded knowledge. At the same time, images and other forms of inscription persisted and influenced alphabetic writing, making Spanish colonial society semiologically plural.[11] Any discussion of indigenous intellectual production in Spanish America must contend explicitly with scholarly debates regarding the relationship of indigenous forms of inscription to alphabetic writing and the longstanding assumption of the superiority of alphabetic writing. Elizabeth Hill Boone, Walter Mignolo, and Frank Salomon have argued persuasively that pre-Hispanic Mesoamerican and Andean peoples wrote without words, thereby countering models that put orality and writing on opposite ends of an evolutionary scale.[12] In the Mesoamerican case, pictographic writing, and in the Andean case *quipus*, represented *semasiographic* forms[13] of communication and record keeping whose independence from speech rendered them legible across geographically expansive and linguistically diverse empires. Like musical notation or chemical formulas, these forms of inscription could be understood by anyone who knew the code, thereby transcending language barriers. For the Inca and Mexica empires—which were highly diverse linguistically—this was crucial. Indeed, one could argue that quipus and pictographic writing served their political and social contexts better than alphabetic writing.

As discussed above, in the early colonial period, Spanish officials recognized the value of indigenous forms of inscription, in part because they served the exigencies of imperial administrative record keeping. But they were also wary of these forms of knowledge, and through the first half of the colonial period, Spanish officials oscillated among encouraging, accepting, and suppressing their production. The commissioning by the viceroy of New Spain Antonio de Mendoza of the pictographic manuscript the *Codex Mendoza*,[14] which recounted the Aztec tribute system, and the acceptance by Spaniards in the Andes of quipus as records of tribute collection, provide perfect examples. Viceroy Francisco Toledo summoned *quipucamayocs* and used their testimonies to rewrite the history of the Inca Empire.[15] Even parish priests suggested that quipus could be used for confession, and in fact it seems that such was the case.[16] However, an ambiguous attitude toward the quipu prevailed, as seen in testimonies stating that the Spanish prohibited the use of quipus, and Toledo ordered their suppression. Historians who have used the "domination versus resistance" paradigm to analyze this process argue that Spaniards forbade the use of quipus and destroyed them en masse. Upon closer scrutiny, however, Spanish attitudes toward quipus were much more complex.

In the case of Mesoamerica, the value that Spaniards placed on pictographic images had as much to do with the high status of the image in the world of the European Renaissance and its truth value vis à vis the written word.[17] Manifestations of disillusion with pictographic writing and other forms of knowledge include the period of the early seventeenth century when Spanish priests and officials in both New Spain and the Andes became increasingly pessimistic about the evangelical enterprise given what they termed the persistence of idolatry, and about the abilities of indigenous people to fully grasp the Christian doctrine. In light of this, Spanish officialdom came to see indigenous forms of inscription as tainted by the brush of pre-Hispanic idolatry, and therefore dangerous.

Despite the oscillation of Spanish attitudes toward indigenous forms of inscription, the alphabetic documents that indigenous intellectuals produced bore the marks of the native genres that provided their sources, models, and inspiration. The authors of this volume's essays provide a range of examples of the ways in which native authors and functionaries drew upon these resources, whether pictographic annals as in the cases of seventeenth-century Nahua historian Chimalpahin (Schroeder),[18] collective oral performance as in the cases of don Juan Buenaventura Zapata's annals (Townsend), mythical accounts in the case of the *Huarochirí manuscript* (Durston), or quipus as in the case of notarial records produced by the *quilcaycamayoc* (indigenous notaries, literally "paper keepers") (Burns). How should we conceive of these forms of intellectual production? They were rendered in alphabetic writing yet some were structured according to older systems of inscription and epistemological forms. Many also bore the stamp of ecclesiastical written forms such as confessional manuals and *doctrinas*. Clearly, these documents belong neither to an indigenous or European archive. In keeping with modern scholarly fashions, it might be tempting to characterize them as hybrid. However, we are sympathetic to Carolyn Dean and Dana Leibsohn's cautionary critique of the misapplication of the term *hybridity*. As Dean and Leibsohn put it, "because cultures are collective, they are inherently heterogeneous."[19] Indeed, the indigenous intellectuals who wrote histories and annals did not likely remark on the heterogeneous nature of their production. Rather, it was part of the fabric of the colonial culture in which they lived and that had

GABRIELA RAMOS AND YANNA YANNAKAKIS

existed prior to European conquest: pre-Columbian Amerinidian empires were multiethnic, linguistically diverse, and culturally plural. Native intellectuals before and after the conquest negotiated heterogeneous forms of power, legitimacy, and authority. An important change that marked the colonial period was that indigenous intellectuals had to negotiate the Spanish idea of the colonial Indian. In doing so, they participated in its construction and ongoing formulation.

Some indigenous intellectuals harnessed Spanish written genres to their purposes, often to chronicle the histories of their ethnic polities or lineages. The important work of scholars who have studied and written about indigenous-language histories and chronicles has widened the tight circle of the early modern literary cannon to include indigenous intellectuals like Felipe Guaman Poma de Ayala, Juan de Santa Cruz Pachacuti Yamqui Salcamaygua, and Domingo Francisco de San Antón Muñón Chimalpahin.[20] Yet as Susan Schroeder notes in her essay, for most modern scholars, the measure of indigenous intellectualism remains Western. And as Alan Durston points out in his essay, in the case of the *Huarochirí Manuscript*, one of the questions about the work is whether or not it constitutes a "book." The chapters in this volume attend to these problems of classification by challenging neat oppositions between European and indigenous forms of knowledge and writing.

Colonialism pushed indigenous people to adapt the directive and organizational roles that existed in their societies prior to the conquest. Some indigenous elites successfully molded their skills and knowledge according to colonial forms, whereas a few remained more loyal to traditional practices. Those few, if caught, incurred the wrath of Spanish authorities, who penalized them. Hereditary leaders were deposed, and ritual specialists were forced underground. In this regard, colonialism worked along two lines: it undermined the authority of some while allowing social mobility for others. This socially mobile group became scribes, notaries, legal agents, and interpreters, and as a group, they constituted the fulcrum of colonial institutions and flourished in the colonial world. One of the innovations of this volume is to conceive of socially mobile colonial functionaries as intellectuals in their own right. Crucially, the knowledge that they produced for administrative and legal purposes—wills, bills of sale, or the records of indigenous municipalities—provided the grist for colonial rule.[21] In particular, their widespread engagement with the law through written documentation produced in the context of notarial record keeping and litigation testifies to the colonial legal system's capaciousness and social depth, and to its centrality as a site for the production of colonial knowledge and the legitimization of colonial rule.[22] That engagement has left us with an archive of indigenous ideas, initiatives, and interpretations.

Networks of Knowledge: Transmission and Circulation

The roughly century-long process of Spanish devaluation of indigenous forms of inscription coincided with the proliferation of indigenous knowledge of alphabetic writing and its recognition by indigenous people as the primary medium for intellectual production and record keeping; although again, we must emphasize that native people continued to use other forms of inscription simultaneously, which shaped alphabetic forms. Now we turn to the question, how did knowledge of alphabetic writing circulate among indigenous people? Here, the contexts of colonial evangelization and education are critically important. From the beginning of the colonial period in both New Spain and Peru, the missionary orders conscripted indigenous allies for the purposes of evangelization; that is, the sons of the native elite would serve as their catechists and assistants. The missionaries established schools (*colegios*) for their education in Christian doctrine, Latin, and Castilian. Colegios represent an early and critical context for transmitting alphabetic writing to the indigenous population, as John Charles's chapter in this volume demonstrates; colegios remained important sites for indigenous education in some locales well into the seventeenth century, as well as sites that produced conflicts among indigenous alumni and their former teachers. In the case of the Colegio de San Francisco Tlaltelolco in New Spain—where Fray Bernardino de Sahagún and his Nahua associates authored *the Florentine Codex*,[23] a twelve-volume compendium of Nahua culture, history, and language—the colegio was also the site for the education of the clergy in Nahuatl and Nahua history and culture, emphasizing that knowledge flowed in both directions. It would be worth tracing the trajectory of official education for indigenous elites in New Spain versus the Andes, as they appear to have had different chronologies and programs.

The colonial state sought to standardize education for indigenous elites, but with the colegios, they did not meet the demand for education in the Spanish fashion, nor did they provide the range of skills that some indigenous individuals sought. Colegios were not for everyone. Those who were not elite and wanted education had to find other means. And some examples suggest that for several who were elite, colegios did not apparently meet their

GABRIELA RAMOS AND YANNA YANNAKAKIS

expectations, so they chose to educate their children or themselves in other ways. Gabriela Ramos's discussion in her essay of the Casa de San Ignacio in Cuzco, a residence for indigenous artisans who collectively studied Christian doctrine when they were not performing their daily work, provides an example. In this case, non-elites used their initiative to create an institutional space in which they could aspire to live a "correct" life and become part of the establishment. These people were not resisting or rebelling against the colonial system; rather, they sought to become a part of it. Their goals were conservative, yet their means were innovative.

In the case of New Spain, informal educational channels such as apprenticeships were also crucial for disseminating knowledge and promoting indigenous literacy. In regions remote from colonial power centers, missionary priests relied on local indigenous elites to help them alphabetize and standardize indigenous languages in order to produce catechisms (*doctrinas*) in a wide array of native languages. In these settings, from the wellspring of the evangelical context, indigenous language writing moved to the setting of the indigenous municipal council, where native scribes and officials employed it for record keeping and in establishing local courts where native legal agents submitted native language petitions and written documents on behalf of native litigants. Informal education—through networks of priests, their native assistants (*fiscales*), indigenous municipal authorities (especially municipal scribes [*escribanos*]), and legal agents (*apoderados*)—facilitated the transmission and circulation of indigenous language writing, Spanish customs, moral attitudes, discursive styles, forms of argumentation, and strategies for dealing with the law. As Yanna Yannakakis demonstrates in her chapter, these local intellectuals in turn transmitted these ideas to local communities. These processes occurred in rural settings, as well as in Mexico City, the heart of New Spain, as exemplified by John Schwaller's chapter on the careers of the Alva Ixtlilxochitl brothers. Bartolomé Alva Ixtlilxochitl, a parish priest who wrote a *confesionario*, and Fernando Alva Ixtlilxochitl, interpreter of the Real Audiencia, provide an example of the intersection of these realms of intellectual production within one family.

The transmission and circulation of different types of knowledge in indigenous languages in New Spain stand in stark contrast with the case of the Andes. Whereas several indigenous languages were alphabetized in New Spain, in the Andes, only a few were. The Spanish placed special emphasis on Quechua. Standard colonial Quechua was used to evangelize, but not often used by indigenous writers, who almost always wrote in Spanish.[24] Scholars have explained the different trajectories of indigenous-produced alphabetic writing in New Spain and the Andes in various ways. In comparison with the quipu, the pictographic traditions of central Mexico and Oaxaca were more commensurate with alphabetic writing, facilitating indigenous adoption of the European form.[25] Furthermore, the more decentralized and urbanized nature of the Mexica Empire facilitated the emergence of a social stratum of religious specialists, administrators, bureaucrats, and intelligentsia among whom ideas circulated and spread. Outside of central Mexico and Oaxaca, the Maya hieroglyphic writing system also appears to have facilitated the transition to the European alphabetic writing system as well as the continuity after the conquest of the key role of Maya intellectuals who produced and circulated knowledge in written form, some of it clandestinely.[26]

The many Mesoamerican pre-Hispanic ethnic polities—*altepetl* (Nahua), *cah* (Yucatec Maya), *ñuu* (Mixtec), and *yetze* (Zapotec)—enjoyed a tradition of political semiautonomy, which entailed record keeping and the intellectual labor of painter-scribes. After the conquest, these ethnic polities became semiautonomous municipalities (*pueblos de indios*) with Spanish-style municipal councils (*cabildos*), staffed by indigenous scribes who produced native-language municipal records.[27] Writing as a practice was thus highly decentralized in Mesoamerica, and due to the standardization of indigenous languages undertaken by the friars and their native assistants, indigenous scribes penned documents in indigenous languages at the municipal level. Through their writing and activities, these figures reinterpreted concepts of authority, persuaded those above and below them regarding appropriate courses of action, and instilled new ideas in their communities.

In the Andes, the more centralized nature of the Inca Empire and its record keeping and more sparse urbanization provided a different framework. In comparison with Mesoamerica, the centralized character of the Inca state probably discouraged the existence of independent intellectuals. Language policy marks an important difference between the two contexts as well. Whereas in the Andes the Spanish required documents written in Castilian, in Mesoamerica, Spaniards accepted indigenous language documentation throughout the colonial period. In the Andes, the Spanish administration's preference for the use of Castilian created a sea change in the role of indigenous intellectuals from the pre-Columbian to the colonial period. The language policy of the Church in the Andes, in particular its decision to standardize a form of "pastoral" Quechua rather than alphabetize the stunning diversity of indigenous languages meant that notarial records were produced

GABRIELA RAMOS AND YANNA YANNAKAKIS

in Spanish. Andean scribes were thus bilingual, which was not necessarily the case in Mesoamerica, and they trafficked in the Spanish language more than their Mesoamerican counterparts. Also fewer indigenous scribes lived in the Andes than in Mesoamerica. In Peru, Viceroy Toledo's ordinances issued in the 1570s attempted to curtail indigenous production of documentation by restricting it to the genre of wills, which may explain fewer municipal-level documents in Peru than in New Spain.[28]

Thus linguistic diversity, language use, policy, and ideology strongly shaped the production and circulation of writing at the local and wider administrative levels in Mexico and the Andes. So too did translation. At the moment of contact, the transformation of indigenous forms of inscription into alphabetic writing itself constituted a particular form of translation: some have argued, a kind of epistemological conquest.[29] In Mesoamerica, once alphabetized, all indigenous-language documents had to be translated into Spanish upon their submission as evidence to a local court. From there, they could circulate more widely through the system of appeal. This exigency required a literate intermediary of a special sort: the court interpreter, a forceful presence in the humblest court of a remote mountain district (alcaldía mayor) to the most powerful court of the realm: the Real Audiencia. As Yannakakis demonstrates, for the Mesoamerican case of Villa Alta, Oaxaca, interpreters—often working in networks—translated oral testimony and indigenous-language documents in multiple languages. In the case of Central Peru, which was even more linguistically diverse, the process of translation is not so clearly delineated in the documents. As Gabriela Ramos points out, for the Audiencia of Lima, legal documentation was submitted in Spanish, so General Interpreters of the Real Audiencia of Lima did not translate the written word. It appears that whatever they were doing linguistically, a significant part of their role was to serve as a cultural broker, introducing indigenous clients to the ways of the high court. Clearly, translation—a crucial factor in knowledge production, transmission, and circulation—operated differently in these two imperial realms. The fact that writing in indigenous languages was more widespread in Mexico suggests that the Andean context facilitated the centralization of the translation process around the lengua general (a standardized form of Quechua), whereas in Mexico, interpreters worked with a wider range of written native languages, thereby facilitating greater linguistic diversity in native writing. The tendency to privilege one language—whether standardized Quechua or Nahuatl—promoted power differentials among ethnic groups and social exclusion.

Having considered indigenous knowledge in terms of its forms, production, and circulation, we must ask for whose consumption indigenous-produced images and texts were intended, and to what ends they were put to use? In sixteenth-century New Spain, micropatriotic boosterism—the trumpeting of the glories of the ethnic polity—provided the rationale for a range of genres of pictographic writing: cartographic histories, annals, genealogies, and conquest pictorials.[30] These genres legitimated the communities' ruling elite and community claims to territory by recounting the ruling lineage's epic migrations, military conquests, and political alliances, often through marriage. Pictographic documents were usually produced for multiple audiences and purposes: for internal consumption as a record of communal history and a legitimating device for community elites, and for use in Spanish courts as a means of documenting claims to land and lineage. Genealogical discourses proved particularly effective in legitimating political claims in both New Spain and the Andes since lineage represented an important point of intersection between Spanish and indigenous understandings of social status and right of rule. Genealogy provides an example of a European device that indigenous people quickly adopted to advance their interests within the colonial system.[31] The intended audiences of indigenous-produced texts clearly shaped their messages and rhetorical strategies. These texts reveal the coexistence of traditional and new ways of thinking, among which indigenous intellectuals made politically significant choices. Representations of gender provide a case in point. As María Elena Martínez argues, in the Mesoamerican genealogical trees and visual succession of Inca rulers—intended to legitimize certain lineages in the eyes of Spanish audiences—female lines of succession were downplayed in favor of the Spanish notion of *linea recta de varón* (direct male line). By contrast, as Susan Schroeder shows us, Chimalpahin, who wrote in Nahuatl, trumpeted the virtues and deeds of female rulers, and at times disparaged them, but ultimately accorded women a hefty role in his historical narratives.

Maps represent another visual genre shaped by indigenous and European traditions that targeted a dual audience: indigenous communities and the Spanish legal system.[32] Through her fascinating analysis of celestial markings on indigenous-produced maps, Eleanor Wake uncovers how native people in central and southern New Spain used astrological knowledge to determine and fix territorial boundaries. Indigenous authorities produced this knowledge through ritualized boundary walking during certain moments of the celestial cycle, reproduced it on maps, and again in primordial titles, which were indigenous-produced land titles based on historical and genealogical claims. Indeed, Wake argues that primordial titles picked up where maps left off as a means of proving and claiming possession in the context of seventeenth-century Spanish encroachment on indigenous lands. The intersection of Spanish and indigenous discourses of territory encouraged the proliferation of written genres such as the primordial titles as indigenous individuals and groups continued to negotiate semiautonomy, land possession, and political authority.

If village scribes, map makers, and interpreters produced documents for local, indigenous consumption, and for Spanish consumption in the legal system, some among a group of self-styled indigenous historians wrote for an indigenous audience. Nahua historians don Domingo de San Antón Muñón Chimalpahin Quauhtlehuanitzin, known as Chimalpahin, and don Juan Buenaventura de Zapata wrote in Nahuatl and operated within the pre-Hispanic tradition of annals record keeping: documenting the important events, past and present, in the life of the ethnic state. As Susan Schroeder demonstrates, in the case of Chimalpahin, he combined references to European classics as well as Nahua painted histories and produced a historical narrative of his home *altepetl* of Amecameca—and notably the deeds of its noblewomen in addition to noblemen—in alphabetic Nahuatl. Camilla Townsend argues that like Chimalpahin, don Juan Buenaventura de Zapata felt a compulsion to record the past of his home altepetl of Tlaxcala, but he eschewed European texts and influences, which he deemed corrupting. According to Townsend, in addition to exalting Tlaxcalan identity and lamenting the diminished authority and legitimacy of the *tlatoque* (noble rulers), his annals point to the new colonial identity of "Indian" in opposition to Spanish and mestizo.

In the Andes, we do not have access to many indigenous-produced chronicles and histories written in native languages. There is nothing analogous to the primordial titles of Mesoamerica.[33] The *Huarochirí Manuscript* provides an exception. For whom was it written, and to what use? Scholars have argued that it was both a record of the history and religious practices of the indigenous people of Huarochirí and an instrument in the extirpation of idolatry. How does the close relationship of Cristóbal Choquecasa (native assistant) and Francisco de Avila (priest and extirpator) bear upon questions of authorship? Alan Durston proposes that we consider the ambivalences in the *Huarochirí Manuscript* in relation to another canonical Andean source (written in Spanish), Felipe Guaman Poma de Ayala's *El primer nueva corónica y buen gobierno* (1615). Durston suggests interesting parallels and divergences between the two authors and their works, including their similarly close relationships with parish priests and the different source material that shaped their writing (Spanish works in the case of Guaman Poma and oral traditions in the case of Choquecasa).

As this volume makes clear, heterogeneous forms of knowledge produced by indigenous intellectuals in colonial Mexico and the Andes connected diverse spheres of power and multiethnic networks. Indigenous intellectuals moved across these networks for source material and intellectual collaboration. The knowledge they produced could be used to critique, resist, and/or accommodate colonialism. Indigenous people used a wide range of strategies and performances in addition to native forms of inscription and alphabetic writing to negotiate collective and individual identities, and the terms of colonial rule. In doing so, they produced what we might call a "colonial culture"—a framework of symbols and meanings forged in the crucible of military conquest, political domination, and overall in the apparent noneventual sphere of daily interaction—whose traces we are fortunate to access in the essays that follow.

Notes

1. Antonio Gramsci, *Selections from the Prison Notebooks*, 6–9.

2. Steven Feierman, *Peasant Intellectuals: Anthropology and History in Tanzania*.

3. The concept of "indigenous intellectual" has generated more discussion for the contemporary context of Latin America. See, for example, Joanne Rappaport, "Between Sovereignty and Culture: Who Is an Indigenous Intellectual in Colombia?," 111–32.

4. See a discussion of the terms *intellectual*, *educated elite*, and *letrado* in Chocano Mena, *La fortaleza docta: Elite letrada y dominación social en México colonial (siglos XVI–XVII)*, especially 30–37. For a discussion of the elite world of letters in Spanish America, and the popular world of letters and other literacies, see Angel Rama, *The Lettered City*; Kathryn Burns, *Into the Archive: Writing and Power in Colonial Peru*; and Joanne Rappaport and Thomas B. F. Cummins, *Beyond the Lettered City: Indigenous Literacies in the Andes*.

5. Nancy M. Farriss, *Maya Society under Colonial Rule: The Collective Enterprise of Survival*.

6. Bernardino de Sahagún, *Florentine Codex: General History of the Things of New Spain*, bk. 11, *Earthly Things*; see also Alfredo López Austin, "Sahagún's Work and the Medicine of the Ancient Nahuas: Possibilities for Study"; Carlos Viesca Treviño, "Los médicos

indígenas ante la medicina europea"; and Carlos Viesca Treviño, *Medicina prehispánica de México: El conocimiento médico de los nahuas*.

7. Antonio de la Calancha, *Crónica moralizada del orden de San Agustín*, vol. 2, bk. 2, ch. 14, 878–79. Other descriptions of medicinal practices can be found in Pablo Josef Arriaga's *La Extirpación de la idolatría en el Perú* (1621); English translation, *The Extirpation of Idolatry in Peru*, 191–277; and Hernando Ruiz de Alarcón, *Tratado de las supersticiones y costumbres gentílicas que hoy viven entre los indios naturales de esta Nueva España* (1629), English translation, *Treatise on the Heathen Superstitions That Today Live among the Indians Native to This New Spain*.

8. Antonio de la Calancha, *Crónica moralizada*, vol. 4, bk. 3, ch. 2, 1248; Rubén Vargas Ugarte, *Concilios Limenses (1551–1772)*, vol. 1, 255.

9. See for example, the case of Joan Enriquez Chuircho, an Indian barber who in 1588 described himself as *bachiller*. Archivo Histórico del Cuzco, Protocolos Notariales, Antonio Sánchez, protocolo 25, f. 693.

10. The famous idolatry extirpator, Francisco de Ávila, aimed to dissuade indigenous parishioners from consulting native healers; see *Tratado de los evangelios que nuestra madre la Iglesia nos propone en todo el año*, 1: 127.

11. Elizabeth H. Boone and Walter D. Mignolo, *Writing without Words: Alternative Literacies in Mesoamerica and the Andes*; Frank Salomon, *The Cord Keepers: Khipus and Cultural Life in a Peruvian Village*; Joanne Rappaport, *Cumbe Reborn: An Andean Ethnography of History*; Rappaport and Cummins, *Beyond the Lettered City*; Frank Salomon and Sabine Hyland, "Graphic Pluralism: Native American Systems of Inscription and the Colonial Situation; and Frank Salomon, "How an Andean 'Writing without Words' Works."

12. Boone and Salomon summarize these debates about the relative value of different forms of inscription, and argue against evolutionary models and the notion that pictographic writing and *quipus* were lesser forms. See Boone and Mignolo, "Introduction," *Writing without Words*; Salomon, *The Cord Keepers*.

13. Semasiographic writing systems are graphic languages independent of spoken language. See Boone and Mignolo, "Introduction," 15–22.

14. Frances Berdan, *The Essential Codex Mendoza*.

15. Pedro Sarmiento de Gamboa, *Historia Indica*; English translation, *The History of the Incas*.

16. John Charles, "Unreliable Confessions: Khipus in the Colonial Parish"; Juan Carlos Estenssoro Fuchs, *Del paganismo a la santidad: La incorporación de los indios del Perú al catolicismo, 1532–1750*; and Juan Pérez Bocanegra, *Ritual formulario e institucion de curas, para administrar a los naturales de este reyno, los santos sacramentos del baptismo, confirmacion, eucaristia y viatico, penitencia, extremauncion, y matrimonio, con advertencias muy necessarias*.

17. Tom Cummins, "From Lies to Truth: Colonial Ekphrasis and the Act of Cross Cultural Translation," 152–74.

18. From here forward, we reference the essays in this volume parenthetically by the author's last name.

19. Carolyn Dean and Dana Leibsohn, "Hybridity and Its Discontents: Considering Visual Culture in Colonial Spanish America."

20. Rolena Adorno, *Guaman Poma Writing and Resistance in Colonial Peru*; Sabine MacCor-

mack, *On the Wings of Time: Rome, the Incas, Spain and Peru*; Pierre Duviols, introduction and ethnohistorical study to *Relación de antigüedades destos reynos del Piru*; and Susan Schroeder, *Chimalpahin and the Kingdoms of Chalco.*

21. Not only were these documents the grist for colonial administration—they have also been the grist for colonial histories. Historians now consider these documentary forms as historical artifacts in their own right, analyzing their formulas, discourses, and circulation. See, for example, Burns, *Into the Archive* and, along very different analytical lines, the work of the new philologists as exemplified by James Lockhart, *The Nahuas after the Conquest: A Social and Cultural History of the Indians of Central Mexico, Sixteenth through Eighteenth Centuries.*

22. Brian P. Owensby, *Empire of Law and Indian Justice in Colonial Mexico*; Yanna Yannakakis, *The Art of Being In-Between: Native Intermediaries, Indian Identity, and Local Rule in Colonial Oaxaca*; and Alcira Dueñas, *Indians and Mestizos in the "Lettered City: Reshaping Justice, Social Hierarchy, and Political Culture in Colonial Peru."*

23. See the twelve-volume translation plus introduction and indices done by Arthur J. O. Anderson et al. and Dibble.

24. Alan Durston, *Pastoral Quechua: The History of Christian Translation in Colonial Peru, 1550–1650.*

25. Boone and Mignolo, "Introduction" in *Writing without Words*; and Boone and Cummins, "Introduction" in *Native Traditions in the Postconquest World: A Symposium at Dumbarton Oaks, 2nd through 4th October 1992.*

26. Dennis Tedlock, *2000 Years of Mayan Literature*; Stephen D. Houston, "All Things Must Change: Maya Writing over Time and Space," 21–42; Ralph Loveland Roys, *The Maya Katun Prophecies of the Books of Chilam Balam*, *The Book of Chilam Balam of Chumayel* and *Ritual of the Bacabs*; Dennis Tedlock, *Popol Vuh: The Definitive Edition of the Mayan Book of the Dawn of Life and the Glories of Gods and Kings.*

27. Lockhart, *The Nahuas after the Conquest*; Robert Haskett, *Indigenous Rulers: An Ethnohistory of Town Government in Colonial Cuernavaca*; James Lockhart, Frances Berdan, and Arthur J. O. Anderson, *The Tlaxcalan Actas: A Compendium of the Records of the Cabildo of Tlaxcala, 1545–1627*; Caterina Pizzigoni, *Testaments of Toluca*; Mathew Restall, *The Maya World: Yucatec Culture and Society, 1550–1850* and *Life and Death in a Maya Community: The Ixil Testaments of the 1760s*; Kevin Terraciano, *The Mixtecs of Colonial Oaxaca: Ñudzahui History, Sixteenth through Eighteenth Centuries*; Michel Oudijk, *Historiography of the Benizaa: The Postclassic and Early Colonial Periods (1000–1600 A.D.)*; and Mathew Restall, Lisa Sousa, and Kevin Terraciano, *Mesoamerican Voices: Native-Language Writings from Colonial Mexico, Oaxaca, Yucatán, and Guatemala.*

28. Lohmann Villena, Guillermo, and María Justina Sarabia Viejo, *Francisco de Toledo: disposiciones gubernativas para el virreinato del Perú*, 1: 476.

29. Serge Gruzinski, *The Conquest of Mexico: The Incorporation of Indian Societies Into the Western World, 16th–18th Centuries.*

30. Elizabeth H. Boone, *Stories in Red and Black: Pictorial Histories of the Aztecs and Mixtecs*; Florine Asselbergs, *Conquered Conquistadors: The Lienzo of Quauhquechollan: A Nahua Vision of the Conquest of Guatemala*; Lori Boornazian Diel, *The Tira of Tepechpan: Negotiating Place under Aztec and Spanish Rule*; Susan Schroeder, *The Conquest All over Again: Nahuas and Zapotecs*

GABRIELA RAMOS AND YANNA YANNAKAKIS

Thinking, Writing, and Painting Spanish Colonialism, 101–23; Stephanie Wood, *Transcending Conquest: Nahua Views of Spanish Colonial Mexico.*

31. María Elena Martínez, *Genealogical Fictions: Limpieza de Sangre, Religion, and Gender in Colonial Mexico.*

32. For a study about mapmaking in colonial Mexico, Barbara Mundy, *The Mapping of New Spain: Indigenous Cartography and the Maps of the Relaciones Geográficas.*

33. Robert Haskett, *Visions of Paradise: Primordial Titles and Mesoamerican History in Cuernavaca.*

Part I

Indigenous Functionaries

Ethnicity, Networks,
and Institutions

CHAPTER 1

Indigenous Intellectuals in Andean Colonial Cities

Gabriela Ramos

In this chapter I examine the background, position, and activities of indigenous intellectuals in the cities of Lima and Cuzco, and discuss the means by which they acquired, developed, and administered the knowledge that allowed them to stand out from their peers. Through the study of several individual cases I aim to show how they were positioned in society, either by gaining a place in the colonial administration, practicing a trade, or associating with others to meet specific ends. Whenever possible, I examine the social relations these individuals established, and assess their participation in and contribution to the production and dissemination of knowledge.

I start by assessing the conditions that allowed indigenous intellectuals to thrive. Briefly comparing the Andes and Mexico, I ask if cities and political centralization played a role in the formation of intellectuals in the period before the Spanish conquest, and hypothesize about the reasons behind the contrasting performance of indigenous intellectuals in the two main centers of Spanish colonial rule. Next, I compare the conditions under which the Andean cities of Lima and Cuzco were created after the conquest, and examine how they affected the position of Cuzqueño and Limeño indigenous elites. I argue that these conditions significantly shaped the kinds of indigenous intellectuals who emerged in each colonial city and the relationship they established with the colonial government and other groups in society. Finally, I consider the instances in which Andean indigenous intellectuals acquired and used the knowledge that allowed them to attain positions of leadership, an achievement that fortified and transformed certain sectors of indigenous society, but ultimately helped to strengthen the colonial system as a whole.

Intellectuals, Cities, and Political Structures

One of the most striking contrasts between pre-Columbian Mexico and the Andes at the time of the Spanish conquest is the abundance of urban centers in Mexico and a correspondingly decentralized political structure, compared with the small number of Andean cities and a governmental structure characterized by a powerful imperial state. To what extent did these differences determine the numbers, behavior, and influence of local intellectuals? Considering the distinct forms in which indigenous intellectuals engaged with Spanish colonial culture and politics in the years immediately following the conquest of Mexico and Peru, I hypothesize that the locations, functions, ways of producing and administering knowledge, and the social relations maintained by both local and imperial intellectuals were greatly influenced by their precontact urban experience and the form of doing politics that city states encouraged, which was dynamic and relied on specialized agents. Although in both Mexico and the Andes local rulers had to negotiate continuously with imperial authorities, it seems that the Inca were more successful than the Mexica at imposing themselves by force upon their neighbors. Perhaps aggressive Incan imperial policy left local Andean intellectuals with more limited means of survival after the Spanish conquest than their counterparts in Mexico. During the early colonial period, specialized knowledge in the Andes rested in very few hands, which, in contrast with the case of Mexico, appears to have limited its endurance and circulation.

The art of record keeping offers a useful comparison with which to examine this question. Although references to Andean cord keepers or *quipucamayocs* appear throughout the colonial period, they are not abundant; nor are they easy to find outside the obvious former imperial center of Cuzco.[1] Compared to Mexico, in the Andes one is far less likely to distinguish a direct link between ancient record keepers and colonial indigenous scribes and notaries (see also Burns, chapter 10). It could be argued that the abundance of indigenous writers in colonial Mexico can be explained by the existence of a greater number of local bureaucracies charged with the rule of city-states and, more important, by the development in pre-Columbian Mexico of forms of representation that engaged better with European writing, drawing, and painting than did Andean devices. For their part, the Spanish were better able to understand Mexican recording systems and allowed them to survive, whereas their attitude toward Andean *quipu* was ambiguous at its best.[2] In addition, precolonial Mexico's political decentralization must have favored the dissemination of knowledge and the formation of a pool of scribes and writers whose duty it was to pass on their skills to the next generation.

Andean Indigenous Power/Knowledge and Early Colonial Urbanism

The spatial reorganization launched shortly after the conquest to facilitate Spanish colonial rule led to the creation of cities and urban settlements in the Andes. Urbanization involved the relocation of both local and foreign populations, the creation of new jurisdictions, and the adaptation of those previously existing to the newly created spatial patterns. These changes were compounded by intense demographic transformations. It was not rare for new indigenous leaders to be brought into the newly created urban centers to take charge of various aspects of their administration. Thus the Andean political landscape was significantly transformed after the conquest. The changes effected had implications for the indigenous elites' participation in government as well as for population distribution and migration patterns.

Pizarro's decision to establish the main colonial administrative center of the viceroyalty in Lima, at a significant distance from the former imperial capital of Cuzco, crucially shaped the social profile of the indigenous intellectuals who in the following years were incorporated into the colonial administration. Aided by the rapid and massive depopulation of the coast, the Spanish easily dispensed with most of Lima's precolonial past as they founded their main political center in the valley of Lima and conducted themselves as if no significant collectivity had ever existed there before their arrival.[3] Thus the city appeared as an innovation, a true starting point of political life.

In contrast, the Spanish could not proceed in the same way in the ancient Inca capital as they did in Lima, because Cuzco and its surrounding area possessed stronger symbolic, material, and human resources, a much denser population, and a cohort of Inca elite intellectuals whose presence could by no means be overlooked.[4] Thus it is worth considering the variances emerging between the two cities that affected the participation of indigenous intellectuals as colonial officers. In both cities the Spanish colonial administration relied on "traditional" and "new" indigenous intellectuals, although in distinct ways. I argue that their function and degree of authority were constructed according to the local sociopolitical conditions existing in each place. Hence it is necessary to explore how these intellectuals and officers were recruited, and how they attained a position within the governmental structure. Focusing on *caciques*, notaries, and interpreters and on their separate or interrelated roles, I further argue that indigenous involvement as colonial officers was dependent upon shifting values assigned to key aspects such as tradition, nobility, language, and social changes surrounding the elusive subject of "race."

A confederation presided over by chiefs or *curacas* ruled the various groups that populated the Lima valley at the time of the Spanish conquest in the early 1530s. Most of these chiefs were related to one another through marriage alliances. Archaeological evidence and early colonial documents suggest that in precolonial times the scope of their activities transcended the boundaries of their own kinship groups to embrace large portions of Peru's central coast and beyond. These chieftains were subordinated to a paramount curaca whose domains encompassed the area that after the Spanish conquest became Lima's city center.[5]

The conquistadors interpreted the paramount curaca's approval of their request for permission to establish a settlement in his jurisdiction as an unlimited authorization to seize land. Soon the Spanish were assigning an increasing number of lots to the new *vecinos*—individual or corporate—and moving the original inhabitants and their authorities to the periphery of the new Spanish city, while the town council issued decrees that shaped the public space and regulated its use.[6] As Rostworowski has noted, in spite of his petitions to defend his land rights and those of his subordinates, within a few years of the founding of Lima the paramount curaca's power was severely weakened.[7] It seems that by the 1560s, a main indigenous authority no longer existed. The several curacas (chiefs), *principales* (authorities), and other elite Indians scattered in the *pueblos* or *reducciones* (settlements) that surrounded the viceregal capital were left with no single, chief indigenous representative. In these new conditions, their political weight was severely diminished. Although these elite Indians performed governmental duties in their respective localities, their position in the public life of Lima was marginal. Most, if not all, were quickly assimilated to Spanish culture. Evidence suggests that

GABRIELA RAMOS

young elite males were taken to the convents where they received religious indoctrination, learned Spanish, and were taught to read and write.[8] These elite Indians, some of whom later became curacas or chiefs, functioned in the colonial administration, and to an extent served as pillars of Spanish rule, promoting the dissemination of Spanish culture and values among their subjects (see also Charles, chapter 3). Curacas and their families maintained a degree of authority and prominence within the boundaries of their own small jurisdictions.[9] However, various circumstances operated to their disadvantage; their proximity to the viceregal capital was only one of them. Over time their position became increasingly precarious because of the acute population crisis, the loss of land, and Christianity's restrictions that forced them to form nuclear families, a mandate that diminished their chances of procreating and increasing the number of their kin. Thus they were left with fewer possibilities of having successors, with fewer subjects to rule, a smaller provision of laborers, and overall with scarce resources to guarantee their support and survival.

The position of curacas in Lima and its surroundings was further weakened by the appearance of individuals occupying posts that the colonial administration created to provide the services the Spanish required to deal with the indigenous population, like interpreters and *alguaciles* (bailiffs). In most cases these posts were new. In other instances they complemented those already existing, and in still others, they replaced indigenous governmental structures. The provenance of indigenous officers settled in Lima suggests that not only did conditions allow upwardly mobile Indians to succeed in finding a placement but also that Spanish authorities found it convenient to promote indigenous individuals foreign to the region to key positions within the colonial administration, as opposed to employing local people. These individuals became instrumental to Spanish colonial rule (see also Yannakakis, chapter 4).

Besides relegating the indigenous curacas to a marginal place, the rapid transformation of the local population contributed to creating conditions that favored the emergence of alternative sources of political authority. Since its founding, Lima had received a flood of migrants coming from most areas of the viceroyalty, to the point that a census taken in 1613 shows that the overwhelming majority of Indians living in the city at that time had been born elsewhere.[10] Although a number of urban Indians were still connected to their places of origin, many had severed their ties with their original authorities.[11] Issues of government, labor and trade, or even survival increased the need for indigenous representatives and intermediaries. In the years following the founding of Lima, different posts, both religious and secular, had been created to lead and channel the indigenous population's participation in urban life. Positions such as alguaciles, confraternity leaders, and *alcaldes* (mayors) were filled up by men who themselves had arrived in Lima as migrants. Given the marginal place local ethnic authorities were allocated within the administration of the viceregal capital, and the consolidation of Lima as the new bureaucratic and ceremonial center, it is not surprising that in the late sixteenth and the early seventeenth centuries, the most important position an Indian could hold in Lima was not that of curaca, but of interpreter general to the Real Audiencia. To understand the significance of this indigenous office, it is worth examining its political, social, and cultural implications (see also Schwaller, chapter 2, and Yannakakis, chapter 4).

The procedures for appointing the General Interpreter show how the post suited the needs of colonial rule and reinforced the conditions of subordination in which the Indian population of Lima lived. In the first place, the pivotal role of the Spanish judiciary and the Real Audiencia was highlighted at the crucial juncture when colonial administration was reformed under Viceroy Toledo (1569–1581) (see also Burns, chapter 10). Toledo endeavored to shape the curacas' role within the Spanish administration, and the appointments he made did much to erode the authority and legitimacy held by traditional indigenous authorities. Unlike other areas of Spanish America like central Mexico, where arrangements to share administrative tasks between Spaniards and locals were fairly common, the Peruvian viceroyalty's indigenous authorities had limited control over the administration of justice, since this function was placed within Spanish hands.[12]

Situated at the top of the governmental hierarchy, second only to the viceroy, the Real Audiencia was the most powerful colonial body the indigenous inhabitants could approach when seeking justice. Often curacas traveled to Lima to follow up their cases, dedicating a significant amount of their time and resources to dealing with the colonial bureaucracy. Thus the individual who acted as a link between indigenous society and the Real Audiencia was unquestionably more influential than any ethnic authority. It is therefore noteworthy that the first interpreter general to the Real Audiencia appointed by Toledo was a man named don Pedro Maíz, a foreigner to the Lima valley. Adding to the distinction attached to the position, when Toledo allocated *mita* or Indian draft laborers to the *vecinos* (elite residents) of Lima, Maíz appears in the colonial registers as the only Indian beneficiary. He also became a

GABRIELA RAMOS

city and religious leader, for soon after his appointment he figured as patron of Nuestra Señora de la Candelaria, the most active Indian confraternity in Lima, sponsored by the Franciscans. His successor, don Diego Solsol, was not born in Lima either. He was the cacique of a *repartimiento* in the remote Chachapoyas province, in the highlands of northeast Peru. His repartimiento was composed of so few people that it is not difficult to understand why he found it more advantageous to move to Lima and become a colonial officer rather than stay in his homeland as curaca. Don Diego Solsol also became a patron of the same confraternity as his predecessor and, besides performing his job at the Real Audiencia, he usually served as interpreter to the few Spanish notaries who offered their services to Indian customers. An additional indicator of the recognition both men enjoyed in the city was that they often acted as guardians of orphaned children, executors, and representatives on behalf of several Indian men and women of varied socioeconomic status.[13]

To better understand the interpreters' significance and long-lasting effect of their function it is necessary to consider the social relations in which they were immersed. These social relations hinged on the knowledge they owned and disseminated, and on the role they performed in their twofold position as representatives of the colonial administration and of the indigenous population. In considering the position of these men, I would like to emphasize three points: first, their relation to writing and to record keeping; second, the social networks they built; and third, the status of the language they spoke (see also Yannakakis, chapter 4).

The use of writing and the extent to which Indian elites managed to learn to read and write was an important factor that affected social and power relations in the colonial Andes. It is likely that the Indian General Interpreters were literate, although it is not known how they learned to read and write, or how they acquired all the other knowledge needed to carry out their tasks successfully. I will come back to the point of education later in this essay. On the question of literacy, it is difficult to ascertain how much *public* use interpreters made of writing, since their work involved delivering oral reports only. In Lima, their duties were closely linked, even subordinate to, the work of notaries. The fact that the job of interpreter was often neatly separated from composing and issuing documents guaranteed at least two closely interrelated results: first, the validity of the enacted business put into writing had to be sanctioned by a Spanish officer; and second, to be legal, all business had to be conducted in Spanish. Crucially, the interpreter's task involved guiding his indigenous clients through the intricate paths of the colonial administration by explaining to them the workings of the system while making them acknowledge its authority and accept its necessity. It was no easy undertaking, for the interpreter's work involved making sense of actions that were unfamiliar to his clients in a culture where writing in the European sense was unknown. Thus in the special circumstances in which they were immersed, the interpreters' relationship with Spanish notaries was crucial since without them the latter could not operate.

Lacking strong bonds with their places of origin, and owing their posts to the colonial administration, social networking was of utmost importance for these indigenous colonial officers. Choosing with whom to establish long-lasting bonds was a pressing question. Maintaining their links with the Spanish had to be balanced with a strong position within the indigenous collectivity because to remain solely as aides of the Spanish administration would have made their position weak and socially isolated. Thus they opted to strengthen, "indigenize," and ennoble their position by establishing ties with powerful curacas. However, for reasons that would need further investigation, the first and most influential interpreters living in Lima during the early colonial period did not make alliances with the indigenous elites from the towns surrounding Lima, but with those from further away. Marriage alliances were crucial.[14] It was only later, when the post of interpreter general of the Real Audiencia saw its importance diminished, that an indigenous man from the Lima valley held the post.[15]

The position of these interpreters toward the question of language is both fundamental and intriguing. As I stated above, the indigenous population of Lima came from different parts of the viceroyalty. Given the great linguistic diversity of the Andean region, it is clear that they were speakers not of one, but of several languages and dialects, some of which were not mutually intelligible.[16] So it is worth asking, what exactly did the interpreter general translate? To what extent did interpreters participate in the formation of a colonial rendering of Quechua, akin to the academic version that in the late sixteenth and early seventeenth centuries the Church created and spread for pastoral needs (see also Durston, chapter 7)?[17] How did linguistic diversity impinge on the interpreter's position—and the knowledge he possessed—in the long run (see also Yannakakis, chapter 4)? Given the lack of intelligibility between, for instance, Chachapoyas Quechua and the variety of Quechua spoken in the central Andes, we must ask how men like don Diego Solsol, interpreter general of the Real Audiencia in the early seventeenth century, dealt with the difficulties involved.[18] I would suggest that the interpreter's task was

GABRIELA RAMOS

primarily to act as a social and political intermediary, and that the linguistic aspect of his job was secondary.[19] This view would be supported by the fact that apparently the problem of linguistic diversity in Lima was solved by the spread of Spanish among the indigenous population. Given that in colonial society (and beyond) the command of Spanish was a sign of acculturation, the growing linguistic *mestizaje* (mixture) among the indigenous population of Lima can effectively be described as a manifestation of ethnic or identity change. The consequences of this transformation were such that in a matter of a few decades the post of interpreter general—and the cultural capital the position involved—significantly diminished in importance. The extent to which this shift in language use affected the relationship between Lima's indigenous elite and its indigenous populace fed by the continuous flow of immigrants to the viceregal capital deserves further investigation.

A comparison with Cuzco can help to illuminate the process of incorporation of indigenous intellectuals into colonial administration. The political significance of Cuzco and the role of its indigenous authorities were central. Even though Pizarro presided over the founding ceremony of Cuzco as a Spanish city, it was impossible to dispossess Cuzco from its preconquest past. In fact, its political symbolism strongly depended on its history. Tradition, whether authentic, redefined, or even invented, supported the persistence of former authorities into colonial rule and often was also invoked to legitimize the role of newly appointed indigenous officers. For example, the descendants of Inca rulers formed part of the core group of indigenous nobles who, through their participation in public rituals enacted regularly in the old Incan imperial capital, guaranteed the loyalty of the indigenous population to the Spanish Crown.[20] When the city was reorganized into parishes in accordance with Spanish ideals of urban planning, a cacique claiming Incan descent was chosen to preside over each parish.[21]

Cuzco's indigenous intellectuals faced difficulties in appropriating writing as quickly and efficiently as did their Mexican counterparts. Even though the knowledge elite Inca men possessed was acknowledged as the colonial administration summoned them to provide historical information recorded in their quipu, it is extremely rare to find notaries among their literate descendants. In Cuzco as in Lima, indigenous use of writing in public situations was restricted.[22]

In significant contrast to the situation in the viceregal capital, though, interpreters proliferated in Cuzco, stimulated by the large demand generated by its large indigenous population. In addition, the absence of a court of justice (such as the Lima Real Audiencia) in Cuzco meant that there was no need for one paramount indigenous intermediary within the judiciary. In a remarkable development, in Cuzco the post of interpreter increasingly became linked to that of notary, instead of the functions being divided between the two posts as alluded to earlier in the discussion of Lima. However, the merging of both functions was not undertaken by elite indigenous intellectuals, but instead became the preserve of mestizos. In their double role as interpreters and notaries, Cuzco mestizos took pride in their partial indigenous origins that allowed them to speak Quechua as if it were their native language and understand the Indians, while their education, social connections, and craft allowed them to move smoothly about the difficult realm of bureaucratic procedures. Thus they took up the ambiguous role of advisers—several had family or business links with Indians—as well as that of gatekeepers who to an extent controlled the Indians' access to literacy and its advantages. Their presence as intermediaries was almost unavoidable in as many official instances as possible in which Spanish was spoken (see also Schwaller, chapter 2, and Yannakakis, chapter 4).[23]

Although Cuzco mestizo notaries and interpreters oscillated between their connections with both indigenous and Spanish relatives and acquaintances, there are signs that they sought to perpetuate their position not by seeking alliances with, for example, elite Indians as the Lima interpreter generals did, or by allying themselves only to the Spanish. Instead their aim was to reproduce themselves as a mestizo group through marriage alliances, a strategy they managed to sustain for most of the seventeenth century, and possibly beyond.[24]

Acquiring an Education in a Transforming World

Having discussed a range of areas where Andean indigenous intellectuals emerged and deployed their expertise, I would like to move on to the question of how and where they acquired the knowledge that allowed them to thrive in colonial society. The experience of Andean indigenous intellectuals calls into question the portrait of the education of indigenous elites which the historiography has presented for colonial Spanish America in general, and the Andes in particular, in at least three important ways. First, historians have tended to view this education as both formal and structured, with a form similar to that of school studies today.[25] Within this model, an institution,

GABRIELA RAMOS

a set of subjects, and a time period during which young men were schooled have been identified to describe and understand the kind of education that both state and church imparted to Indian pupils. This institutionalized view of education has prevented us from understanding how studies were conducted in the past when, for example, the idea of reading and learning at one's own pace was the rule, a practice very different from today's, when the needs of the institution or of the educational and disciplinary machinery as a whole often prevail over the interests and wants of both student and teacher. Although I am not suggesting that colonial Indians were able to pursue their learning activities in an accommodating environment, I would like to highlight the fact that the lack of structured programs of study did not consist only of drawbacks, as scholars of colonial education have suggested, but also could offer learning opportunities. Thus, when speaking about education in the colonial Spanish American world, it is first necessary to admit that it is more likely that, for indigenous people, learning did not occur within clearly defined programs and solid institutions, but was instead haphazard and that, although *colegios* (schools) were important (see also Charles, chapter 3), a good part of education, knowledge, and learning took place elsewhere.[26] Second, historical studies of the education of indigenous people in the colonial period assume that there was little social mobility within this sector of society. Historians who have focused on the education of the indigenous elite also seem to conceptualize it as a "finished product": a group who already existed and continued to exist as such after its members attended the schools that were set up for them. The process by which different individuals *became* part of an indigenous elite, as a consequence of acquiring a specific type of knowledge, has been overlooked. Finally, and as a result of the two previous points, the indigenous men—and possibly women—who acquired a Spanish education during the colonial period are generally portrayed as passive recipients of whatever both colonial authorities and ecclesiastics were willing to teach them.

The conjunction of these views on the education of indigenous elites in the colonial context prevents us from considering a wide range of learning and educational experiences, including those individuals to whom I have referred in this essay. The indigenous intellectuals I have studied did not attend schools for elite Indians, nor did they follow structured and formal programs of study, and some were not even part of the elite when they started their careers. Spanish professionals and mestizo teachers were among the providers of nonformal education in Andean colonial cities.[27] The knowledge they acquired was not determined only by what Spanish authorities were willing to offer them, but was instead the result of a laborious search, and of building effective social networks, as well as the outcome of patient observation, perhaps oriented by wisdom, possibly fueled by opportunism.

Religious Education and Learning to Play by the Rules

Other nonconventional, noninstitutional initiatives that emerged in colonial cities can be missed if we limit ourselves to an institutional approach. An example from Cuzco in 1636 illustrates what I have in mind. In February of that year, a group of indigenous men and one woman, all residents of the parish of Nuestra Señora de Belén, bought a house situated in the popular Limacpampa square, founded a *casa de recogimiento*[28] (house of devotion), which they named Casa de San Ignacio, and placed it under the spiritual care of the Jesuits. Ethnic and gender rules of the house were stringent, as only Indian males would be allowed to live there. The men would live in the house and work daily at their trades in the city. They would return home in the evening to discuss and examine one another about their knowledge of the *doctrina cristiana*. Overall, the purpose of the house was simple: the men would live exemplary lives and stay away from women and other distractions, they would learn in depth the Christian doctrine, confess and take communion regularly, listen to the sermon that the Jesuits delivered to the Indians every Sunday evening in their church, and although these young men would live saintly lives, they would not aspire to take vows, much less start a journey that would end in their ordination as priests. Although the men were expected to remain celibate as long as they lived in the house, they were free to leave and marry once they had communicated their decision to the chaplain and received his authorization.[29]

Even though at first glance the idea of the casa de recogimiento looks unexciting and possibly out of place in a discussion about indigenous intellectuals, a consideration of the local context and of the individuals involved should help to explain why the case is meaningful. To start, taking into account that the Jesuits in Cuzco are known for having been in charge of the Colegio de San Borja,[30] the school for caciques, the Casa de San Ignacio stands out as an exception. The founders of the house were a group of artisans, farmers, and traders, and it is apparent that they did not form part of the Cuzco indigenous nobility. The beneficiaries were urban Indians and Indians from the countryside who were willing to move to the city, young artisans who would earn their living through practicing their trade while dedicating their lives to learning, discussing, and putting into practice the Christian doctrine. According to the conditions established by the founders, the bishop could claim no jurisdiction over the house, which was under the auspices of the Society of Jesus. This clause of the agreement is surprising, considering that, in the history of the Andean Church, the 1630s are often considered as a juncture when diocesan authorities had established their religious orders as they competed to gain control over the indigenous population. In addition, although a Jesuit priest was appointed as patron, the master and teacher of the house was not a Spanish Jesuit father, but Lorenzo de Jesús, an Indian man from La Paz (then known as Chuquiabo), reputed to be a knowledgeable, good Christian.

Unfortunately, we don't know how successful the house was or how long the experience lasted. What this example illustrates, though, is an angle of the indigenous experience in regard to knowledge that shows an attempt, even in the midst of a society as highly hierarchical as colonial Cuzco, by a group of Indians to acquire a kind of knowledge considered "right," indeed conventional, and thus necessary to achieve a "good life." In their quest they challenged significant conventions of the time, such as the idea that only noble, elite Indians should have access to education, that only clergymen could be reliable spiritual leaders and teachers, and that Indians had no capacity to aspire to saintly lives, much less live them successfully.[31] These are significant points that would need careful examination, placing them alongside the experiences of no small number of indigenous men and women of humble origins who lived in the Cuzco and Lima convents as *donados* (gifted to live religious lives but unable to take vows), or independently or in small communities as *beatas* (women consecrated to religious life, although not in a convent and likewise unable to ever take vows).[32] It is likely that several of these individuals were literate, had access to the cultural goods produced in the convents or within the sphere of the Church, and served as their transmitters and interpreters to a wider indigenous, plebeian world.[33]

This essay has attempted to give an overview of the ambits and conditions in which Andean indigenous intellectuals lived during the early colonial period, with a focus on those intellectuals who established themselves in the cities. I started by hypothesizing about the reasons behind some significant contrasts between the indigenous intellectuals in colonial Mexico and those in the Andes. These contrasts are noticeable, for example, in the degree of involvement Mexican indigenous intellectuals had with official procedures to which Andeans had less access. While the contrasts observed could be related to differences in the timing, strategies, and forms in which Mexicans and Andeans related to the Spaniards, it is also possible to think that the conditions developed under Spanish rule could be explained in part by circumstances to be found in the pre-Columbian past. Was the proliferation of urban centers and the presence of decentralized political structures like those of pre-Columbian Mexico more favorable for local intellectuals to thrive? Did limited Inca interest in promoting urbanism in areas beyond Cuzco and a few ceremonial and administrative centers, coupled with their aggressive imperial policies, have a different impact on the conditions in which local intellectuals developed, created, and disseminated knowledge and engaged with political power in the Andes? Further and comparative studies of pre-Columbian imperial bureaucracies should cast some light on these questions.

The status and functions of urban indigenous intellectuals under Spanish rule depended on factors as diverse as political and spatial organization, the shifting values that the colonial administration assigned to tradition, and the cultural, racial, or ethnic make-up of the cities resulting from the transformations brought about by processes unleashed by conquest and colonial rule. To secure their position in the former imperial capital of Cuzco, the Spaniards felt compelled to establish a link with the existing indigenous authorities and their intellectuals. Although foreigners were brought into the city to perform certain administrative tasks — a practice the Inca used as they built their empire — the importance of lineage, tradition, and the paramount role of Inca descendants could not be dismissed. In contrast, in Lima, the center of Spanish rule, demographic and political changes precipitated the decline of the local indigenous elites and their demotion to marginal status.

Migration was crucial in shaping the ethnic composition of Andean cities — Lima in particular — and had a profound impact on language, a pivotal marker of ethnic ascription: becoming fluent in Spanish represented a significant step in abandoning Indian status. Indians foreign to the region came to occupy the posts of leadership in the religious and political spheres. Particularly important in the viceregal capital was the post of interpreter general. Given that the Real Audiencia was second only to the viceroy in the governmental hierarchy, the post of interpreter general to the Real Audiencia became the most important position available to indigenous people. Foreign Indians also held this post during the early colonial period. In Cuzco, because there was no Real Audiencia and because it had a much higher proportion of indigenous dwellers in comparison to Lima, interpreters proliferated in that city. A significant terrain of dispute over knowledge and power is represented by the competition to control the post of notary and the successful bid by mestizos to monopolize the position in Cuzco in the seventeenth century.

For indigenous intellectuals, acquiring an education that would be considered valuable from a European viewpoint and that would allow them to attain influential positions did not depend exclusively on the institutions officially created by the Church and the colonial government. Aspiring indigenous men and women found opportunities for informal education in convents, in the studies of notaries, in the homes of mestizo teachers who imparted private lessons, and by entering houses of devotion with stringent rules of conduct, with the aspiration of living saintly lives and exploring the sacred Christian realm on their own. Their goal as intellectuals was not necessarily to contest the sociopolitical system, but to understand and interpret it to themselves and to their peers. In pursuing this goal, they strengthened colonial society, though not without taking part in its transformation.

Notes

1. News about active cord keepers or *quipucamayocs* often appear in early colonial sources but become elusive as Spanish colonization progressed. References to quipucamayocs appear in sixteenth-century documents from the central and southern Andes (Xauxa, Chucuito, Huarochirí, and Cuzco), see Martti Pärssinen and Jukka Kiviharju, *Textos andinos: Corpus de textos khipu incaicos y coloniales*; Garci Diez de San Miguel, *Visita hecha a la provincia de Chucuito*; Sarmiento de Gamboa, *Historia Indica*; John V. Murra, *Formaciones económicas y políticas del mundo andino*, 243–54. For an excellent, thought-provoking anthropological and historical study of the *quipu*, see Frank Salomon, *The Cordkeepers: Khipus and Cultural Life in a Peruvian Village*; see also Gary Urton and Jeffrey Quilter, *Narrative Threads: Accounting and Recounting in Andean Khipu*.

2. Tom Cummins, "Representation in the Sixteenth Century and the Colonial Image of the Inca"; Salomon, *The Cordkeepers*.

3. María Rostworowski de Diez Canseco, *Señoríos indígenas de Lima y Canta*; Paul Charney, *Indian Society in the Valley of Lima, Peru, 1532–1824*; and Lyn B. Lowry, "Forging an Indian Nation: Urban Indians under Spanish Colonial Control (Lima, Peru, 1535–1765)."

4. Catherine Julien, "La organización parroquial del Cuzco y la ciudad incaica"; Gabriela Ramos, *Death and Conversion in the Andes: Lima and Cuzco, 1532–1670*.

5. Rostworowski de Diez Canseco, *Señoríos indígenas*, 76–77; Charney, *Indian Society*; Lowry, "Forging an Indian Nation"; Miguel Cornejo, "Pachacamac y el canal de Guatca."

6. Enrique Torres Saldamando, Pablo Patrón, and Nicanor Boloña, *Libro primero de cabildos de Lima*.

7. Rostworowski de Diez Canseco, *Señoríos indígenas*, 89.

8. Rostworowski de Diez Canseco, *El señorío de Pachacamac*.

9. Rostworowski de Diez Canseco, *Señoríos indígenas* and *El señorío de Pachacamac*; Charney, *Indian Society*.

10. Noble David Cook, *Padrón de los indios de Lima en 1613, por Miguel de Contreras*.

11. Gabriela Ramos, "'Mi Tierra': Indigenous Urban Indians and Their Hometowns in the Colonial Andes," 128–47.

12. Charles Gibson, *The Aztecs under Spanish Rule: A History of the Indians of the Valley of Mexico, 1519–1810*; Woodrow Borah, *Justice by Insurance: The General Indian Court of Colonial Mexico and the Legal Aides of the Half-Real*; David Garrett, *Shadows of Empire: The Indian Nobility of Cusco, 1750–1825*, 70.

13. Gabriela Ramos, *Death and Conversion*, 191–93.

14. See my discussion of the cases of two indigenous interpreters of Lima's Real Audiencia, each married to a daughter of a principal of the central highlands in Ramos, *Death and Conversion*, 192.

15. According to the will of one of his daughters, don Martín Capuy, interpreter general of Lima's Real Audiencia and a resident in the town of Surco, was born in Lima. Archivo General de la Nación, Protocolos Notariales (henceforth AGN-PN), Alonso Durán Vicentelo 422, 1662–69, testament of Luisa Miña, Lima, July 1, 1666. Capuy was active in the 1620s. AGN-PN, Francisco de Bustamante 235, 1621, f. 194v. Unfortunately, I have found no records showing his intervention in public affairs.

16. On language diversity in the Andean region, see Willem F. H. Adelaar, and Peter Muysken, *The Languages of the Andes*; on Quechua, see Rodolfo Cerrón Palomino, *Lingüística quechua*; Bruce Mannheim, *The Language of the Inka since European Invasion* and "The Inka Language in the Colonial World." On the relationship between Spanish and indigenous languages in early colonial Lima, see Gabriela Ramos, "Language and Society in Early Colonial Peru," 19–38.

17. On the use of Quechua for missionary purposes, see Alan Durston, *Pastoral Quechua: The History of Christian Translation in Colonial Peru, 1550–1650*.

18. Taylor, personal communication, 1995; Alan Durston, commentary at the 2010 Cambridge symposium.

19. The sociopolitical significance of the post of General Interpreter in the colonial Andes has not been investigated. On its ritual and political importance in Mexico City in the eighteenth century, see Edward W. Osowski, "Indigenous Centurions and Triumphal Arches: Negotiation in Eighteenth-Century Mexico City," 79–105.

20. Donato Amado González, "El alférez real de los incas: Resistencia, cambios y continuidad de la identidad indígena"; Carolyn Dean, *Inca Bodies and the Body of Christ: Corpus Christi in Colonial Cuzco*.

21. Ramos, *Death and Conversion*, 169.

22. For an informed discussion of the transition from Andean preconquest to post-

conquest indigenous systems of representation, the work of Tom Cummins is fundamental: "'Let Me See! Writing Is for Them': Colonial Andean Images and Objects 'Como Es Costumbre Tener Los Caciques Señores,'" 91–148, and *Toasts with the Inca: Andean Abstraction and Colonial Images on Quero Vessels*; see also Pärssinen and Kiviharju, *Textos andinos*; and Galen Brokaw, *A History of the Khipu*. Frank Salomon, *The Cord Keepers*, argues convincingly that quipus and writing existed in parallel, although the former remained only within the indigenous domain. Examining Indian wills from Cuzco, I have suggested that indigenous issuers and executors of testaments who admitted being illiterate kept records of possessions and debts possibly using quipus. See also Ramos, *Death and Conversion*, 184–85, and note 81.

23. Notary records show that an interpreter was summoned even if an Indian issuing a document was fluent in Spanish. This was particularly true if the issuer was a woman and was dressed in indigenous clothing.

24. One of the most salient examples in seventeenth-century Cuzco is that of the mestizo interpreter Lucas Gutiérrez de Melo and his extended family. AHC-PN, Alonso Beltrán Luzero 8, 1642–43, f. 55.

25. Lino Canedo Gómez, *La educación de los marginados durante la época colonial: Escuelas y colegios para indios y mestizos en la Nueva España*; and Monique Alaperrine-Bouyer, *La educación de las elites indígenas en el Perú colonial*.

26. Pilar Gonzalbo Aizpuru has pointed out this feature for Mexico, although she envisions only or mainly religious education; see *Historia de la educación en la época colonial el mundo indígena*.

27. The study of a notary could also be the place a curaca would choose for the education of his heir. Since there were no schools for women, elite indigenous females were educated in convents. See, for example, the last will of don Martín Chaucaguaman, cacique or curaca of Sisicaya, in the highlands of Lima, who charged the executor of his will with placing his older son in the care of a notary in Lima, while his daughter would be sent to a convent in the same city: Testament of don Martín Chaucaguaman, Sisicaya, May 17, 1619, AGN-PN, Gabriel Martínez 1087, n. p. An example of a mestizo teacher in Cuzco is that of Juan Gómez de León, who was also an interpreter. He might originally have been Indian, but likely became a mestizo because of his education, wealth, and occupation. See his last will and testament issued on July 12, 1630, in AHC-PN, Alonso Beltrán Luzero 1, f. 301.

28. On casas de recogimiento in colonial Peru (although for women) see Nancy Van Deusen, *Between the Sacred and the Worldly: The Institutional and Cultural Practice of Recogimiento in Colonial Lima*.

29. "Venta, fundación e institución de obra pía: Mateo Quispe Juan Baptista y otros yndios en una casa para recogimiento y buena enseñanza de yndios." Cuzco, February 29, 1636, AHC-PN, Joseph Navarro, 230, 1635, f. 694.

30. The best study of the Jesuit Colegio de San Borja is Alaperrine-Bouyer, *La educación de las elites*.

31. On this subject, see Juan Carlos Estenssoro Fuchs, *Del paganismo a la santidad: La incorporación de los indios del Perú al catolicismo, 1532–1750*.

32. On women religious and knowledge sharing in colonial Lima, see Nancy Van

Deusen, "Circuits of Knowledge among Women in Early Seventeenth-Century Lima," 137–50. Her examination of the relations established and the conditions in which religious women coexisted leads Van Deusen to argue that race was not a primary category in use among them.

33. In her fascinating study of indigenous religious women in Cuzco, Kathryn Burns argues that the main motive for setting up the beaterios and casas de recogimiento was the interest of patrons in building and safeguarding the highly valued concepts of honor and decency. While I agree with this view, I would stress that these institutions offered those who joined them opportunities to acquire knowledge and potentially to gain power and prestige. These aspects were as important as honor and decency, as the example of the Casa de San Ignacio demonstrates; see "Andean Women in Religion: Beatas, 'Decency' and the Defence of Honour in Colonial Cuzco," 81–91. Examples of beatas, donados, and donadas in Cuzco, most of them of indigenous origin, are found in notary registers. An interesting case is that of Domingo Mayta Carrasco, AHC-PN, Cuzco, April 20, 1656, Lorenzo de Mesa Andueza 182, f. 816. Although Mayta Carrasco was a donado brother at the Franciscan convent, he was a wealthy, entrepreneurial man. Mayta Carrasco's will stated that he did not know how to sign his name. References to donadas close to the Inca nobility in the early seventeenth century can be found in doña Inés Chimbo Quipe's will in AHC-PN, Cuzco, March 27, 1633, Luis Diez de Morales 75, f. 897. According to Burns, beaterios for indigenous women in Cuzco flourished in the late seventeenth and eighteenth centuries.

GABRIELA RAMOS

CHAPTER 2

The Brothers Fernando de Alva Ixtlilxochitl and Bartolomé de Alva

Two "Native" Intellectuals of Seventeenth-Century Mexico

John Frederick Schwaller

In the waning decade of the sixteenth century and the first three decades of the seventeenth, Mexico saw the emergence of a group of highly literate persons of native descent. Important among these were the Alva brothers, Fernando de Alva Ixtlilxochitl and his younger brother Bartolomé de Alva. These two men occupied mid-range positions in the imperial bureaucracy. Fernando was a governor of native provinces and eventually an interpreter in the Indian court. Bartolomé was an ordained priest and became the bene-ficed curate of the parish of Chiapa de Mota. But beyond this, they were both deeply involved in the intellectual and literary culture of their time and were critically important figures in the resurgence of interest in Nahuatl and pre-Columbian history in the middle decades of the seventeenth century. What makes these men even more interesting is that they were descendants of the famous poet-kings of Texcoco, Nezahualcoyotl (Fasting Coyote) and his son, Nezahualpilli (Fasting Child/Lord).

Nezahualcoyotl and the Lords of Texcoco

To better understand the cultural and historical environment from which the Alva brothers emerged, a quick survey is in order of the exploits of their famous forbears who helped to forge the Triple Alliance that ruled the Valley of Mexico from 1428 until its defeat by the Spanish conquistadors. Nezahualcoyotl became the ruler of the pre-Columbian city-state (*altepetl*) of Texcoco in the fifteenth century. Texcoco was one of several city-states located in what is now called the Valley of Mexico. These included Tenochtitlan, now Mexico City, capital of the Mexica; Azcapotzalco, capital of the Tepaneca; and Texcoco, capital of the Alcolhua. Among the three *altepeme* that formed the Triple Alliance, Texcoco was second only to Tenochtitlan in terms of size, prestige, and power. Culturally speaking, its rulers had pretensions to superiority over Tenochtitlan.

Nezahualcoyotl was known as the principal architect of his capital, filling it with elaborate palaces and impressive temples. In the realm of laws, he is credited with having developed the most advanced system among the pre-Columbian groups of central Mexico. Closely related to the legal code was the system of councils that Nezahualcoyotl established to help him administer justice throughout his realms. This struck a particular chord among the Spanish observers after the conquest since they too favored a conciliar judicial administrative system. Lastly, Nezahualcoyotl is credited with authorship of scores of poems: a true poet-king.

Nezahualcoyotl's son, Nezahualpilli, succeeded his father in the leadership of Texcoco. Nezahualpilli followed in his father's footsteps by focusing internally on capital projects, laws, culture, and the arts. The two men resembled each other to such a degree that historians have had difficulty determining which person accomplished which deed. Nezahualpilli was a respected poet, like his father. He also embarked on an impressive construction campaign, central to which was the renovation of the main temple in Texcoco. Nezahualpilli expanded and revised the legal code established by his father to keep up with changing times. He held that the law had to be enforced among the nobility just as among the commoners. Having governed forty-four years, Nezahualpilli died in 1515.

Following Nezahualpilli's death, a struggle for power ensued in Texcoco among his sons and other claimants to the throne. The ruler of Tenochtitlan, and Nezahualpilli's cousin and brother-in-law, imposed one of Nezahualpilli's numerous sons on the throne. Yet because the new ruler was a son by a concubine and not a son from the principal marriage, many Texcocoan nobles rebelled, including Ixtlilxochitl (Black Faced Flower), one of Nezahualpilli's sons by his principal wife. In the negotiations that ensued, Ixtlilxochitl was made governor of the northern Texcocoan provinces under the

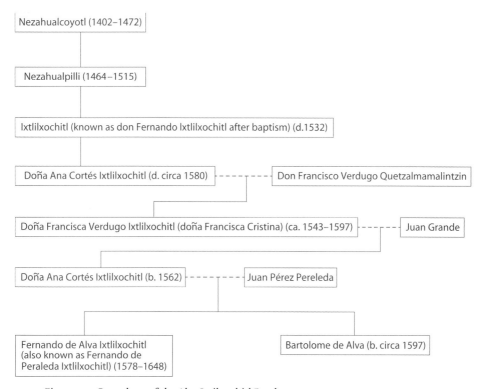

Figure 2.1. Genealogy of the Alva Ixtilxochitl Brothers.

rulership of his half-brother, Cacama (Little Ear of Corn). When the Spanish arrived, while a few Texcocan princes remained faithful to the Mexica of Tenochtitlan, Ixtlilxochitl sensed an opportunity and allied with the Spanish. Yet in the aftermath of the conquest, the leader of the Spanish conquest of Mexico, Hernán Cortés, recognized the traditional ruler, Coanachoch (Serpent Ear-Plug), who had fought against the Spanish. When it later became clear that Coanacoch was involved in a plot to overthrow the Spanish, Cortés had him executed. After several years of uncertainty and in-fighting for power, Ixtlilxochitl received the appointment from Cortés and was baptized as don Fernando Ixtlilxochitl.[1]

Don Fernando Ixtlilxochitl founded the lineage from which the later *mestizo* intellectuals, Fernando de Alva Ixtlilxochitl and Bartolomé de Alva, would descend (see figure 2.1).[2] In the two decades immediately following the conquest, the lines of succession to the Texcocan throne became quite twisted because Ixtlilxochitl had no sons. Don Fernando dictated that upon his death, in 1532, the governorship would pass to his younger brothers. Yet he named his young daughters, doña Ana and doña Luisa Cortés Ixtlilxochitl, as his universal heirs.[3] Doña Ana married don Francisco Verdugo Quetzalmamalintzin in about 1540. He was the *cacique*[4] of Teotihuacan, one of the territories of the northern section of Texcoco. Upon Verdugo's death in 1563, doña Ana became *cacica*. She died in about 1580 and the *cacicazgo* of Teotihuacan passed to her daughter, doña Francisca Verdugo Ixtlilxochitl, also known as doña Francisca Cristina, who was born in about 1543.

Doña Francisca Cristina initiated the family's mestizo line by marrying a Spaniard, Juan Grande, who served the Real Audiencia (the Spanish high court of justice in Mexico City) as a Nahuatl translator.[5] The marriage of doña Francisca Cristina to Grande represents the shifting social patterns of New Spain in the mid-sixteenth century. This marriage represented an alliance of a traditional Nahua family with a mid-level royal bureaucrat. Each party to the marriage brought some real advantages. On the native part there was social prestige in the native community, a small income from their lands, and traditional dues. The Spaniard brought a steady income, a small degree of social prominence among the Spanish, and a network of peers and friends who could be of great assistance in dealings with the Spanish authorities.[6]

The eldest of their children, doña Ana Cortés Ixtlilxochitl (born 1562), inherited the cacicazgo in 1597 upon the death of her mother, even though doña Ana was no longer fully native. In 1576, doña Ana married a Spaniard, Juan Pérez Pereleda (also known as Juan Pérez de Peralta), who served for a time as *maestro de obras* (chief of works) for the city of Mexico.[7] The pressures that brought about the marriage of Juan Grande and doña Franciscan Cristina also played a role in the wedding of her daughter. Although the royal court had ruled that persons of mixed blood could not serve as traditional nobles in native villages, the courts were actually unwilling to intervene. The marriage of doña Ana and Pérez Pereleda helped to strengthen the family by reinforcing ties between the native and Spanish communities: a traditional native noble with a government bureaucrat, who in the case of Pérez Pereleda was also involved in the potentially lucrative construction business.[8] Their two eldest sons, Francisco de Navas Pereleda and Fernando de Peraleda Ixtlilxochitl (also known as Fernando de Alva Ixtlilxochitl) were born one year apart, right after their parents' marriage, in 1577 and 1578, respectively. Their younger brother, Bartolomé de Alva, was born sometime around 1597, about the time their mother inherited the cacicazgo of Teotihuacan.[9]

JOHN FREDERICK SCHWALLER

Fernando de Alva Ixtlilxochitl and Bartolomé de Alva were two of the leading lights of an intellectual movement of the early seventeenth century, which saw the flowering of a literary tradition that in many ways synthesized the pre-Columbian Nahua tradition of Texcoco with the new Spanish culture. The great difference in age between the brothers meant that later scholars frequently misunderstood their relationship, at some times making Bartolomé the child, rather than the brother, of Fernando. Each brother made significant contributions to the realm of colonial letters and has deeply affected the way in which modern scholars understand both the pre-Columbian past and the native tradition in the middle-colonial era.

In spite of the important contributions of Fernando de Alva Ixtlilxochitl (also referred to hereafter as Alva Ixtlilxochitl), no definitive biography of him exists. The closest thing to a biography is the chronology of his life and times compiled by Edmundo O'Gorman for the publication of his works.[10] Alva Ixtlilxochitl did not enter into the public record until 1596, when his grandmother left him some houses that she owned in the village of San Juan Teotihuacan. In the document he is called Hernando de Peraleda Izquisuchitl [sic].[11] O'Gorman concluded that shortly thereafter Alva Ixtlilxochitl began to redact various historical works that would appear in his *Sumaria relación*, his earliest attempt at history.

The *Sumaria relación* deals with the history of the Texcoco region from the fall of the Toltec Empire, in about 1000 A.D., until the arrival of the Spanish. Alva Ixtlilxochitl created a work that followed a European model of chronological narrative history, largely focusing on events in the territory, specifically on the reigns of the various native leaders. It consists of five distinct narratives which, in all likelihood, were oral histories collected by Alva Ixtlilxochitl from the elders still living in Texcoco in the late sixteenth century. As a result, one should consider Alva Ixtlilxochitl more as a compiler and translator than as the principal author.[12]

Beyond his work as a historian, Fernando de Alva Ixtlilxochitl also served as a government functionary. In 1612 he served as a *juez gobernador* (judge-governor)[13] of Texcoco for a year. His letter of appointment noted that he was a descendent of the ancient kings of Texcoco. In 1616 he became the juez gobernador of Tlalmanalco, serving until 1618. The following year he was appointed juez gobernador of the province of Chalco.[14] These positions were important ones within the Spanish system of government, which was grafted on top of the traditional Nahua state. In general a native city-state was governed by a *tlahtoani* (king or ruler). As seen in the discussion of the Alva family the powers of these pre-Columbian rulers continued in the colonial state, under the title of cacique. Most of the native altepeme enjoyed a tlahtoani who was also accorded the Spanish title of gobernador. In the latter sixteenth century the two offices began to be separated. Especially in the region around Mexico City, the Spanish authorities would appoint an external, native governor to rule the territory, the juez gobernador.[15] Consequently, one can see through these appointments that the Spanish royal officials considered Alva Ixtlilxochitl to be an indigenous person from the ruling elite, rather than a Spaniard, in spite of his mixed-ethnic ancestry.

Fernando de Alva Ixtlilxochitl exhibited considerable ambition to rise in the colonial administration. Building on his appointments as gobernador, he submitted a *relación de parte y de oficio* (also known as a *relación de méritos*, or "account of merit") with the Royal Audiencia seeking additional royal appointments.[16] In 1620 the Council of the Indies issued a decree asking local authorities to grant him appropriate offices and other favors. While he undoubtedly held other official posts it was not until around 1640 that he became an official court interpreter in the Royal Indian Court of Mexico. Coincidently, his grandfather, Juan Grande, had held a similar position in the Real Audiencia more than half a century earlier. Alva Ixtlilxochitl and his grandfather served in two distinct courts. In all likelihood it was a coincidence that they were both interpreters, but significant because of the role of cultural intermediary played over several generations in the family.

Also in about 1640, Fernando and Bartolomé's mother, doña Ana Cortés, died, an event that signaled a fortuitous shift in the fortunes of the mestizo brothers. In her will she listed all of her children, including both Fernando and Bartolomé, naming all of them using the honorific "don" or "doña." She left several pieces of property in San Juan Teotihuacan, Mizquitlan, and other places to Fernando, while Bartolomé received her principal residence in Teotihuacan, along with several other properties. She also named them as executors of her will. In spite of her important social standing, and the accomplishments of her sons in the world of letters, doña Ana was illiterate and could not sign her own will.[17] In 1643, after several suits claiming that the family was no longer native, the royal court named Fernando and Bartolomé's older brother, Francisco de Navas, as cacique of San Juan Teotihuacan, succeeding their mother in the post. Fernando had married at some point after 1624, to Antonia Gutiérrez, and they had several children, at least the first of which was born out of wedlock. Fernando died in 1650 and was buried in the parish church of Santa Catarina Mártir in Mexico City.[18]

Historical Works of Fernando de Alva Ixtlilxochitl

Fernando de Alva Ixtlilxochitl was one of a few persons of mixed-ethnic heritage in colonial Mexico who sought to recapture the history of the natives prior to the arrival of the Spanish. In this he consulted several of the pictorial manuscripts that were still extant and sought native assistance in interpreting them. In addition he carried out interviews with native elders and others who had knowledge about the ancient past.[19] The result of his efforts was a series of works that have been collected together under two different titles: *Relaciones* and the *Historia chichimeca*. The *Relaciones* might be thought of as an eclectic collection of shorter narrative histories. It consists of some five works itself: *Sumaria relación*, five pieces telling the history of the Toltecs; *Historia de los señores chichimecos*, a history of Texcoco from the time of the progenitor ruler, Xolotl, up through Nezahualcoyotl, based on the *Codex Xolotl*, with a continuation up to the time of the conquest; *Noticias de los pobladores*, extracts of names from pre-Columbian painted manuscripts, specifically of conquered places along with specific documents such as the Ordinances of Nezahualcoyotl; *Relación sucinta*, a brief summary history of Texcoco in thirteen sections; and *Sumaria relación de la historia general*, another summary of the history of Texcoco. These parts of the *Relaciones históricas* can be aggregated into three larger works. One is a history of Texcoco with two parts (a history of the Toltecs and one of the Chichimecs) along with a documentary appendix (the first three parts of the *Relaciones*). The *Relación sucinta* and the *Sumaria relación* then stand as independent works covering much of the same topics, with the *Sumaria relación* being more extensive than the *Relación sucinta*.

His other work is the *Historia chichimeca*, consisting of ninety-five chapters, tracing native history from earliest times, on to the Toltecs, through the Acolhua of Texcoco, into the conquest period. This more unified work remained unfinished at his death. Alva based this work in part on certain pictorial manuscripts including the *Codex Xolotl*, the *Mapa Quinatzin*, and the *Mapa Tlotzin* as well as on information gleaned from oral histories of the region passed down by the elders.[20] Through his writings Alva Ixtlilxochitl became one of the most important conduits of information about Mexico's pre-Columbian past and especially one of the major sources of information about ancient Texcoco.

The historical works of Fernando de Alva Ixtlilxochitl fit into a model that emerged in the late sixteenth and early seventeenth centuries. A small group of mestizo and native writers engaged in capturing the indigenous history of New Spain from native sources. Others involved in this endeavor include Diego Muñoz Camargo, for Tlaxcala, Hernando Alvarado Tezozomoc, for Tenochtitlan, and Diego de San Antón Muñón Chimalpahin, for Amecameca (see also chapter 2). Both Chimalpahin and Alvarado Tezozomoc were natives and both wrote in Nahuatl. Muñoz Camargo and Alva Ixtlilxochitl were both of mixed heritage and wrote in Spanish. Each of these authors approached writing history in a slightly distinct manner. Chimalpahin produced one of the most complete set of narratives, and drew heavily on the annals form of history whereby events were recounted strictly chronologically, year by year. He drew upon both painted manuscripts and the recollections of elders as he composed his history, writing in Nahuatl. Recent scholarship has questioned whether the work attributed to Tezozomoc might actually be from the hand of Chimalpahin, either in whole or in part. Alva Ixtlilxochitl seems to have also collected some of the Chimalpahin and Alvarado Tezozomoc materials for use in his own histories. Muñoz Camargo was from Tlaxcala, outside of the Valley of Mexico, but lived for a time in Spain while seeking royal preferences for the city of Tlaxcala from the Crown. His work is similar to that of Alva Ixtlilxochitl in that it contains different accounts of the same or similar events, along with genealogies, some of which contradict one another. This suggests that Muñoz Camargo was drawing upon multiple native sources, informants, and pictorial manuscripts, which differed from one another. Alva relied on several sources for his history of ancient Texcoco, including pictorial manuscripts, oral histories, and accounts retained by the elders. Evidence of this is found in the writings themselves. While numerous examples exist, one notice comes at the end of one of the various accounts within the *Sumaria relación*, when Alva concludes the section on the death of Tezozomoc, ruler of Azcapotzalco, and the rise of Nezahualcoyotl: "With this the author, or authors, who painted this original and ancient history ended, for nothing further occurred."[21] It is quite possible that the components of the work that we know of as the *Sumaria relación* were not just different drafts of the same story, but versions of the stories taken from different sources, some from pictorial manuscripts, others from different oral histories provided by different, now anonymous, informants. Camilla Townsend has posited that the frequent appearance of multiple versions of a common story reveals vestiges of the author, or more precisely the compiler, having used many different informants, each representing multiple entities within the polity. For example, in Tlaxcala where internal political divisions recognized four constituent polities, the narratives provided perspective from each of these polities (see Townsend, chapter 6).

Fernando de Alva Ixtlilxochitl listed the various elders from whom he learned the history of Texcoco: "This is the true history of the Toltecs as best as I have been able to interpret and those elderly nobles with whom I have communicated have declared it to me." Among them were don Lucas Cortés Calanta, 108 years old, and lord of Conzoquitlan near Tototepec; don Jacobo de Mendoza Tlaltecatzin, nearly ninety years old, noble, and native of Tepepulco; and don Alfonso Izhuezcatocatzin, also known as Axayacatzin, son of the last emperor, Cuitlahuac, nephew of Moctezuma, and lord of Iztapalapa.[22] These informants were both elders in their communities and were also part of a network of traditional nobles within the old kingdom of Texcoco, who remained linked by ties of marriage and common social and political gain.[23] Alva Ixtlilxochitl helped to carry on the vision of the pre-Columbian past from the perspective of the nobility, not of the *macehualtin*, the common people.

The impact of the works of Fernando de Alva Ixtlilxochitl was to make the preconquest history of Texcoco understandable to a wider audience. Although it is treacherous attempting to determine intentions over five centuries, Alva Ixtlilxochitl seems to have been responding to several things. On the one hand, he believed that in the historical literature written up to his time Texcoco had been largely ignored, due to the Tenochtitlan-centric histories that emerged immediately following the conquest. In this he was similar to Muñoz Camargo and Chimalpahin, who sought to raise their particular homelands to the attention of the leadership of the colony. By writing a narrative history in a European style, rather than the annals style of native pictographic histories, Alva also sought to incorporate the history of the New World into the world (Christian) history brought by the Spanish. He did this by referencing European chronologies in reference to events in Mexico.[24] Alva Ixtlilxochitl also sought to save for posterity the exploits and accomplishments of his immediate forbears, namely Nezahualcoyotl, Nezahualpilli, and Ixtlilxochitl, and particularly the latter's contributions in assisting the Spanish in the conquest.[25] As noted, he submitted a relación de méritos in 1620 to secure royal preference for himself and his family based upon his descent from the Texcocan ruling family, also documenting for all times his tie to that heritage.

Much of what we know about the rulers of Texcoco we know from the writings of Fernando de Alva Ixtlilxochitl. He portrayed these leaders, and especially Nezahualcoyotl and Nezahualpilli, in a favorable light. Alva Ixtlilxochitl rather clearly stated that this was his goal when he wrote:

> Certainly it has seemed to me that the ancient historians who depicted the life of this singular prince [Nezahualcoyotl] did what was ascribed to Xenophon that in the biography which he wrote of Cyrus, King of the Persians, it was not so much his intent to write about the particular man, as it was to depict a great king manifesting those aspects which he should have, and thus it seems that whomever might wish to depict and write about a good monarch, even a barbarian, of all those who lived in the New World, he would need to go no further than to present the life of King Nezahualcoyotzin, because he was the example of the good and excellent prince.[26]

Fernando de Alva Ixtlilxochitl functioned as a translator and interpreter on several levels. His actual function in the government bureaucracy was as a mediator between the native populations and the Spanish royal government, first as governor of various native provinces, then later as a court functionary (see also Ramos, chapter 1, and Yannakakis, chapter 4). In his work on the Indian court he literally was a translator. But on a different level, his writings served to interpret and translate the native history into models that were understood by the Spanish rulers of the colony. He consulted native pictographic materials and translated these into prose history. He consulted with native elders and interpreted native customs and culture into a matrix understood by the Spanish. Alva Ixtlilxochitl was well placed to collect the history of the native peoples of Texcoco and publicize them among the Spanish. A mestizo by birth, he obviously identified with the native population, since he served in many posts generally reserved for natives. Yet at the same time he was fully a member of Spanish society, with only one grandparent who was native, as best we can determine. He clearly saw that he could occupy an important mediating position between the dominant Spanish culture and the colonized Nahua culture of Texcoco.

Bartolomé de Alva: Priest and Scholar

Whereas Fernando de Alva Ixtlilxochitl served the colony's civil administration, his younger brother, Bartolomé de Alva (also referred to hereafter as Alva), served the Catholic Church. Alva, as noted, was born about 1597. In all likelihood he was the youngest of the children of doña Ana Cortés Ixtlil-xochitl and Juan Pérez de Pereleda, although it is possible that he had a younger sister. There is no indication in the record how either of the Alva sons received their early education. Clearly Fernando was competent in both Spanish and Nahuatl, since he went on to have a successful career as a court interpreter. Bartolomé attended the University of Mexico and received his baccalaureate degree in arts in 1622, when he was a respectable twenty-five years old. By about 1643 he completed the requirements and was awarded the licentiate degree.

Bartolomé de Alva entered the priesthood in 1625, after the required course of study and presentation of his qualifications, including evidence that he held a secure ecclesiastical income based on chantries established by his family and had been ordained to the minor orders of sub-deacon and deacon. Alva was ordained a priest at a time when very few persons of mixed-ethnic heritage achieved that status. Local canon law restricted ordination to only pure-blooded Spaniards, although there is ample evidence that this restriction was selectively ignored by the 1630s.[27] He then entered into the competitive exams through which clerics were chosen for appointment as parish priests. The records of the exam show that he was extremely competent in Nahuatl, but his preparation in moral theology and the adminis-tration of the sacraments was only moderate. The examining tribunal was also aware of his descent from the Texcocan nobility, since he had provided them with a copy of the royal decree issued to his brother for favor in offices and grants. After the examination, the tribunal approved him as the bene-ficed curate of Zumpahuacan in 1627. He served that parish only until 1631 when he received an appointment as the beneficed curate of Chiapa de Mota, located to the north and west of Mexico City.[28]

Works of Bartolomé de Alva

Although Bartolomé de Alva pursued a successful career as a parish priest, like his brother, he also was interested in various types of literature. He is known for two very different works. His only published work was his *Guide to Confession Large and Small (Confessionario mayor y menor)* (1634). This confes-sional guide was printed at a time when there was a resurgence of interest in Nahuatl among the lettered classes of New Spain and publishers in particu-lar. The first-generation confessional guides, published in the early sixteenth century, were essentially Spanish catechisms translated into Nahuatl. These were followed by works that had a better grasp of Nahuatl, but still focused more on orthodox Christian beliefs than on addressing confessional issues among the natives and date from the 1570s and later. Alva, like others of his era, began to address traditional native practices that were at odds with orthodox Christianity and used the confessional guide as a means to coax these out. In his confessional guide, Alva demonstrated his familiarity with native practices, which he used as a springboard to teach Christianity to the natives who were already nominally Christian.

Bartolomé de Alva's confessional guide falls within a tradition known in Perú as "the extirpation." The extirpation was a movement in which parish priests became more forceful in their attempts to eradicate the last vestiges of traditional native religions and spirituality (see also Charles, chapter 3, and Durston, chapter 7). In New Spain, efforts were mostly vested in the local parish priest. Alva's confessional guide had as one of its goals providing assistance to the parish priest in discovering the last remnants of the old religious practices.[29]

Early on in the confessional guide, Bartolomé de Alva posed model questions designed to elicit responses concerning idolatry, a violation of the First Commandment. When asking if the person confessing had worshipped something other than God, Alva had the penitent answer: "Yes, I have loved Him with all my heart, but at times I have believed in dreams, [hallucinogenic] herbs, peyote, and *ololiuhqui* and other things." Ololiuhqui was an herb used to provoke hallucinations. He then had the priest ask about specific idols: "Are you guarding in your home [idols called] 'turquoise children' and 'turquoise toads'?"[30] A bit further on he had the priest inquire about the continuation of the cult of Tlaloc, the god of rain, and specifically ask if the penitent prayed to the demigods called the *ahuaques*. These deities lived on high mountains and were responsible for the condensation that created rain. They were propitiated by offerings of candles, incense, and beer.[31] Alva also focused on mortuary practices and asked if when the penitent buried his or her dead, they accompanied it with traditional grave goods such as: "henequen cloaks, tobacco, tumplines, sandals, money, water, food." He also asked a woman regarding a dead child: "did you put your breast milk on him with a reed: do you go there [to the grave] to spill and pour your breast milk on him?"[32] Many other questions sought to discover drunkenness on the part of the natives and using drunkenness as a means of avoiding responsibility for sin. Against this Alva contrasted ancient Nahua practices where moderation was the rule and when drunkenness was punished by execution.[33] Obviously, like his brother, Bartolomé helped to bring the culture of the New World into the Christian ecumene. In writing his confessional guide Alva clearly benefitted from his extensive knowledge of Nahuatl and of traditional native religious practices. Nevertheless, he chose to use these strengths in the furtherance of the colonial state.[34]

Shortly after the publication of the confessional guide, Bartolomé de Alva embarked on a project in which he translated various peninsular Spanish theatrical pieces into Nahuatl. In particular he adapted works by Calderón de la Barca, Lope de Vega Carpio, and Antonio Mira de Améscua for presentation in Mexico to persons who spoke Nahuatl.[35] What he developed was quite unlike anything in the corpus of Nahuatl theater, in particular, and Nahuatl literature, in general. While many religious plays have been cast in Nahuatl, along with various types of devotions and confessional guides, these works stand in stark contrast, being plays written for the Spanish theatre, which Alva translated and adapted to Nahuatl. Analysis of these texts also demonstrates that Alva was a member of a small group of scholars of Nahuatl, the most famous of whom was the Jesuit Horacio Carochi. Carochi is credited for recognizing the importance of vowel length and the glottal stop as crucial features of spoken Nahuatl. Carochi developed a system of diacritics to mark these features of the language, a system that was used by Alva. In marginal notes in Alva's works, we find references to Carochi, and in marginalia in Carochi's works, we find references to Alva. There are also references to a "don Fernando," who one can rightly assume was Bartolomé's brother, Fernando de Alva Ixtlilxochitl, who was also consulted by both regarding the fine points of Nahuatl grammar.[36] Last, Bartolomé de Alva served as one of the official examiners of Carochi's grammar prior to it being published. He wrote that far from criticizing it "I am moved by admiration to praise it instead."[37]

This moment in Nahuatl letters has been characterized by Angel María Garibay as the "Vuelo roto," or broken flight.[38] As noted, Bartolomé de Alva's *Confessionario* belonged to the third generation of such works. By the second and third decade of the sixteenth century a significant number of intellectuals were literate in Nahuatl. The grammars and confession manuals from this period reflect a heightened interest in the Nahuatl as a nuanced and subtle means of communication, thanks in part to Horacio Carochi, who sought to have a deeper understanding of Nahuatl than any of his predecessors. As part of his research he came to know the Alva brothers and drew upon their intimate knowledge to recover important nuances that the early missionary friars who first copied the language in European characters had failed to notice.

This group, consisting of a Florentine Jesuit and two Nahuatl-speaking Mexican mestizos, represents a unique moment in Mass colonial history. While many of the early friars had worked with native informants (as did Fernando de Alva Ixtlilxochitl), they claimed the work product for themselves. In this instance each participant provided insights to the group, which then served to illuminate their own work. As a result, in his work Bartolomé de Alva not only sought to improve the method of confessing native peoples, drawing upon his own cultural background, but he also sought to provide European-style entertainment in Nahuatl. While the final version of his *Confessionario* does not include many of the diacritics developed by Carochi, the plays do. It is not clear what impact this had on his older brother, Fernando, who died some five years after Carochi published his famous grammar of Nahuatl.

Within Bartolomé de Alva's adaptations of Spanish Golden Age plays, one can easily see his transformation of European images into a Nahuatl vernacular. Louise Burkhart, in her analysis of the plays, noted that Alva modified the dialogue of the plays to reflect Nahua sensibilities, even adapting the stage directions to the local context.[39] Evidence of Alva's hand as a cultural translator can be seen in much of the dialogue. In Nahua poetry, for example, flowers, birds, and precious stones are commonly used as metaphors for beauty. In the opening lines of "The Animal Prophet and the Fortunate Patricide," the sweetheart in the play extols the summer saying: "Everything sprouts anew in summer. At that time the *chachalaca* bird goes about chattering. Flowers burst into bloom and the rain falls lightly in the place of delight. Here my heart takes pleasure in smelling the flowers. And now red popcorn flowers and golden flowers guard my heart and my words." Later, lamenting her lost love she cries, "Let me remain hopeful in the garden, here where the golden flowers lie sprouting like emeralds, and the sacred popcorn flowers lie hatching like roseate spoonbills."[40] Compare this to a passage from the famous collection of Nahua poetry, the *Romances de los señores de la Nueva España*: "Let there be popcorn flowers, cacao flowers. Let them scatter, let them sprinkle down beside the drum. Let's be pleasured. There! The turquoise swan, the trogon, the roseate swan is singing, warbling, happy with these flowers."[41] Alva took descriptive passages from the European tradition and translated them into the Nahua context, using metaphors appropriate for Nahua listeners, rather than simply translating word for word from Spanish to Nahuatl. Thus, in his work in translating the Golden Age dramas he pursued a very similar course to that which he followed in writing his confessional guide, of situating the new Christian, and Spanish, world in a valid

Nahua context. He went about translating European culture in a manner that would have the greatest impact on native readers and hearers, since he made the foreign culture appear in the trappings of the Nahua.

The Alva Brothers as Intellectual Leaders

While both Fernando de Alva Ixtlilxochitl and Bartolomé de Alva served as cultural intermediaries between the dominant Spanish culture and the colonized Nahua culture, the direction of their discourse of mediation differed one from the other. Fernando, the elder, by and large sought to inform the dominant culture about the richness and glory of the colonized. He used his skills as an intermediary to chronicle the history of his ancestors and the nobility of Texcoco for a Spanish audience. By having a relación de méritos drawn up, he did this formally, in a legal dialog with the Crown. He also did it in his histories for the broader public. His history put the events and cultures of the New World into a context like that of European history, and in fact he even developed correlations between the two histories. By telling of the history and glory of Texcoco and its leaders he was aggrandizing his own place in society as an heir to that tradition. His younger brother, Bartolomé, on the other hand, engaged in a process of communicating the dominant culture of the Spanish to the colonized Nahuas. The essence of the *Confessionario* is a dialog in which the old native culture is stripped away and replaced with the new Christian religion and culture. His translations of the plays similarly provided examples of European culture to the natives of New Spain, presented in a manner that was intelligible to them.

Bartolomé de Alva and Fernando de Alva Ixtlilxochitl were critically important figures in the resurgence of interest in Nahuatl and pre-Columbian history in the middle decades of the seventeenth century. Each of the brothers seems to have been driven by a slightly different set of impulses. Fernando sought to recover the splendor of pre-Columbian Texcoco for posterity. He had a personal reason for doing this, insofar as he was descended from the ancient kings, notably from Nezahualcoyotl. Intimately linked to this, and heightened by the colonial environment, Fernando sought to demonstrate his own descent from Nezahualcoyotl to justify seeking preference from the Spanish Crown (see also Martínez, chapter 8). As a functionary in the colonial administration he was well aware of the criteria used for preference within that system. Even though he was mostly of Spanish descent, he could point to his native forebears as traditional leaders and important figures prior to the arrival of the Spanish. His grandmother, mother, and brother were traditional native lords, which reinforced his claim to preference. Adding luster to the name of Texcoco had the benefit of adding luster to his family because of their descent.

Bartolomé de Alva also responded to some of the same pressures as his brother. He was also a government functionary, a parish priest. He does not seem to have used his descent from native kings quite as much to his advantage as his brother did. At the same time, by the early seventeenth century, while prohibitions on the ordination of persons with native blood were no longer as actively followed, it was a possible complication for Bartolomé. Yet when he presented himself for examination regarding his knowledge of Nahuatl, he could note his native ancestry as a positive element. What Bartolomé sought to do was to mediate between the dominant culture of the Spanish and the subordinate culture of the natives, but according to specific rules. He was a priest and thus charged with the spreading of the gospel. He used his knowledge of Nahuatl and the Nahua culture to interpret orthodox Christianity in a manner that would be more easily understood by the natives. His efforts did not stop with simply doctrinal issues. Rather he also sought to expose native peoples to the broader Hispanic culture. To further this second end, he translated several Golden Age plays into Nahuatl, and also adapted them to Nahua culture. Furthermore, he also assisted Horacio Carochi in making Nahuatl better understood by Spanish speakers. He worked to record the rules and nuances of the language for posterity, an effort in which his brother also joined, but as an advisor. While both Fernando and Bartolomé occupied a space ethnically between the Spanish and the natives, their work also mediated between these two colonial worlds.

The Alva brothers also occupied different worlds in the cultural dialog between the natives and the Spanish. Just as Fernando sought to explain the native history and culture to the Spanish, so in his career he also translated the native culture, and language, for the Spanish courts. First as an appointed governor in native districts, he became a legal representative for an altepetl before the Spanish authorities, as well as governing the natives within his district. Assuredly later, once he was a court interpreter, the direction of his discourse was more important from the natives to the court.

The context of Bartolomé de Alva's mediation was the Catholic Church. Within the evangelical model of the day, his role was clearly more of teacher and guide than spokesperson for the natives. While his brother's court actively managed the full dialog between colonizer and colonized, Bartolomé

JOHN FREDERICK SCHWALLER

could not. His function was to spread the gospel and teachings of the Church. As a result his participation in the Carochi circle and his efforts to translate works of Golden Age drama stand in stark contrast to his clerical duties. In assisting Carochi, he stepped away from his normal role and was able to look at the language from outside of the cultural dialog—to examine it as an artifact. The translation of the plays was an outgrowth of his work with Carochi, where Bartolomé then took the rediscovered elements of the language and applied them to a specific task. Yet the end result was a product that maintained the direction of the cultural dialog within which he had already been operating, that is, to provide Spanish cultural information to the native peoples.

One family produced two sets of leading intellectuals in two very distinct periods: Nezahualcoyotl and Nezahualpilli in the late fifteenth early sixteenth century; Fernando de Alva Ixtlilxochitl and Bartolomé de Alva in the seventeenth. The cultures in which they lived were radically different. Of the older pair, both were highly respected noblemen, rulers of their community. In many ways they exemplified the poet-king. The latter two were both functionaries of the colonial government, yet men of malleable social status. While both Fernando and Bartolomé had one grandparent who was fully native, they also moved easily within local Spanish society. In their lives and work they served as intermediaries between the dominant Hispanic colonial culture and the subject native culture.

The Alva brothers were unique in midcolonial Mexico. Although intermediaries and of a vague social status in a system of ethnic identity because they did not fit easily into either the model of creole or of native noble, they were secure in the social system dictated through corporate identity. Fernando was a respected government functionary who moved through a series of viceregal appointments into positions of increasing responsibility. Bartolomé was highly educated and a member of the clerical estate. He won a beneficed curacy in a period when not all priests could secure such a plum appointment. There was no hint of illegitimacy in their ancestry. The marriages of their parents and grandparents seem to have been conducted according to the norms of the time. Yet in the end, these men did not easily fit anywhere. They were of mixed-ethnic heritage, descended from the rulers of an important pre-Columbian altepetl, brothers and uncles of Indian nobles, yet themselves functionaries of the Spanish colonial apparatus. Perhaps as a result of this unique status, their writings, their libraries, and their manuscripts did not pass to their children, or nieces and nephews. They, instead, were entrusted to a creole intellectual, don Carlos de Sigüenza y Góngora, who served as legal counsel to several branches of the family.[42] The Alva heirs seem to have followed a path similar to Fernando and Bartolomé. One of Fernando's children, don Juan de Alva Cortés, became an interpreter in the Royal Indian Court, like his father. The nephews of Fernando and Bartolomé continued as the caciques of San Juan Teotihuacan well into the eighteenth century.[43]

Persons of mixed-ethnic heritage could find a niche in the colonial society, mediated by their social rank, wealth, skills, and occupation or corporate identity. The Alvas, while well-to-do by native standards, were middling on the Spanish social scale: comfortable but not rich. They were able to translate their language skills into stable, well-paying careers. Others of a similar ethnic background were not so fortunate because they had insufficient wealth to reach a position where their unique skills could prove to be advantageous.

Notes

This study began with funding from the National Endowment for the Humanities as part of a large project on Nahuatl manuscripts in the United States. In this project, as in all my work on Nahuatl, I am eternally grateful to R. Joe Campbell for having served as my mentor and friend. I also thank Frances Karttunen for her continuing assistance with the fine points of Nahuatl. Yanna Yannakakis and Gabriela Ramos have been fantastic colleagues, and I thank them for having organized the conference in which this paper was presented and for their editing skills afterward.

1. Eduardo de Jesus Douglas, *In the Palace of Nezahualcoyotl: Painting Manuscripts, Writing the Pre-Hispanic Past in Early Colonial Period Tetzcoco, Mexico*, 8–10; and Patricia Lopes Don, "The 1539 Inquisition and Trial of Don Carlos of Texcoco." With the conquest a shift occurred in the method of determining the native leader. Before the conquest, elders would choose a male from the ruling family to take the leadership, usually preferring a brother, and then a son or nephew. Under the Spanish, succession came to mirror Spanish rules of inheritance.

2. In the colonial period the honorific "don" was an important signifier. Thus to a person in the colonial period don Fernando Ixtlilxochitl and Fernando Ixtlilxochitl were clearly two different people.

3. Fernando de Alva Ixtlilxochitl, *Obras históricas*, 1: 493.

4. A *cacique* was a traditional native ruler. The term itself was Arawak and adopted by the Spaniards while still in the Caribbean and then imposed on the rest of their territories in the Americas.

5. The historical record about Juan Grande is nearly empty. However, history records an early settler, possibly a member of the Narváez expedition, named Alonso Grande

from Moguer, who married a native woman and had six children. He did not list an occupation; Icaza, *Diccionario de conquistadores de Nueva España*, 2: 201. Alonso's brother, Juan, was one of the pilots who sailed with Columbus on the third and fourth voyages; Peter Boyd-Bowman, *Índice geobiográfico de cuarenta mil pobladores españoles de América en el siglo XVI, 1493–1519*, items 1945 and 1946, 67. This might possibly be the man, or at least a kinsman of him, who ends up marrying doña Francisca Cristina.

6. A good overview to the dynamics of the colonial cacique, and the presence of persons of mixed race in their ranks, can be found in James Lockhart, *The Nahuas after the Conquest: A Social and Cultural History of the Indians of Central Mexico, Sixteenth through Eighteenth Centuries*, 133–34; and Charles Gibson, *Aztecs under Spanish Rule: A History of the Indians of the Valley of Mexico, 1519–1810*, 161–65.

7. Juan Pérez Pereleda worked for the city from 1592 to 1594 on a variety of projects; Edmundo O'Gorman, *Guía de las actas del cabildo de la ciudad de México, Siglo XVI*, items 5329, 5377, 5384, 5432, 5474, and 5537.

8. Robert Haskett, *Indigenous Rulers: An Ethnohistory of Town Government in Colonial Cuernavaca*, 138–40.

9. John F. Schwaller, "Don Bartolomé de Alva, Nahuatl Scholar of the Seventeenth Century," 8; and Fernando de Alva Ixtlilxochitl, *Obras históricas*, ed., Edmundo O'Gorman, 1: 9–21. All of the children used various forms of their names throughout their lifetimes.

10. Alva Ixtlilxochitl, *Obras históricas*, 1: 17–42.

11. Alva Ixtlilxochitl, *Obras históricas*, 2: 289.

12. Alva Ixtlilxochitl, *Obras históricas*, 1: 197–201.

13. An external, native governor appointed by Spanish authorities to rule a territory, generally not the home region of the person.

14. Alva Ixtlilxochitl, *Obras históricas*, 2: 24–27.

15. Lockhart, *Nahuas after the Conquest*, 30–35; Gibson, *Aztecs under Spanish Rule*, 167–68; and Yanna Yannakakis, *The Art of Being In-Between: Native Intermediaries, Indian Identity, and Local Rule in Colonial Oaxaca*, 11–14.

16. The relación de parte y de oficio consisted of formal testimony taken under the supervision of a royal court judge as to one's service to the Crown. Yannakakis sees the relación de méritos as the basis for many petitions of native communities to the Crown for the defense of their privileges; Yannakakis, *Art of Being In-Between*, 41–42, citing Alva Ixtlilxochitl's work specifically.

17. Alva Ixtlilxochitl, *Obras históricas*, 2: 347–48.

18. Alva Ixtlilxochitl, *Obras históricas*, 1: 27–36. It is not clear if Antonia Gutiérrez was a Spaniard, *india* (Indian woman), or *mestiza* (a woman of mixed Indian-Spanish descent).

19. Alva Ixtlilxochitl, *Obras históricas*, 2: 235.

20. Charles Gibson and John B. Glass, "A Census of Middle American Prose Manuscripts in the Native Historical [sic] Tradition," 337–38, esp. 15; and Eduardo de Jesus Douglas, "Pictorial History in the 'Quinatzin Map' of about 1542," 286.

21. Alva Ixtlilxochitl, *Obras históricas*, 1: 371, "Con esto acabó el autor o autores que este original y antigua historia pintaron por no haber sucedido más."

22. "Esta es la verdadera historia de los tultecas según yo lo he podido interpreter, y los viejos principales con quien lo he comunicado me lo han declarado," Alva Ixtlilxochitl, *Obras historicas*, 1: 285–87.

23. The importance of these ties in the period after the conquest is outlined in Lopes Don, "The 1539 Inquisition and Trial."

24. For example in discussing the period in which the Chichimeca nobles lived in Tulancingo prior to departing for Tula he wrote: "en el año de la encarnación de Christo nuestro señor, 13 acatl, y a la nuestra 542, siendo sumo pontífice Virgilio, romano, al segundo año de su pontificado, y a los doce años del imperio de Justiniano, y en España, el rey Theudio, a los doce de su gobierno. . . ." Alva, *Obras históricas*, 1: 291; Salvador Velazco, "La imaginación historiográfica de Fernando de Alva Ixtlilxochitl," 34.

25. Rolena Adorno, "Arms, Letters, and the Native Historian in Early Colonial Mexico," in *1492–1992: Re/Discovering Colonial Writing*, 213–15; Lisa Voigt, "Peregrine Peregrinations: Rewriting Travel and Discovery in Mestizo Chronicles of New Spain," 9–11.

26. "Cierto, muchas veces me ha parecido, que los historiadores antiguos que pintaron la vida de este singular príncipe hacen lo que se cuenta de Xenofonte, que todos dicen de él, que en la vida que escribió de Ciro, rey de los persas, no fue tanto su intento escribir vida de un hombre en particular, cuanto pintar un buen rey en las partes que conviene que tenga, y así parece que quien quisiera pintar y hacer relación de un buen monarca, aunque bárbaro, de cuantos hubo en este nuevo mundo, no tenía que hacer más de poner delante la vida del rey Nezahualcoyotzin, porque fue un dechado de buenos y excelentes príncipes," Alva Ixtlilxochitl, *Obras históricas*, 1: 439.

27. By the 1620s mestizo sons of the native elite were being ordained; Francisco Morales, *Ethnic and Social Background of the Franciscan Friars in Seventeenth Century Mexico*, 38–47.

28. John F. Schwaller, "Don Bartolomé de Alva, Nahuatl Scholar of the Seventeenth Century," 6–8.

29. The best-known work in Mexico of this genre is Hernando Ruiz de Alarcón, *Treatise on the Heathen Superstitions That Today Live among the Indians Native to This New Spain*.

30. Schwaller, "Don Bartolomé de Alva," 74–75.

31. Schwaller, "Don Bartolomé de Alva," 78–79.

32. Schwaller, "Don Bartolomé de Alva," 82–85.

33. Schwaller, "Don Bartolomé de Alva," 92–97.

34. Natives of the Texcoco region continue this pre-Hispanic religious tradition believing that the ahuaques control the moisture in the heights of the mountains behind the city. Another example of works written at this time to be used in rooting out traditional native religious practices was Ruiz de Alarcón's *Treatise on the Heathen Superstitions*. Interestingly enough, Ruiz de Alarcón's brother was Juan Ruiz de Alarcón, who became a famous playwright of the Spanish Golden Age.

35. Barry Sell, Louise Burkhart, and Elizabeth R. Wright, *Nahuatl Theater*, 3.

36. Schwaller, "Don Bartolomé de Alva," 12–13.

37. Horacio Carochi, *Grammar of the Mexican Language: With an Explanation of Its Adverbs*, 8–9.

38. Angel María Garibay, *Historia de la literatura Nahuatl*, 2: 339–68.

39. Sell, Burkhart, and Wright, *Nahuatl Theater*, 3: 35.

40. Sell, Burkhart, and Wright, *Nahuatl Theater*, 163–65, 197. The original Spanish version of the first passage reads; "Beautiful and verdant garden whose beauty rivals Aphrodite's gardens on Cyprus so celebrated by the Ancients. Rose bushes, who in defense of the felicitous rose buds, arm yourselves with sharp and slender thorns. Beautiful pink flowers, you blush on hearing me, for your white blossoms are tinged with purple." The Spanish version of the second passages is: "These beguiling brooks stir my feelings, as does this myrtle, and the jasmine that steals the sweet perfume of amber. All the forest shelters me, while this green laurel provides a rich canopy shaded by these flowers."

41. *Ballads of the Lords of New Spain*, 86–87. This particular passage then goes on to praise Alva's forbear, Nezahualcoyotl. "There! A flower tree stands beside the drum. The plume swan is in it. It's Nezahualcoyotzin. He's like a bird, flower-chirping, happy with these flowers."

42. For his part, Sigüenza y Góngora also drew on Fernando de Alva's works in writing his own historical treatises; Pablo García, "Saldo del criollismo."

43. Alva Ixtlilxochitl, *Obras históricas*, 1: 39–42.

CHAPTER 3

Trained by Jesuits

Indigenous *Letrados* in Seventeenth-Century Peru

John Charles

In 1540, the Society of Jesus was founded with a mission to spread Catholicism to peoples and places throughout Reformation Europe and beyond, and to non-Christians in contact with or living under the imperial rule of Portugal and Spain. The transoceanic voyages of Spain's Jesuit missionaries began without delay. In 1541, they journeyed to India and to the Far East; and in 1549, to the Americas, first Brazil and Florida, then to Peru in 1568 and New Spain two years later. The Jesuits' ministry in the Peruvian viceroyalty started with great promise and triggered the optimism of Crown and Church authorities, whose success in evangelizing native Andeans had been limited in the turbulent postconquest period of civil war and Inca revolt. From their base in Santiago del Cercado, the indigenous district of the Lima capital, the Jesuits baptized and preached to neophytes, heard confessions, and celebrated Mass. Groups of priests also traveled to the highland communities of the interior to teach native Andeans about the errors of the ancestral divinities and the rewards of Christianity.[1] But the establishment of schools in urban centers, for Spanish and Indian youth, was a hallmark of the order's ministry and a key part of its strategy to transform the manners and customs of colonial society.[2]

Indigenous elites were the focus of the Society's designs from the start, for ties between the Jesuits and native Andean chieftains made it possible for the order to assume positions of authority over local communities in the absence of the former Inca governors. One of the most celebrated ventures in this regard was the royal boarding school, the Colegio del Príncipe, which was inaugurated in 1618 by order of King Philip III to educate the sons of the indigenous nobility of the Lima archdiocese. It was here that adolescent notables of the Pacific coast and central Andean highlands undertook schooling in Castilian literacy and Christian doctrine, on the condition that upon completion of the course of study, they would return to their home villages and serve at the behest of Spanish provincial governors (*corregidores*) and the clergy in temporal and spiritual administration. The Jesuits at the colegio planned to mold a select cadre of hereditary chiefs (*curacas*) who would teach and personify orthodox Christian values and practices in local native communities that were seen as politically resistant and prone to religious error. As Viceroy Francisco de Borja y Aragón, the school's leading patron, expressed in the school's charter, the native students under Jesuit care had the promise to become living examples of virtue for all indigenous subjects.[3] The Royal Audiencia and Lima Church were also eager to begin a positive new chapter in the story of evangelization and, after long debate over the school's financing and administration, the two bodies agreed that the Society of Jesus was the missionary group best suited for the assignment.[4] So suited, that in 1621, the Jesuits opened a homologous institution in Cuzco, the ancient capital of the Incas, to educate the sons of ethnic lords in the dioceses of Cuzco, Huamanga, and Arequipa. The Colegio del Príncipe and Cuzco's Colegio de San Francisco de Borja thus added to the number of prototype colegios that the order had already established at their various South American missions.[5]

The optimistic portrait of the Jesuit education program in statements by the viceroy and by other colonial authorities continues to echo in modern historical scholarship, which has largely presumed that the native students were obedient cultural ambassadors, strictly aligned with the goals of Spanish colonialism. Studies of the "education as conquest" variety have stressed, as did colonial policymakers, the caciques' overwhelming effectiveness as agents of acculturation.[6] For example, a landmark study of neo-Inca intellectual movements in the eighteenth century excludes the Andean nobles schooled by Jesuits from analysis, describing the ethnic lords of this type as "more Catholic and better Christians than the Spaniards themselves," who probably "knew little or nothing of the pagan practices of their tributaries."[7] To be sure, numerous historical studies produced in the last decades have identified the variable cultural and social positions that caciques in general occupied as intermediaries between Europeans and Andeans in provincial settings, as well as the pathways of advancement that their Spanish education afforded them in colonial society.[8] Yet with regard to those trained by Jesuit priests, in particular, the category of the fully Hispanized subject, loyal to Spanish rule and Catholic teachings, has been difficult to revise, and the stories of the students themselves have not figured as points of departure for grasping a more complete view of the schools' colonizing function and of the Jesuits' role in the development of Peru's native governing class.

Andean nobles who were schooled by Jesuits no doubt held understandings of Catholicism that differed from those of Indian tributaries. But little is known about the specific contours of that Catholicism or about how their learning impinged on issues of local culture and politics in native pueblos. Fortunately, new studies about the education of indigenous elites have begun to locate by name a small but significant number of former Jesuit students in the bureaucratic papers of the colonial archive. The most notable is Monique Alaperrine-Bouyer's longue durée institutional history of the schools in Lima and Cuzco, which has identified in judicial records thirteen former students of the Colegio del Príncipe out of the 280 listed on the school's official matriculation registries for the period 1621–1656.[9] Although relatively few in relation to the total number enrolled, these case studies nevertheless present an invitation to correct well-rehearsed assumptions and examine the actual historical situation of caciques who acted as cultural brokers amid the competing political and economic forces of the "república de indios." The evidence of their varied participation as plaintiffs and defendants in colonial tribunals, at times in support of the conquering authority and at other times in opposition, speaks in large part to the new powers that their Jesuit education provided them.[10] What appears from the vantage point of the legal docket is a side of the colegio that was marked by opposition and controversy, whose graduates used their knowledge of Spanish values and legal principles, and not always to serve colonizing agendas.

Trial records concerning the extirpation of idolatries in the archive of the Lima archdiocese, together with parish inspection reports and lawsuits against Crown authorities and the clergy, expose a broader sweep of social interactions that are missing in the official histories and pronouncements, as well as a sharper picture of the caciques' historical role in the evangelization process as they themselves understood it. The focus here centers on the Colegio del Príncipe's first half century, from 1618 until roughly the end of Archbishop Pedro de Villagómez's tenure in 1671, with special attention given to the troubling nexus, from a colonialist perspective, between education and empowerment. Starting with the case of one heretofore unknown graduate, Antonio Chupica, the goal is to examine the students' attempts to protect indigenous autonomy in negotiation with Spanish rule, and to pose new questions about the impact of their Jesuit training on day-to-day administration in native communities far from the empire's metropolitan centers.

A Jesuit Curriculum for Noble Lords

How did the Jesuits prepare their students to speak for the Church and the Crown within native society? Partial answers can be found in the guidelines that Fathers José de Acosta and Juan de la Plaza drew up for future schools in Lima and Cuzco following the order's provincial congregation of 1576. According to the instructions, only the eldest sons of hereditary elites (*caciques principales* and *segundas personas*) were to be admitted, entering between the ages of nine and sixteen, and remaining cloistered for a period of six years.[11] The proposed curriculum, similar to the liberal arts curriculum of a minor seminary, emphasized training in Castilian literacy, insisting that the students speak and write exclusively in Spanish among themselves. They were to learn Christian doctrine for work as catechists, in Spanish and in their native language of Quechua, and receive instruction in arithmetic and music. Catholic liturgy, devotional readings, and spiritual exercises rounded out the structured daily regime.[12] The program to instill civility (*policía cristiana*) in the young charges also had a Christian humanist dimension: "The [Indian boys] should not be deprived of the laws and customs and way of governing of their lands, provided they are not contrary to natural and Christian law. Nor is it wise to transform them completely into Spaniards, which not only would be difficult and cause of discouragement for the students but also a great obstacle to their government."[13] In Acosta and Plaza's view, there was no quick fix for transforming barbarous habits into Christian ones; they believed that to create an Andean Catholic society, the future caciques should impose the new laws and customs gradually upon the conquered groups with patience and flexibility. While the Jesuits advocated forcefully the suppression of traditional beliefs and rites, such as ritual drunkenness and ancestor worship, the strategy was to tolerate more innocent native routines and guide them slowly toward Christian ends.[14]

A corollary aim of the school was for the padres to acquire the indigenous cultural knowledge and language skills they needed for Andean ministry. The reciprocity between the Jesuits and their native students is perhaps most evident in the sizable corpus of catechisms and pastoral complements they produced jointly in the recently alphabetized languages of Quechua, Aymara, and Guaraní. Jesuit linguists—Diego González Holguín (1607, 1608), Ludovico Bertonio (1612), Antonio Ruiz de Montoya (1640), and others— praised the mostly unnamed literati of Lima, Cuzco, and Juli, who taught them how to use Andean languages to communicate Christian doctrine and denounce false religion.[15] Given the intellectual achievement of the indigenous collaborators, it is not surprising that some Jesuits hoped that their native students might prove capable of entering the priesthood.[16] In 1582, this idea for the future schools was presented by the Jesuit attorney Diego de Torres before the Spanish Crown and Roman Curia. However, previous bans by Lima's First and Second Church Councils against the ordination of Indians, and Philip II's decree of 1583 that prohibited instruction of indigenous neophytes in the "supremas facultades" (highest faculties) on the reasoning that native exposure to higher disciplines and the Scripture could lead to heresies, created hurdles too powerful to overcome.[17] The legislation thus helps to explain why no evidence surfaces in Jesuit records to confirm that Latin grammar, logic, theology, rhetoric, or other subjects of the universities and seminaries were taught to Andean nobles on a formal basis in the order's missions and schools.

Judging from the principles outlined by Acosta and Plaza, it seems that the colegios had a more ordinary purpose. The intention was to equip young leaders for the routine tasks of enforcing parish obligations, such as attendance at Mass and catechesis, recording native corvée labor and tribute payments, and updating corregidores and priests on the status of natural and human resources in regional parishes and administrative districts (repartimientos). This included, above all, setting a Christian example for common Indians and reporting to the extirpating clergy the occurrence of any clandestine beliefs and ritual activities among the villagers, and the locations of ancestral divinities and shrines. In this sense, the colegio's graduates were to serve as de facto legal agents, maintaining community records, keeping watch over the native tributaries and parishioners, representing them before colonial authorities, and denouncing public crimes that fell under the purview of Spanish justice. They would be letrados on a minor scale, but without a law degree: interpreters and producers of legal, religious, and political discourses in the service of colonial municipal officials and priests (see also Yannakakis, chapter 4).

Acosta returned to Spain in 1586 before the schools' founding, but the Lima see's systematic campaigns to extirpate Andean idolatries, initiated by Archbishop Bartolomé Lobo Guerrero (1609–1622), provided the necessary momentum for the Jesuits' plan. In 1618, under the direction of Acosta's intellectual heir in the Peruvian province, Pablo José de Arriaga, the Colegio del Príncipe was built in the Cercado, together with the Casa de Santa Cruz, a neighboring house of reclusion for convicted idolaters that was also run by the Jesuits.[18] The *carta annua* of that year from the Lima residence celebrates the two-month anti-idolatry mission of Father Juan Vázquez, which resulted in recruiting fourteen students for the school and the detention of forty "sorcerers and witches" who would be the first to carry out their criminal sentences at the prison.[19] According to Arriaga, instruction and persuasion, rather than judicial punishments, were the preferred instruments for educating young caciques, and separating them from the bad influence of native religious specialists in the colonial Indian settlements (*pueblos de indios*) was central to this goal. At the same time, in the highland communities, the nurturing approach to evangelization, which relied heavily on the mediating work of the noble lords, existed in constant tension with the Inquisitorial mechanisms of the extirpation-of-idolatries trial complex. A look at the papers of the ecclesiastical archive casts light on the opportunities and challenges that the colegio's graduates met as the face of these at times mismatched programs of catechesis and extirpation.

Making Legal Prosecutions

On July 25, 1623, Antonio Chupica, a descendant of the noble line of San Francisco de Ihuari, in the region of Checras, registered in the Colegio del Príncipe's sixth class of boarders.[20] At the time of his enrollment, support for the colegio among native elites was uneven. The curacas of Cuzco, for example, saw the schools as a key to obtaining Spanish recognition of their noble status. In a 1601 letter to the Crown, they petitioned the creation of a colegio for noble lords under the direction of the Jesuits, as had been promised to them since the time of Viceroy Toledo. But lingering resentments existed, in particular over the caciques' ongoing exclusion from the priesthood, and over the viceroy and archbishop's use of the overstretched indigenous community funds (*cajas de comunidad*) for the school's financing.²¹ In the Colegio del Príncipe's first four decades, the school received on average only eight new students per year, with forty being the peak number that was enrolled at one time.²² The modest proportion of caciques aside, one can presume that Chupica's family was among those who foresaw the social and economic benefits that a Jesuit education promised. In return for supervising local parishes and municipalities, major native functionaries of noble status received salaries and exemptions from tribute payments and forced labor service (*mita*), as well as opportunities for lucre in extralegal business dealings at the local level.

The extant writings of the colegio's graduates, while relatively scarce, verify that the students did, in fact, receive superior training in Castilian literacy. These writings, which appear in judicial dossiers, reveal across the board elegant script, a firm grasp of Spanish notarial rhetoric and officialese, and certain knowledge of royal law and Church canons.²³ Nothing would distinguish the papers they authored from those of the ubiquitous Spanish notary or legal functionary. Much like the practitioners (*prácticos*) in early modern Iberia who produced legal-aid texts in the vernacular but without formal training in law,²⁴ the native collegians probably acquired legal knowhow outside formal educational channels. In all likelihood, they learned to write petitions due to their contact with Spanish attorneys and royal protectors (*protectores de naturales*), and their work as assistants of royal and Church inquests and municipal tribunals. While many of the Jesuits' students composed manuscripts independently without Spanish legal mediation, Chupica sought out scribal assistance; he had his known legal papers drafted via an ecclesiastical notary. The signatures and rubrics he added to the documents, however, attest to a hand quite proficient in notarial operations (see also Burns, chapter 10).²⁵

Informing on spiritual customs forbidden by the Church was one of Chupica's duties as governor and cacique principal in Checras, although he is so far the only colegio graduate to be located in the archival record who brought idolatry charges in the role of ecclesiastical prosecutor, or *fiscal de la idolatría*. On December 22, 1644, the native fiscal presented a criminal accusation (*causa criminal*) against a secret ritual complex in the town of San Pedro de Pacho—which involved men and women tributaries, a municipal magistrate (*alcalde*), and a rival cacique—for venerating a *huaca*, or traditional Andean deity, in ways that connected with pre-Hispanic custom. Chupica's accusation, received by the priest and vicar of the town, Pedro de los Ríos, and then remitted to Archbishop Villagómez, began with the moralizing boiler-plate found in contemporary sermons of extirpation: "It has come to my attention that some Indians of the province, with little fear of God, and in defiance of the Holy Catholic Faith, have practiced idolatry in ancient rites and ceremonies and huacas, sacrificing animals, offering chicha and other ceremonies to the devil, without regard to this being an offense against God Our Lord and His Holy Catholic Faith."[26] Chupica named Juan de la Plata as recording notary and two language interpreters (one of whom was Antón Angola, a ladino African) for the examination of witnesses. The fiscal then ordered local native parish officials to arrest the accused, confiscate their properties, and confine them in the public jail of Ihuari, without recourse to immunity or other church privileges, for what turned out to be an almost two-year inquiry and trial.

The records of idolatry prosecutions are rarely straightforward, however; orthodox perspectives expressed in the documents typically overlapped with the material and political interests of the actors involved. In this case, the counterarguments of the indicted point to crucial facts that were excluded from the original accusation. Chupica's assistants executed the order of arrest, but Pedro Mais, the chief minister, fled capture. Most of the remaining detainees were pressed under torment to admit their guilt in the prosecutor's terms. According to Mais's wife, the devil had prompted the group to worship the stone Pariaguanca, with ritual drinking and dance, and offerings of cuy, flowers, worms, spiders, and chicha.[27] Meanwhile, a few defendants held firm, claiming the reason for their indictment and detention was personal; they had refused Chupica's demand to leave their pueblo and join his workforce in Ihuari, despite viceregal provisions that sanctioned their right to provide mita labor in their home village of Pacho.[28] But additional turns of the rope by Chupica's assistants, under the watch of Checras's extirpating judge, Tomás de Espinosa, eventually produced the desired confessions: that at the group's behest, Mais had indeed performed sacrifices for Pariaguanca in the hope of obtaining legal victory in the dispute with the governor.[29] In the absence of the fugitive ringleader, Espinosa found three conspirators guilty of idolatry and issued a standard punishment: one hundred lashes and a procession of shame on mules, with a town crier broadcasting their offense; this was to be followed by compulsory attendance at a feast-day Mass, while stripped to the waist and with their necks bound in a noose.[30]

A few years later, in 1655, Chupica turned up again in the ecclesiastical courts, but this time as a native authority criminally charged with the theft of livestock. The prosecution of the charge stemmed from a grievance filed by the veteran extirpator and beneficiary of the parish of Ihuari, Bartolomé Jurado Palomino, who had assumed the post in 1650.[31] As stated in the grievance, upon returning to the parish after being away on church business in Lima, Jurado Palomino learned from the chief attendants (*mayordomos*) of a local confraternity that, without authorization, Chupica had taken possession of 130 llamas belonging to the religious association and then sold them to a Jesuit hacienda in the coastal valley of Chancay.[32] According to the complaint, the priest quietly confronted Chupica about the misconduct following the next Mass, asking why the native governor insisted on meddling in the assets of the church, when he, Jurado Palomino, left Chupica free to govern and collect tribute in the secular domain as he wished. And at this the cacique flew into a rage, Jurado Palomino's diplomacy notwithstanding:

> [Don Antonio] stated he had taken the llamas, and that he could do so, and I said to him "Señor Don Antonio, you cannot, look at the books and the orders left by the church inspector," and he responded in great anger, "I can do it as the governor I am, and I have no need for books," and other foolish statements, to which I replied, "Let me speak, Don Antonio," . . . Then, he came towards me, putting on his hat and twirling a staff he held in his hands, and stomping the floor, he said that I should know whom I was talking to, and "We'll see if you dare to talk that way in the Audiencia," addressing me with "tú" and "vos," contradicting me many times, and with many other bad words, both he and his brother Don Pedro Chupica [had], against Doctor Pablo Reino de Castilla, the canon of the Holy Church of Lima. . . . And gathering his native officials, he left with them in tow, and according to my information, he then opened a wineskin and gave out aguardiente and chicha, and in the company of the mestizo Roque de Ávalos, who is married to one of his sisters, [Don Antonio] ordered a grievance to be written up, and they sent it to Lima, threatening me, saying that I would pay dearly for it, . . . and all the Indians and others present were astonished and frightened to see with what liberty and shamelessness he spoke to me. And the hatred and bad will he has for me is not only because I brought charges of witchcraft and idolatry against one of

his friends, but also because he generally despises the parish clergy, as he has [despised] all who have been priests in this benefice since he became governor.[33]

Jurado Palomino's statement—which was corroborated by eyewitnesses, including native church personnel; members of the municipal council hierarchy; and Pedro Quispe Condor, a recent graduate of the Colegio del Príncipe[34]—adds further dimensions to the evolving portrait of Chupica, whose relationship with the new parish and extirpation authorities was soured by legal actions and fights over income and property ownership. The testimony discloses the cacique's ties to the Jesuit hacienda, antagonisms toward Checras's secular clergy, associations with drunkards and religious backsliders, and a willingness to manipulate the legal system (through use of the Indian court of the Lima Royal Audiencia) in order to blackmail political adversaries. Chupica thus positioned himself tactically in relation to Spanish authority in multiple and shifting ways. While at first he employed the law of the Church in order to advance the cause of extirpation and his power as fiscal, he later asserted his ethnic authority and legal acumen to strengthen ties with native kin groups and limit the influence of extirpators and priests. Chupica's numerous involvements with the royal and ecclesiastical courts suggest that disputes over cultural and religious boundaries and their representations in the legal dossiers were as much about the erratic nature and structure of local political authority as about the actual fitness or corruption of native Andean practices (see also Yannakakis, chapter 4).[35] That a former student of the Jesuit colegio in Lima would defend Jurado Palomino's account of what happened in Ihuari indicates, furthermore, that the school's graduates did not necessarily speak with one voice.

The conflict in Checras was by no means the only conflict involving graduates of the colegio in the pueblos of the central highlands during the school's first fifty years. Other trials tell the story of Sebastián Quispe Ninavilca, successor of Huarochirí's chief noble dynasty and a "mortal enemy of priests," who was accused of inciting rebellion against the clergy in the region, while concealing information from church investigators on traditional beliefs and ceremonies.[36] His contemporary Rodrigo de Guzmán Rupay Chagua, the governor of Huamantanga in Canta province, battled Mercedarian friars, extirpators, and competing nobility for more than three decades as both an accused idolater and a plaintiff against bad priests.[37] Yet another former student, Rodrigo Flores Caja Malqui, the governor and cacique principal in Santo

Domingo de Ocros, Cajatambo, fought the depredations of parish clergy and was prosecuted, in turn, for religious crimes.[38] A testimony by Juan de Mendoza, the cacique and governor of Lampas in the 1650s, hints that the Jesuits' students appropriated the forms of learning that brought the most immediate and practical benefits. Mendoza explained to an inspector of idolatries that his son, Alonso, had enrolled in the colegio to "learn to read and write and become a good letrado and rise to the office of cacique and governor."[39] For many noble lords, Jesuit schooling was first and foremost a path of social preservation that allowed their offspring in time to learn the law and writing so as to protect local self-rule as well as the family's interests and investments. The more cynical view, expressed by countless Spanish authorities, was that the Indians desired letters, not to understand better the catechism, but instead to make better lawsuits.[40]

Still, generalizations about the collective action of the colegio's alumni become impossible to draw, even within a single case study. It seems that the noble lords crafted strategies of action in terms of ever-changing individual needs and circumstances, rather than according to unified political or religious agendas. The trial records underscore a dynamic ethnic activity, which was not necessarily separate from their formal practice of Catholicism, however doctrinaire or ambiguous this may have been, or from their political and economic dealings with Spanish authorities (see also Yannakakis, chapter 4).[41] Also striking is that the caciques who were incriminated by Spanish justice seem to have defied their colonial mandate openly, knowing full well that their misbehavior could be taken as violations of royal and ecclesiastical law. The ubiquity of curacas who defied brazenly the Church and its ministers has led scholars such as Karen Spalding to speculate that they did so to remind native tributaries of their power over the local clergy, or perhaps to draw Church authorities into lawsuits they saw as winnable.[42]

A School in Controversy

The result of Chupica's dispute with Jurado Palomino is unfortunately missing from the legal dossier, but there is good reason to believe that Archbishop Villagómez would not have hesitated to bring judgment against the defiant cacique. In the Lima Church's anti-idolatry fervor from the 1640s to the 1660s, when indigenous elites were badly needed to reinforce the actions of extirpating authorities, Villagómez was angry at the pervasive reality of caciques who, in his view, misdirected their energies away from native religious error and toward lawsuits against the clergy. The prelate's disdain for native litigation was clear in his response to a series of lawsuits in the 1650s that native lords, including two graduates of the colegio, Francisco Chavín Palpa and Gabriel Camacguacho, brought against the parish priest of San Juan de Huariaca for economic abuses and sacramental neglect.[43] Outraged by what he felt were false allegations that tarnished an exemplary minister, Villagómez took the unusual step of entering a reprimand of the caciques into the court record, which offered harsh words for native litigants in general; plaintiffs of this type, he declared, were "not just bad [Christians], . . . but the worst kind," who dishonored the priests in order to replace them with ones agreeable to their schemes and interests.[44] Using similar language, Cuzco's Archbishop Fernando de Vera wrote to the Spanish monarch in 1639 and 1645 concerning the injurious activism of the "demonios" educated at the Colegio de San Francisco de Borja and their mistreatment of indigenous tributaries.[45] From the standpoint of the high clergy, the caciques' penchant for troublemaking inflicted political turmoil on native parishes, making it unfeasible for the *curas de indios* to carry out their role as Christian examples and monitors of religious orthodoxy.

Long-standing disagreements between the Society and secular Church powers on a host of issues relating to indigenous ministry provide some necessary background for the archbishops' rancor. Vera and Cuzco's ecclesiastical council, for example, railed against the order's refusal to contribute monies to the diocesan seminary or to allow pastoral inspections (*visitas*) of their missions.[46] Villagómez, Vera, and their predecessors in the Lima and Cuzco sees also defended the Church's episcopal jurisdiction over the coveted parishes of San Lázaro, Lambayeque, and Andahuaylillas in the face of Jesuit attempts to claim them as missionary centers outside diocesan control.[47] The tense relations touched a flash point, in particular, over the return to systematic persecution of traditional Andean beliefs and customs in the central highlands. One of Villagómez's core policies was to revitalize the extirpation-of-idolatries campaigns, at a time when the Jesuits, who had been active supporters of the campaigns under Lobo Guerrero, began to distance themselves from their increasingly punitive character.[48] While Jesuit priests continued to accompany the extirpating judges on inspections and oversee the teaching of religious offenders at the Casa de Santa Cruz, they did so in fewer numbers, prompting the archbishop to denounce the Jesuits' waning commitment in a 1654 letter to the Crown. The *cartas annuas* for that time period confirm the Peruvian province's concerns that association with the harsh methods of extirpation's juridical apparatus was endangering the padres' status as trusted confessors and preachers in the view of native communities.[49] Moreover, to a number of Jesuits, the continuing problem of idolatries was caused largely by the incompetence and double standards of secular priests; in this perspective, the visita was a course of action that should not only correct religious error but also hold accountable the clergy.[50]

Signs also point to the fact that Jesuit priests may have encouraged the caciques to use Spanish justice to protect native communities from corrupt priests and functionaries.[51] In 1637, after learning reports that former students of the schools for noble lords were using their education to file lawsuits against corregidores and clergymen, in great detriment to colonial governance, Philip IV asked Viceroy Cabrera y Bobadilla to determine if it was not best to shut down the Jesuit colegios altogether. The viceroy's response, in resolute support of the schools' continuation, enlisted the opinion of Antonio Vázquez, the provincial of the Peruvian province, who praised the caciques' Christian leadership and assistance in destroying the Andeans' sacred idols, which was the principal objective of the institutions. Furthermore, Vázquez stated that native judicial actions were a much-needed remedy against Spanish abuses of power: "The corregidores, and priests, and other Spaniards attack [the caciques for their education] because [the former] wish to be absolute lords in the pueblos, without having anyone there to defend the Indians or bring their lawsuits, as these caciques do by protecting [the Indians] from the humiliations they endure; and [the Spanish authorities] fear that [the caciques] will seek reparation for the offenses by going to the Superior Tribunals with their complaints."[52] Vázquez was not alone in his conviction; for example, in 1661, Lima's Protector General of the Indians, Diego de León Pinelo, called for more rigorous inspections of the corregidores and parish clergy while simultaneously defending the Christian example of the Colegio del Príncipe's alumni.[53]

The Ambiguity of Indigenous Education

The extent to which the Jesuit order as a whole embraced the native lords' defense of their prerogatives through the courts remains foggy. What connection existed, if any, between Jesuit ideas about native education and the activities of the colegio's graduates? Was legal activism against the immoral conduct of corregidores and churchmen a part of the order's sense of its religious mission? On the one hand, as Sabine MacCormack has noted, the

Jesuits traveled to Peru in the king's service, with orders from the Society's general not to interfere in politics, and as a result they were generally reserved about expressing public criticisms of Crown and Church policies and practices.[54] The continued involvement of Jesuits in the extirpation campaigns in the mid-1600s, albeit without direct participation in its juridical component, and the general silence of the annual letters on the issue of indigenous lawsuits, suggest the absence of a stable trend or systematic call to activism. On the other hand, however, the Jesuits struggled to reconcile matters of policy with matters of conscience. It was common to find in their writings direct and well-informed condemnations of the Indians' poor treatment at the hands of the rapacious provincial governors and clergy.[55] And the activism of the colegio's graduates undoubtedly carried on, whether animated or not directly by Jesuit opposition to Spanish abuses. In 1665, the extirpator Juan Sarmiento de Vivero faced separate lawsuits by three Andean noblemen, all of them former Jesuit students—Rodrigo de Guzmán Rupay Chagua, the governor of Huamantanga; Francisco Gamarra, segunda persona in Ihuari; and Cristóbal Carhuachin Pariasca, the curaca of San Juan de Lampián–owing to the inspector's alleged punishments and extortions while conducting visitas in the areas of Canta and Checras.[56]

There is an added methodological problem of establishing what, precisely, the stories of a handful of former collegians represent. The group of graduates known to scholars appear in the legal record because they were litigious. But are they typical of the colegio's students in general? However representative the caciques identified in tribunal records might have been, it is evident that they were, in fact, lightning rods in the volatile early history of the Peruvian Church. What is more, their actions point out, as does the generalized activism of ethnic lords outside the sphere of Jesuit influence, a basic contradiction that attached to the Spanish education of the indigenous nobility: Although schooling in Christian laws and customs was imparted to native elites, originally, in order to rule and manage the tributary populations, it was later withheld from them because the students had come to learn too well. Alaperrine-Bouyer has noted the steady drop in the colegio's enrollment when the influence of extirpation began to diminish, from 1660 onward,[57] which may serve as partial indication of the shift in Spanish attitudes on the merits of teaching literacy to native Andeans and of indigenous frustrations with their own unmet demands for instruction in supreme disciplines and access to higher offices. By 1657, when the curacas Luis Macas and Felipe Carhua Mango wrote to Philip IV in protest of the threadbare education that their sons received at the colegio, despite rising tuitions,[58] it was already obvious that the Jesuits' attempt to remake Andean evangelization through the boarding schools for noble lords had lost its utopian attraction.

The ambiguity of indigenous education comes through in a scene from the 1621 annual letter of the Jesuits of Lima's Cercado, which reports on the order's triumphs at the Colegio del Príncipe and at its highland mission among the neophytes and religious offenders in the province of Huarochirí. It first describes the students of the colegio, so quick to learn and pious that they equal the Spanish, and then goes on to describe the capture and imprisonment in Huarochirí of eleven chief sorcerers, who through committed instruction by the padres are soon expected to confess their sins. One night at the mission, the letter states, a Jesuit father awoke to hear devout Catholic songs coming from the prisoners' quarters, and he wondered how a people as loyal to Satan and indifferent to Christianity as this could know such beautiful hymns. When he confronted the huaca specialists, they explained to him: "Almost forty years earlier, when [we were] children, the Jesuit fathers who were the priests in the pueblo taught them [to us], but after the padres left, the devil tricked [us] and made [us] his ministers."[59] Characteristically, the emphasis falls on the stark opposition between two types of Andeans: the fervent Christians of the colegio and the recidivist elders of the parish, whom, it is hoped, the future caciques will one day turn back to Catholicism. As the ecclesiastical trial records make clear, however, even for the highly educated noble lords, no amount of education about Spanish Christian ways could prevent the impact of indigenous judgments and volitions on the "Andean interculture" that was born of colonialism.[60] While the colegio and the sorcerers' prison might at first suggest, in this sense, two divergent chapters in the history of native Andean responses to evangelization, the papers of the archive reveal a more complicated narrative about the distance between the school's educational ideals and the graduates' everyday situations, in which the extremes of loyalty and resistance seem conventional and out of place.

Notes

The following two archives were consulted for this chapter: Archivo Arzobispal de Lima (AAL) and Biblioteca Nacional del Perú (BNP).

1. Rubén Vargas Ugarte, *Historia de la Compañía de Jesús en el Perú*, 1: 43–54.

2. John O'Malley, *The First Jesuits*, 239–42; and Teófanes Egido, Javier Burrieza Sánchez, and Manuel Revuelta González, *Los jesuitas en España y en el mundo hispánico*, 107,

cites the Jesuit Pedro de Ribadeneira's letter to Philip II on the Society's overriding dedication to schools for the youth.

3. Anonymous, "Colegio de caciques," 796.

4. Monique Alaperrine-Bouyer, *La educación de las elites indígenas en el Perú colonial,* 47–75, recounts the fifty-year struggle to bring the Colegio to fruition. Vargas Ugarte, *Historia de la Compañía,* 2: 225, describes the enthusiasm for the school in secular and ecclesiastical circles at the time of its opening.

5. Peru's Jesuits first established schools for indigenous neophytes in provincial areas such as Huarochirí (1570) and Juli (1576). See Vargas Ugarte, *Historia de la Compañía,* 1: 63, 2: 212; and Juan B. Olaechea Labayen, "La política selectiva de los jesuitas en los colegios de hijos de caciques," 423–33. Olaechea Labayen also details the founding of Jesuit schools for noble lords in other regions of the Spanish Indies.

6. Mario Cárdenas Ayaipoma, "El Colegio de caciques y el sometimiento ideológico de los residuos de la nobleza aborigen"; and Virgilio Galdo Gutiérrez, *Educación de los curacas: una forma de dominación colonial.* Louise Burkhart, *Holy Wednesday: A Nahua Drama from Early Colonial Mexico,* 59, notes similar approaches in studies of Mexico's Colegio de Santa Cruz de Tlatelolco, namely José María Kobayashi's *La educación como conquista: Empresa franciscana en México.*

7. John H. Rowe, "El movimiento nacional inca del siglo XVIII," 22; translations of Spanish quotations are by the author; see also Pierre Duviols, *La destrucción de las religiones andinas (conquista y colonia),* 338.

8. Pioneering studies in this vein include Carlos J. Díaz Rementería, *El cacique en el virreinato del Perú;* María Rostworowski de Diez Canseco, *Estructuras andinas de poder: Ideología religiosa y política;* and Karen Spalding, *Huarochirí: An Andean Society under Inca and Spanish Rule.*

9. Alaperrine-Bouyer, *La educación de las elites,* 207–22. As Pablo Macera, "Noticias sobre la enseñanza elemental en el Perú durante el siglo XVIII," 342, points out, the Colegio del Príncipe educated a minority of the indigenous nobility, serving only forty students at the height of its enrollment. The school's matriculation records for the years 1618–1802 are reproduced in Anonymous, "Colegio de caciques," 800–829. Other studies that identify alumni of the Colegio in the colonial archives include Monique Alaperrine-Bouyer, "Saber y poder: La cuestión de la educación de las elites indígenas," 145–67; Manuel Burga, *Nacimiento de una utopía: Muerte y resurrección de los Incas;* John Charles, *Allies at Odds: The Andean Church and Its Indigenous Agents, 1583–1671* and "'More Ladino than Necessary': Indigenous Litigants and the Language Policy Debate in Mid-Colonial Peru"; José De la Puente Brunke, "'Los vasallos se desentrañan por su rey': Notas sobre quejas de curacas en el Perú del siglo XVII"; and Alcira Dueñas, "Ethnic Power and Identity Formation in Mid-Colonial Andean Writing."

10. Burkhart, *Holy Wednesday,* 59, makes this observation about the Nahua students of the Franciscan's Colegio de Santa Cruz.

11. According to Vargas Ugarte, *Historia de la Compañía,* 2: 223, the school would also admit younger sons of the indigenous nobility, provided that the families bore the cost of their education.

12. Sketches of the educational program appear in Xavier Albó, "Jesuitas y cultu-

ras indígenas Perú 1568–1606: Su actitud, métodos y criterios de aculturación," 273–76; Macera, "Noticias sobre la enseñanza," 340; Luis Martín, "The Peruvian Indian through Jesuit Eyes: The Case of José de Acosta and Pablo José de Arriaga," 205–14; and Alaperrine-Bouyer, La educación de las elites, 181–82.

13. Antonio de Egaña, Monumenta Peruana, 2: 460; and cited in Martín, "The Peruvian Indian through Jesuit Eyes," 211.

14. See José de Acosta, De procuranda indorum salute o Predicación del evangelio en las Indias," 1: 587, 591. The educational plan was then brought by Plaza to Mexico, where during his tenure as provincial of the Mexican province, the order established a colegio for indigenous youth at San Martín de Tepotzotlán. See Peggy K. Liss, "Jesuit Contributions to the Ideology of Spanish Empire in Mexico: Part I. The Spanish Imperial Ideology and the Establishment of the Jesuits within Mexican Society," 329.

15. Bertonio's Aymara coauthor and translator, Martín de Sancta Cruz Hanansaya, of the Society's mission in Juli, is one of the few mediators of this stratum known by name; see Ludovico Bertonio, Libro de la vida y milagros de Nuestro Señor Jesucristo en dos lenguas, aymara y romance, 5.

16. Pedro Guibovich, "La educación en el Perú colonial: Fuentes e historiografía," 277; referenced in José De la Puente Brunke, "'Los vasallos se desentrañan por su rey': Notas sobre quejas de curacas en el Perú del siglo XVII," 460n5.

17. Juan B. Olaechea Labayen, "La política selectiva de los jesuitas en los colegios de hijos de caciques," 423. The royal decree is transcribed in Richard Konetzke, Colección de documentos para la historia de la formación social de Hispanoamérica, 1493–1810, 1: 550.

18. Anonymous, "Colegio de caciques," 780–83. Albó, "Jesuitas y culturas indígenas," 275. On the colegio's rules of admission, see Macera, "Noticias sobre la enseñanza," 341; and Vargas Ugarte, Historia de la Compañía, 2: 223–24.

19. Mario Polia Meconi, La cosmovisión religiosa andina en los documentos inéditos del archivo Romano de la Compañía de Jesús (1581–1752), 437. The Lima Jesuits' annual letter of 1621 reports the enrollment of more than thirty boys at the colegio and the custody of more than 140 sorcerers at the house of reclusion. See Laura Gutiérrez Arbulú and Javier Flores Espinoza, "Dos documentos sobre los jesuitas en Huarochirí," 202.

20. Anonymous, "Colegio de caciques," 801.

21. Juan B. Olaechea Labayen, "La política selectiva de los jesuitas en los colegios de hijos de caciques," 423; Alaperrine-Bouyer, La educación de las elites, 141, 143, and "Saber y poder," 157, 162.

22. Macera, "Noticias sobre la enseñanza," 342.

23. For recent linguistic studies of native Andean uses of Spanish in the colonial period, see Rodolfo Cerrón-Palomino, Castellano andino: Aspectos sociolingüísticos, pedagógicos y gramaticales; and José Luis Rivarola, Español andino: Textos bilingües de los siglos XVI y XVII.

24. Richard Kagan, Lawsuits and Litigants in Castile, 1500–1700, 148; see Kathryn Burns, Into the Archive: Writing and Power in Colonial Peru, for the history of notaries and legal functionaries in colonial Peru.

25. AAL, Hechicerías e Idolatrías, Leg. 2, Exp. 3, fol. 1v; AAL, Hechicerías e Idolatrías, Leg. 2, Exp. 4, fol. 1r.

26. AAL, Hechicerías e Idolatrías, Leg. 2, Exp. 3, fol. 1r.

27. AAL, Hechicerías e Idolatrías, Leg. 2, Exp. 4, fols. 1v, 2r.

28. AAL, Hechicerías e Idolatrías, Leg. 2, Exp. 4, fol. 7r; see also fols. 10v, 18r.

29. AAL, Hechicerías e Idolatrías, Leg. 2, Exp. 4, fols. 17r–18v, 24v–25v, 32v.

30. AAL, Hechicerías e Idolatrías, Leg. 2, Exp. 4, fol. 35r. In 1647, Chupica assisted Judge Espinosa's inquiry into charges that Tomás de Acosta, *segunda persona* in the district of Checras, practiced witchcraft and ancestor veneration. In strongly denying the charges, Acosta stated that Chupica targeted him because he resisted Chupica's exclusive claim on power in regional native governance. See AAL, Hechicerías e Idolatrías, Leg. 2, Exp. 7, fols. 1v, 47r–48r; and description of the trial in Nicholas Griffiths, *The Cross and the Serpent: Religious Repression and Resurgence in Colonial Peru,* 171–72.

31. AAL, Concursos, Leg. 4, Exp. 9. Jurado Palomino is also recognized for his Quechua translation, published in 1649, of an Italian catechism by the Jesuit theologian Roberto Bellarmino; see Alan Durston, *Pastoral Quechua: The History of Christian Translation in Colonial Peru, 1550–1650,* 170.

32. AAL, Criminales, Leg. 19, Exp. 6, fols. 1r–2v. The hacienda, unidentified in the complaint, may refer to the Jesuit ranch in Huaura, which contained many livestock, according to Nicholas Cushner, *Lords of the Land: Sugar, Wine, and Jesuit Estates of Coastal Peru, 1600–1767,* 73.

33. AAL, Criminales, Leg. 19, Exp. 6, fols. 1r–1v.

34. AAL, Criminales, Leg. 19, Exp. 6, fols. 3v–6r. Quispe Condor matriculated at the Colegio in 1649. See Anonymous, "Colegio de caciques," 805.

35. See Lauren Benton, *Law and Colonial Cultures: Legal Regimes in World History, 1400–1900,* 2.

36. AAL, Criminales, Leg. 16, Exp. 6; AAL, Hechicerías e Idolatrías, Leg. 2, Exp. 2; see Spalding, *Huarochirí,* 227, 261.

37. AAL, Hechicerías e Idolatrías, Leg. 3, Exp. 9; AAL, Hechicerías e Idolatrías, Leg. 5, Exp. 4; AAL, La Merced, Leg. 7, Exp. 42; AAL, Visitas Eclesiásticas, Leg. 23, Exp. 30; see also Charles, *Allies at Odds,* 42–43, 53–57, 67–69, and "More *Ladino* than Necessary."

38. AAL, Capítulos, Leg. 9, Exp. 13; AAL, Capítulos, Leg. 11, Exp. 1; AAL, Capítulos, Leg. 15, Exp. 7; AAL, Civiles, Leg. 67, Exp. 1; AAL, Criminales, Leg. 9, Exp. 31. See Manuel Burga, *Nacimiento de una utopía: Muerte y resurrección de los Incas,* 362–64; and Charles, *Allies at Odds,* 123–29.

39. AAL, Hechicerías e Idolatrías, Leg. 3, Exp. 11, fol. 37v; see Burga, *Nacimiento de una utopía,* 365.

40. Bartolomé de Álvarez, *De las costumbres y conversión de los indios del Perú: Memorial a Felipe II* (1588), 268–69.

41. In contrast, Burga, *Nacimiento de una utopía,* 393–94, interprets the conflict between Chupica and Jurado Palomino as indication of the diminished standing of the traditional ethnic order.

42. Karen Spalding, "La otra cara de la reciprocidad," 61–78.

43. AAL, Capítulos, Leg. 15, Exp. 4 and 7.

44. AAL, Capítulos, Leg. 15, Exp. 4, fol. 28r.

45. Vargas Ugarte, *Historia de la Compañía*, 2: 225; see also Olaechea Labayen, "La política selectiva de los jesuitas," 426.

46. Norman Meiklejohn, *La Iglesia y los lupaqas de Chucuito durante la colonia*, 196–98.

47. Alaperrine-Bouyer, *La educación de las elites*, 236–37.

48. Duviols, *La destrucción de las religiones andinas*, 225–30; Griffiths, *The Cross and the Serpent*, 44; and Kenneth Mills, "The Limits of Religious Coercion in Mid-Colonial Peru," 90.

49. Mills, "The Limits of Religious Coercion," 90; and Vargas Ugarte, *Historia de la Compañía*, 2: 134–35.

50. Paolo Broggio, *Evangelizzare il mondo: Le missioni della Compagnia di Gesù tra Europa e America (Secoli XVI–XVII)*, 174.

51. Álvarez, *De las costumbres y conversión*, 269.

52. Vargas Ugarte, *Historia de la Compañía*, 2: 332; also transcribed in Eguiguren, *Diccionario histórico cronológico de la Real y Pontificia Universidad de San Marcos y sus colegios*, 2: 876; and Alaperrine-Bouyer, *La educación de las elites*, 241.

53. Diego de León Pinelo, *Mandó que se imprimiesse este escrito el Excelent mo señor Conde de Alva de Aliste, y de Villaflor, grande de Castilla: Virrey destos Reynos del Peru, en la Iunta, que se ha formado, por cedula de Su Magestad, de 21 de setiembre de 1660 años*, 2v.

54. Sabine MacCormack, "Grammar and Virtue: The Formulation of a Cultural and Missionary Program by the Jesuits in Early Colonial Peru," 576–601.

55. See, for example, Acosta, *De procuranda indorum salute*, 1: 579–83, 2: 323–25.

56. BNP, B 1282; AAL, Hechicerías e Idolatrías, Leg. 5, Exp. 9 and 10. See Kenneth Mills, "Bad Christians in Colonial Peru," 8; Griffiths, *The Cross and the Serpent*, 193–94.

57. Alaperrine-Bouyer, *La educación de las elites*, 144.

58. De la Puente Brunke, "'Los vasallos se desentrañan por su rey,'" 465–66; Alaperrine-Bouyer, *La educación de las elites*, 144–45, 198, and "Saber y poder," 158.

59. Gutiérrez Arbulú and Flores Espinoza, "Dos documentos sobre los jesuitas," 202.

60. For a study of Andean Catholicism as part of an "Andean interculture," see Kenneth Mills, "The Naturalization of Andean Christianities," 508–39.

CHAPTER 4

Making Law Intelligible

Networks of Translation in Mid-Colonial Oaxaca

Yanna Yannakakis

Throughout Spanish America, the law provided an institutional space in which indigenous people expressed, shaped, and resolved conflict. Native litigation and the legal system itself facilitated the negotiation of colonial rule, including the growth and transformation of legal institutions and practices, and the relationship between Indian and Spanish jurisdictions.[1] One of the central facts of indigenous engagement with the legal system was that although Indians turned to courts in large numbers, most of them did not speak Spanish. Translation is therefore central for understanding the relationship between indigenous people and the law. How did non-Spanish speakers make their disputes intelligible to court officials? How did language use and translation shape the relationship between law and society at the local level?

In order to answer these questions, we must consider native people not only as parties to legal disputes but also as legal, administrative, and church functionaries who through their intellectual activities and social networks created a communicative bridge between indigenous society and the law. In this essay, I examine indigenous participation in interethnic networks of translation in legal settings in the multilingual district of Villa Alta, Oaxaca, Mexico during the late seventeenth and early eighteenth centuries. My analy-

Map 4.1. Oaxaca and Villa Alta.

sis focuses on two interlocking social groups: first, official court translators, including General Interpreters and court-appointed interpreters who
brokered power regionally; and second, native municipal and church functionaries who leveraged the power of the district court to shape community-
level politics. By reconstructing translation networks and their practices, my
essay suggests how colonial law gained traction in some of New Spain's most
remote *pueblos de indios* (Indian municipalities), and how native legal functionaries shaped interethnic relations and hierarchies at a regional level.

Court Interpreters and Language Use

From the perspective of the legal archive, translation in colonial courts appears to have been the work of an official interpreter who translated an original text in an indigenous language into Spanish, or in the case of spoken testimony, the words of an indigenous witness or litigant into Spanish. Upon
closer inspection, this act of translation was but one step in a larger process,
and the official court interpreter, one player in a larger network of translators. Who participated in this network, and how did their work facilitate
court translation? General Interpreters[2] and other court-appointed interpreters[3] provide a vantage point from which to survey the practice of trans-

YANNA YANNAKAKIS

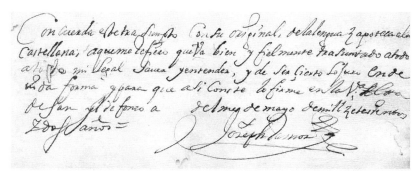

Figure 4.1. General Interpreter Joseph Ramos's signature. Courtesy of the Archivo Histórico del Poder Judicial de Oaxaca.

lation at a regional level. Their ethnic identities, linguistic competence, and language use shaped legal culture and, more broadly, the hierarchy of ethnic groups in the district (see also Ramos, chapter 1).

Joseph Ramos, General Interpreter of the district court of Villa Alta from 1685–1709 was one of the region's most significant translators during the colonial period (figure 4.1). His tenure coincided with the demographic recovery of the region's indigenous population following its nadir in the early seventeenth century, a mid-colonial extirpation campaign from roughly 1660–1710, and the secularization of the Dominican parishes of Villa Alta after 1705.[4] This historical conjuncture engendered land disputes and power struggles among and within Villa Alta's pueblos de indios, increasing the civil and criminal caseload in the district court. Not surprisingly, this period also witnessed the flowering of native language notarial writing in the region. Although Villa Alta's Indian *cabildos* (municipal councils) authored notarial documentation from the sixteenth through nineteenth centuries, the bulk of these records, many of which entered the district court as evidence, were produced from roughly 1680–1750.[5]

During this busy time for the court of Villa Alta, Joseph Ramos worked in more cases than any other court interpreter who served during the same years.[6] In addition to translating in civil and criminal litigation ranging from land disputes to sedition, and helping with tasks critical to civil administration such as the maintenance of tribute rolls and tribute collection,[7] Ramos translated in cases that were watersheds in the colonial history of the region. Notably, he served as interpreter during the ecclesiastical inspections of Villa Alta's one hundred indigenous pueblos during the extirpation campaign that followed the indigenous uprising in 1700 known as the Cajonos Rebellion. As official translator, he translated the "confessions" of *sierra cabildos* (highland municipal councils) which revealed the communities' sacred spaces and the identities of their "maestros de idolatría," and facilitated the surrender of the communities' sacred objects, calendars, and ritual texts.[8] He also translated during the trial of twenty-five defendants accused of fomenting the rebellion, which included confessions under torture and a grisly death sentence for fifteen of the accused.[9]

Joseph Ramos hailed from the barrio of Analco, an indigenous settlement adjacent to the district seat of Villa Alta, founded by the region's central Mexican Indian conquistadors—allies of the Spanish conquerors—and home to their descendants.[10] The barrio of Analco was strongly identified with the *indios conquistadores*, but by the mid-colonial period was also home to a mixed population of indigenous people from the region.[11] When Ramos began his tenure as General Interpreter, the Spanish magistrate of Villa Alta identified him as a "mestizo," signaling a social network that stretched across Spanish and native worlds (see also Ramos, chapter 1). The magistrate also identified him as "ladino en la lengua castellana," which meant that Spanish was not his native language.[12] I will return to this point later.

Joseph Ramos had strong cultural and political connections to the barrio of Analco, serving as an *alcalde* (magistrate) in its cabildo during his tenure as General Interpreter.[13] His service as alcalde is significant to our understanding of Ramos's social identity given that the barrio of Analco was understood to be Indian. Ramos had equally strong ties to the culturally Spanish world of the district seat of Villa Alta, and he enjoyed an important place in that world, owning land and, like other colonial officers, a house in the center of town.[14] Joseph Ramos's father, Nicolás de Chaves, was also identified by the court of Villa Alta as a "ladino in the Castilian language, native and resident of the barrio de Analco" and as a "mestizo." According to scattered legal documents, Chaves possessed ample resources and land, which he passed onto his son and other descendants. He was also reputed to enjoy close relations with the lieutenant of the Spanish magistrate, and with "*las justicias*" (Villa Alta's court functionaries), a social network that may have helped his son Joseph Ramos to secure the prestigious post of General Interpreter.[15]

Like his father, Joseph Ramos situated himself among the powerful and cliquish court functionaries of Villa Alta. These multilingual figures, belonging to a few families, dominated the district court as interpreters, untitled lawyers, court witnesses (in lieu of an official notary), and legal agents. They owned houses near and around the town plaza, involved themselves in the politics and business of the region's pueblos de indios, and made good off of the region's robust textile trade and other forms of commerce. They became an increasingly diverse group over the course of the eighteenth century, as indigenous people entered their ranks, particularly in the post of General Interpreter. This network of legal functionaries defined Joseph Ramos's social identity as saliently as the labels "mestizo," "ladino," or "Indian."

Joseph Ramos also had strong relations with native elites throughout the district. References to his roles as legal executor and legal agent for indigenous groups and individuals appear in the legal record.[16] He also served as an intermediary figure between native people and the court (see also Ramos, chapter 1, and Schwaller, chapter 2). On a few occasions, a court case opened with correspondence penned by a municipal scribe reporting a crime or conflict in a local community, directed not to the Spanish magistrate, but to Joseph Ramos.[17] In one of these letters dated May 21, 1702, the municipal authorities of San Juan Yae addressed Ramos as "our lord"; begged his pardon that "because you are our interpreter you must bear the burden of our written accounts"; and reminded him that as our interpreter "all eyes of the jurisdiction are on you as you go before the magistrate."[18] In another letter dated May 14, 1703, the municipal authorities of San Juan Tabaa who were in prison for creating a civil disturbance entreated him with "you, our interpreter of this, our jurisdiction, must translate in front of the magistrate the account that we have related to you."[19] In both cases, the language of the municipal authorities—part beseeching, part cajoling—makes clear that they expected Ramos not only to translate, but also to mediate and advocate on their behalf.

As discussed above, Joseph Ramos was ladino, meaning that Spanish was not his first language. As was true of many of the district's interpreters and court functionaries, he was multilingual, translating in three languages of the region: Zapotec, Nahuatl, and Spanish. Given his origins in the barrio of Analco, Nahuatl was likely one of his mother tongues.[20] Small errors in article usage, misusing vowels or consonants in spelling certain words, and the nuances of his translations in written Spanish suggest that Zapotec may have been another of his mother tongues. At least six native languages were spoken in Villa Alta (three varieties of Zapotec, Mixe, Chinantec, and Nahuatl); but with a few exceptions, only Zapotec and Nahuatl were ever written during the colonial period, and until the eighteenth century, the district's General Interpreters only translated written and oral testimony in Nahuatl and Zapo-

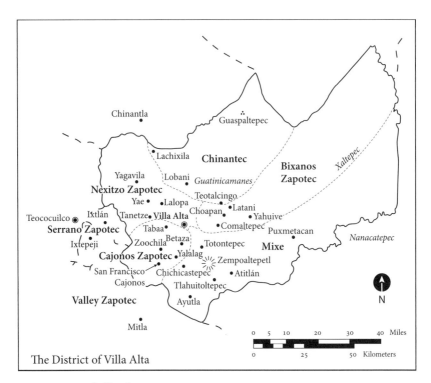

Map 4.2. Map of Villa Alta.

tec (in its three varieties). The Chinantecs used Bijanos Zapotec as an intermediary language with the court,[21] and the Mixe used Nahuatl.

Translation through the intermediary language of Nahuatl marks an important aspect of the work of court interpreters and of language politics in Villa Alta.[22] Nahuatl was not the first language of any ethnic group in the Sierra Norte of Oaxaca. Unlike the Mixteca Alta of Oaxaca, where Nahuatl was used as a lingua franca,[23] the Sierra Norte was never conquered by the Triple Alliance, so Nahuatl was not introduced to the region by force during the pre-Hispanic period, though it was used as a language of trade.[24] How, then, did Nahuatl become a legal-administrative language in the region? Following the conquest, the Spaniards' Nahuatl-speaking central Mexican allies became part of the colonial administration. They served as intermediaries with the local indigenous population in their roles as governors in rebellious pueblos, interpreters, tribute collectors, bailiffs, messengers, schoolmasters, and spies.[25] Nahuatl speakers thus became the primary face of Spanish colonialism in the early years after the conquest, and may

YANNA YANNAKAKIS

have introduced Nahuatl to the local population, or at least expanded its use as a lingua franca.

Dominican friars constituted another group of Nahuatl-speaking colonizers, who used Nahuatl to evangelize in response to the challenges posed by Oaxaca's many indigenous languages.[26] In 1570, in response to a request by Bishop Albuquerque of Oaxaca, the Crown decreed that all Indians in Oaxaca must learn Nahuatl so that the friars could more effectively do their work.[27] Similar complaints by regular clergy throughout New Spain about the difficulties of mastering so many native languages persuaded Philip II to make Nahuatl the official language of New Spain's Indians, though this policy was later reversed in favor of Spanish.[28] Although it is impossible to gauge the effectiveness of such language policies, it is notable that the Church sought to institute Nahuatl as a lingua franca in Oaxaca.

In the Zapotec areas of Oaxaca, Nahuatl quickly gave way to Zapotec as a language of evangelization and written standard. By 1567, three years prior to Philip II's decree, Dominican friar Pedro de Feria produced a catechism in Valley Zapotec, and in the late seventeenth century secular priest Francisco Pacheco de Silva published a bilingual catechism in Spanish and Nexitzo Zapotec, a variant of the district of Villa Alta.[29] By the middle of the sixteenth century, the native elite in the valley and the sierra came to use written Zapotec to record official business, including the accounts of the municipal treasury, the administration of local justice, and the creation of last wills and testaments of town residents.

By contrast, no extant documentary evidence exists in the archive of Villa Alta that Mixe municipal authorities wrote in their own language during the colonial period. Dominican friars, who complained that Mixe was difficult to write due to its grammar, did not publish pastoral literature in Mixe until the mid-eighteenth century.[30] Nahuatl thus became the written register into which Mixe elites were socialized. From the friars, they learned to write using Nahuatl, and continued to do so over time in Spanish notarial genres.

Nahuatl found a receptive audience among Nahuatl-speaking General Interpreters of Villa Alta's district court, like Joseph Ramos and Nicolás de Bargas, a Spanish *vecino* (resident) of Villa Alta who served the court during the same period as Ramos. In this way, the exigencies of evangelization coincided with the linguistic competencies of the region's General Interpreters to perpetuate the use of Nahuatl among the Mixe in the legal-administrative realm. Nahuatl also found a receptive audience among las justicias, the legal functionaries in the district seat discussed above, most of whom were Spanish vecinos of Villa Alta. How did they acquire Nahuatl? Many of Villa Alta's Spanish vecinos were merchants, and likely used Nahuatl, the language of trade, in their long-distance commerce.

Ramón de Vargas, a vecino of Villa Alta, provides a perfect example of one of the region's Spanish *nahuatlatos*.[31] Vargas, along with his nephew Nicolas de Bárgas, the General Interpreter mentioned above, were members of a powerful Villa Alta family who controlled many of the district's legal and administrative posts. Although a vecino of Villa Alta, Ramón de Vargas was also a resident of the Mixe community of San Pablo Ayutla where he engaged in commerce. The alcalde mayor appointed him as an interpreter in the investigation of the death of a resident of Ayutla because he spoke both Mixe and Mexicano (Nahuatl).[32]

Ramón de Vargas was not the only translator in this case. Spanish law required that the court appoint two interpreters to translate in criminal cases involving Indian witnesses. In the case cited above, Luis Basques, governor of the Mixe community of Tlahuitoltepeque, and a speaker of both Mixe and Mexicano, served as the second court-appointed interpreter.[33] Mixe elites like Luis Basques were important links in a chain of translation that brought Mixe criminal cases to the district court.

Mixe scribes who produced notarial records for their communities in Nahuatl provided another important link in the chain of translation. One of the puzzles of their translation work is that although the court identified some Mixe scribes as Spanish speakers, they used written Nahuatl for notarial purposes.[34] The court identified some of the court-appointed interpreters in the Mixe zone as Spanish speakers as well. Although the scribes and interpreters in question, and other Mixe elites—at least in the larger pueblos— spoke Spanish, they did not, could not, or chose not to write in Spanish. This may have been because they knew only how to write in Nahuatl and not Spanish. Mixe elites may also have used spoken and written Nahuatl as a sign of prestige and as a strategy for social exclusivity and political power.

Mixe elites used Nahuatl to engage with the local colonial bureaucracy, to translate, and to speak for non-Nahuatl-speaking Mixes. Mixes who did not speak Nahuatl were sometimes excluded from the legal record because of local translation practices and language politics. For example, in a case of murder along the Camino Real, a *pardo* (mixed-race person of African descent) who spoke and understood Zapotec and Nahuatl served as a court-appointed interpreter. Among the witnesses were Zapotecs and Mixes. One Mixe witness could speak Nahuatl, so his testimony was recorded. But another Mixe witness could not speak Nahuatl, so his voice remained unheard.[35] This basic fact makes clear the implications of a regime of Nahuatl among the Mixe: Nahuatl allowed access to the legal system, the vehicle for negotiating power in the colonial period. Those who monopolized Nahuatl—interpreters in the district seat, the Indian conquistadors of the barrio of Analco, Dominican friars, Spanish vecinos, and Mixe elites from the larger pueblos and cabe-ceras—exercised control over important material and political struggles: land disputes, fights over municipal elections and local leadership, and the determination of crime and punishment. In these struggles, Mixe who were not Nahuatl or Spanish speakers were marginalized, more so than their Zapotec counterparts who had access to the courts through direct Zapotec-Spanish translation. Alonso Barros argues that differential access to the law due to language use had material implications, facilitating Zapotec appro-priation of Mixe lands through the Spanish legal system over the course of the colonial period.[36]

A final implication of the use by General Interpreters, court-appointed in-terpreters, and Mixe elites and functionaries of written and spoken Nahuatl as a language of interface with the law concerns what sociolinguists call "iconicity": "the assumption that the essential characteristics of groups of people (e.g., civility, barbarism) are reflected in the languages they speak."[37] Due in part to tenacious Mixe resistance to the conquest, the Spaniards from the outset of colonial rule in Oaxaca considered the Mixe "barbaric," more so than their Zapotec and Mixtec counterparts. The use of written Nahuatl rather than an alphabetic form of Mixe for the purposes of municipal record keeping and engagement with colonial courts and the use of spoken Nahuatl for communication with colonial officials implied a lesser standing for Mixe as a language in relation to Nahuatl and Zapotec, and a corresponding as-sumption of the persistence of Mixe "barbarity" and "rusticity" in relation to the more "civilized" Zapotecs.[38] It also implied the cultural superiority of Nahuatl speakers.

The end of Joseph Ramos's career in 1709 coincided with changes in the shadow regime of Nahuatl in Villa Alta's district court and in the Mixe region. In 1705, the district court employed its first Mixe General Interpreters: Juan de la Cruz, a native of Totontepec, and Juan Marcos, whose origins were not noted, but whose name suggests Mixe origins.[39] Their presence in the dis-trict court added more indigenous personnel to the tight circle of court func-tionaries. Cruz and Marcos translated spoken testimony from Mixe to Span-ish, without the mediation of Nahuatl speakers like Joseph Ramos.

Court translation of written testimony from the Mixe region during the eighteenth century was a different matter. As discussed above, there is no evidence that the Mixe ever produced notarial documents in their own language during the colonial period. Rather, they continued to author Nahuatl-language documents well into the eighteenth century. An interpreter "en la lengua Mexicana" remained in the district court until at least 1816, the latest reference to such a figure that I have found.[40] Like Joseph Ramos, he was a native of the barrio of Analco, and served as its alcalde in 1816.[41]

Zapotec Church and Municipal Functionaries as Translators

Native church and municipal functionaries constituted a network of translators who intersected with court interpreters. In contrast with the case of the Mixe, the Zapotecs of Villa Alta wrote in their own language thanks to the production by Dominican friars of Zapotec pastoral literature such as dictionaries, grammars, confessional guides, and catechisms. As the friars translated the Christian doctrine into indigenous languages, they relied heavily on elite native assistants who had a strong command of Spanish and the "high" registers of their native languages. Although these native assistants in many ways coauthored native-language pastoral texts, they remain anonymous to us, the friars' names appearing alone on the finished products. Zapotec church and municipal functionaries put the alphabetic writing born of Christian translation to a range of uses, producing administrative, notarial, and criminal records, some of which were authored for the courts and some of which ended up in the courts as evidence.[42]

Given the disparity between Christian and indigenous cultural and linguistic frameworks, translation from Spanish to native languages involved what William Hanks in his study of evangelization among the Maya calls "commensuration," that is, "aligning the two languages so that one could translate between them." In this way, writes Hanks, "European and Christian meanings were converted into Maya utterances."[43] Hanks argues that through this initial process of commensuration, Maya-language Christian discourse served as a "vector" for all other forms of Maya writing, including notarial writing. Scholars of other Mesoamerican regions have noted the strong relationship between Christian discourse and legal and notarial discursive forms.[44] In criminal records, the languages of sin, guilt, and deviance provide important examples.[45] The strong connection between concepts of sin and criminality—indeed, they were practically one and the same—is not surprising given that Christianity provided the ideological foundations of Spanish law, and that parish priests and native church and civil functionaries policed moral behavior in their overlapping roles as judges and spiritual authorities in rural communities.

Dominican Fr. Juan de Córdoba, with the help of native assistants, produced a Spanish-Zapotec dictionary, *Vocabulario En Lengua Zapoteca*, published in 1578.[46] Córdoba identifies a number of Zapotec concepts in an effort to give meaning to the Spanish concept of "sin." There is quite a bit of slippage in Córdoba's vocabulary as he lists multiple terms to signify sin in the general sense, suggesting the uneasy process by which commensuration took place. The Zapotec terms *tola* and *xihui* figure most prominently in Córdoba's translations. Of these two terms, my analysis will focus on the use of xihui. Athough tola, like xihui, appears with great frequency in ecclesiastical writings and Zapotec criminal records of the seventeenth and eighteenth centuries, xihui has a broader semantic range, in part because it was most often used as a modifier. In addition to connoting sin and evil, xihui also meant "false" in certain contexts, further widening its range of usage.[47]

Dominican friars refined and adapted their translation strategies over time in response to their engagement with indigenous communities in their roles as spiritual fathers, teachers, and judges. Confessional manuals provide excellent sources with which to trace these strategies, as their authors were often explicit about the logic that undergirded their approaches. In a confessional manual from 1633, *Manual breve y conpendioso para enpezar a aprender Lengua Zapoteca y administrar en caso de necesidad*, written by Fray Alonso Martínez who worked in the Valley of Oaxaca, the friar provides a Zapotec vocabulary, grammar, and guide to confession, with a section describing "sins frequently committed by Indians." These sins included drunkenness, adultery, abuse of authority, and trouble making, which not surprisingly corresponded with some of the major categories of crimes prosecuted in the district court. Finally, the manual includes some additional advice and information for parish priests.[48] At the end of this section, as was typical of confessional guides, the friar includes a full-page warning (*advertencia*) regarding certain words used in confession. In his advertencia the friar explains how a parish priest could translate sinful behaviors. The key was the term *xihui*. The friar writes: "*Xihui* is an adverb that is used with almost all verbs that relate to sin because even though the verb's meaning may be neutral, when joined with *xihui*, the verb takes on 'a bad sense'; 'it wears an evil appearance' (*in malam partem*)." Martínez goes on to provide examples in which xihui (and its opposite, chahui) serve as modifiers that when used in joint constructions with verbs produce meanings that correspond to sin and virtue.

Using xihui and chahui to mark out a Manichean Christian universe appears in other seventeenth-century Zapotec ecclesiastical writing. Don Francisco Pacheco de Silva, the parish priest of San Juan Yae-San Juan Tanetze in the Sierra Norte, published a bilingual catechism in 1687 in Nexitzo Zapotec, a different Zapotec variant than that spoken in the valley where Córdoba and Martínez worked. In his *Doctrina cristiana en lengua zapoteca nexitza*, Pacheco uses xihui and *tzahui* (the Nexitzo Zapotec equivalent of chahui) in an even wider range of constructions than seen in Martínez's confessional manual to connote "sinful" and "virtuous."[49] A small sampling of constructions with xihui (including noun + xihui and xihui + proper noun) appears below:

Pontio Pilato = Xihui Poncio Pilato
pecador (sinner) = benne huexijhui[50] (a person who acts in a bad way)
culpas (sins) = ielahuexijhui (the doing of bad things)

The example of "Xihui Pontio Pilato" proved to be particularly resonant with the political situation in the late seventeenth and early eighteenth century Sierra Norte. Pontius Pilate, a Roman imperial functionary, provided an exemplar, in the words of Friar Martinez's 1633 confessional, of a "magistrate or leader who exceeded his authority," a "sin frequently committed by Indians." As we will see in the examples below, the trope of the "sin" of "exceeding authority" undergirds Zapotec-language criminal documentation deployed in intrapueblo conflict, suggesting the ways in which confessional and catechistic discourse provided a template through which Zapotec elites expressed pueblo politics.[51] By using xihui and tzahui to communicate notions of sin and virtue, Zapotec caciques and cabildo officers filtered local conflict through the ideological lens of Christianity.

In 1695, the Nextizo Zapotec pueblo of San Juan Yatzona was in the thick of a pitched political battle for control over the community's municipal government. From 1687 to 1702, Yatzona's political conflicts generated cases of sedition and abuse of authority in the district court that intersected with political tensions in the region as a whole, characterized by the extirpation of idolatry and the Cajonos Rebellion.[52] During this period, three prominent caciques, don Felipe de Santiago, don Joseph de Celis, and don Pablo de Vargas, engaged the district court of Villa Alta and the Real Audiencia in order to influence the outcome of Yatzona's village elections and neutralize their political rivals by charging them with a range of crimes.[53] In three of these cases, the parties involved submitted Zapotec-language *memorias* (accounts/records), which the court's General Interpreters Joseph Ramos and Nicolás de Bargas translated into Spanish.[54] In these memorias, the Zapotec authors—Yatzona's cabildo (municipal) officers—marked the crimes of their political enemies with xihui, the language of sin. They were not the only authors of Zapotec criminal memorias to do so. Within a corpus of thirty Zapotec criminal memorias, about one-third employ expressions with xihui as a narrative strategy.[55]

How did Zapotec municipal officers acquire facility in Zapotec-Christian discourse? How did they localize that discourse in a narrative about village politics? These are important questions considering that the memorias' native authors lived at a marked cultural and geographical distance from Spanish religious and administrative centers. In comparison with their counterparts in late seventeenth-century central Mexico and the Mixteca Alta of Oaxaca, the Zapotecs of the remote Sierra Norte of Oaxaca did not have as frequent contact with Spaniards and mestizos, nor did they live as proximately to them. Almost all of Villa Alta's handful of Spaniards lived in the district seat, and until 1705 there were only eight Dominican doctrinas that ministered to one hundred pueblos de indios scattered across some of the colony's most rugged terrain. Many native villagers saw their parish priest only a few times a year.[56]

In the absence of parish priests, native church functionaries provided the rudiments of Christian moral education. Native *fiscales* (priest's assistants), *cantores* (church singers), *maestros de doctrina* (lay catechists), *maestros de capilla* (choir masters), and *sacristanes* (sacristans) oversaw the administration of the church, made sure that villagers complied with their Christian responsibilities, served as the priest's eyes and ears, and taught the doctrine to village youth and adults, mainly through rote oral recitation of the catechism (see also Charles, chapter 3, and Burns, chapter 10). Of these native church posts, that of fiscal was the most prestigious and powerful. Fiscales were usually one of a handful of village notables distinguished by their literacy. Fiscales and other native church functionaries rotated in and out of positions in native municipal councils, helping to make ecclesiastical discourse a resource for the rhetoric of criminal records and other kinds of notarial documents produced by native cabildos. In practice, then, the separation of the civil and ecclesiastical jurisdictions at the local level of the rural parish did not exist; they were one and the same.

Neither were religion or local politics separable. Even if they were not a constant presence in sierra pueblos, parish priests often meddled in village affairs, throwing the weight of their personal prestige and that of the local Catholic cult behind a favored cacique and his faction. For their part, caciques often engaged priests as powerful allies in internecine struggles. Don Pablo de Vargas, one of the main actors in Yatzona's political drama, epitomized a native ally of the church who dominated indigenous municipal government. Vargas served as governor of Yatzona more or less continuously from 1684 to 1696 with the backing of three consecutive Spanish magistrates and the region's Dominican friars.[57] In a 1687 case against him for abuse of authority, a witness who testified on his behalf stated "while he was governor, don Pablo de Vargas made sure, through his own hard work and solicitousness, that the fiestas were celebrated with great splendor and that the children were taught the Christian doctrine, paying a teacher to do so, which is why don Pablo has been and is loved and esteemed by all of the priests and magistrates of this province."[58] Vargas's close relations with parish priests were made manifest in the same case by a letter written to him in florid Zapotec by Dominican Friar Alonso de Bargas, praising him for his work on behalf of the church and disparaging his political enemies. The letter was submitted as evidence in support of don Pablo's good conduct as governor.[59]

In 1695, governor don Pablo de Vargas and the municipal government of San Juan Yatzona brought a case against Yatzona's municipal authorities of the previous year—don Francisco de Paz, don Juan de Santiago, and Pedro Jimenez, the governor and alcaldes of Yatzona—for abuse of authority. Don Joseph de Celis, another cacique of Yatzona and their legal agent at the time, was also a main target of this criminal case.[60] To initiate the case, they produced an elaborate eight-page criminal complaint—which they identified as a "memoria"—that is one of the richest and longest of its kind in Villa Alta's colonial archive (figure 4.2).[61]

The 1695 document authored by don Pablo de Vargas, the municipal authorities, and 113 caciques and principales of San Juan Yatzona conforms to the Spanish notarial genre of memoria through its opening and closing formulas, and the structure of its body, which appears in the form of an enumerated list. The list details thirteen incidents in which the former authorities and their legal agent committed crimes against the community or individuals therein. The memoria is chock full of details of village life, social conflicts and alliances with powerful Spaniards, and struggles for power. In the interest of space, I have boiled these narratives down to their essential elements, summarizing the causes of action: They (don Francisco de Paz et al.) did not

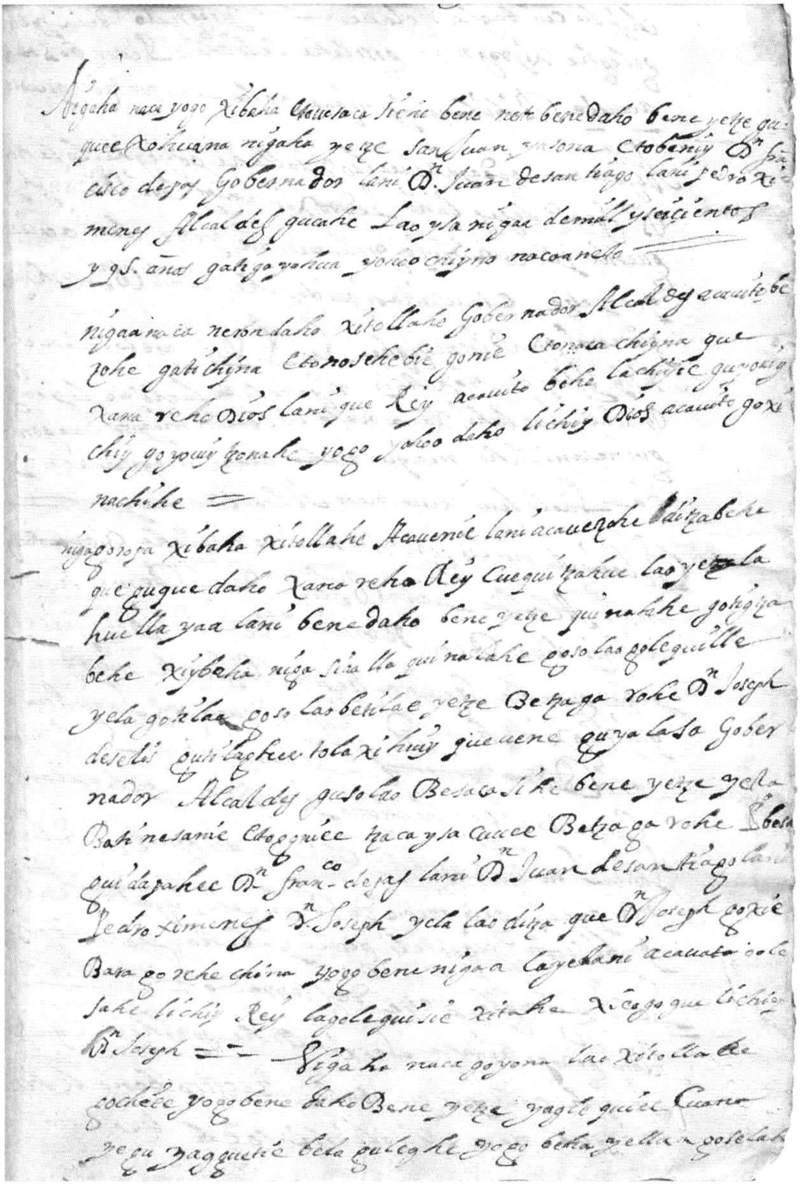

Figure 4.2. Zapotec-language *memoria de cabildo* from San Juan Yatzona used as evidence in the 1695 criminal case against don Francisco de Paz et al. Courtesy of the Archivo Histórico del Poder Judicial de Oaxaca.

exercise their obligation to serve God and King; they raised false accusations against past officials; they allowed Pedro Boza, lieutenant of the alcalde mayor, and Joseph de Celis, a village cacique, to advise them and usurp their authority by giving them power of attorney in the name of the pueblo without the pueblo's consent; they imposed an illicit head tax (*derrama*) on the villagers to pay for litigation; they practiced nepotism in the appointment of church functionaries; they abused their political opponents; they robbed the villagers by keeping money for themselves from *the repartimiento de mantas* (forced production of textiles), and imposed a repartimiento for Pedro Boza and don Diego de la Sierra, son of the chief bailiff, saying they were for the alcalde mayor, and keeping money for themselves.

At the conclusion of the memoria, don Pablo de Vargas and his allies demand that don Francisco de Pas pay back the money (two hundred pesos) that his government forcibly collected for the cacique don Joseph de Celis to go to Mexico City on legal business on behalf of the pueblo, and that don Francisco de Pas and his government pay back the money they pocketed from the repartimiento de mantas.

In this litany of alleged abuses, the authors of the memoria make frequent use of constructions with xihui, expanding its pragmatic and semantic range beyond the context of the catechism into the realm of notarial writing and Spanish law. As one compares the translations of specific constructions with xihui in Pacheco's bilingual catechism with those of the Zapotec criminal memoria and its Spanish translation, it becomes clear that the language of sin helped the memoria's authors to connect local politics with the broader colonial context by communicating messages about the legitimate exercise of power and use of the legal system by Indians that squared with Spanish perceptions of Indian behavior: Indian leaders either upheld Christian precepts and colonial law or abused their authority and used the law for nefarious purposes. In short, Christian discourse helped to make the narrative translatable at the hands of the court interpreter and intelligible to a Spanish audience; the language of sin was a framework through which the Spanish magistrate could understand local circumstances. It also helped to construct and reinforce for Spaniards ideas about Indians in Manichean terms: they were either good or bad, virtuous or sinful, with us or against us. In the context of extirpation and social tensions around "idolatry," this view proved to be both convenient and incendiary.[62]

For example, the authors of the Zapotec memoria refer to don Joseph de Celis as *bene xihui* (bad man) because he made trouble for the village by counseling its leaders to go to Mexico City and spend two hundred pesos on a lawsuit. Bene xihui is a translation for "sinner" in Pacheco's catechism. As used in this context, bene xihui retains the moral dimension of "sinner" while adding political dimensions to the term, locating don Joseph outside the moral boundaries of the community by virtue of exercising his power and influence against its interests. In this regard, the use of bene xihui in the memoria resonates with the meaning conveyed by *Xihui Pontio Pilato* in Pacheco's catechism: a leader who abuses his authority. The court interpreter translated "bene xihui" as "hombre malo" (bad man).

The memoria's authors use the expression "tola xihuiy" (false guilt) to allege that don Joseph de Celis and don Francisco de Pas had falsely accused the former municipal officials of certain misdeeds. "Xihui" ("false") and "tola" (guilt/sin) are also used in a joint construction in Pacheco's translation of the eighth commandment (thou shalt not bear false witness or lie): "El octavo, no levantarás falso testimonio ni mentirás: Goxoono xibaa, acca gogooaxihuilo *tolla* lezahalo, tzela aca gonixee lachilo" (italics, my emphasis). The usage in the catechism and the memoria resonate quite strongly with each other. The court interpreter translated "tola xihuiy" as "delitos falsos" (false crimes).

In the memoria, xihui marks speech that leads to abuse of authority: "xihuiy ditza" (bad word). The semantic field of the term "ditza" ("word," also written as "titza") had deep resonance in Zapotec and Spanish, indexing a range of meanings associated with authority and the realm of the sacred. For example, in his catechism, Pacheco used "titza" as a translation for "commandment." In the memoria, "xihuiy ditza" appears in the context of the allegation that don Francisco de Pas and the other officials got together with don Joseph de Celis in Celis's house to instigate the illicit head tax. According to the Zapotec narrative, Celis advised the men ("hue xiha xihuiy ditza," literally "making good and bad words," figuratively "weighing the good and the bad"), the end result being the instigation of the head tax. The court interpreter translated "hue xiha xihuiy ditza" as "consultar" (to consult/advise).[63]

The cabildo further broadened the usage of xihui by pairing it with Spanish loanwords to create mixed constructions unique to the legal context. In all of these constructions, xihui connotes "false" rather than "bad/evil." For example, the cabildo used "puder xihuiy" to refer to when the cabildo gave don Joseph power of attorney by recourse to a notary in Oaxaca City in the name of the pueblo without the pueblo's consent. The court interpreter translated "puder xihuiy" as "poder falso" (false letter of attorney). They used "pleyto xihuiy" to refer to the disputes that the past officials and Pedro Boza, to whom they gave power of attorney, fomented. The court interpreter translated "pleyto xihuiy" as "pleito o falsedad" (dispute or falsehood). They used "justicia xihui" to refer to the past officials' mistreatment of the people of the community. The court interpreter translated "justicia xihui" as "ynjusticias" (injustices). Finally, they used "juramento xihuiy" in reference to when the officials attempted to force villagers to give false testimony in the case against a former governor. The court interpreter translated "juramento xihuiy" as "jurar falso" (to swear falsely). By pairing Spanish legal lexicon with xihui, the Zapotec authors of the memoria created new meanings and communicated the moral parameters of Zapotec political authority in relation to Indian engagement with colonial law. More specifically, these mixed constructions helped to tell a story of abuse of authority through misuse of the law, while underscoring the sinfulness and criminality of the accused.

As the examples above make clear, the varied use of xihui throughout the memoria was not a mere parroting of the catechism back to colonial administrators. Rather, xihui formed part of a rhetorical strategy. By conveying ideas of moral and immoral behavior in a Christian register of Zapotec, Yatzona's municipal officers aimed to persuade a Spanish magistrate (via a court interpreter) of their good governance (policía) and respect for the laws of God and King in order to shore up their local authority during a period of regional political strife inspired in part by a war against idolatry. In this regard, the authors of the memoria attempted to convince the court that their political objectives supported the colonial objectives of order and control.

In the making of their discourse of criminality, Zapotec municipal authorities drew not only from ecclesiastical sources but also from Spanish legal language, as demonstrated in the last set of examples above. How did Spanish loanwords make their way into Zapotec discourse? Most likely, frequent litigation socialized Zapotec authorities into the use of legal terminology. Zapotec discourses of criminality therefore emerged in the context of a network of translation involving Zapotec church and municipal functionaries, Dominican friars, parish priests, and legally literate individuals who William Taylor Taylor has coined "legal entrepreneurs": natives and Spaniards well-versed in legal procedures and formulas who guided their native clients through the legal system (see also Ramos, chapter 1, Charles, chapter 3, and Burns, chapter 10).[64] Some of these legal entrepreneurs, like don Joseph de Celis, the much maligned cacique of Yatzona who played a starring role in the 1695 criminal complaint analyzed above, came from the high echelons of

YANNA YANNAKAKIS

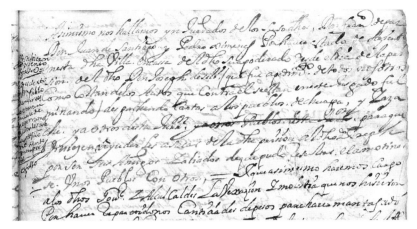

Figure 4.3. Marginalia in 1695 criminal case against don Francisco de Paz et al.
Courtesy of the Archivo Histórico del Poder Judicial de Oaxaca.

native society. Others, like Pedro Boza, lieutenant of the Spanish magistrate who also appears in the 1695 memoria, came from the ranks of Villa Alta's Spanish vecinos who served as district court functionaries.

Others, like Joseph Ramos, the General Interpreter of Villa Alta with whom this essay began, were court interpreters. In Nicolás de Bargas's Spanish translation of the Zapotec memoria analyzed above, anonymous marginalia refuting many of the causes of action appear (figure 4.3). In the margin alongside the accusation that don Francisco de Pas and his government went to the house of Pedro Boza and then to that of don Joseph de Celis to concoct unauthorized lawsuits, the following rebuttal appears in a cramped hand: "it is false that they [don Francisco de Pas et al.] governed from this person's [Boza's, and then Celis's] house; what is true is that don Pablo and his associates were in the house of Chepe Ramos, who made the petitions, being Interpreter."[65]

Some interested party in the court—perhaps Pedro Boza—was the author of the marginalia. His written retort hurled the same accusation back at the accusers: that they were conspiring in the home of one of las justicias to bring legal action against their rivals. Whether this counteraccusation was true or not, it reinforces the idea that Joseph Ramos moved easily between the role of court interpreter and *apoderado* (legal agent), mediating between his indigenous clients and the legal system by drafting petitions for submission to the court. Clearly, the activities of interpreters extended well beyond translation into the realms of judicial and political activism. This is not surprising.

As I have argued throughout this essay, translation in mid-colonial Villa Alta constituted an ideological and political activity in which interpreters played only the most visible role.

Networks of translation peopled by court interpreters, legal agents, Dominican friars, parish priests, and native church and municipal functionaries made Villa Alta's legal system function. The interethnic and multilingual character of translation networks allows us to perceive translation as a wide-ranging social and cultural process premised upon the institutionalization of languages of interface with the district court—in this case, Nahuatl and Zapotec—to the exclusion of others, like Mixe and Chinantec. In the case of Nahuatl, a synergy of forces explain its durability as a legal lingua franca: the history of the conquest of the region featuring Nahuatl-speaking central Mexicans who helped govern the district during the colonial period, the longstanding use of Nahuatl as a language of trade, and the use of Nahuatl as a language of Christian evangelization. Christian translation had a strong role to play in court translation, especially where native-language notarial documentation was concerned. In the case of Zapotec, Christian-Zapotec discourse shaped discourses of criminality articulated in the Spanish genre of the memoria. When submitted as evidence in criminal litigation and translated by court interpreters, these documents brought village and regional politics to bear upon one another.

The case of Villa Alta demonstrates that although translators extended the reach of Spanish law deep into Villa Alta's lettered mountains, the process could differ sharply across the space of a single district. The use of Nahuatl and Zapotec rather than Mixe as languages of the court shaped social differentiation within Mixe communities and among the Mixe, Zapotecs, and descendants of central Mexican Indian conquistadors. And without Mixe-language notarial writing, the Mixe did not develop a legal idiom in the same manner as their Zapotec neighbors; instead, it was mediated through Nahuatl. The work of translators thus cut two ways. Translators facilitated indigenous engagement with colonial courts, with advantageous results for those native litigants who found themselves on the winning side. At the same time, translators brokered regimes of language and a legal system in which they played a range of roles (like that of legal agent) that enhanced their material and political status, and helped create new forms of inequality within communities and across ethnic groups.

YANNA YANNAKAKIS

Notes

The following archives were used in this chapter: Archivo Histórico Judicial de Oaxaca (AHJO), Archivo del Poder Judicial de Oaxaca, Archivo de Villa Alta (APJO, AVA), and Archivo General de las Indias (AGI). Please note that from 2001 to 2003, the APJO created a separate historical archive, the AHJO. In this process, they recatalogued the AVA. My citations reflect both the pre-2001 (APJO) and post-2003 (AHJO) systems.

1. Carlos Sempat Assadourian, "Los señores étnicos y los corregidores de indios en la conformación del Estado colonial"; Carlos Sempat Assadourian, *Transiciones hacia el sistema colonial andino*; Woodrow Borah, *Justice by Insurance: The General Indian Court of Colonial Mexico and the Legal Aides of the Half-Real*; Alcira Dueñas, *Indians and Mestizos in the "Lettered City": Reshaping Justice, Social Hierarchy, and Political Culture in Colonial Peru*; Bernardo García Martínez, *Los Pueblos de la Sierra: El poder y el espacio entre los indios del norte de Puebla hasta 1700*; Bernardo García Martínez, "Jurisdicción y propiedad: Una distinción fundamental en la historia de los pueblos de indios del México colonial"; Susan Kellogg, *Law and the Transformation of Aztec Culture, 1500–1700*; Margarita Menegus Bornemann, *Del señorío indígena a la república de indios*; Brian P. Owensby, *Empire of Law and Indian Justice in Colonial Mexico*; Ethelia Ruiz Medrano, *Mexico's Indigenous Communities: Their Lands and Histories, 1500–2010*; Ethelia Ruiz Medrano and Susan Kellogg, eds., *Negotiation within Domination: New Spain's Indian Pueblos Confront the Spanish State*; Sergio Serulnikov, *Subverting Colonial Authority: Challenges to Spanish Rule in Eighteenth-Century Southern Andes*.

2. General Interpreters were salaried figures appointed by the Spanish magistrate based at the district court.

3. In legal proceedings that took place outside the district court and in which a General Interpreter could not be present, such as a murder investigation, the attending court functionary (generally the bailiff or the lieutenant of the Spanish magistrate) appointed an interpreter, usually a local in whom he "had confidence."

4. Marcello Carmagnani, *El regreso de los dioses: el proceso de reconstitución de la identidad étnica en Oaxaca, siglos XVII y XVII*; John K. Chance, *Conquest of the Sierra: Spaniards and Indians in Colonial Oaxaca*; José Alcina Franch, *Calendario y religión entre los Zapotecos*; Yanna Yannakakis, *The Art of Being In-Between: Native Intermediaries, Indian Identity, and Local Rule in Colonial Oaxaca*; Thomas Calvo, *Vencer la derrota: Vivir en la sierra zapoteca de México (1674–1707)*; and David E. Tavárez, *The Invisible War: Indigenous Devotions, Discipline, and Dissent in Colonial Mexico*.

5. Michel Oudijk has transcribed much of the extant Sierra Zapotec notarial documentation (his corpus totals 314 documents), which span the years 1537–1824. Of these, 170 were produced between 1680 and 1750. Una Canger and Michael Swanton's forthcoming study has identified roughly one hundred Nahuatl language notarial documents for the Sierra Norte produced between 1564 and 1750, the bulk in the seventeenth and eighteenth centuries; Michel Oudijk, Wiki-Filología, Instituto de Investigaciones Filológicas, UNAM; Michael Swanton, personal communication, February 26, 2013.

6. My narrative of the work of Villa Alta's interpreters and court translation from the 1670s to the first decade of the eighteenth century is based on the following cor-

pus of cases (106 civil cases, 129 criminal cases; 235 total cases): AHJO Villa Alta Civil: Legajo 2 1672–1685; Legajo 3 1689–1694; Legajo 4 1694–1698; Legajo 5 1698–1702; Legajo 6 1702–1706; Legajo 7 1706–1722. Criminal: Legajo 3 1675–1685; Legajo 4 1685–1694; Legajo 5 1695–1698; Legajo 6 1698–1701; Legajo 7 1701–1703; Legajo 8 1703–1706; Legajo 9 1707–1709. Joseph Ramos translated in more cases in the district court than any of his fellow interpreters. Between 1685 and 1709 he translated in 74 out of 116 criminal cases, and 30 of 62 civil cases. Civil and criminal cases came primarily from the Zapotec zone (about two-thirds of civil cases and four-fifths of criminal cases), and then from the Mixe zone (about one-third of civil cases and one-fifth of criminal cases). A negligible number came from the remote Chinantla lowlands.

7. AHJO Villa Alta Civil Leg. 28 Exp. 16.14 (1709), "Maria Martín, viuda de Joseph Ramos y Juan Miguel dan poder a Capitán Don Joseph Rodriguez de Ledesma para que en su nombre recaude y cobre los salarios que les pertenecen por la interpretacion que dicho Joseph Ramos hizo y la que ha hecho dicho Juan Miguel en la cuenta y matricula de los yndios desta jurisdiccion."

8. AGI México 882 (diciembre de 1704). The testimony of the Villa Alta cabildo officials translated by Joseph Ramos appears in 1,544 pages at the end of this legajo.

9. APJO AVA Criminal (uncatalogued) (1701), "Contra los naturales del pueblo de San Francisco Cajonos por sedición, sublevación e idolatría."

10. AHJO Villa Alta Criminal Leg. 5 Exp. 2 (1695), "Contra los de Yate por robo": Nombramiento del ynterprete, f. 3v.–4.

11. Chance, *Conquest of the Sierra*, ch. 2.

12. AHJO Villa Alta Criminal Leg. 4 Exp. 3 (1686), "En Averiguación de un incendio que hubo en Tagui," f. 1v.

13. AHJO Villa Alta Criminal Leg. 4 Exp. 16 (1698), "Entre Jayacotepeque y Ocotepeque sobre tierras." In this case, Joseph Ramos serves as a "testigo de asistencia" (court-appointed witness in lieu of an official notary) during a "vista de ojos" (land survey). The court identifies him as a current alcalde of the barrio of Analco.

14. AHJO Villa Alta Civil Leg. 28 Exp. 16.42 (1699), "Venta de Casa." In this document, Juan de la Sierra y Vargas, vecino of Villa Altas sells his house to Sevastian de Roa, Joseph Ramos's son-in-law. According to Sierra, the property shares a border with the house of Joseph Ramos and other prominent vecinos of Villa Alta. Details about Joseph Ramos's landholdings can be found in a 1713 property agreement and 1732 property dispute among his children: AHJO Villa Alta Civil Legajo 7 Exp. 17.06 (1713) "Acuerdo entre los herederos de Joseph Ramos"; APJO AVA Civil Exp.141 (1732), "Los hermanos Ursula María y Anastasia María contra Nicolás Ramos por tierras, todos del barrio de Analco."

15. AHJO Villa Alta Civil Leg. 28 Exp. 16.36 (1695). In this notarial document, Nicolás de Chaves, "ladino en la lengua castellana, natural y vecino del barrio de Analco," gives property to his granddaughter Barbara de la Cruz, daughter of Joseph Ramos and wife of Sevastian de Roa. APJO AVA Civil Exp. 5 (1665), "Contra Nicolás de Chavez por despojo de dos terrenos en perjuicio de Juan de la Cruz, ambos de Analco." In this case, Juan de la Cruz claimed that the reason that Chaves (identified by the court as a mestizo) was

able to secure title to the land was because of his close relations with the *teniente* of the *alcalde mayor*, and with las justicias.

16. APJO AVA Civil Exp.141 (1732), Petición de Juan de los Santos; AHJO Villa Alta Criminal Leg. 5 Exp. 3 (1695), "Contra Don Francisco de Paz, Don Juan de Stgo y Pedro Jimenez Gobernador y alcaldes de Yatzona por derramas economicas, agravios y vegaciones."

17. AHJO Villa Alta Criminal Leg. 4 Exp. 11 (1688), f. 3; AHJO AVA Criminal Leg. 8 Exp. 6 (1704), f. 1; AHJO AVA Criminal Leg. 7 Exp. 6 (1702), f. 5v–6; AHJO Villa Alta Criminal Leg. 7 Exp. 11 (1703), f. 1–3.

18. AHJO Villa Alta Criminal Leg. 7 Exp. 6 (1702), "Contra Francisco Canseco de Yaee por robo," f. 6–7.

19. AHJO Villa Alta Criminal Leg. 7 Exp. 11 (1703), "Contra la republica de Taba por varios hechos," f. 1–3.

20. John Chance notes that the natives of the barrio of Analco used Nahuatl within their settlement throughout the colonial period; *Conquest of the Sierra*, 21–22, 124–25, 155, 175.

21. Chance, *Conquest of the Sierra*, 124.

22. For case studies of Nahuatl as lingua franca and intermediary language in New Spain, see Robert Schwaller, "A Language of Empire, a Quotidian Tongue: The Uses of Nahuatl in Colonial New Spain."

23. Kevin Terraciano, *The Mixtecs of Colonial Oaxaca: Ñudzahui History, Sixteenth through Eighteenth Centuries*, 45–48.

24. Fr. Francisco de Burgoa writes: "y por el pasaje del camino real de este reino para Guatemala, casi ordinarias en la villa la necesidad de confesar indios arrieros y viandantes, que para este trajino [*sic* trajín], y ejercicio lo general es hablar la lengua Mexicana. . . ." Francisco de Burgoa, *Palestra historial de virtudes y ejemplares apostólicos fundada del celo de insignes heroes de la sagrada Orden de Predicadores en este Nuevo Mundo de la America en las Indias Occidentales*, 500.

25. Chance, *Conquest of the Sierra*, ch. 2; and Yannakakis, *The Art of Being In-Between*, ch. 6, and "The 'Indios Conquistadores' of Oaxaca's Sierra Norte: From Indian Conquerors to Local Indians," 227–53.

26. For Dominican friars who used Nahuatl in the sierra, see Chance, *Conquest of the Sierra*, 21–22, 124–25, 155, 175.

27. Chance, *Conquest of the Sierra*, 155.

28. Shirley Bryce Heath, *Telling Tongues: Language Policy in Mexico, Colony to Nation*, 26.

29. Pedro de Feria, *Doctrina christiana en lengua castellana y zapoteca* (México, Pedro Ocharte, 1567). Francisco Pacheco de Silva, *Doctrina christiana, traducida de la lengua castellana, en lengua zapoteca nexitza. Con otras addiciones utiles y necessarias para la educacion catholica y excitacion a la devocion Christiana* (México, 1687). Feria's and Pacheco's doctrinas are only two among a larger corpus of Valley and Sierra Zapotec pastoral literature (see the next section of this essay in which some others are discussed).

30. *Confesionario en lengua mixe; con una construcción de las oraciones de la doctrina christiana y un compendio de voces mixes para ensenarse a pronunciar la dicha lengua; escrito todo por el R. P.*

Augustín de la Quintana, cura que fué de la doctrina de San Juan Bautista de Xuquila, año de 1733. 202 pp. BR498.35 MQ45a. The Library of Daniel Garrison Brinton, The University of Pennsylvania Museum of Archaeology and Anthropology.

31. For information on the Vargas family of Villa Alta, see APJO AJVA Criminal Exp. 30 (1670), "Contra Juan Díaz por muerte de Nicolás Vargas vecino de Villa Alta," 47 ff. The plaintiff, Nicolás Vargas (the elder), was the Interpreter General of Villa Alta prior to his son Nicolás de Bargas. The details of the case include the identification of his family members, who according to the accused, Pedro Dias, controlled all business "having to do with papers in this Villa," so that under no circumstances could he enjoy a fair treatment by the court in Villa Alta; see also APJO AVA Civil Exp. 17 (1682), "Libro conteniendo varios testamentos de diferentes personas." This book of wills includes that of Margarita de Cardenas, the matriarch of the Vargas clan, and makes clear the identities and occupations within the colonial administration of her husband Juan de Vargas, and her seven sons, Alonso, Juan, Jacintho, Nicolás, Lorenso, Domingo, and Miguel.

32. AHJO Villa Alta Criminal Leg. 4 Exp. 1 (1685), "En Averiguación de la muerte de Domingo Nicolás de Ayutla," f. 4.

33. AHJO Villa Alta Criminal Leg. 4 Exp. 1 1685, f. 4.

34. AHJO Villa Alta Criminal Leg. 9 Exp. 8 (1707), "Contra los alcaldes de Tepuxtepec por ocultar un delito." In this murder case, the court identified a Mixe scribe who served as a witness as a Spanish speaker.

35. AHJO Villa Alta Criminal Leg. 6 Exp. 3 (1698), "En averiguación del robo que sufrieron Baltasar Miguel y Sebastian Gomes de Totontepeque."

36. Alonso Barros van Hövell tot Westerflier, "Cien años de guerras Mixes: Territorialidades prehispánicas, expansión burocrática y Zapotequización en el istmo de Tehuantepec durante el siglo XVI."

37. Judith Irvine and Susan Gal, "Language Ideology and Linguistic Differentiation," 35–83, see esp. 10.

38. Fray Francisco de Burgoa articulates Spanish ideas about Mixe "barbarity" in his chronicle of Dominican evangelization of Oaxaca, *Geográfica Descripción: de la parte septentrional del polo ártico de la América y nueva iglesia de las Indias Occidentales, y sitio astronómico de esta provincia de predicadores de Antequera, Valle de Oaxaca*, 11: 188–203, 232–52.

39. The Mixe district interpreters first appear in the following criminal case: AHJO Villa Alta Criminal Leg. 8 Exp. 11 (1705), "Sobre la muerte de Jacinto Mathias natural del pueblo de Xareta contra Jacinto Miguel y consortes."

40. AHJO Villa Alta Civil Leg. 40 Exp. 21 (1816), "Sobre un despacho que se les estrabió a la Republica de Yaa." The municipal officials of the pueblo of San Andrés Yaa accuse Teodoro Solano, "el ynterprete de la Mexicana" of stealing a Real Decreto from them.

41. AHJO Villa Alta Civil Leg. 40 Exp. 20 (1816), "Por bienes hereditarios. Lachirioag." Solano serves as interpreter in this case as well and is identified as an alcalde of the barrio of Analco.

42. Literate Zapotecs used alphabetic writing for other purposes as well, authoring a corpus of ritual texts that drew upon pre-Columbian discursive and ritual traditions

that circulated clandestinely in the seventeenth and early eighteenth centuries; see Ta-várez, *The Invisible War*.

43. William F. Hanks, *Converting Words: Maya in the Age of the Cross*, XVII.

44. Susan Kellogg and Matthew Restall, *Dead Giveaways: Indigenous Testaments of Colonial Mesoamerica and the Andes*.

45. Kevin Terraciano, "Crime and Culture in Colonial Mexico: The Case of the Mixtec Murder Note"; and Lisa Sousa, "The Devil and Deviance in Native Criminal Narratives from Early Mexico."

46. Juan de Córdoba, *Vocabulario en lengua zapoteca*.

47. The analysis of *xihui* in this section derives from a collaborative research project on Zapotec-Spanish translations at the intersection of ecclesiastical and legal settings conducted by Schrader-Kniffki and Yannakakis; see Martina Schrader-Kniffki and Yanna Yannakakis, "Sins and Crimes: Zapotec-Spanish Translation from Catholic Evangelization to Colonial Law (Oaxaca, New Spain)." I thank Professor Schrader-Kniffki for allowing me to use some examples from our work.

48. Library of Congress, Indian Languages Collection, box 57.

49. Copies of Pacheco's *Doctrina* can be found in the Biblioteca Fray Francisco de Burgoa, Oaxaca, and in the John Carter Brown Library.

50. The orthography of *xihui* is irregular in Pacheco—sometimes it is written as xijhui, the "j" indicating a glottal stop.

51. Confessional manuals could also provide more concrete guidance; some of them contained templates for notarial documents (see also Burns, chapter 10).

52. For accounts of electoral strife in San Juan Yatzona, see Chance, *Conquest of the Sierra*, 135; Yannakakis, *The Art of Being In-Between*, ch. 1; and Calvo, *Vencer la derrota*, 2010.

53. Yannakakis, *The Art of Being In-Between*, ch. 1.

54. AHJO Villa Alta Criminal Exp. 59 (1687), "Contra Don Pablo de Vargas por peculado y robo de la caja común"; AHJO Villa Alta Criminal Leg. 5 Exp. 3 (1695), "Contra Don Francisco de Paz, Don Juan de Stgo y Pedro Jimenez Gobernador y alcaldes de Yatzona por derramas económicas, agravios y vegaciones"; AHJO, Villa Alta Criminal Leg. 5 Exp. 4 (1695), "Contra Jose Mendez y socios de Yatzona por sedicioso."

55. Schrader-Kniffki and Yannakakis, "Sins and Crimes."

56. Chance, *Conquest of the Sierra*, 159.

57. Yannakakis, *The Art of Being In-Between*, ch. 1.

58. AHJO Villa Alta Criminal Exp. 59 (1687), f. 17v–18.

59. AHJO Villa Alta Criminal Exp. 59 (1687), f. 12–13v.

60. AHJO Villa Alta Criminal Leg. 5 Exp. 3 (1695).

61. AHJO Villa Alta Criminal Leg. 5 Exp. 3 (1695), f. 11–14v.

62. Yannakakis, *The Art of Being In-Between*, chs. 1 and 2; Tavárez, *The Invisible War*.

63. For a more fulsome linguistic analysis of these examples, see Schrader-Kniffki and Yannakakis, "Sins and Crimes."

64. William B. Taylor, *Magistrates of the Sacred: Priests and Parishioners in Eighteenth-Century Mexico*, 376–84.

65. AHJO Villa Alta Criminal Leg. 5 Exp. 3 (1695), 15–18.

Part II

Native Historians

Sources, Frameworks,
and Authorship

CHAPTER 5

Chimalpahin and Why Women Matter in History

Susan Schroeder

By any standard, the seventeenth-century Nahua historian Chimalpahin was Mexico's foremost indigenous intellectual. But how do we understand indigenous intellectualism in the seventeenth century? In Chimalpahin's case, the measure is Western. Although an autodidact, Chimalpahin was well read, and he cited classical authors such as Sophocles, Plato, and Ovid, as well as the Old Testament and the writings of the great church fathers, Saint Augustine and Saint Thomas Aquinas. He was also familiar with some of the finest secular and theological works of his day.[1] Doubtless he was fluent in Latin and Spanish as well as his native Nahuatl. Moreover, he could read and interpret the sophisticated pictorial accounts from precontact Mexico and amassed dozens, if not hundreds, of manuscripts in order to write an authoritative history of Indian Mexico.[2] An erudite, epic work, it is the only extant account by a known author in his native language and signed by the man himself.

A native of Amecameca Chalco, Chimalpahin moved to Mexico City in 1593 at the age of fourteen to work as a *fiscal* (priest's assistant) at the tiny church of San Antonio Abad in the district of Xoloco, located about two kilometers due south of the city traza. While at San Antón, in addition to his other duties, he began to collect and copy ancient Nahuatl pictorial manuscripts, transforming them into Roman alphabetic script. These were annals, the traditional form of indigenous recordkeeping, and they were rich in the histories and royal lineages of the great *altepetl* (kingdom[s], corporate state[s]) of central Mexico (see also Townsend, chapter 6). There were other Nahuas and mestizos writing histories, but those works were largely in Spanish for a Spanish readership (see also Schwaller, chapter 2).

The hub of all indigenous intellectual activity in Mexico City was the San Francisco church, whose library housed manuscripts along with published books in Latin, Nahuatl, and Spanish.[3] La Capilla de San Josef, the chapel for indigenes at San Francisco, was said to accommodate thousands for mass. We know that Chimalpahin was a member of the San Josef congregation, and I believe that he may well have used the library as a resource. He also interviewed elders and relatives, trying to corroborate the sometimes conflicting information contained in his many sets of annals. He tells how he came by the annals about Amecameca, and he carefully describes the methodology he used to write the history. How the treasure trove of manuscripts about the Mexica fell into his hands he does not say, but they may have been at the San Francisco church library. His church, San Antón, was a small facility with only one friar, Agustín del Espíritu Santo, who was trying to start a branch of his religious order in New Spain. The friar was engaged with the local Nahua community, though, and by all appearances supportive of Chimalpahin's history-writing avocation.

In one set of his annals, Chimalpahin documented events in Mexico City, roughly from the time he arrived in the capital until 1615, and we therefore know that he was a man about the city. He may have been engaged with a circle of other native intellectuals, men such as don Hernando de Alvarado Tezozomoc, don Fernando de Alva Ixtlilxochitl (see also Schwaller, chapter 2), don Gabriel de Ayala, and Cristóbal del Castillo, for he used some of their materials as sources, but this is unlikely since there is no mention of him in the historical record by any of his contemporaries. This void may be attributable to the marginal location of his church and his humble background as a commoner in Amecameca.

Optimistically, he wrote in Nahuatl for a Nahua audience. His annals go back to Adam and Eve and the beginning of time, and there is also rather profound theological commentary. But his interest, always, was in the great Nahua kingdoms of central Mexico. The annals follow the ancient Mesoamerican calendar juxtaposed to Julian and Gregorian dates. The entries are typically about a particular event at a particular time and depend almost en-

SUSAN SCHROEDER

tirely on his interpretation of the painted images in his documents. There was notably as well an oral component that allowed for alleged verbatim speeches by rulers and deities. He collected, sorted, and compared the many annals and usually selected the oldest manuscript as his copy text. He checked with other authors along with elders and, when possible, was a firsthand observer. He then "renewed," as he said, and rewrote the annals. What we have is Chimalpahin's version of what he believed to be the most authentic and truest history. But annals, for our purposes, are too often too brief and even incomplete.

Chimalpahin's oeuvre comprised more than fifteen hundred pages, and all are now available in reliable Spanish or English translation.[4] It is an extraordinary history that often contains information that cannot be found elsewhere or furnishes a new perspective on an old topic. Chimalpahin was a devout Christian, which only indirectly affected the content of his writing.[5] He knew that the history of ancient Mexico was extraordinary, and he wanted to be certain that his hometown, Amecameca, was a part of it. But that same history, in spite of Chimalpahin's best efforts to exemplify Mesoamerican traditions, had its share of adultery, concubinage, ethnoracism, illegitimacy, incest, murder, and political intrigue, all of which are present in his annals.

Remarkably, and contrary to other Nahuatl accounts, women have a place in nearly every aspect of his annals,[6] and he wrote of women from all walks of life: blacks, Jews, mestizos, and both high- and low-ranking Spaniards. But of course his primary interest was in the Nahuas, and it is obvious that women mattered enough in the precontact era to be represented in even the earliest pictorial manuscripts. I do not believe that Chimalpahin was necessarily a feminist or that there was a historical bias favoring women of his time. Indeed, Mesoamerican women were essential to Nahua history, and they were therefore a part of each autochthonous couple in their primordial home at Chicomoztoc Aztlan, for example, and when it came to the actual pictorial manuscripts, Chimalpahin points out that metaphorically it was *both* the old Teochichimeca women and the old Teochichimeca men (*yn illamatque in huehueyntin teochichimeca catca*) who compiled, recorded, and updated the official ancient accounts.[7] How could he not acknowledge one half of the history he was writing? And the women's names are recorded, almost endlessly, as essential wives, mothers, sisters, and daughters. Through the medium of his annals, therefore, a prospect exists of an ideal that corroborates Chimalpahin's staunch traditionalism while affording transparency and a view of the reality of women's lives in early Mexico.

Of course, the greatest detail and richest information are about noble-women, of which two Nahuatl categories exist: the *cihuapipiltin*, the noble-women, who by definition were born of an official, legitimate royal husband and wife,[8] and the *tlatocacihuapipiltin*, the royal noblewomen who were also the descendants of legitimate royal parents but were eligible to succeed their fathers or husbands as full-fledged rulers in their home altepetl, or who could marry a man, even a commoner, in another locale and start a new royal lineage and altepetl while ruling together as tlatoque.[9] In both instances the rulership passed to their heirs and both are excellent examples of political dominance through the female line (see also Martínez, chapter 8). Although kings were *always* the rule in Nahua Mesoamerica, there were enough queens in the early annals to remind us of their vital role in sociopolitical affairs, and, as will be seen, it was the Nahua queens who were the whole point of Chimalpahin's history.

First Women

Before discussing the royal women, I would like to furnish some background on how women figure more generally and inclusively in the Nahuatl annals. Going way back, there is Eve, our first mother (*yn achto tonantzin Eva*) of that essential founding dyad, Adam and Eve[10]; and the first parenthood is recycled too, with considerable discussion of the prophet Noah and the deluge. But Chimalpahin also furnished the names of Noah's sons, Sem, Cam, and Jafet, and their wives, Titea Magna, Pandora, Noela, and Noegla, with a grandson, the patriarch Tubal, making his way to Spain with his wife, children, and many other peoples, becoming the founding fathers and mothers there and in Chimalpahin's way of thinking, perhaps, somehow legitimizing the Span-ish invasion of North America.[11]

As noted, there were first-founding couples in Chicomoztoc, and mi-grating groups setting out from there were often accompanied by women.[12] Chimalpahin notes that the Azteca Mexitin numbered ten thousand, includ-ing women and children.[13] Some of these women were credited as serving as guides who showed groups the peril involved in crossing bodies of water to escape their enemies.[14] Among others, a Chimalman is identified and a man named Mario[15] who served as *teomamaque* (godcarriers). Chimalman was carrying the omnipotent god Huitzilopochtli, a mindboggling undertaking in its own right.[16] That it was a woman who was given the charge of carry-ing this formidable deity warrants further investigation.[17] A migrating god-

SUSAN SCHROEDER

Figure 5.1. A royal mother and the founding of the First Mexica Dynasty, 1227–1299, according to Chimalpahin.

carrier was also sometimes described as *hueltiuhtli* (older sister), which is a complex, multipurpose term discussed further below. Mesoamerican first women, then, had taken on crucial familial, political, and spiritual responsibilities even before they reached their final destinations.

Moreover, the great founding rulers were dependent on royal mothers for their status. Most notable are the Mexica, who twice began their royal rulerships with commoner males and high-ranking, non-Mexica females from high status altepetl. The first *tlatoani* (king, ruler), Huehue Huitzilihuitl (r. 1227–99), was the son of a Mexica Chichimeca; in other words, a commoner, and a noblewoman, Tlaquilxochtzin, the daughter of King Tlahuizcalpotonquiteuctli of Tzompanco. It was said that he became ruler because his mother belonged to a great lineage and was the daughter of the *huey* (great) tlatoani of Tzompanco.[18] The Mexica were still migrating southward and got as far as Acocolco, near Chapoltepec, when Huitzilihuitl, his daughter, Chimallaxotzin,[19] and his elder sister (*yhueltiuh*) were captured, stripped naked, and sacrificed by King Coxcoxtli (r. 1281–1307) of Colhuacan.[20] According to the annals, Huitzilihuitl begged Coxcoxtli to cover his daughter's nudity and spare her, but to no avail. Huitzilihuitl left no heirs,[21] and it was incumbent on the Mexica to regroup (see figure 5.1).[22]

The new, second Mexica royal genealogy was established upon the installation of Acamapichtli the younger as tlatoani (r. 1367–87) of the recently established island altepetl of Mexico Tenochtitlan.[23] The Mexica prevailed on the Colhuaque who although obviously treacherous were also at the time the most prestigious people in central Mexico, with powerful ennobling ties and believed to be of Toltec heritage.[24] On this occasion the Mexica started their royal lineage with Atotoztli, a royal noblewoman from Colhuacan as founding wife and mother. She was the daughter of the same King Coxcoxtli, and her stature was such that she could marry a man who was "only a Mexica Chichimeca," a *quauhpilli*, "a person with status earned by rank and not inherited."[25] It was a classic example of first founders of preeminent altepetl tracing their nobility through the female line (see also Martínez, chapter 8). Yet it was the same heraldic pedigree as that of the great Mesoamerican emperor, Moteuczoma Xocoyotl (r. 1502–20), and it continued for 198 years, until 1565 when the last legitimate noble Mexica descendant died.[26] In Tetzcoco, the great king Nezahualcoyotzin (r. 1431–72) was the son of Huehue Ixtlilxochitzin and Matlalcihuatzin, the daughter of tlatoani Huitzilihuitl the younger (r. 1391–1415) of Mexico Tenochtitlan, generations later but of the same ennobling, founding female line as that of the Mexica discussed above (see figure 5.2).[27] Thus the essential cornerstone of the eminent rulerships and lineages of the Aztecs and Tetzcoca was a woman, a point to which I shall return (see also Martínez, chapter 8).

Commoner Women and Others in Their Milieu

Chimalpahin's annals identify other women, some of whom I shall refer to as "collectives." For example, in Four Rabbit, 1522, when Hernando Cortés ordered that Mexico Tenochtitlan/Mexico City be repopulated after the destruction of the Aztec regime, Chimalpahin poignantly recorded that it was the women who returned to their homes, carrying their children and their belongings. He added that they found only bones scattered all about.[28] In other instances, when a complaint regarding the relocation of the markets was registered before Audiencia judges, women were successful in their petition to prevent the move,[29] and when the wife of King Philip III (r. 1598–1621), *tohueycihuatlahtocatzin* (our great queen) doña Margarita de Austria, died (1612), noblewomen and noblemen and commoners all dressed in mourning clothes and traveled from Amecameca to Tlalmanalco, a considerable distance, for the funeral service.[30] Otherwise native women were to cover themselves with a white tilma when they were in a church.[31] Annals, being terse, episodic reports, seldom furnish all the information that we would like about Nahua women. Yet they tell of a wide range of their experiences. For example, we read that women suffered during the flower wars, but to what extent is not known, only that when they went to collect water their pots and jugs were broken and that when their children went to gather firewood it was taken from them and burned.[32] Still, women frolicked in the lakes in Patzcuaro,[33]

SUSAN SCHROEDER

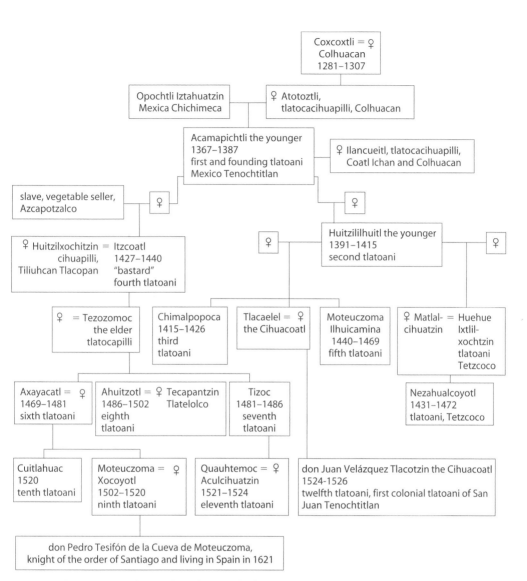

Figure 5.2. Another royal mother and the founding of the Second Mexica Dynasty, 1367–1621, according to Chimalpahin.

or used the *temazcalli* (steam house) for themselves and their newborns[34]; and some women served as wet nurses.[35] But elsewhere women of the *tecpan* (palace) were robbed,[36] and female tribute collectors could be killed by angry debtors.[37] In addition, women were expected to continue to spin and weave even in times of severe political upheaval,[38] and some women suffered abuse by their husbands. On one occasion the ruler don Juan Bautista Toyaotzin (r. 1548–64, 1565–76) of Tequanipan, in Amecameca, killed his Cuitlahuac wife. He was forced to abdicate his throne but was eventually absolved of any crime. Also during the colonial period, don Josef del Castillo Ecaxoxouhqui (1548–64, 1570–76), ruler of Tzaqualtitlan Tenanco in Amecameca, was arrested for living in concubinage and abusing of the women. When he escaped from jail, the Tenanca, his subjects, did not want him back, but after being pressured by their priest, Father Juan Páez, he was installed as ruler one more time. His wife, doña María Itzmiquilxochitzin, a noblewoman of higher-ranked Tenanco Texocpalco, died as soon as he returned.[39] What brought on the wrath and cruelty of these men is not stated. Nonetheless, when Tetzcoca King Nezahualpilli's (r. 1472–1515) high-status Mexica wife committed adultery, it was cause enough for him to have her put to death.[40]

Surely one of the most interesting but wrenching stories about commoner women was when Cortés and his Spaniards first stopped at Amecameca, Chimalpahin's hometown. The Spaniards were given forty attractive and well outfitted local female commoners, made up to look like noblewomen. Chimalpahin described how it was accomplished: The rulers and their legitimate sons solicited women from across the altepetl, specifying that they were to be young. They had the girls bathed in the temazcalli and cut their legs.[41] They dressed them in beautiful skirts and huipiles, coiffed their hair, and put makeup on them—adornments customarily worn by the wives of rulers. Two Amecameca kings took the girls, along with three thousand pesos' worth of wrought gold jewelry, to the outskirts of town as gifts for the conqueror. The Spaniards probably never knew that commoner females had been substituted for nobility. We can only imagine how terrified the girls must have been.[42]

Nevertheless, some commoner women did become royal mistresses and the mothers of future kings, although they were never recognized as official wives. Take, for example, the Mexica king Acamapichtli who through an arranged marriage came to have noblewoman Ilancueitl, his aunt, as his legitimate wife. But Ilancueitl was childless, and her young husband became smitten with a slave, a vegetable seller from Azcapotzalco. Their child, Itzcoatl (r. 1427–40), referred to as a bastard, nevertheless became a valiant warrior, acceded to the throne, and eventually had many notable heirs.[43] But the Mexica nobility were seriously concerned about the royal line possibly having been compromised by Acamapichtli's association with a slave, so royal daughters from across central Mexico were sent to King Itzcoatl, and the offspring of these unions thus were responsible for establishing the new

SUSAN SCHROEDER

altepetl and royal lineages of Itztapalapan, Xilotepec, Apan, and Atotonilco, to name just a few. It was said that Ilancueitl, Acampichtli's sterile wife, lay with each newborn in her arms, pretending it was her own.[44]

Women on Their Own
THE HUELTIUHTLI

One puzzling Nahuatl category of women is the hueltiuhtli, the older sister, which always appears in the possessive form. It occurs with some frequency in Chimalpahin, who has three uses for the term. "Older sister" can be quite literally a sibling relationship, as when the Aztec emperor Axayacatzin arranged for the marriage of his older sister Chalchiuhnenetzin to King Moquihuixtli of Tlatelolco (r. 1460–73), the altepetl to the north with which Tenochtitlan shared the island. The hueltiuhtli of a sibling relationship was also associated with sedentary polities.[45] It was a pro forma arrangement, but even though Moquihuix had a child with the older sister, he did not like her, because, it was said, she was flat chested, bony, not pretty, and had bad breath. He took away the precious gifts that her brother sent to her,[46] giving them to his other women. He badly beat Chalchiuhnenetzin and cast her and their child out of the palace to live amid the grinding stones. At the same time, Moquihuix decided to go to war against Mexico Tenochtitlan, and the older sister alerted her brother Axayacatzin, who brought her home and rewarded her lavishly with goods to provide for her and her child. Axayacatl investigated her report, had a war song created to challenge the Tlatelolca, and performed the song before going to battle.[47] The Tlatelolca were overwhelmed, and Moquihuixtli leaped from a high place to his death. His followers were driven into the swamps and made "to quack like ducks," or so it was said. The annals conclude that "there was ruin because of a concubine."[48] Thereafter the Tlatelolca were without influence. However, the conspicuous sexism in blaming the fall of a state on a woman confounds Chimalpahin's otherwise idealizing portrayal of women and obfuscates the blatant political machinations of triumvirate empire building.[49]

In the next two examples of hueltiuhtli, the older sister serves less in a family capacity and instead takes on more of a sexual role, with religion, as gods, godcarriers, and sorcerers—all of whom could be women—becoming more prominent. These older sisters all appear to be specific to migrating groups. In the first example, the older sister is the only female named among a migrating group; she meets a leader of an established altepetl and becomes impregnated by the man, after which the migrating group is given land and allowed to settle there. The child of the relationship inevitably succeeds to office in a new altepetl, starting a legitimate royal rulership and lineage. One example is from Amecameca in 1295, when the ruler and godcarrier Tziuhtla-cauqui Yaopol Tzompahua led the migrating Tequanipan people along with his daughter (name unknown), who is described as *ynhueltiuh*, "the older sister [of the Tequanipan people]," to Itztlacoçauhcan, the leading polity in Amecameca. They encountered a migrating group leader, Tliltecatzin Yaote-quihua, who was out hunting and who soon impregnated their older sister. The rulers of Amecameca then conferred and decided to permit the Tequani-pan people to stay, granting them a generous amount of land in Amecameca territory. Tziuhtecatl (r. 1304–?), the child of Tliltecatzin and the older sister, was installed as first ruler of the newly established polity of Tzompanhuacan Tequanipan Amecameca.[50]

Later Tziuhtecatl married Cilcuetzin Matlaltzin, daughter of the ruler in Tzaqualtitlan Tenanco, the second-in-rank altepetl in Amecameca, thus bringing together and mixing the lineages of three Amecameca polities.[51] Their son, Xonecuiltzin, succeeded his father as ruler in Tequanipan.[52] A daughter, Miztliyauhtzin, married Itztlotzinteuctli (r. 1348–1417), tlatoani of Tzaqualtitlan Tenanco, and their son, Quauhtlehuanitzin (r. 1418–65), also became ruler in Tzaqualtitlan Tenanco.[53] First-cousin marriages every second generation or so tended to be a pattern in Amecameca.[54] In sum, the older sister was a migrating woman responsible for the founding of an altepetl. In this instance she was of a lesser rank, but such a woman was almost always also affiliated with a man who was a godcarrier, or she was one herself.[55]

The third example pertains exclusively to older sisters as deities. In 1064 all seven *calpolli* (group of families, territorial unit) departed from Aztlan Chicomoztoc accompanied by Malinalxoch, the elder sister of the Mexica god Huitzilopochtli. She was attended by a cohort of advisers, and all were said to be wicked sorcerers. It was for this reason that Huitzilopochtli aban-doned his older sister at Patzcuaro, and she subsequently moved on with her subjects and established the polity of Malinalco, after being impregnated by the ruler and then bearing a son, Copil.[56] Yet the account becomes more troubling and even gruesome, since Huitzilopochtli ended up beheading his mother, Coyolxauhqui,[57] and eating her heart and those of his uncles, the Centzonhuitznahua. His mother was said to be the older sister of his uncles. It may well be that migrating Coyolxauhqui, Malinalxoch, and even the elder sister of the above-mentioned first Mexica tlatoani Huehue Huitzili-

SUSAN SCHROEDER

huitl, who was killed at Chapoltepec, were to serve as sexual carrots to entice local rulers into accepting newly arrived peoples in their home regions. As I noted, King Coxcoxtli of Colhuacan obviously would have none of Huitzilihuitl's sister and saw to her death, eschewing any sort of political or territorial concession to the Mexica. It was only later that he relented and married his daughter to a Mexica. On the other hand, Coyolxauhqui, Malinalxoch (an evil sorcerer and yet a pregnant migrating older sister), and Huitzilopochtli, a god turned wicked, may be nothing more than Nahua Mesoamerica's first dysfunctional family.[58] Thus, these older sisters could have either negative or positive attributes. Yet by no means should the concept of the Nahuatl older sister be considered in the abstract. In her various forms, she was definitely an essential part of Nahua society and spirituality in spite of the deficiency of the English definition of the term.

MALINTZIN

If anyone was ever on her own, it was Malintzin, the Nahua girl gifted to Cortés in 1519. Chimalpahin describes her work with Cortés as that of an interpreter (*Mallintzin nahuatlahtohua*), and in his annals he consistently calls her Malintzin and not Marina, her baptismal name and that used by the Spaniards. He includes Cortés's pronouncements as they have come to us through Malintzin's Nahuatl voice. In addition, she was the spokesperson on the installation of kings in their offices, and she served as the translator for lawsuits before the viceroy in Mexico City as late as 1530. Chimalpahin also recorded that she served as the interpreter during the interrogation and torture of the Aztec ruler Quauhtemoc and other imperial leaders (also see Ramos, chapter 1, Schwaller, chapter 2, and Yannakakis, chapter 4).[59] Yet she does not seem extraordinary. It is of interest, however, that in the anonymous Nahuatl Tetzcoca annals in the *Codex Chimalpahin*, she is referred to only as Marina, and here she is even more authoritative, issuing directives, questioning rulers, serving as a messenger for Cortés, and seeing to it that things were done as he wished.[60] She is singularly supportive of the Spaniards' needs and wishes, without exception.

In contrast, Chimalpahin was somewhat less constrained in his treatment of Malintzin in the course of his rewriting of Francisco López de Gómara's Spanish-language *Conquista de México* (1552). On the one hand, there are numerous references to her (far more than Cortés's scant mention), and she appears as both Malintzin and Marina. She was typically translating for Cortés, and Chimalpahin added in Spanish that "[she] was always there to help the Captain."[61] On the other hand, he makes a point of dignifying her by giving her a second name, Tenepal, a term of uncertain meaning, yet an attempt to professionalize her actions and portray her less as Cortés's pawn and more the indispensable aide that she had turned herself into.[62] During the first encounters and conquests, then, women were indispensable to the purposes of both the natives and the Spaniards. In general, in his *Conquista* book Chimalpahin makes a point of portraying native women favorably whenever possible, which is what we have come to expect in his histories over all.

Continuities in the Seventeenth Century

Obviously, individual women were not without agency; nor did they hesitate to speak out against abuse, even during the colonial era. Chimalpahin furnishes a classic example from 1612, when a María López, a chocolate seller, went directly to the Real Audiencia to register a complaint against fray Gerónimo de Zárate, the chaplain at the Capilla de San Josef, the Franciscan center of all native religious activity in the capital. It seems that fray Gerónimo had stripped her ailing husband of his clothing, tied him to a stone pillar in the church, and whipped him, nearly killing him. The friar then had her husband put in jail, accusing him of squandering *cofradía* (confraternity, religious brotherhood) funds. Other Nahuas registered complaints against Zárate as well. María Constanza had been taken from her home and put on public display with her breasts exposed because she had not come to Mass. And a man, Josef Gómez, was abused because he talked back to the friar. Chimalpahin added that the friar was relieved of his duties at San Josef because María López had the courage to confront the Audiencia judges while they were in session and persuade them to launch an investigation.[63] Of course, fray Gerónimo did not go away for long. Chimalpahin was evidently supportive of these women, whom he doubtless knew well, since he too was part of the congregation at San Josef.

Spanish Women

Spanish women were also in the annals. Peninsular viceroys came and went with their wives, and their daughters formed important marital alliances with prominent New Spanish men. Major events in faraway Spain, such as royal births, deaths, and marriages, were duly recorded and celebrated with

SUSAN SCHROEDER

rooftop bonfires across the city and with church bells ringing. As noted, the deaths of Spanish queens were cause for mourning by even their most humble royal subjects. Chimalpahin is also quite taken with the doings of nuns and *beatas* (pious lay females), and he carefully noted all of Moteuczoma's daughters who either founded or entered convents, furnishing the names of the women and their establishments.[64] Of great interest was when a group of nuns moved from one convent to another, which was cause for celebration and a procession, with all regular clergy participating and everyone else watching.[65] The saints, their feast days, and the Virgin Mary received respectful mention on numerous occasions, and Guadalupe was noted twice.[66]

Creole women could be found throughout New Spain, but generally Chimalpahin had little to say about them, unless they violated the norm. There were two cases concerning unruly women that caused him considerable consternation, nevertheless. These were women living with male relatives in Nahua neighborhoods, and in both instances they behaved badly and suffered dire consequences. Spanish women were also portrayed as emotionally labile, that is, shouting, crying, and hiding on occasions of eclipses, earthquakes, and rebellions—all reasonable cause for concern.[67]

Mariana Rodríguez lived in Chimalpahin's Xoloco neighborhood, and she and her husband vociferously opposed placing a holy cross next to their house. The land belonged to the community, and the community wanted to erect a cross right there. Mariana spoke out repeatedly against the cross, even using what Chimalpahin witnessed as "filthy" language. However, she was immediately stricken with a disease and died within days. A judge declared in favor of the cross and the community, giving the Nahuas the land in perpetuity.[68] Likewise, a Nahua woman, María, a seller of bitter *atole* (maize gruel), also lived in Chimalpahin's neighborhood, and she too went to great lengths to protest placing a cross next to a road near her house, complaining to the cabildo that it was on her property. She had two men arrested for erecting the cross there. She scolded and swore, and used foul language. It was Chimalpahin's priest at San Anton who intervened and set the matter straight. But the damage was done. Chimalpahin recorded that "all the bad and filthy language with which she went scolding [the two men] cannot be said or told. She showed great disrespect for them, for she was a woman."[69] María, along with her son-in-law, who supported her, became ill and died. Chimalpahin noted that God had sent down his wrath, since obviously their willful behavior violated Nahua social conventions.[70]

Jewish women were noted only in passing, and that was when they were being investigated by the Inquisition. In 1601, one woman, Isabel Machado, young, unmarried, and the daughter of a tailor, was displayed, along with a beata, a nun, and a priest.[71] Earlier, in 1596, other Jews were burned as idolaters, four of whom were Spanish women.[72] Chimalpahin offered no personal opinion of the Holy Tribunal's actions.

However, in 1609 and again in 1612 Chimalpahin went to great lengths to describe the terror felt by the Spaniards when they learned of the possibility of blacks rebelling in the capital. Doubtless always living on the edge because they were outnumbered by non-Europeans, by 1612 they were convinced that an uprising was imminent and that they would be targeted. Spanish men would be castrated, even killed, and all the pretty Spanish women would marry black men. Nuns would be spared since they could serve as teachers of the black children, and black women would finally be allowed to take the veil. The Europeans were terrified. Spanish women were said to be weeping, doors were bolted, and Spanish soldiers were posted everywhere. Reportedly, a black had been elected king, and a *morisca* (descendant of conquered Muslims) named Isabel was to be his queen. Other blacks were to be the dukes, counts, and marquises to help rule Mexico. It was said that rebels and runaways were coming from both Acapulco and Veracruz to join forces with the blacks in the city.

It all happened during Holy Week, and the city was brought to a standstill, at least for the Spaniards. Was there such a plot, or was it all an excuse to intimidate New Spanish blacks and keep them in their place? We do not know. But the next month, in May, twenty-eight black men and seven black women were hanged. Chimalpahin offers no commentary regarding the possible truth of the rumors or the punishments meted out; he emphasized the foolishness of the Spaniards' behavior, though, noting that the Nahuas were not in the least bit concerned about any of it, which is of course telling in itself.[73]

Royal Nahua Women

It goes without saying that women are everywhere in Chimalpahin's history of Indian Mexico, and his inclusiveness seems natural. But was he really that objective? Might he have had an ulterior motive for depicting women in a positive light? The annals speak for themselves, as do their many authors! The trendy trope, "gender conscious," seems superfluous.[74] Nevertheless, regal women, queens especially, were crucial to the majesty of Amecameca history, and his six-times-removed grandmother Xiuhtotoztzin the Tlailotlacteuctli

SUSAN SCHROEDER

(r. 1340–48) was one of those queens. Chimalpahin was proud that Xiuhtotoztzin was installed as ruler in his hometown of Tzaqualtitlan Tenanco in Amecameca. She ruled because there was no male to succeed her father, and her son acceded to the throne on her death.[75]

Elsewhere in Amecameca, in Tlailotlacan Teohuacan a very young boy was installed in office because his father was forced to go into exile. His mother, royal noblewoman Tlacocihuatzin (r. 1411–19), was charged with his care and went to Mexico Tenochtitlan to be invested with a royal title and installed as queen, serving as regent until he reached his majority.[76] Both queens were vested with titles and all the authority and pomp enjoyed by their male counterparts, and both maintained their respective rulerships and royal lineages.

There were other Mesoamerican queens.[77] Of those noted by Chimalpahin, Mexica King Itzcoatl's daughter left Tenochtitlan and traveled about searching for a husband. She found him, a commoner, in Atotonilco, and together they ruled as tlatoque there, initiating a rulership and official lineage and having a son (named Itzcoatl after his grandfather) who succeeded his parents on the throne.[78] Another queen was Ilancueitl, of Acolhuacan Cohuatlichan, who may have left some sort of record regarding the Mexica conquest of Azcapotzalco in 1428. Unfortunately, the relevant folios are missing from Chimalpahin's history.[79] A fifth queen was Tlapalizquixotzin, who succeeded her brother and was the third ruler (*cihuatlatoani*) at Ecatepec. She married the great emperor Moteuczoma Xocoyotl, obviously giving up her throne though forming an important and lasting alliance with Mexico Tenochtitlan. They had a daughter, doña Francisca de Moteuczoma, who married don Diego de Alvarado Huanitzin, formerly tlatoani of Ecatepec (r. 1520–38) and the first governor of Mexico Tenochtitlan (r. 1538–41) in the colonial era.[80] Their son was don Hernando de Alvarado Tezozomoc (fl. 1598), Moteuczoma Xocoyotl's celebrated grandson and the chronicler of ancient Mexico. In spite of being a scion of distinguished ancestry, it is obvious that doña Francisca was not a primary wife, for Alvarado Tezozomoc was never considered as a candidate for succession to his grandfather's throne, though the authorities were desperate to fill the position.[81] Rather, it seems that Moteuczoma Xocoyotl's primary wife (name unknown) may have been the daughter of his uncle Ahuitzotl, a former king of Mexico Tenochtitlan. She and Moteuczoma had at least one child, Teucichpochtzin, later known as doña Isabel de Moteuczoma, who was first married to her cousin Atlixcatzin,[82] son of the late King Ahuitzotl, then to tlatoani Cuitlahuac, her father's brother, and finally to Quauhtemoc, her cousin and the half-brother of her first husband,[83] all

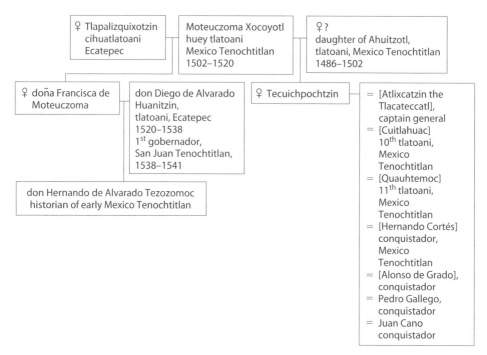

Figure 5.3. Some of the important women in Moteuczoma Xocoyotl's royal family, according to Chimalpahin.

before the arrival of the Spaniards; she ultimately had six husbands by the time she was in her early twenties (see figure 5.3). It was said that her third husband, Quauhtemoc, upon assuming the rulership of both Mexico Tenochtitlan and Tlatelolco (1521–24),[84] systematically put to death all of Moteuczoma Xocoyotl's descendants who were rivals to his own dynastic heritage.[85] Doubtless, since she was a member of the family and a potential queen, Quauhtemoc was partial to Teucichpochtzin and spared her. Her stature was such that even Hernando Cortés had a child with her and then saw that she married well and was provided for.[86]

It is obvious that noble mothers and daughters played valuable roles in their society.[87] Royal daughters crisscrossed Nahua Mesoamerica, forming a crazy quilt of sexual politics based on inviolable traditions that reinforced altepetl alliances and consolidated political confederations. Chimalpahin championed those traditions through his reiteration of rank, class, status, office, and title.[88] There are abundant examples to support Chimalpahin's point. For example, in Tepexic Mixtlan, Toçancoztli was installed as ruler only because of his wife[89]; Quauhtemoc was installed as tlatoani of Tlate-

SUSAN SCHROEDER

lolco because his mother was from there[90]; Chimalpilli the younger ruled Ecatepec because his mother was from there, and later, don Diego de Alvarado Huanitzin ruled Ecatepec as well because his mother was from there[91]; don Antonio de Valeriano the younger became judge-governor of Azcapotzalco (1611) because his mother was from there[92]; Huetzin, as far back as the year 1130, became the first tlatoani of Colhuacan because his mother was from there[93]; Popocatzin, a commoner, became ruler of Atlauhtlan Tzaqualtitlan Tenanco because he was so rich that King Cohuazacatzin the Teohuateuctli of Tlailotlacan Teohuacan married his royal noblewoman daughter to him in order to gain access to his wealth[94]; Moquihuixtli became tlatoani of Tlatelolco because of his high-status mother and his marriage to the sister of King Axayacatzin of Mexico Tenochtitlan[95]; during an outbreak of war, Toltecatl, son of the ruler of Chiyauhtzinco Huexotzinco, came with many nobles, noblewomen, and commoners to seek safe haven in Amecameca because his mother was from there[96]; Miccacalcatl Tlaltetecuintzin the Chichimecateuctli ruled Tequanipan (r. 1492–1522) in Amecameca because his mother was from there[97]; don Esteban de la Cruz de Mendoza was installed as ruler of Tequanipan (r. 1575–88) because of his wife[98]; don Juan Bautista Toyaotzin became tlatoani of Tequanipan because of his mother[99]; and the infamous Quetzalmaçatzin (r. 1522–47) and Tequanxayacatzin (r. 1525–65) of Itztlacoçauhcan and Tlailotlacan Teohuacan Amecameca, respectively, would not have dreamed of taking over the rulerships there if they had not been their mother's homes.[100]

Close examination of Chimalpahin's annals reveals, however, that even in Mesoamerica rules were made to be broken, and it would seem that continuity and conformity prevailed over legitimacy in the survival of royal rulerships.[101] But in the 1540s when Viceroy don Antonio de Mendoza sent a judge to restore all rightful rulerships to the respective kings in his hometown, a dispute ensued over who should be installed on the throne in Panohuayan, the fifth altepetl in Amecameca. The obvious eligible candidate was don Josef de Santa María Teuctlacoçauhcan, whose lineage was traced through the female line. His mother was a noblewoman, but she had married a *quauhpilli*, a man who had earned his position through merit, not inheritance. The judge abhorred don Josef's entitlement since his lineage was compromised by his mother's marriage.[102] Of course, we already know that the great rulerships in central Mexico were founded on succession through the female line, a practice that traced back twice to the origins of the infamous Mexica royal lineage (see figures 5.1 and 5.2).

The judge, though, after inspecting all the ancient genealogies and histories, offered the throne to someone else, don Mateo Tetlilnelohuatzin the
Tecpanecatlteuctli, who traced his lineage through the male side of his family
(see also Martínez, chapter 8), but he declined the position. The judge went all
the way to Tlalmanalco to find a suitable tlatoani, don Juan de Ojeda Quauhcececuitzin, but this man refused as well. With no takers, only reluctantly was
the judge forced to install don Josef (r. 1548–64).[103] And it was here that Chimalpahin found his cause. He was upset with the judge's reasoning and determined to set the record straight. Hence his history of Amecameca, which
only came to be after he collected, transliterated, and analyzed all the dozens
of annals about Indian Mexico that he could get his hands on. The judge was
wrong, said Chimalpahin, when he invalidated the tradition of royal succession through the female line. After all, his grandmother had ruled as queen.
But the judge already knew of the Amecameca queens, and he would not
change his mind. Fortunately, Chimalpahin was well read; he turned to the
dynastic history of Spain for substantiation. He began with King Roderic and
the Godos, "Goths," knowing that don Pelayo, Roderic's younger brother,
was succeeded as ruler of León by his daughter Ormisinda. Accordingly, her
husband, Alonso I el Católico, ruled with her but was not eligible to ascend
the throne, which was to pass to their heir.[104] Spain's long history includes
many more great female rulers, but Chimalpahin was mostly interested in the
Trastámara dynasty and the rulership of Queen Isabel and her daughters.[105]
Isabel succeeded her brother Henry IV to the throne of Castile in 1474. It was
not an easy undertaking, for there was resistance to her rule in various quarters. But Isabel shrewdly married Ferdinand II of Aragón and used him to her
best advantage. The credibility and authority of both rulers was enhanced by
their complementary offices, and together they came to fashion their kingdoms into admirable imperial thrones. Chimalpahin documented Isabel and
Ferdinand's rule and furnished considerable detail about the birth rank and
royal marriages of their daughters. Their second daughter, Juana, was the
designated successor to the throne of Castile on the death of Isabel in 1504.
Juana and her husband, Philip I, were living in Flanders, and thus there was
a long delay before their arrival in Castile. Ferdinand served as regent, then,
along with his second wife, Germana (Germaine). Chimalpahin knew of
Juana's incapacity and noted that on Ferdinand's death in 1516, Juana's son,
the illustrious Holy Roman Emperor (1519) Carlos V, became king of Spain.

Chimalpahin championed the rule and accomplishments of the Catholic

SUSAN SCHROEDER

kings and their daughters, having no trouble making comparisons with the situation in Amecameca. Thinking of exemplary Queen Isabel in Spain, he asserted that there should be no challenge to descent and rule through the mother's line in Amecameca. And, just in case and to shore up his argument, he invoked the Catholic faith, stating that now the holy sacrament of marriage afforded additional legitimacy and a royal noblewoman should be able to marry anyone at all, and their heirs were entitled to full authority, rights, and privileges.[106]

Chimalpahin wrote his history so that future generations of Nahuas would know the wonder of their past, and it concerned him that Amecameca's history was accurate and complete. He wrote, "It will never be forgotten."[107] His collection of painted manuscripts from his hometown as well as Mexico Tenochtitlan, Tetzcoco, and elsewhere was already rich in information about the world of Nahua women since the beginning of their history. These manuscripts were not still-life drawings but pictorial representations of real life. Of course, everyone thought that the preferred form of descent reckoning was through the male line, and it probably was. But the annals reveal that in many instances women were the founders of those same lineages. There was no reason for Chimalpahin to think that the women of Amecameca were any less active or important, especially when so many parallels could be drawn between the royal houses in Spain and his hometown. Was there really any difference between the Roman goddess of love and the Tetzcoco Venus?

At best, Chimalpahin can be described as an accidental intellectual. It is true that he came up with a famous pen name for himself and it is true that he seemed to spend as much time at the San Francisco church as he did at San Antón. But his purpose was never anything more than to write a true and best history of Amecameca and situate it in the greater scheme of what he and others knew about the world. As far as he was concerned, women mattered from beginning to end.

Notes

1. It is apparent that Chimalpahin was familiar with many of the works of the Franciscan friars in New Spain as well as, for just one example, Henrico Martínez's *Reportorio de los tiempos e historia natural de Nueva España*.

2. For a list and analysis of these works, see Susan Schroeder, "The Truth about the Crónica Mexicayotl."

3. Susan Schroeder, "Chimalpahin, don Carlos María de Bustamante and *The Conquest of Mexico* as Cause for Mexican Nationalism," 288–89; and "Chimalpahin Rewrites the Conquest," 101–23.

4. Domingo Chimalpahin, *Las ocho relaciones y El memorial de Colhuacan* (hereafter DC); don Domingo de San Antón Muñón Chimalpahin Quauhtlehuanitzin, *Codex Chimalpahin* (hereafter CC); *Annals of His Time* (hereafter AHT); and *Chimalpahin's Conquest*.

5. For one theory about how Chimalpahin could write about the ancient history of Mexico and not have his papers confiscated, see Schroeder, "Chimalpahin Rewrites the Conquest."

6. Compare, for example, the Nahuatl annals of Puebla and Tlaxcala, in which there is scant mention of native women. See Camilla Townsend, ed. and trans., *Here in This Year: Seventeenth-Century Nahuatl Annals of the Tlaxcala-Puebla Valley*, 37. All data in this essay are from Chimalpahin, including dates, spellings, and interpretations. For studies of gender complementarity and issues of women as separate but equal in Mesoamerica, see any number of articles in Susan Schroeder, Stephanie Wood, and Robert Haskett, *Indian Women in Early Mexico*. These topics are not specifically addressed in this essay for lack of space, but it is evident, still, that Chimalpahin generally thought of women in terms of gender equality. There are numerous examples. For a more theoretical and feminist approach, see Rosemary A. Joyce, *Gender and Power in Prehispanic Mesoamerica*.

7. DC, 2, 272.

8. See Camilla Townsend, "Don Juan Buenaventura Zapata y Mendoza and the Notion of a Nahua Identity," 168.

9. Chimalpahin is not entirely consistent in his usage, but enough examples exist to unequivocally support this position. The inconsistency can likely be traced to the gaps in the information about primary wives. See DC, 2, 47, 105; and Bernardino de Sahagún, *Florentine Codex: General History of the Things of New Spain*, bk. 10, *The People*, 45–50, which discusses many categories of noblewomen as well as a *tlatocacioatl* (hereinafter Sahagún).

10. DC, 1, 30, 38. Susan D. Gillespie, *The Aztec Kings: The Construction of Rulership in Mexica History*, also treats "founding queens" but with a different purpose.

11. DC, 1, 311–13. Stafford Poole, C.M., tells me that women are seldom listed in Old Testament genealogies, and that none is mentioned in Genesis, ch. 10. He feels that most of the names are legendary. Titea Magna is Latin, with Magna meaning "great," but there is no information about Titea. Pandora is Greek for "all gifts"; and Noela seems to reflect Christmas (in spite of its being supposedly Old Testament information), and we have no idea what Noegla would mean. None of the names are Hebrew. Poole adds that legends were in wide circulation in medieval and early modern times, and it was common for people to invent them, Saint James (Santiago) reportedly having introduced many of them to Spain. Saint Paul was even said to have gone to Spain, but there is no evidence that Tubal went there.

12. DC, 1, 183, 189, 213; CC, 1, 29, 183.

13. "Azteca Mexitin" was the original name for the Mexica when they departed Chicomoztoc Aztlan; DC, 1, 67–69; 2, 18. Their deity officially changed the name of the migrating group from Azteca to Mexitin, i.e., Mexica, in Five Flint 1068, CC 1, 73.

14. CC, 1, 99, 207–9 states that the woman was "painted in the traditional manner."

15. No explanation exists about how the Spanish name Mario worked its way into the annals, other than as a corruption of the Nahuatl spelling. One set of annals states that the wife of Hueymac, ruler of Tula (r. 993–1029), was also named Mario; DC, 1, 77.

16. CC, 1, 71, where four godcarriers are named, with Chimalman serving as the only female of the group.

17. It is worth noting that some women proceeded only with trepidation, asking Huitzilopochtli about food sources and where they were to live; DC, 1, 213–15.

18. DC, 1, 113, 167–69; 2, 227–29.

19. Her name is also spelled Chimallaxochtzin on one occasion. Another annal states that her name was Azcatlxochtzin, and yet another source identifies the older sister as Chimallaxotzin and that Huehue Huitzilintzin was the middle child with two sisters; DC, 1, 167–69; CC, 1, 223.

20. DC, 1, 171 also shows that the elder sister, here named Cuetlaxoch, escaped by hiding in the tules. See also CC, 1, 223.

21. CC, 1, 205, and DC, 1, 171. But see DC, 1, 213, which speaks of a "son" crying because his father and sister were killed at Chapoltepec. See also DC, 1, 167, n.13, which states that while at Chapoltepec Huehue Huitzilihuitl married a Mexica woman, and they had four children: a son, Acolnahuacatl, and his three older sisters: Tozpanxochtzin, Chimallaxochtzin, and Cohuaxochtzin. DC, 1, 169, states that the three girls were sacrificed at three different locales, while their younger brother hid among some tules in Azcapotzalco.

22. CC, 1, 93, 95, states that the Mexica "now tarried, took Culhuaque girls as daughters-in-law, and the Colhuaque took young Mexica men as sons-in-law. Now their children mingled."

23. DC, 1, 227; 2, 47; CC, 1, 37–45; 2, 91.

24. See Lori Boornazian Diel, *The Tira de Tepechpan: Negotiating Place under Aztec and Spanish Rule*, 23, 33–34; and Sahagún, bk. 3, *The Origin of the Gods*, 14–15. See also DC, 2, 294, where Chimalpahin's ancestors even included the Tolteca in their heritage group, "tulteca Tzaqualtitlan Tenanco Chiconcohuac Amaquemecan."

25. Her husband was Opochtli Iztahuatzin; DC, 1, 356–57; CC, 1, 35. For an alternate version of Acamapichtli II's ancestry, see Ibid., 1, 225, which states that he was the product of three generations of marriage affiliation between Mexica male commoners and Colhuaque noblewomen, with his parents as first cousins.

26. CC, 2, 43. "Eight House 1565. Don Luis de Santa María Nanacacipactzin (r. 1563–65) died . . . With him the last of the great lords of Tenochtitlan came to an end."

27. DC, 2, 53, 75.

28. DC, 2, 165.

29. AHT, 39; and DC, 2, 217, where both Mexica women and men pummeled the palace at San Juan with stones to vociferously protest tribute assignments.

30. DC, 1, 429; AHT, 211–13.

31. DC, 2, 187.

32. DC, 1, 359–61.

33. CC, 1, 77, 187.

34. CC, 1, 99–101, 209.

35. CC, 2, 89–91.

36. DC, 1, 266. Apparently, there was a distinct category of palace women, the *tecpancihua*, who were among the original migrating *calpolli* and tribute payers.

37. DC, 1, 274.

38. CC, 2, 199.

39. DC, 2, 237, 245. It was a good match for don Josef, for doña María was the daughter of the tlatoani there. However, one cannot help but be suspicious of the circumstance of his return, his history of abusing women, and her death.

40. DC, 2, 115, 117.

41. The Nahuatl here is *quinyecxoteçonhuique*, which Rafael Tena defines as *tallar*, "to cut [their legs]," DC, 2, 331. See also Sahagún, bk. 6, *Rhetoric and Moral Philosophy*, 210–11; bk. 2, *The Ceremonies*, 7, 53; and bk. 3, *The Origin of the Gods*, 14, who notes that thorns were used to lacerate calf muscles for blood offerings to the gods. Book 8, *Kings and Lords*, 47, treats women's makeup and hairstyles. Of twenty-one chapters in this book, only two concern women. See also bk. 9, *The Merchants*, 18, 60, for more about women's hair, jewelry, and outfits. Book 10, *The Merchants*, 18, 60, states that the breasts of Otomi women were painted and the painting was scratched and scarified. And see CC, 1, 139, for leg painting as a spa ritual; and AHT, 171, 173, for Chimalpahin's description of the faces of Chinese men whom, he thought, looked like girls.

42. DC, 2, 330–31. On certain occasions, Cortés also specifically asked for women, and in one case they were the daughters of King Nezahualpilli of Tetzcoco. But three of the girls died when the Spaniards were forced to retreat to Tlaxcala after the Noche Triste rout; CC, 2, 187.

43. Ilancueitl was described as formerly the queen (*reyna*) of Colhuacan. She had helped to raise Acamapichtli. See CC, 1, 35–39, 115; DC, 2, 79–81. Huehue Tezozomoctzin is surely the most notable of Itzcoatzin's sons, since he fathered three Mexica emperors: Axayacatl (r. 1469–81), Tizoc (r. 1481–86), and Ahuitzotl (r. 1486–1502).

44. CC, 1, 39. Chimalpahin devotes considerable space to a royal love affair in his own Amecameca that involved a young pregnant girl being given to a king who then adopted the child as his own and brought to the fore issues of legitimacy, succession, adultery, and murder, causing so much grief that the viceroy became involved in the matter. See DC, 1, 353–55; 2, 173–75, 177, 179, 181, 251, 271, 299, 301–3, 311, 313, 321, 333–45, 349–57; AHT, 135.

45. See Pedro Carrasco, "Royal Marriages in Ancient Mexico," 41–81, for an analysis of the politics of royal marriage. Chalchiuhnenetzin's influence was such that during a period of famine (1450), King Moteuczoma Ilhuicamina shared his tribute with four of his grandchildren, three of whom—Axayacatzin, Tizoc, and Ahuitzotl—were future Mexica emperors, as well as with Chalchiuhnenetzin as the older sister of one of them; CC, 1, 233.

46. These were likely a part of her dowry; see DC, 2, 145, for further evidence of dowries. For additional information about the Chalchiuhnenetzin and Moquihuixtli's marriage, see Susan Schroeder, "The First American Valentine: Nahua Courtship and Other Aspects of Family Structuring in Mesoamerica."

47. CC, 1, 135–39; 2, 93. The lyrics of a famous war song by the Amaquemeque were composed to exalt a Mexica ruler but use Chaca women as a vehicle for both eroticism and politics. See Camilla Townsend, "'What in the World Have You Done to Me, My Lover: Sex, Servitude and Politics among the Pre-Conquest Nahuas as Seen in the *Cantares Mexicanos.*'"

48. CC, 2, 93.

49. For additional examples of the hueltiuhtli as sibling, see CC, 2, 191, 209; DC, 1, 213; 2, 93, 167, 351; AHT, 177. For another example of Mexica statecraft, see the fascinating account of Tlatoani Huitzilihuitl's (r. 1391–1425) efforts to take over Quauhnahuac (Cuernavaca) by commandeering and seducing the daughter of the local ruler, Oçomatzin, CC, 1, 119–23; and Schroeder, "The First American Valentine."

50. DC, 1, 341–45, 353–55.

51. The uniting and mixing of lineages, *ynic onenepaniuh ynic oneneliuh in tlahtocatlacamecayotl in tlahtocaeztli*, is extremely important to Chimalpahin and is a topic to be explored more fully in the future; DC, 2, 284, 292. In CC, 1, 119, the mingling of Mexica rulers' lineages is noted.

52. DC, 1, 337–43, 355.

53. DC, 1, 355.

54. See Susan Schroeder, "The Noblewomen of Chalco."

55. See CC, 1, 73, for another example of a migrating Mexica group of teomama, the Mimixcoa, and their elder sister, Teoxahual.

56. DC, 1, 183; CC, 1, 81.

57. DC, 1, 183; CC, 1, 83, has Coyolxauhcihuatl.

58. DC, 1, 183. For additional deities and hueltiuhtli, Tezcatlipoca and his older sister who was fasting are discussed in DC, 1, 217. And see Sahagún, bk. 6, *Rhetoric and Moral Philosophy*, 164, who also furnishes examples of hueltiuhtli.

59. DC, 1, 411–13; 2, 157–59, 181.

60. CC, 2, 187–89, 193, 197–99.

61. Chimalpahin, *Chimalpahin's Conquest*, 279.

62. Speculation exists that Tenepal is no more than Chimalpahin's invention of a term to signify "translator." However, throughout López de Gómara's chronicle he uses only the Spanish terminology for interpreter, following Gómara. In his Nahuatl annals, he uses only *nahuatlatoa*. See Camilla Townsend, *Malintzin's Choices: An Indian Woman in the Conquest of Mexico* for more information about Malintzin.

63. AHT, 195–97, 201.

64. DC, 2, 231; AHT, 299–301.

65. AHT, 29, 71, 91, 213, 251, 273, 291, 299–301; DC, 2, 257.

66. For example, AHT, 29, 31, 33, 47, 61, 75, 261, 271, 289; DC, 2, 211.

67. AHT, 181, 189.

68. AHT, 255–57.

69. AHT, 251–55.

70. AHT, 253.

71. AHT, 73–75.

72. AHT, 59.

73. AHT, 155, 215, 219–27.

74. Karen Olsen Bruhns and Karen E. Stothert, in *Women in Ancient America*, 3–25, focus on the role of gender in archaeology and the American past.

75. DC, 2, 41, 363–65.

76. DC, 2, 63, 365–67; see also 1, 233–35.

77. Bruhns and Stothert, *Women in Ancient America*, speak generally of many queens but do not offer specifics or the essential references, unfortunately.

78. CC, 2, 101; DC, 2, 81.

79. DC, 1, 247.

80. CC, 2, 101; DC, 2, 135. Alvarado Huanitzin was the grandson of Emperor Axa-yacatl, hence the prestigious position of governor while maintaining Mexica dynastic continuity, CC, 1, 165.

81. CC, 1, 63.

82. CC, 1, 167, states that Atlixcatzin had children and grandchildren but makes no mention of Teucichpochtzin as their mother.

83. See Carrasco, "Royal Marriages in Ancient Mexico," 41–82, for information about doña Isabel.

84. CC, 1, 57–59.

85. See Donald E. Chipman, *Moctezuma's Children: Aztec Royalty under Spanish Rule, 1520–1700*, 41; CC, 1, 167.

86. CC, 1, 53–57; Chipman, *Moctezuma's Children*, 49, 51, 96.

87. Townsend, "Don Juan Buenaventura," 145, 149, 169, 178n75, 179n83, where descent through the female line was also important.

88. Susan Schroeder, *Chimalpahin and the Kingdoms of Chalco*, 154–97.

89. CC, 1, 133–35.

90. CC, 2, 79.

91. DC, 2, 155.

92. AHT, 193.

93. DC, 1, 99.

94. DC, 2, 83.

95. DC, 2, 93.

96. DC, 2, 135.

97. DC, 2, 97, 117.

98. DC, 2, 243.

99. DC, 2, 357.

100. DC, 2, 167, 283, 349. The list of such examples of women's role in engendering rulership continuity is nearly endless.

101. DC, 2, 297, for 369 years "at no time was the lineage interrupted."

102. This judgment, even though don Josef had distinguished himself by going to war with the Spaniards and fellow natives on behalf of Viceroy Mendoza; DC, 2, 201.

103. DC, 2, 357–61.

104. DC, 2, 371; and see Peggy K. Liss, *Isabel the Queen: Life and Times*, 114.

105. DC, 2, 371–75. Chimalpahin was mistaken that Ferdinand and Isabel had no

male heir. Their son and heir, Juan, was born in 1478 but died in 1497. Juan's wife, Margaret, miscarried not long after his death. Next in line was the eldest daughter, Isabel, queen of Portugal, but she died in childbirth a few months after Juan's death; see Liss, *Isabel the Queen*, 167, 367.

106. DC, 2, 367–69.

107. DC, 2, 295.

CHAPTER 6

The Concept of the Nahua Historian

Don Juan Zapata's Scholarly Tradition

Camilla Townsend

Don Juan Zapata came from a long line of indigenous nobility who made their home among the four hills of Tlaxcala for at least three centuries.[1] In 1675, he lived on a street in town just below the Franciscan monastery, near the row of arches that ran along the base of the complex. One May morning just before dawn, the aging don Juan and his wife were assaulted in their beds. "Six thieves entered our home. Two came in the window. First one came in . . . he grabbed me. When I was on the point of overpowering him, he called to his friend, so that they doubled up on me."[2] Yet afterward, in the clear light of day, don Juan's primary reaction seems to have been one of relief. Despite recent tensions between Tlaxcala's *pipiltin* (nobility) and *macehualtin* (commoners), the interlopers had wanted only money. They did not beat him or his wife. They took only cash and left all the valuable clothing and handwoven textiles. "Not a rag did they remove," he reiterated. Amid don Juan's treasured raiment were the traditional, symbol-laden indigenous costumes he loved to wear at important ceremonies. And among his important papers lay his great oeuvre, a history of the *altepetl*[3] that he had been working on for decades. These lay safe where they were stored, not a box or drawer violated. Don Juan certainly felt a need to describe the incident in his history and to record the fact that he had attempted to fight back. That done, however, his sense of self as a valuable and valued member of the pipiltin does not seem to have been diminished. In his next entry, he wrote of the work that he and others of the governing nobility were doing to prevent encroachments against Tlaxcala's historic border with Tepeyacac, including not just paperwork, but also a long, hot hike out to the site in question, where formal speeches were undoubtedly exchanged.[4]

The governing nobles were members of the indigenous council or cabildo established by the Spaniards in the sixteenth century. Zapata referred to them as the tlatoque, the plural of tlatoani, meaning "king," or "ruler," or more literally, "he who speaks [on behalf of others]." When Zapata invoked the term "tlatoque," he on one level meant merely, "cabildo members," but older associations must surely have lingered on. The pictorial we know as the Lienzo de Tlaxcala was commissioned by the cabildo mid-sixteenth century, and some version of it was probably still hanging in the cabildo building in his lifetime.[5] The central scene outlined the old political structure in a way that even outsider Spaniards could understand the message—and thus by good fortune we can comprehend it today as well. All Nahuas built their lives according to a sort of cellular principle (all wholes being composed of constituent parts), and Tlaxcala was no exception. Their greater altepetl was composed of four individually governed altepetls (Ocotelolco, Quiahuiztlan, Tepeticpac, and Tizatla), and each of these in turn consisted of a number of teccalli, lordly houses or lineages ruling over the common farmers. The people of these lineages were the pipiltin, each individual being called a pilli, literally meaning "child" or "offspring" ("of someone important" being implied). When the Spaniards first arrived, for example, the subaltepetl of Quiahuiztlan apparently had twenty-nine chiefly lines; in the Lienzo, they are represented as twenty-nine cells or blocks, each personified by an individual (figure 6.1). These individuals would have been responsible for leading war parties, making peace when necessary, and maintaining order at home through equitable rotation—in such matters as assigning usufruct rights to communally owned land, collecting tribute, and bringing people to contribute to public works (building temples), etc. From one of these lineages don Juan Zapata was descended, as were—theoretically at least—all other cabildo members. The pipiltin elected each other to office on a rotating basis and together managed the altepetl's affairs.[6]

And there was yet another aspect of the lives of the pipiltin that was crucially important in the mind of don Juan Zapata: they traditionally comprised the community's intelligentsia. It had been understood before the conquest

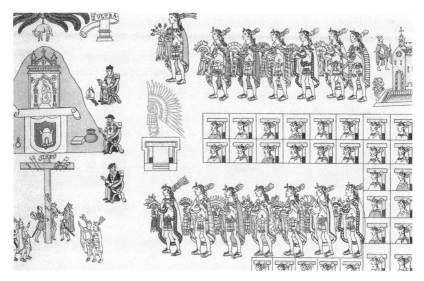

Figure 6.1. The quadrant of Quiahuiztlan in the Lienzo de Tlaxcala.

that within each teccalli, certain people would be responsible for the community's intellectual life, helping to guide social memory and expectations for the future. Priests, of course, took charge of reading the heavens and other elements of the natural world, of noting omens and issuing prognostications (or alternatively, of offering comforting explanations after the fact). By the 1670s, however, communal memory of the priests' doings was shadowy at best. The words of other intellectuals were remembered better: men other than priests had once been charged with preserving the people's history, and their works were by no means entirely lost. Spanish priests and lawmakers had expressed interest in their accomplishments rather than condemning them, thus encouraging the preservation of their labor. Some of the history keepers—or historians—had been painters who produced timelines recording events of interest to the community as a whole along lists of dates written on unfolding strips of bark, maguey paper, or cloth. Others were performers who could look at these glyphic representations and recall detailed accounts, often including vivid dialog suggestive of the political tensions at play.

This was the art of the *xiuhpohualli* or yearly account. In public performances, more than one teccalli or subaltepetl would present their histories, one right after the other, so that the same chronological ground was covered from varying points of view. To the Nahua mind, any higher truth was inherently multiple—how else could a narration inspire the loyalty of all elements

CAMILLA TOWNSEND

of a fractured group of people? During the colonial period, such composite histories, now written out in Roman letters rather than glyphs, remained a central element of the community's intellectual identity. Though they most likely were not performed, they were widely passed from hand to hand.[7] It was in this arena that don Juan Zapata came to play a vital role. The set of historical annals he authored is one of the richest to have survived and illuminates his own and his community's beliefs about indigenous intellectuals.

Don Juan Zapata's Life and Work

Our historian's full name—don Juan Buenaventura Zapata y Mendoza of Quiahuiztlan—was itself suggestive of both alliance building and dedication to tradition, two hallmarks of the pilli class from which he came. His grandfather, don Buenaventura Zapata, had married doña Magdalena de Mendoza (probably related to don Juan de Mendoza, the last man to act as hereditary tlatoani of Quiahuiztlan in the 1580s) and had himself served as a high office holder on the cabildo before dying suddenly in the middle of his term. His father, also named don Juan Zapata, had likewise been active on the cabildo until he gave up serving there in favor of becoming *fiscal*, or managing officer, in the local church. Our don Juan Zapata thus grew up in close proximity to Spanish church officials. In his text, he would later express both affection for and resentment against some of these, but most certainly he did not follow the path of becoming more closely involved in church affairs.[8]

His parents both died in an epidemic in 1641, when he was still a young man. So it was, in his father's absence, that he became a *regidor*, or cabildo councilman, in 1645, and an *alcalde* (cabildo officer) in 1646. He must have been widely respected, for by 1651 he had already attained the prestigious position of *gobernador*, or head of the council. He later served as alcalde numerous other times, and toward the end of his career, he took on the important positions of treasurer and then cabildo notary. He was thus constantly involved in public affairs—collecting taxes, petitioning the Spaniards, organizing public ceremonies and participating in them (sometimes in traditional garb), helping to orchestrate the building and rebuilding of bridges, fountains, churches, and belltowers, sending delegations to Mexico City or Puebla to conduct business, and occasionally visiting those places himself. Even when he was temporarily out of office (or "resting," as he put it), he remained active in municipal affairs, as did his peers. Zapata was a sort of patron of indigenous artists and artisans, frequently noting and emphasizing their contributions. While he served as governor in 1651, for example, he made it his business to get back for the altepetl a beautiful cloak that had been made years before for the icon of "our precious revered mother" Santa María Asunción and then pawned in Mexico City by a profligate former governor.[9] A lover of music, he also saw to it that the musicians in two different indigenous chapels learned to play the chirimía.[10]

In the 1550s, about the time he made plans to marry doña Petronila de Paredes, daughter of another leading family, don Juan made the decision to compile a xiuhpohualli to preserve the history of Tlaxcala.[11] He had been exposed to the tradition through copied histories and fragments of histories shown to him by older men—old oral performances or memories or explanations of once extant visual texts written down in the Roman alphabet. He began to collect and copy these with gusto. Zapata was born too late ever to have known someone who had been present at a historical performance before the conquest, but among the papers he had in his possession was at least one statement clearly dictated by a man who remembered those years, apparently speaking to someone in the generation of Zapata's grandfather or great-grandfather. He said, for example, "The ruling lords (tlatoque) were baptized when three of the ones called 'friars' came. One was fray Juan. We did not know the name of the second, and the third was called fray Pedro de Gante. The late fray Juan was really joyful. He really wanted to teach people. But he could not yet speak Nahuatl. . . . He would point towards mictlan and say, 'snakes, toads.'"[12] Other documents were more recent productions; a few included preconquest stories that were probably many generations old. Most were pastiches, for these papers had been passed from hand to hand and copied and recopied so many times that the trail was dizzying. Indeed, an earlier study has demonstrated that all twenty-some surviving sets of annals from the Tlaxcala-Puebla region are "genetically related," that is, that strands of copied material bind all of them together, in the sense that not one stands alone as a creation entirely independent of all the others.[13]

In the vicinity of Mexico City, the tradition of sharing and preserving historic annals seems to have peaked with Chimalpahin (see also Schroeder, chapter 5) at the turn of the seventeenth century and then to have died out. This was not the case, however, in Tlaxcala. There, we remember, the indigenous nobility had early on capitalized on their decision to ally with Hernando Cortés at the stage when he most needed allies. They extracted as recompense after the conquest an agreement that they would not be given out in encomienda as tribute payers to an individual Spaniard but rather would pay

CAMILLA TOWNSEND

their tribute directly to the Crown. In connection with this, few Spaniards came to live among them for the first century. Thus it is perhaps not surprising that it is in Tlaxcala, with its self-conscious history and its combination of proximity to power and yet relative isolation, culturally speaking, that we find in the seventeenth century a sort of renaissance of the tradition of the xiuhpohualli. Zapata either had been given some of the older documents from the central valley or knew someone who had, for the beginning of his study includes fragments of texts from that area.[14] Certainly his text reveals that he and close friends of his traveled to Mexico City on official business, once indeed in the mid-1650s, the very period when he seems to have begun to write his own annals entries. It is also clear, however, as I have indicated, that don Juan had in his possession annals that had been worked on by older men of his acquaintance in Tlaxcala itself for many years, though they were not nearly as extensive as the ones he himself was determined to produce.

Choosing Sources: Listening to the Tlatoque

The old tradition of multivocality in historic performances of the xiuhpohualli demanded that speakers from various subentities of a community each present their own separate versions of the same events.[15] Zapata likewise placed varied accounts of the same period in series. How much he knew of this format it is impossible to say; to some extent, he probably simply copied what he received from others without full comprehension. Modern historians have failed to recognize the phenomenon where it appeared in sixteenth-century productions, because the original writers themselves never thought to make an issue of it and explain what they were doing. They just unceremoniously backtracked and began covering the same period again, albeit from a slightly different perspective, giving modern readers an impression of disorganization. Undoubtedly many of the earliest copyists themselves failed to understand what had been occurring originally and simply passed on to others what already seemed to them a somewhat confusing text; Zapata may have been following suit. Yet on another level he seems to have been making conscious decisions about including varied voices, even as he sometimes presses them into a linear format.

Specifically, Zapata covers the Chichimec migrations through the Spanish conquest once, then backtracks and begins all over again, this time continuing not only through the conquest but also up to his own present day. It was customary to cover particularly important and/or contentious periods from multiple perspectives even if the rest of the account was linear, and his approach is in keeping with such a phenomenon, the origins of Tlaxcala's political structure being determined between about 1330 and 1530. Beyond this, in the first segment, several distinct voices emerge, with drastically different styles and interests. Even if the same years are not explicitly covered more than once, I believe they in effect were, though different angles were pegged to different years. (An affectionate former student of the friars is quoted in 1520–21, for example, while a man raging about the unnecessary hangings the friars and their indigenous students were responsible for is copied out in the entries for 1526–27.) And in the second segment as well, in the period of Zapata's own lifetime, at least six first-person narrators beyond Zapata himself are identified. Here, too, no year is explicitly covered more than once, but on the other hand, within several year entries, more than one person clearly speaks, as we shall see.

Zapata's work covering his own century is worth exploring in some depth in our efforts to understand his notions of history and the historian. Though genetically related to the other surviving annals of the Tlaxcala-Puebla region, as well as to certain central valley documents, Zapata's text nevertheless contains extensive material assiduously gathered by himself, as it appears nowhere else. What then—other than the papers of the "ancients"—did he consider a worthy source? Elsewhere I have demonstrated what he would not use.[16] He would have had access to the indigenous cabildo records—which survive even to our own day—but did not use them. He would have had access to local church records, but did not use them. He almost certainly knew of the work of Diego Muñoz Camargo, but apparently did not read it.[17]

He seems to have sought only statements from tlatoque, that is, from the ruling lords who, by definition of the word itself, and according to social expectation, had a right—even a duty—to speak on behalf of their people. His history would be a collection of their voices, a continuation of what the "ancients" had left for posterity concerning their era. All six of the recognizable figures whom he quotes fit squarely within this category. The backbone, as it were, of Zapata's annals is a recitation of the tlatoque elected to fill each important position in the year-by-year march through time. The altepetl continues ever forward, with the component parts justly represented in an ongoing rotation. Someone began to keep this record almost as soon as the cabildo was fully organized in the 1550s, and others continued it in greater or lesser detail in various periods. Until Zapata's voice takes up the register, it is largely an anonymous record, but there are moments when distinct speakers are heard.

Early in the seventeenth century, in 1609, someone who called himself a fiscal of an unnamed church spoke "here in Tizatlan," explaining, "We were asked to pay [the tithe] every week."[18] Zapata's wife's family was from Tizatlan, so such a segment could have come from her father or grandfather—but also from any of various other good friends. In 1616–17, a man calling himself "I, Sebastián de Rosas" contributed text.[19] He lived in the city of Tlaxcala and was "escribano de la cárcel" and later the cabildo's "teniente" in charge of work parties, apparently an assistant to the governor. In the 1620s and 30s someone contributed who clearly had a close relationship with the Spanish church hierarchy in downtown Tlaxcala: he reported on who filled various church positions with almost as much interest as he showed in the indigenous cabildo.[20] Zapata's father, we remember, served as fiscal in this generation; this could have been his work, or that of some close acquaintance of his. In 1643—in the wake of the death of Zapata's father and numerous others in a major epidemic—one Antonio Diego spoke in the first person, explaining that he had often acted on behalf of the governor and his teniente as well as the cabildo's notary because he could write well.[21]

From early in the seventeenth century, comments are often made from the reference points of Topoyanco or Acxotlan, both pueblos in Ocotelolco and both homes to branches of the Salazar family, with whom Zapata was on intimate terms. Don Bernabé Salazar, who also served as governor of the cabildo at one point, seems to have been Zapata's closest friend, and his son, don Manuel Santos Salazar, actually managed to attend university and become a priest. They each contributed first-person statements. Others in their extended family or circle of friends probably added statements as well, but these are two of whose participation we can be certain.[22]

All six distinguishable contributors were of sufficiently noble status to fill important posts. Antonio Diego might possibly have been an exception, might not have been of the pipiltin—given his undistinguished last name and his own commentary—but he was both educated and close to powerful men, so most likely he, too, was born a pilli; and if not, he had proven his worth in a time of need. Nor were these just any noblemen; of the six, the only one who was *not* a scholar of sorts (a man qualified to serve as a scribe or a fiscal or even a university student in the one case) was don Bernabé Salazar, and he had the prestige requisite to be elected governor of the cabildo.

Zapata's manuscript, in short, was the work of the elect, of those anointed through their line of descent to speak for others and keep the community's history.

Who Are "We"? Zapata Decides Who Counts, and Why

We do, fortunately, have ways of exploring Zapata's thinking as he made his decisions about whom to ask for statements for his history. Despite the text's multiplicity in some regards, it does remain first and foremost Zapata's. Although the work includes statements from those whom Zapata perceived as qualified pipiltin of the various subaltepetls, the vast majority of the work from the 1650s onward was clearly authored—not just copied out—by Zapata himself (see also Durston, chapter 7). This is made clear in what he says when he speaks in the first person.[23] He relied on a closed circle of sources, and he himself was the leading one, producing a rich and often self-revealing text. Thus it is that through his work we have access to the extended thoughts of an individual scholar. We can learn something of how a particular indigenous intellectual envisioned himself and his own role in relation to his community. Listening to his thoughts, it becomes clear that although he believed that only certain people could contribute meaningfully to his history, his conviction stemmed not from arrogance or a bent toward exclusivity. Rather, it was a mark of his belief in the *responsibility* of the pilli class to represent their people effectively and preserve the community. Indeed, his greatest fear was that they themselves would relinquish this responsibility and lose the trust of the commoners. And if they faded from the scene, there would be no one else who could maintain the intellectual life of the community. It was not that the elderly male pipiltin were the only people of value. In Zapata's text, women can be important for their lineage and for the children they bear, and laboring men honored for their work. Certain Spaniards can be loved, and certain Africans respected. But none of them can be the indigenous people's history keepers. It was simply not the role assigned to them—and, as Zapata well knew, it was never likely to be.

How do we come to the conclusion that Zapata was not exclusionary in the sense of that word today, that he in fact categorized people in rather expansive ways? Clues to his perspectives on his relationships with others may be found in his use of the term "we." The vast majority of his uses of the first-person plural connected him to other Christians, and especially, other Catholics. Examples occurring throughout the text include "our precious mother" (totlaçonantzin), "our saviour" (totlaçotemaquixticatzin), "our guardian" (toguardian), and "our father" (totatzin). A closer reading, however, shows that the majority of these references are not to the Virgin Mary or the Savior writ large, for example, but to icons of Mary or Jesus that the altepetl cares for assiduously. The guardian is *guardián* in the Spanish sense, the local head of the Franciscan order, and "our father" is of course their priest, not Our Lord. Thus in effect Zapata is tying himself to other people in his indigenous congregation, not to Catholics the world over. Never was he more delighted to belong to such a group when they purchased a bell, for he had long been a lover of the chimes. "The bell came to our chapel, and we could no longer hear what we said to each other!" he reported gleefully.[24] (Sometimes Zapata referred not to the local indigenous chapel, but to the larger parish of the church of San José, though in such cases he said not "we" but "here in San José." It was to him a place, not a social grouping.) Other related uses of the first-person plural reference musicians playing together in processions, or people of Quiahuiztlan who participated in public works together. The various groups included in these uses of the word "we" were probably largely overlapping: that is, all designated groups of neighbors among whom Zapata lived, worshipped, and worked.

Sometimes Zapata's "we" referred to the indigenous people of Tlaxcala as a whole, not just of his chapel or neighborhood. For instance, some officials traveled to Puebla to try to bring back some Tlaxcalans who had left secretly to take up their abode in that town, hoping to avoid paying tribute in either place. He called them "our Tlaxcallan children [or descendants]" (topilhuan tlaxcalteca).[25] Another time he mentioned that through a legal battle conducted by the cabildo on behalf of Tlaxcala "we were given possession" of all "the woodland that the Spaniards had made their own" in a particular locale.[26] And once he even reported on a *self-conscious* use of the notion of "we Tlaxcalans," claiming that he and his peers continued to follow in the loyal tradition of their ancestors. The viceroy was on his way to deal with a social disturbance on the coast and was making a stop near Tlaxcala. Zapata and his colleagues put on a miniature drama for him:

> On Saturday, February 15, at 11 o'clock the tlatoani [meaning the viceroy] entered San Juan Atlancatepec. And this is what happened when we—the governor and the other pipiltin—went to meet the entourage. The governor was don Francisco Ruiz from Tepeticpac, governor for the first time; the alcalde of his subaltepetl was don Martín Pérez, the regidores don

Nicolas Salvador and don Francisco Hernández. For Quiahuiztlan, there was the alcalde don Juan Buenaventura Zapata y Mendoza, don Francisco Pascual, and other nobles from Quiahuiztlan, together with the residents of San Juan Atlancatepec. Everybody got undressed down to the *sotanilla* or *ropilla* [meaning short doublets—they had removed their outer garments] and everybody carried a walking stick to meet him at the bridge. And our king said, "Why do you do this?" And they answered him, "We will accompany you wherever you go. We are already aware of your concerns. Thus did our ancestors, so that the Marqués conquered all the altepetls." He was very grateful for these words. He said, "Truly you are impressive, you Tlaxcalans. You demonstrate both the respect you deserve and the respect you give to others. May our Lord God keep you. I thank you deeply."[27]

Zapata's frequent use of the phrase "our tlatoani" to refer either to the viceroy in Mexico or the king in Spain might be interpreted to mean that he is categorizing himself with all people who are ruled by the monarch, but ample evidence suggests that in his mind, he meant "the king upon whom we Tlaxcalan indigenous bestow our loyalty." First, he insistently uses the Nahuatl term "tlatoani," when the word "rey" was well known to him. Second, there are subtleties evident in the examples themselves that seem to emphasize a connection to other Tlaxcalan indigenous who owe fealty to the same king, rather than a connection to all the residents of the region. In the instance noted above, after insisting that "our Tlaxcalan children" must be brought home, he explains that this is in order that they may pay the tribute they owe as indigenous residents of the town to "our tlatoani." In another instance, "our ruling lady queen" over in Spain (*toçihuatecuiyotzin reyna*, half Nahuatl, half Spanish, though speaking of the Spanish queen) has sent a letter specifically to the indigenous cabildo of Tlaxcala, thanking them for orchestrating such grand funeral celebrations in honor of her husband, the late king. "She sent the document so as to honor the altepetl of Tlaxcala. The Spanish governor gave it to us by his own hand."[28] And the ruling lords, among whom sat don Juan Buenaventura Zapata y Mendoza, felt the full honor of her compliments, and a genuine pride in being an essential part of a great kingdom. "All the tlatoque cried when they heard her letter." These were ceremonial tears, shed on all such great public occasions.[29]

What is especially interesting about Zapata is that in a purportedly highly micropatriotic world, he sometimes seems to have meant an all-inclusive "we indigenous people of Mexico" or at least "we Nahuas"—not just "we the people of Tlaxcala"—when he used the first-person plural. In 1669, he was thinking about the Nahuatl language a good deal, for example. He mentioned that the priest began a sermon in Spanish "but finished in our Nahuatl language."[30] Such things were on his mind when he wrote the entry because later that year he traveled to Mexico City with a small group to be questioned by the Real Audiencia. He happily reported that they had asked him, "Do the priests know enough of our language to preach to us and confess us?" But Zapata had noted with enthusiasm the use of Nahuatl in church matters even before the year of the trip and he often mentioned the appearance of indigenous insignia in parades, or the participation of indigenous artisans in town projects.

His insistence on a category of "we the indigenous" is rendered more clearly visible in his use of the word *indio*, or as he would have it, the more reverential form *itiotzin*, or, in first-person plural, *tindiotzintzin*, as he uses it the first time.[31] Over the course of the period from the 1660s to the 1680s, when he is largely composing his own entries, Zapata uses the term at least a dozen times.[32] The word, so prevalent among Spaniards, appears rarely in most Nahuatl texts produced by indigenous peoples in the colonial era. Generally, when the Nahuas wished to distinguish between the Spaniards and themselves, they used the word *macehualli* or "commoner" in the old tongue.[33] But this would not do for Zapata, as his social existence was steeped in the distinctions between macehualli and pilli. He was aware that *macehualli* could be used to describe indigenous people in general, placing them in opposition to their Spanish overlords: at least once he used the word that way. But he needed to have recourse to another, less confusing term to apply to indigenous people in general whenever he wanted to distinguish them from Spaniards or mestizos or Africans, for more often than not, distinctions within the indigenous world were uppermost in his mind, or were at least an equally relevant variable in whatever situation was at hand.[34]

Zapata's *itiotzin* did not have a pejorative connotation, as *indio* did for most Spaniards. And it certainly did not imply that the person or people in question were of the macehualli class. It meant only that they were indigenous. He used it to categorize people of whom he approved and of whom he disapproved. It was an explanatory label, a social category, nothing more. A craftsman who helped raise a beautiful new set of church bells was itiotzin, as was the unfortunate mother of a mixed-blood criminal. Most often, if there was any subtext at all, the use of the word implied a positive statement about the worth of the indigenous—that they had participated in creating art, or music, or had heard the word of the king from the town crier alongside all the other peoples of the realm. But Zapata's term was by no means ostentatiously proud. He used the words "mestizo" and "mulato" in comparable situations. The point is that Zapata had a definite category of "Indians" in his mind. Neither the traditional word for "commoner" nor the word for "person of a certain altepetl" would do for him, as it had often done for Chimalpahin, for example. He needed a more inclusive rubric.

Perhaps the crux of the matter, in considering Zapata's understanding of his relations with others, lies in his concept of tlatoque specifically. Clearly, he felt at one with the people of his immediate community and with the indigenous people of Tlaxcala as a whole and with Nahuatl-speaking Indians writ large. But within this generous-spirited connectedness, what do we make of his conviction that only certain people could rule, and only certain people could give voice to history? How important was it to him to define himself in opposition to, and as superior to, the macehualli majority around him? What do we make of his certainty that he had a right to represent them both intellectually and politically, but not the other way around?

Who, in short, were his tlatoque? The tlatoque of his narrative are by no means all-powerful. Indeed, in the second half of the sixteenth century and the first half of the seventeenth, their primary role was to be periodically taken prisoner (and occasionally executed) by the Spanish state when they could not manage to deliver whatever the Spanish overlords demanded from their people.[35] In the 1670s, when the tax crises erupted during Zapata's political career, tlatoque are once again subject to such dangers.[36] If the tlatoque speak on behalf of their people, and organize their people and give orders to them, they are likewise the ones held responsible when all does not go well.

Nor are the tlatoque of Zapata's narrative consistently honorable and good. In the preconquest period, many are dreadful schemers, and in his own lifetime, he does not hesitate to criticize indigenous governors whom he feels to have been irresponsible or profligate. He tolerates a mestizo who enters the cabildo and even ends up serving as governor for many years until he is caught in a corruption scandal; then he turns on him bitterly, calling him "that mestizo from hell." "At his hands were destroyed the inheritance of the pipiltin . . . That one, he destroyed everything."[37] Communal funds were lost and the people's trust irreparably hurt. His views echo those of another traditional Nahuatl annalist writing a century before him, one who railed against a drunken and abusive Spanish official:

CAMILLA TOWNSEND

He should not be chosen [to lead] if his life is not righteous, even if he is a nobleman. He should not guide the community. He who scoffs at other people should not perform any post. Even if he is the viceroy or the visitador, if he doesn't do his job rightly, if he afflicts people, then he is from hell. He belongs in hell. He will go to hell, and will be forever imprisoned there.[38]

In Zapata's mental world, what he saw clearly when he thought of the tlatoque was apparently not their power and wealth, but rather their vulnerability to crisis and their responsibility to others. Such men owed much to posterity, not least rectitude and the use of their intellects.

Breaking Faith: The Risks of Losing the Trusted Tlatoque

Most telling of all, perhaps, for Zapata the word "tlatoque" referred to a social role exclusively, not to the actual humans who temporarily filled that role. The tlatoque represented all the people; in effect, they *were* the people as a whole. Individuals thus *could not identify themselves as tlatoque.* For semantic reasons, it was *grammatically impossible* to do so. In the Nahuatl language, all nouns are in effect predicates, and must have an accompanying subject pronoun. "We [who are] musicians played our instruments," Zapata might say. Or: "He [who is] the governor gave the orders." On numerous occasions, Zapata would list all those who had been elected to office in a given year, including himself. Then he would describe a procession in which all cabildo members participated. He would say "they [who are] the tlatoque" gathered or went in procession, and in the very next sentence, something to the effect that, "we [meaning the individuals walking] went around the building" or "we went in a line."[39] In context, the fact that the preceding sentence always read simply as *in tlatoque* ("they the tlatoque") rather than *titlatoque* ("we the tlatoque") is notable indeed. A clear example occurs in the dialog cited above in which the tlatoque go to meet the visiting viceroy and put on a little skit for him. "We [that is, certain named individuals] went to meet the entourage," says Zapata. But then, a moment later, "They [the tlatoque] answered him. . . ." On one occasion, Zapata avoided a grammatically awkward situation—when the word "tlatoque" was needed but using the third person was going to be horribly unclear—by saying *timochitin cavildo* ("all of us of the cabildo").[40]

Yet this construct was shattered in 1671—a few years before the house robbery. Zapata could not say (or think) "titlatoque" ("we the tlatoque") as long as the tlatoque were understood to be the *equivalent* of the people, the stand-in for the whole. He could do so, however, once a great social crisis occurred, and the macehualli people began to place themselves in opposition to the governing pipiltin, to the tlatoque. In February of 1671, popular anger over increasing taxes on maguey plants—increases that the tlatoque had in fact vainly attempted to stave off—boiled over. "Everyone got angry and confronted us," Zapata wrote. "They really shouted."[41] He did not say that everyone confronted the Spanish or the government or even the cabildo. They simply confronted "us," the tlatoque. This is a first in his lengthy text. He is now aware that the people are blaming (as it was a new social phenomenon, not a permanent state) their own leaders, that they no longer trust them to speak on behalf of the community.

One might assume that the people were angry because their noblemen had proven to be ineffective advocates, but the situation was worse than that. They were convinced that it was their own tlatoque who desired to see them pay higher taxes (so as to further enrich themselves), and the Spanish were only too happy to exploit this popular distrust. In May, viceregal officials issued a statement declaring that they themselves were attempting to lower the per capita tax by taking a new head count (in that the city's total quota would remain the same but be divided by the greater number of people uncovered in the count) and that the people's own governors were attempting to prevent such a change. Rumors ran rife: "The people of all four altepetl and from all the villages went inventing things about us, that we were taking money from them and that the [Spaniards] were going to lower the tribute by half."[42] It is clear that Zapata feared social chaos would result from the kind of talk being instigated by the Spanish authorities against his newly defined "us," but the Spaniards remained blithely unaware of any danger. Responding with alacrity to the people's suspicions concerning their governing nobles, Mexico City sent auditors to the cabildo. "They came to investigate us about everything," wrote Zapata.[43]

What the tlatoque had been saying soon proved to be correct: the Spanish had no real intention of lowering individual tax payments, and in 1672, as soon as the new census was complete, they raised the total amount of tribute due considerably. The city exploded in riots, which Zapata had been expecting. This time, however, the people laid the blame at the feet of the Spanish and surged toward the royal offices. "It was a real war that was made," commented Zapata laconically.[44] The violence was soon put down. As treasurer, it fell to Zapata to deliver the newly collected taxes not long after. He could

barely contain his loathing for the royal officials who had caused these problems. He and his peers deposited the money and "left without further ado."[45]
(He expressed the latter in a sentence of perfect alliteration and rhythm, "çan
iuhqui yaque.")

The next year it came out that the long-time mestizo governor had in fact
been involved in racketeering of some stripe, and, as we have said, Zapata's
pain and anger knew no bounds. But he and his community worked to put
their lives back together, and at the time of the robbery, he was relieved that
his assailants had not come to wreak any real destruction, but just to gain
some much-needed cash. He continued his labors on behalf of the altepetl.
In some ways, no real changes were discernible in his day-to-day life. Yet certain subtle shifts were occurring for Zapata. He largely replaced his use of
the word "tlatoque" with "pipiltin," and he began to comment with bitterness when mestizos or people of the macehualli class rose to political prominence, usurping the positions of the pipiltin.[46] He continued to work hard on
his set of traditional annals and prepared to pass it on to younger men in his
family and circle of friends. If Zapata seems to have felt just a touch besieged
by changes that were occurring, he was quite justified, in the sense that these
changes existed in the minds of others as well.[47] And if the pipiltin were
losing their status as defenders of the altepetl, and anyone wealthy enough
could claim the title, then they must also have been losing their position
as its legitimate historians, preservers of its memory. Once that was gone,
the pipiltin would eventually be envisioned only as parasites, as collectors of
tribute produced by the sweat of other people's brows. The word itself would
fade from use, and the notion of entrusted representatives of the indigenous
community who were inherently wise, who knew how to speak on behalf of
others, both in the present and across the generations, would disappear. In
the plaintiveness of some of his last entries, Zapata seems to have foreseen
this. And indeed, history proved him right. It would take the political movements of the late twentieth century to reintroduce the notion of the indigenous intellectual to the world stage.

Notes

1. For a detailed biographical study of this figure, see my article, "Don Juan Buenaventura Zapata y Mendoza and the Notion of a Nahua Identity," 144–80.

2. Don Juan Buenaventura Zapata y Mendoza, Historia chronológica de la noble Ciudad de
Tlaxcala, 534. Reyes and Martínez provide a transcription of the Nahuatl with certain

edited corrections as well as a Spanish translation on the facing page. I am largely in accord with their translation, but have provided my own direct translation to English, as their editing out of Zapata's punctuation has, I believe, led to occasional errors in the division of clauses. I advise interested parties to consult the original in the Bibliothèque Nationale de France, Paris, Collection Goupil, Méxicain 212.

3. This is the Nahuatl word for the small ethnic states into which their world was divided. It continued to be used throughout the colonial era, often with the sense of "town" or "community."

4. Zapata, *Historia*, 536.

5. For a full treatment of the Tlaxcalan conquest pictorials, see Travis Barton Kranz, "Visual Persuasion: Sixteenth-Century Tlaxcalan Pictorials in Response to the Conquest of Mexico," 41–73. On Tlaxcala's strategic positioning of itself as a helpmeet to Spain, see Michel Oudijk and Mathew Restall, "Mesoamerican Conquistadors in the Sixteenth Century," 28–64.

6. On the formation of the cabildo and the political situation in the first century after conquest see Charles Gibson, *Tlaxcala in the Sixteenth Century*; and James Lockhart, Frances Berdan, and Arthur J. O. Anderson, *The Tlaxcalan Actas: A Compendium of the Records of the Cabildo of Tlaxcala, 1545–1627*.

7. For more on the tradition of the xiuhpohualli see my "Glimpsing Native American Historiography." The best treatment of the colonial Nahuatl alphabetic annals remains James Lockhart's chapter in his *The Nahuas after the Conquest: A Social and Cultural History of the Indians of Central Mexico, Sixteenth through Eighteenth Centuries*, and the best overall discussion of the pictorial annals is Elizabeth H. Boone, *Stories in Red and Black: Pictorial Histories of the Aztecs and Mixtecs*.

8. For all details concerning Zapata's life, see my article "Don Juan Buenaventura Zapata." The information in that piece is drawn from Zapata's own text as it intersects with material found in legal documents housed in the Archivo General del Estado de Tlaxcala.

9. See Zapata, *Historia*, 254 and 292.

10. This was a wooden wind instrument, the ancestor of the oboe. It was invented in France and was brought to Mexico sometime in the sixteenth century. There, the indigenous peoples of Oaxaca and Tlaxcala made it their own, making certain adjustments to its form and playing it in conjunction with their traditional *huehuetl*, or great drum.

11. We know that he began to write in this period because the entries become much longer and more detailed. He even occasionally writes in the first person.

12. Zapata, *Historia*, 96–98. Several other such instances appear in which it becomes clear that an older person is speaking to a younger about his memories of the time before conquest or the conquest itself.

13. Frances Krug, "The Nahuatl Annals of the Tlaxcala-Puebla Region." Krug completed extensive work analyzing the language content of twenty-three surviving annals (or fragments of annals) from the region before the project was interrupted. For a summary of her major contributions, see Frances Krug and Camilla Townsend, "The Tlaxcala-Puebla Family of Annals."

14. Luis Reyes García and Andrea Martínez Baracs in their introduction to Zapata's

Historia, 37–44, note the overlap with a document in the Bibliothèque Nationale that was published by Alfredo Chavero as the "Anónimo Mexicano." Frances Krug in her dissertation first noted the overlap with a document from Tula published by Robert Barlow, "Anales de Tula, Hidalgo, 1361–1521."

15. For a detailed study of this subject, see my "Glimpsing Native American Historiography."

16. See my "Don Juan Buenaventura Zapata."

17. Diego Muñoz Camargo was a mestizo who wrote a detailed narrative history of Tlaxcala in Spanish. Extant legal documents and Zapata's own text demonstrate that his family and the Zapata family knew each other. But a careful study of the Muñoz Camargo work proves that Zapata did not follow its narrative arc in the slightest degree. For an excellent edition and introductory study, see Diego Muñoz Camargo, *Historia de Tlaxcala*.

18. Zapata, *Historia*, 212–14.

19. Zapata, *Historia*, 222–24.

20. Zapata, *Historia*, entries beginning 232.

21. Zapata, *Historia*, 276 and 282.

22. For a full treatment of the Salazar family, including their relationship to Zapata and to his text, see my *Here in This Year: Seventeenth-Century Nahuatl Annals of the Tlaxcala-Puebla Valley*, 21–27.

23. For example, he refers to a woman in his grandmother's family as "my aunt," notes the birth of those known to be his sons, etc. He also signs his work periodically.

24. Zapata, *Historia*, 384.

25. Zapata, *Historia*, 350.

26. Zapata, *Historia*, 446.

27. Zapata, *Historia*, 444. The last sentence in the paragraph says in a literal sense, "Your heart has granted things, has been generous." This was used to express deep thanks.

28. Zapata, *Historia*, 394.

29. A full study of ceremonial weeping in the Nahua culture could easily be made. One of the most famous documents is "And Ana Wept," appearing *In the Language of Kings*. This piece, concerning the 1583 grant of a house-site to a bereft branch of a noble family in the Tetzcoco region, was first transcribed, translated, and published by Lockhart in *Nahuas after the Conquest*, 455–59.

30. Zapata, *Historia*, 422.

31. Zapata, *Historia*, 269.

32. Zapata, *Historia*, 336, 386 (twice), 458, 500, 520, 536, 554, 560, 600, 604, 632.

33. For commentary on this subject, see Lockhart, *Nahuas after the Conquest*, 114–15; and introduction by James Lockhart, Susan Schroeder, and Doris Namala to *Annals of His Time*, 17.

34. For a complete discussion of his use of this word, see my "Don Juan Buenaventura Zapata," 162–64.

35. Zapata, *Historia*, 196, 212, 216, 260, 264, 272.

36. Zapata, *Historia*, 485.

37. Zapata, *Historia*, 510. The mestizo in question was the half-Portuguese Nicolás Méndez de Luna, who lived in Quiyahuiztlan and was wealthy and influential enough to rise to importance on the cabildo. For more on this crisis see Andrea Martínez Baracs, *Un gobierno de indios: Tlaxcala, 1519–1750*, 365–91.

38. Luis Reyes García, *¿Cómo te confundes? ¿Acaso no somos conquistados? Anales de Juan Bautista*, facsimile folio 31v. In the mid-1560s, the nobly born artisans of Mexico City were suddenly faced with an order to begin paying a head tax. This caused a great social crisis, and some of the men involved made an extensive record of the events in Nahuatl in traditional annals format, complete with detailed dialog exchange. The source is thus invaluable to us today. The man speaking in this selection had been delegated to go address a council of religious men on behalf of his brethren, and he had apparently been thrown in jail as a reward. Numerous other instances record in extant Nahuatl sources of tlatoque (or any race or ethnic group) being measured and evaluated by the depth of their sense of responsibility, but this passage jumps out for having so much in common with Zapata's own utterance.

39. For examples, see Zapata, *Historia*, 363, 367, 373, 375, 423.

40. Zapata, *Historia*, 388.

41. Zapata, *Historia*, 462.

42. Zapata, *Historia*, 464.

43. Zapata, *Historia*, 478.

44. Zapata, *Historia*, 482.

45. Zapata, *Historia*, 486.

46. In the past, Zapata had been somewhat tolerant of mestizos, for example, as long as they did not interfere with indigenous ways. Now he not only referred to "that mestizo from hell" but also even lobbied against an elected governor who was not born a pilli, but had gained influence merely because he was raised by Spanish priests in the Spanish world. However, Zapata's tone was mild compared to that of his young friend, don Manuel de los Santos Salazar, who received Zapata's work after he died and put editorial comments in the margins that were laced with contempt for mestizos. Don Manuel went to university and became a priest; perhaps his closer proximity to the Spanish world intensified his bitterness.

47. For more on the shifts that were occurring, see the last chapter of Martínez Baracs, *Un gobierno de indios*.

CAMILLA TOWNSEND

CHAPTER 7

Cristóbal Choquecasa and the Making of the *Huarochirí Manuscript*

Alan Durston

Cristóbal Choquecasa, an indigenous nobleman from Huarochirí in highland Peru, has arguably influenced our understanding of the Andean past more than any other indigenous writer with the exception of Felipe Guaman Poma de Ayala.[1] I base this claim on the compelling evidence that Choquecasa wrote the *Huarochirí Manuscript* (ca. 1608), a book-length Quechua compendium of the mythology and rites of Huarochirí that has been the object of seminal research since the 1960s.[2] Here I would like to move beyond the technical issues of authorial identification to reflect on (1) the role of Francisco de Avila, Choquecasa's parish priest, in the creation of the *Huarochirí Manuscript*; (2) what the *Huarochirí Manuscript* can tell us about Choquecasa; and (3) what purposes guided Choquecasa in writing the *Huarochirí Manuscript*. Finally, in an effort to put Choquecasa in a broader frame of reference as an early colonial Andean intellectual, I develop a brief comparison with the life and work of Guaman Poma. I hope to show that new perspectives emerge on both Choquecasa and the *Huarochirí Manuscript* when we link them more directly and firmly than has been the case so far. Given the nature of the available sources a certain amount of speculation is involved, but my hope is to stimulate renewed debate and creative re-readings of the *Huarochirí Manuscript*. The exercise is merited not just by the extraordinary importance of this text for Andean ethnohistory, but also by the prospect of adding Choquecasa to a short list of indigenous intellectuals from the early colonial Andes who left us major works and whose lives and agendas we can hope to reconstruct.

Cristóbal Choquecasa, Francisco de Avila, and the Huarochirí Manuscript

The *Huarochirí Manuscript* is an untitled and anonymous text that deals with the *huacas*, or divine ancestors, of the people of Huarochirí, a highland province east of Lima.[3] It relates both their deeds in the mythical past and how they continued to be worshipped at the time of writing. Its author knew full well that the information it contained would be used to root out these cults, but at the same time was writing to preserve the mythohistorical memory of his people for its own sake.[4] The *Huarochirí Manuscript* was written during Francisco de Avila's tenure as priest of San Damián de Checa (also known as San Damián de los Checa or San Damián de Urutambo), one of the parishes of Huarochirí, from 1597 to 1608, and was probably completed in 1608.[5] It survives along with other texts in a volume that belonged to Avila and is now in the Spanish national library. It is ninety-six pages long, divided into thirty-one chapters, followed by two untitled sections known as supplements, and is written entirely in Quechua with the exception of the early chapter titles and the marginalia.

Francisco de Avila, a secular priest born in Cuzco who appears to have been a mestizo, is best known as a key architect of the extirpation of idolatries, an inquisitorial and punitive approach to native religious backsliding that was practiced in the archdiocese of Lima at various points in the seventeenth century (see also Charles, chapter 3).[6] In late 1607, when he had been priest of San Damián for ten years, a crisis occurred in his relationship with his parishioners. He was sued by a group who accused him of a long list of abuses before the archdiocesan authorities in Lima. Around the same time, and probably not coincidentally, he began formal anti-idolatry proceedings in his parish.[7] Cristóbal Choquecasa played a key role supporting Avila in both battles. A few months after the lawsuit began several retractions were submitted by Avila's accusers, two of which were penned by Choquecasa, one of them in Quechua.[8] In an account of his experiences as an extirpator in Huarochirí written in 1645 Avila claimed that it was Choquecasa who first revealed to him the existence of large-scale idolatry in Huarochirí.[9] He did not mention the *Huarochirí Manuscript*, but it was being written around this time and must have contributed to Avila's success as an extirpator.

ALAN DURSTON

The identification of Choquecasa as author of the *Huarochirí Manuscript* hinges on paleographic, linguistic, and stylistic similarities between the Quechua retraction written by Choquecasa for Avila's trial and the *Huarochirí Manuscript*. I also make the independent argument that the scribe who penned the *Huarochirí Manuscript* did much more than that, and can be considered the book's author. I refer the reader to my article "Notes on the Authorship of the *Huarochirí Manuscript*" for the details of these arguments. However, I will repeat and expand on certain points because they are germane to my purposes here. I begin by addressing two apparent obstacles to the identification of Choquecasa as scribe and author of which readers familiar with the *Huarochirí Manuscript* will be aware. First, the marginal annotation reads "by the hand and pen of Thomas." On closer inspection this turns out to be a random scribble of later date.[10] Second is the fact that Choquecasa is the protagonist of chapters 20 and 21, which recount his struggles with a huaca in the third person. I argue that Choquecasa constructed a third-person narrative here, even administering a judicial-style oath on the cross to himself, because he did not want to be identified as the work's author. Avila would later state that Choquecasa feared for his life if his role in uncovering idolatry became known.[11]

There can be no doubt that Choquecasa worked with a number of different informants, and he may have had assistants or collaborators. What seems unwarranted is the belief that the *Huarochirí Manuscript* contains transcripts of oral narratives and/or that a group of indigenous contributors were involved in the conceptualization and composition process.[12] We are on more solid ground when it comes to Avila's contributions. How much influence Avila exercised over Choquecasa's work is an issue of broad relevance, as indigenous authors from the colonial period often had some sort of intellectual association with clergymen, and the relationship between Choquecasa and Avila is a prominent example of such collaboration.

A key source that merits close examination in this regard is the *Tratado y relación de los errores, falsos dioses y otras supersticiones y ritos diabólicos en que vivían antiguamente los indios de las provincias de Huaracheri, Mama y Chaclla y hoy también viven engañados con gran perdición de sus almas.*[13] This Spanish-language manuscript, which is dated 1608, is in Avila's hand and was included in the same volume as the *Huarochirí Manuscript*. The title page states that Avila gathered its contents from "persons" who had themselves practiced the false religion before being illuminated by God. The *Tratado y relación* is thus presented as Avila's own work based on the testimony obtained from his informants. In reality, it is a translation of the first six chapters of the *Huarochirí Manuscript* to which Avila added a running commentary that transformed it into an apology for extirpation (which the *Huarochirí Manuscript* was not).[14] Avila's intention appears to have been to publish the *Tratado y relación* for a peninsular audience, but he left it unfinished.[15]

What is most interesting about the *Tratado y relación* is that it shows that Avila viewed the *Huarochirí Manuscript* itself as a form of error. The tales of the huacas were amusing and instructive on the lamentable state of Andean souls and minds, but not impressive, and there was no possible relation between them and Christian truth. The *Tratado y relación* directly refutes the *Huarochirí Manuscript* on several points, for instance, the suggestion that the biblical flood and the death of Christ were recorded in the mythical memory of the people of Huarochirí.[16] (It is worth noting that later on in his long life Avila appears to have become more amenable to such efforts to bridge Andean and European sacred history, as one of the Quechua sermons he published in 1647 goes on at length about a visit by St. Thomas the apostle to Lake Titicaca on the basis of indigenous oral tradition.[17]) It is also apparent from various omissions and additions that Avila found the *Huarochirí Manuscript* amusingly pretentious. The famous prologue that equates the deeds of the ancestors of the people of Huarochirí to those of the Spaniards is left out entirely, and a thread of sarcasm runs through the text. For instance, Avila points out that Pariacaca's mythical journeys spanned a mere twenty leagues, and calls another huaca *valiente y respetado* immediately before reminding the reader that he demanded child sacrifices and drank human blood.[18] It is unfortunate that the *Tratado y relación* only gets as far as chapter 6 and that we do not have Avila's responses to the rest of the *Huarochirí Manuscript*.

This critical and ironic distance between the *Tratado y relación* and the *Huarochirí Manuscript* indicates that Avila did not oversee the writing of the latter very closely.[19] Avila's numerous notes in the margins of portions of the *Huarochirí Manuscript* convey the impression that he merely commented or requested clarification on Choquecasa's work in the process of planning his *Tratado y relación* and/or extirpation activities. It is sometimes assumed that Avila was directly involved in gathering (or extracting) information from the numerous informants whose testimonies went into making the *Huarochirí Manuscript*.[20] This assumption conflates the formal extirpation process that Avila began only in mid-to-late 1608, culminating in 1609, with researching and writing the *Huarochirí Manuscript*, which must have begun earlier.[21] It seems far more plausible that Choquecasa, a local of high rank who by his own account was

ALAN DURSTON

no stranger to the sin of idolatry, carried out his own independent "field-work." And finally, the fact that the only extant copy of the *Huarochirí Manuscript* is among Avila's papers should not lead us to assume that it was written specifically and exclusively *for* him. It is possible that other copies existed, or that Choquecasa had not intended for Avila to keep the text.

This is not to say that Avila and his interest in idolatry did not have a crucial role in the genesis of the *Huarochirí Manuscript*. One possible scenario is that Avila asked Choquecasa to provide him with written information on specific topics, and that in fulfilling these requests the project of writing a book on the huacas of Huarochirí developed. The two "supplements," untitled sections describing specific rites that were arguably written before the rest of the *Huarochirí Manuscript*, may provide important clues in this regard.[22] The first supplement deals with the rites that were performed after the birth of twins, and Avila mentions preaching on this topic to his parishioners in San Damián prior to his "discovery" of idolatry.[23] This raises the possibility that the genesis of the *Huarochirí Manuscript* is to be sought in Avila's sermons rather than his extirpation campaigns. Avila was a renowned Quechua preacher whose strong suit was to draw on a detailed knowledge of Andean religious error in order to refute it in dialogical fashion. His magnum opus, the *Tratado de los evangelios*, is a massive bilingual sermonal published at the end of his life in the late 1640s.[24]

A final question concerning participation structure is readership: what sort of audience did Choquecasa envision? Very little can be said about this key issue. However, the opening paragraph of the *Huarochirí Manuscript* indicates that Choquecasa anticipated a readership beyond Avila himself and even expected his work to be read in a remote posterity:

> If the ancestors of the people called Indians had known writing in earlier times, then the lives they lived would not have faded from view until now. As the mighty past of the Spanish Vira Cochas is visible until now, so, too, would theirs be. But since things are as they are, and since nothing has been written until now, I set forth here the lives of the ancestors of the Huaro Cheri people, who all descend from one forefather: What faith they held, how they live up until now, those things and more; village by village it will be written down: how they lived from their dawning age onward. (HM 1–2)[25]

How Choquecasa expected the *Huarochirí Manuscript* to reach readers other than Avila, and what sort of readers he envisioned, is unclear. Perhaps he was aware of the fact that Avila meant to publish a Spanish version aimed at a peninsular readership. As will be seen below, indications also show that Choquecasa sought to use the *Huarochirí Manuscript* to strengthen his position as a political and religious leader within his community. This in turn suggests an expectation that the manuscript would reach a local audience, consistent with the caution Choquecasa exercised to keep it anonymous.

Cristóbal Choquecasa through the Lens of the Huarochirí Manuscript

In 1645 Avila described Choquecasa as a Christian nobleman from San Damián who was still alive at his time of writing.[26] From the *Huarochirí Manuscript* we know that he was the son of Gerónimo Canchoguaman, the head cacique or *curaca* of the Checa, one of five units that made up the Huarochirí "people" (HM 247). These units were referred to as *huarangas* (thousands), administrative units of (hypothetically) one thousand households. When Viceroy Francisco de Toledo implemented *reducción*, or forced resettlement and concentration, in the 1570s, the village of San Damián became the core settlement of the Checa and the seat of what would later be Avila's parish.[27] Choquecasa was born there and wrote the *Huarochirí Manuscript*, or parts of it, in the same town.[28] Given that he was still alive in 1645 he must have been born after the middle of the sixteenth century—his father had been born ca. 1530 and lived until at least 1588. Canchoguaman never learned Spanish or became literate, and Choquecasa belonged to the first generation of the Huarochirí nobility to receive a colonial education (possibly one influenced by the Jesuits who were active in the area in the 1570s) (see also Charles, chapter 3).[29]

It appears that Choquecasa never succeeded his father as cacique of the Checa. At least two other individuals held the lifelong post prior to the conclusion of the *Huarochirí Manuscript*, and Choquecasa holds no title of any kind in Avila's trial record. He appears as *teniente de Don Carlos Marçelo*, the *alcalde* or mayor of San Damián (who also used the last name Canchoguaman), in a petition from 1631.[30] *Teniente* was not one of the usual cabildo posts and it sounds like Choquecasa was serving as an assistant to a more prominent kinsman. It is nonetheless significant to find him still active in community government and litigation over twenty years after Avila's trial, as this points to a lifelong involvement in local politics.

What sort of picture of Cristóbal Choquecasa emerges from the *Huarochirí Manuscript*? Most striking is the ambivalence of a fervent Christian regarding the work's subject: the huacas. There are certainly passages where the huacas are denounced, most prominently in the narrative of Choquecasa's own struggle with Llocllayhuancupa. The supplements have a sermon-like tone and refer to the huacas as *supay* ("demon" or "devil" in the Christian Quechua lexicon). However, this is not the case in the rest of the manuscript and Choquecasa seems to relish and even feel a sense of pride in the deeds of the huacas.[31] It is also clear that the huacas were very much alive to him—his accounts have a striking immediacy, as when he describes the light blue smoke that came out of their mouths when they spoke, or the sound they made when they consumed their offerings of *mullu* shells and coca leaves, reproduced as *cap cap* and *chac chac*, respectively (HM 101, 265).

It is worth revisiting the (disguised) autobiographical narrative of chapters 20 and 21, where Choquecasa recounts his struggle with Llocllayhuancupa, a son and emissary of the great coastal huaca and oracle Pachacamac. Chapter 20 begins by describing Llocllayhuancupa's appearance in the area and the tenacity of his hold on the Checa people into recent times. His defeat is due to "a certain man who converted to God with a sincere heart" (HM 246):

> There was a man named Don Cristóbal Choque Casa, whose father was the late Don Gerónimo Cancho Huaman . . . This man lived a good life from his childhood onward because his father bitterly scorned all these huacas. But when he was about to die, Don Gerónimo was deceived by these evil spirits and fell into this same sin . . . The deceased man's son . . . is still alive. It was he who saw the demon Llocllay Huancupa with his own eyes, when he was also deceived by the same evil spirits because of his father's death. (HM 247–48)

In his first encounter with Llocllayhuancupa, the huaca appears to Choquecasa during a nighttime visit to an abandoned building that had been Llocllayhuancupa's temple. Choquecasa's motives for visiting the building are unclear. He expels Llocllayhuancupa, who flies out in the shape of an owl, by reciting the Salve Regina in Latin, after first uttering a long series of Christian prayers in Quechua. The next morning he preaches to the town:

> "Brothers and fathers, the Llocllay Huancupa whom we feared has turned out to be a demonic barn owl. Last night, with the help of the Virgin Saint Mary our mother, I conquered him for good. From now on, none of you are to enter that house. If I ever see anybody enter or approach that house, I'll tell the *padre*. Consider carefully what I've said and receive it into your hearts completely!" Thus he admonished all the people. Some people

probably assented, while others stood mute for fear of that demon. (HM 257–59)

That night, however, Llocllayhuancupa attempts to reclaim Choquecasa's loyalty in a terrifying dream narrated in chapter 21. Choquecasa is summoned to Llocllayhuancupa's temple where he delivers a short sermon berating the huaca, but this time it is he who ends up fleeing. Prior to the encounter Choquecasa searches frantically for a four-*real* coin he had been holding—an offering for Llocllayhuancupa, in Frank Salomon's exegesis (HM 262–63).[32] We are then told that Choquecasa went on to defeat many other huacas in his dreams, telling the people about his victories, and has continued to do so up to the present (HM 272).

Salomon's analysis of this narrative stresses the inconclusiveness and ambiguity of Choquecasa's victories. In the dream Choquecasa has to flee Llocllayhuancupa's temple, a victory only in the sense that he has resisted the huaca's demand for worship. Other huacas continue to visit him with nightmares in which he "defeats" them again and again. Salomon argues that this inconclusiveness is inherent to Choquecasa's status as a "colonial propagandist and collaborator." His conversion can never be complete; instead it is constantly replayed in dreams and public performances: "The convert publicly displays the elements of his selfhood as error, what he abjures becomes his stock in trade."[33] If Choquecasa were to truly put the huacas behind him, or seek to definitively destroy them, he would endanger his ability to communicate with potential followers who lived in a fluid religious world.

Choquecasa's self-presentation in chapters 20 and 21 also reinforces the argument that the *Huarochirí Manuscript* reflects an agenda independent of Avila's. He is not acting as an extirpation assistant—he does not seek out the huacas and call for a priest when he finds them. Instead, it is the huacas who accost him, testing his strength as a convert. His victory (unaided by a priest) consists in reaffirming his Christian identity, not in destroying huacas. These are narratives of (re)conversion, not extirpation. Also, Choquecasa claims more independent religious agency than most priests would have been comfortable with, improvising his own prayers and sermons and serving as a spiritual guide to his people. The clergy were becoming increasingly hostile to such efforts at what Kenneth Mills calls self-Christianization (indigenous religious agency that deviated from a set script or was not under clerical supervision).[34] As Salomon notes, Choquecasa's use of dreams both in the *Huarochirí Manuscript* and in his preaching was particularly problematic given that dream interpretation was proscribed as a sin in the confession manual of the Third Lima Council, as well as later Quechua manuals. The very title of chapter 21 tells the reader that he is aware of the prohibition but has decided to ignore it.[35]

The language of the *Huarochirí Manuscript* can also reveal much about Choquecasa. The linguistic research of Gerald Taylor indicates that the people of Huarochirí spoke forms of Aymara and Central Quechua. The *Huarochirí Manuscript*, however, is written in a form of Southern Quechua known to modern scholars as *lengua general*.[36] Following Rodolfo Cerrón-Palomino, I have argued that this variety was a written standard developed by the Spanish clergy on the basis of the Quechua of Cuzco, and proposed calling it Standard Colonial Quechua.[37] By the early seventeenth century Standard Colonial Quechua had established itself not just as the language of Christian instruction and liturgy among the Spanish and mestizo clergy and their indigenous assistants, but also as a medium of written communication among the indigenous elite, who used it for private correspondence and petition writing.[38] Choquecasa's use of Standard Colonial Quechua provides additional evidence of his proximity to the Church, and he probably acquired it by reading the catechisms, sermons, and confession manuals published in the 1580s by the Third Lima Council.[39]

As James Lockhart has noted, the Quechua of the *Huarochirí Manuscript* is also characterized by a surprising degree of Spanish influence: a large number of loanwords of different kinds and even conjunctions are used redundantly alongside roughly equivalent Quechua suffixes.[40] This is not a characteristic of the Third Lima Council texts, where Spanish loanwords are used only for key religious terminology. Lockhart suggests that the *Huarochirí Manuscript* records a sociolect that developed in a sector of indigenous society that was in close interaction with the Spanish. This certainly would apply to Choquecasa, but we cannot assume much of a relation between the Quechua he wrote and the Quechua he spoke. I would suggest instead that the Hispanisms in the *Huarochirí Manuscript* reflect the habits of someone who was more accustomed to writing in Spanish than Quechua. The clearest evidence for this is the fact that one of the two retractions penned by Choquecasa for Avila's trial is in fairly good Spanish.[41] It is clear that Choquecasa had had some practice writing petitions and possibly other sorts of documents in Spanish. Why then did he write the *Huarochirí Manuscript* in Standard Colonial Quechua? While this form of Quechua was distinct from the variety he spoke natively and in which he must have interviewed many of his informants, they were nonetheless closely related. These similarities would have facilitated the composition process. The fact that Avila wrote and preached in Standard Colonial Quechua may also have been a factor, especially if the hypothesis associating the genesis of the *Huarochirí Manuscript* to Avila's sermon writing is correct.

Summing up, Choquecasa was born into a family of the highest rank and was literate in both Spanish and the variety of Quechua favored by the church. He probably had close links to the clergy since childhood. It may thus seem striking that he should have been seduced by the huacas. However, scholars of the extirpation trials have noted the absence of a clear boundary between Christian orthodoxy and "idolatry" in seventeenth-century Andean parish life, arguing that how Andeans positioned themselves along a continuum of religious practices often had more to do with local politics than with the fundamentals of faith (see also Charles, chapter 3).[42] Assuming positions of leadership in the colonial Andes often required acknowledging the huacas, and Choquecasa's "lapse" into idolatry, which he associates with his father's death, may have been part of an unsuccessful bid for political power. Similarly, his later antihuaca activities could have been part of an effort to undermine his political opponents—idolatry accusations were a common weapon in succession battles.[43] The *Huarochirí Manuscript* often appears to serve this purpose, as it is highly critical of Canchoguaman's successors, Juan Sacsalliuya and Juan Puyputacma, who are presented as inveterate idolaters, while partially exonerating Canchoguaman, who hated the huacas and only succumbed on his deathbed (HM 231, 235, 244–45).[44] Choquecasa himself appears as a leader of his people in the struggle against idolatry and as the vanquisher of Llocllayhuancupa, a huaca whose cult had been resurrected by Juan Sacsalliuya. It may be of some significance that Juan Puyputacma's death occurred right around the time when Avila began formal extirpation proceedings and the *Huarochirí Manuscript* was being completed—the curaca's passing could have unleashed a power struggle between religiously identified factions.[45]

Making the Huarochirí Manuscript

To what degree, and how, does the *Huarochirí Manuscript* hold together as a book rather than a compendium of lore? According to what criteria was the rich and complex information it contains chosen and organized (see also Schroeder, chapter 5, and Townsend, chapter 6)? If we cannot understand the *Huarochirí Manuscript* exclusively in terms of its utility to Avila, what purposes did it serve?

ALAN DURSTON

The manuscript reflects different stages of composition and the differing and changing agendas of both Choquecasa and Avila—a thorough analysis of the evidence concerning the composition process (variations in handwriting, possible variations in the type of paper employed, text added after a first writing, internal cross references, the distribution of Avila's marginalia . . .) still needs to be carried out. However, there is an overall consistency to the *Huarochirí Manuscript*—Salomon sees in it a totalizing quality that makes it a book in the full sense of the word.[46] Where does this totalizing quality come from?

A small part of the *Huarochirí Manuscript* reproduces the typological structure of contemporary idolatry manuals, which were organized according to universally applicable sets of categories such as life events (birth, marriage, death, and such) and objects of worship (celestial bodies, plants, and animals).[47] Toward the end of the manuscript, chapters 27–29 and the two supplements deal with beliefs and rites concerning death, the llama constellation, twin births, and the birth of babies with an unusual pattern in their hair. These chapters, whose themes and sequencing otherwise seem somewhat random, appear to reflect Avila's line of questioning. Chapters 1–4, on the other hand, deal with assorted "first things" in the mythical memory of the people of Huarochirí: the first huacas, a previous humanity that was immortal, and local recollections of biblical events. Although he disapproved of Choquecasa's efforts to connect local pagan history to universal Christian history, Avila's influence is apparent in the concern for chronological order that characterizes these chapters (cf. HM 7 and Avila's marginal notes in HM 7 and 9).

The bulk of the book tells the stories of the huacas who founded the living communities of Huarochirí. Issues of chronology and universal history barely come up. Structure is provided by the mythic cycles themselves and by the kinship relations among the various huacas, particularly the siblings and sons of Pariacaca, the dominant huaca of the region, and his female counterpart Chaupiñamca. Each of these myths pertains to the status and patrimony (especially lands and irrigation systems) of a community, and the narrative thus shifts smoothly and frequently to descriptions of contemporary huaca worship. The theme is not "idolatry" or "religion" but rather the mythological and ritual foundations of Huarochirí society, especially as they pertained to the relations between an invasive highland ethnicity and a local lowland one.[48] As Choquecasa himself put it, his objective was to set down, "village by village," the "lives" (*causascan*) of the ancestors of the people of Huarochirí, and how these people continue to "live" until the present day (*yma yñah canancamapas causan*) (HM 2). In one of his invaluable philological essays, Taylor argues that *causa-* (to live) can refer to an entire "way of life": norms, traditions, and everything necessary to the survival of a community.[49] This historical-ethnographic way of framing the material allows Choquecasa to set aside any hint of proselytism and even the most perfunctory condemnation of the huacas in most of the work. It is not so much (or not just) that he still "believes" in the huacas, but that their stories provide the only comprehensive explanation for the social world in which he lives.

One of the most striking aspects of the *Huarochirí Manuscript* is the precision and highly localized character of the information it conveys. Whatever universalizing ambitions Choquecasa may have had were sacrificed to this meticulosity, making the *Huarochirí Manuscript* both inexhaustibly rich as an ethnohistorical source and, at times, all but impenetrable. Choquecasa's descriptions of huaca worship employ numerous terms that were uniquely local (especially terms for ritual objects), resulting in passages that are extremely challenging for modern translators. Such terms are especially abundant in the two supplements describing the rites that were performed after ominous births, requiring Avila to insert several glosses in the margins. Choquecasa's meticulosity is perhaps most in evidence when it comes to geographical references. Not only is the *Huarochirí Manuscript* chock-full of place-names, but also the exact location of mythical events or ritual activities is often further specified by reference to prominent landmarks and to roads (e.g., HM 42, 69, 79, 119). Finally, it is particularly noteworthy that Choquecasa did not iron out divergent accounts of key myths to create a seamless narrative—instead, he made note of the divergences and explained that they were tied to different groups. For instance, chapter 13 begins by explaining that the mythology contained in it concerning the huaca Chaupiñamca is specific to the town of Mama and diverges from the accounts already given (e.g., HM 172 and 188).

This meticulous localism certainly had much to do with Avila's requirements. Some of his marginal comments request place-names and locations that are not provided in the text (e.g., HM 54, 109), probably because he anticipated that the information would be useful for extirpation activities. Much the same can be said for the names of ritual objects, variations in the beliefs of different communities, and so forth. However, the abundance of certain types of information also served Choquecasa's textual project of laying out the mythohistorical foundations of local society. In particular, mythical narrative and ritual action were inextricably tied to the landscape and could not be explained without reference to that landscape (see also Wake,

ALAN DURSTON

chapter 9). The geography of Huarochirí has provided an essential cotext with which modern scholars have deciphered Choquecasa, requiring much (literal) legwork. Spatial references also serve important validational functions in the narrative. Mythical events had left visible traces, especially in the rock formations into which the huacas had been frozen.

An important example of the validational role of the landscape appears in chapter 1, which describes a previous age when overpopulation had forced people to cultivate even the rocky mountain heights, the remains of their fields being visible up to the present day (HM 5). Avila dismissed the plausibility of this narrative as well as the chapters on the flood and the five days of darkness following the death of Christ, noting that the people of Huarochirí were easily deceived by the Devil. The Andes could not have been peopled before the flood, and how could they have known that the darkness had lasted five days when they had no clocks to measure the passage of time? If "some Indian" were to point to the remains of agricultural structures at high altitudes as evidence of the previous humanity, Avila's rebuttal was that the Devil could easily have fabricated these remains.[50] This imaginary dialogue may well reproduce the tenor of Avila's conversations with Choquecasa. The implication of Avila's critique is that the people of Huarochirí knew nothing about their own past. Choquecasa sought to establish that even though his people had lacked writing they did indeed have a history—one that was inscribed in the landscape itself.[51]

Finally, it is worth exploring the possibility that much of the information contained in the *Huarochirí Manuscript* was put there because of its political and legal importance. It was on the basis of the mythology contained in the manuscript that Huarochirí communities established their right to exist and their claims to resources into the seventeenth century and (in some cases) up to the present day. Salomon has studied a mid-seventeenth-century lawsuit between two villages in the vicinity of San Damián in which the parties reproduced, in some detail, the narratives concerning the creation of these communities and their irrigation infrastructure, contained in chapter 31 of the *Huarochirí Manuscript*. Huaca narratives were presented as straightforward "history" to a colonial legal system that adjudicated such conflicts on the basis of "immemorial" custom and tradition (see also Wake, chapter 9).[52] The detailed geographical information contained in the *Huarochirí Manuscript* takes on an entirely new meaning in the context of competition for territory and resources. Huaca narratives had enormous practical importance for colonial caciques who mediated internal conflicts and served as community advocates in external ones. In setting down these narratives Choquecasa may have sought to establish particular versions of them that were coherent with a specific agenda and interests. The historical-ethnographic project described above would thus also have served as a charter for local governance.

Choquecasa and Guaman Poma

Felipe Guaman Poma de Ayala's massive illustrated history of the Andes, the *Primer nueva corónica y buen gobierno*, completed in 1615, is our most fundamental source on colonial Andean culture, and Guaman Poma himself an icon of the struggle of bicultural, Spanish-speaking elite Andeans to make sense of and reshape the colonial world. Choquecasa and Guaman Poma are rarely put in the same frame of reference, but they had much in common. Like Guaman Poma, Choquecasa was a scion of a provincial elite and it is probable that he, too, felt disinherited. Like Guaman Poma, Choquecasa was bilingual and highly literate, and in all likelihood had acquired these skills by working closely with clergymen from an early age. Because of their literacy and their social position they were both involved in litigation, probably more so than we know. It is to be hoped that further examples of Choquecasa's involvement before the colonial courts lie waiting to be discovered and will help fill in crucial biographical details, as has happened with Guaman Poma.[53]

Among the experiences that set them apart from thousands of other literate Andeans whom we know only as litigants were their relationships with priests of unusual intellectual ambition. Recent research by Thomas Cummins suggests that Guaman Poma's apprenticeship with the Mercedarian chronicler Martín de Murúa was crucial to the creation of the *Primer nueva corónica*. Murúa produced two extant illustrated chronicles of the Incas and Guaman Poma assisted him in making the drawings of one of these chronicles, known as the *Galvin codex*. The style of illustration that Murúa developed provided a template for the drawings in the *Primer nueva corónica*, and Guaman Poma also drew freely on Murúa's texts.[54] We do not know how much Avila contributed to the training that allowed Choquecasa to write the *Huarochirí Manuscript*, but there was probably a crucial relation between the genesis of the manuscript and Avila's ambitions as an extirpator and expert on Andean idolatry. But if Choquecasa and Guaman Poma received their impetus from Avila and Murúa, they both went on to craft brilliantly original works based on their own experiences and agendas.

Obviously, these works are different. The *Primer nueva corónica* is a work of much greater scope, providing a systematic history of the central Andes from the first people to the conquest followed by a highly critical portrait of colonial society. The *Huarochirí Manuscript* makes only brief references to the Spanish colonial world or to events beyond the confines of the province. José María Arguedas, one of the few people to compare the two works, contrasted Guaman Poma's "somewhat bookish wisdom" to the demotic, oral authenticity of the *Huarochirí Manuscript*.[55] Guaman Poma did indeed draw on an extensive library to write his chronicle.[56] But if Choquecasa did not cite any written sources it was out of choice—it seems fair to assume that he had read books before he was able to write one.

These contrasts may have much to do with the fact that Guaman Poma, unlike Choquecasa, was of *mitmaq* (Inca-period colonist) origin. His immediate ancestors had been transplanted in Inca times from Huánuco to Huamanga, where he grew up. He consequently had two different homelands, which would have made him less inclined, and able, to produce a deep provincial history. Additionally, in 1600 Guaman Poma was exiled from Huamanga for fraudulently presenting himself as a cacique in a failed lawsuit over lands. Rolena Adorno argues that it was only at this point, having exhausted his legal recourses, that Guaman Poma began working on the *Primer nueva corónica*, greatly embittered by his experiences with the colonial system. Many of the travels that gave him such a broad perspective on the Andean world were forced upon him, first by the need to litigate and then by his exile.[57] We may one day discover that a similar shift from litigation to history lies behind the *Huarochirí Manuscript*, but the crucial difference is that Choquecasa came from a lineage long established in Huarochirí, and every reference we have puts him in his home village of San Damián. While there were certainly other factors involved, this biographical contrast helps us understand why Choquecasa wrote, in Arguedas's words, "a small regional bible"[58] rather than a wide-ranging history of the Andes.

By way of a conclusion I would like to stress a couple of general points about Choquecasa. First, he produced a work that is far more grounded in local indigenous tradition than that of any other Andean writer even though he was much like other bicultural nobles of his time in terms of his intellectual background and skills. A second point is that while Avila may have been the catalyst behind it, the *Huarochirí Manuscript* reflects an independent intellectual project stressing the validity of the historical experience expressed in the huaca tales. Both observations point us toward Choquecasa's bids for local leadership, a topic that we need to know more about. New archival explorations and re-readings of the *Huarochirí Manuscript* should reveal further clues in this regard. Taking a page from the scholarship on Guaman Poma, the *Huarochirí Manuscript* can be fruitfully approached as the outcome of an Andean nobleman's concrete experiences and agendas, agendas that were also expressed through litigation and other forms of activism.

Notes

I thank Frank Salomon for his comments on a draft and Peter Gose for sharing with me a transcription of Francisco de Avila's trial.

1. Choquecasa also appears in the colonial record as "Choquecassa," "Choquicassa," and "Choqqueccaça." These are all fairly predictable orthographic variants. Among the modern scholars of the *Huarochirí Manuscript*, Gerald Taylor writes "Choquecaxa," whereas Frank Salomon prefers "Choque Casa" to indicate there are two separate morphemes in the name (one possible gloss is "golden thorn"). I have opted for what could be considered the simplest spelling, and to not insert the morpheme division as it is not reflected in contemporary documents and might create the impression that they are two separate names.

2. Alan Durston, "Notes on the Authorship of the *Huarochirí Manuscript*." Several editions and translations of the *Huarochirí Manuscript* have been published. Frank Salomon and George Urioste's English edition provides the most complete analysis of the work's content and context: *The Huarochirí Manuscript*. Gerald Taylor's Spanish edition is the outcome of groundbreaking dialectological and philological research: *Ritos y tradiciones de Huarochirí: Edición bilingüe*. Nonetheless, many Spanish readers continue to prefer José María Arguedas's much older translation, and the *Huarochirí Manuscript* is best known under the title *Arguedas* invented for it; see José María Arguedas and Pierre Duviols, *Dioses y hombres de Huarochirí: Edición bilingüe. Narración quechua recogida por Francisco De Avila (1598?)*.

3. Huacas had different physical manifestations. The most important huacas were major mountain peaks, others could be rock formations or mummies.

4. Salomon, "Introductory Essay," in Salomon and Urioste, *The Huarochirí Manuscript*, 2.

5. In my 2007 article on Choquecasa and the *Huarochirí Manuscript* I argued that the date suggested by Antonio Acosta, 1608, be corrected to ca. 1600 (Durston, "Notes on the Authorship," 229–30). This argument did not take into account some crucial evidence that points to a later date—see Alan Durston, "Rectification of 'Notes on the Authorship of the *Huarochirí Manuscript*,'" 249–50.

6. On Avila see Antonio Acosta, "Francisco de Avila, Cusco 1573(?)–Lima 1647," 551–616. The classic study of the extirpation of idolatry campaigns is Kenneth Mills, *Idolatry and Its Enemies: Colonial Andean Religion and Extirpation, 1640–1750*.

7. Cf. Acosta, "Francisco de Avila," 584–85, 587.

8. Archivo Histórico Arzobispal de Lima, Capítulos I:9. Causa de capítulos seguidos contra el doctor Francisco de Avila, cura de la doctrina de San Damián y anexos, ff. 92–92v (in Spanish, cf. 90v) and 100–101 (in Quechua).

9. Avila, *Tratado de los evangelios que nuestra madre la Iglesia nos propone en todo el año . . . Tomo primero*, n.p.

10. Durston, "Notes on the Authorship," 232–33.

11. Avila, *Tratado de los evangelios*, n.p.

12. Durston, "Notes on the Authorship," 231–32. This view has surely been strengthened by the fact that authorial self-references in the *Huarochirí Manuscript* almost invariably use the first-person plural. However, the pragmatics of the person system in the *Huarochirí Manuscript* are complex. It is the inclusive form of the first-person plural (*-nchic*) that is used rather than the expected exclusive (*-ycu*), as if the intended readers had also been involved in the writing process (the "we" of *-nchic* includes the addressee, whereas that of *-ycu* excludes the addressee). There is often some contextual variability in the way person forms are used (*–nchic* and its equivalents can serve as a polite second person in some modern varieties), and it would not be surprising if, in a perhaps unprecedented literary enterprise like the *Huarochirí Manuscript*, they functioned in unpredictable ways. César Itier has suggested that the use of *–nchic* in the authorial self-references may have been intended as a *pluralis auctoris* or authorial "we" borrowed from Spanish (personal communication). An alternative interpretation is suggested by Bruce Mannheim, who proposes that the use of *–nchic* in the *Huarochirí Manuscript* may reflect interference from a local language in which the person system worked somewhat differently (personal communication).

13. Avila, "Tratado y relación de los errores, falsos dioses," in Arguedas and Duviols, *Dioses y Hombres de Huarochirí*, 199–217.

14. Duviols, "Estudio biobibliográfico," in Arguedas and Duviols, *Dioses y Hombres de Huarochirí*, 236–37; Roswith Hartmann, "El texto quechua de Huarochirí: Una evaluación crítica de las ediciones a disposición." Gerald Taylor has rejected Duviols's and Hartmann's arguments that the *Tratado y relación* is based on the *Huarochirí Manuscript*. Initially Taylor suggested that the similarity between the two texts could be explained by their use of a hypothetical common source: the "field notes" compiled by Avila and an indigenous assistant (Gerald Taylor, *Ritos y tradiciones de Huarochirí. Segunda edición revisada*, xv–xvi). More recently, however, Taylor has argued that the *Tratado y relación* predates the *Huarochirí Manuscript* and served as a model for it (*Ritos y tradiciones de Huarochirí*, 10). Suffice it to say that the similarities between the two texts are indeed compelling and that the *Tratado y relación* even reproduces what could be considered errors or deficiencies in the *Huarochirí Manuscript*, such as the sequence of chapters 3 and 4 and the omission of the name of the huaca Tamtañamca (Avila, "Tratado y relación," 209), which is present in the corresponding passage of the *Huarochirí Manuscript* but is clearly a later addition. The fact that the *Tratado y relación* bears the late date of 1608 and embroiders and comments on the *Huarochirí Manuscript* indicate that the former postdates and is based on the latter.

15. Duviols, "Estudio biobibliográfico," 237.

16. Avila, "Tratado y relación," 206–8.

17. Avila, *Tratado de los evangelios*, 234–35.

18. Avila, "Tratado y relación," 214.

19. Cf. Salomon, "Introductory Essay," 2. Salomon suggests that Avila may have

deliberately given the author(s) of the *Huarochirí Manuscript* a certain amount of leeway as a means of increasing the intelligence value of the text.

20. Most recently by Taylor, *Ritos y tradiciones de Huarochirí*, 9–10.

21. Given that Avila's *Tratado y relación* is dated 1608 it seems fair to assume that the *Huarochirí Manuscript* had been largely completed by that year. Cf. Durston, "Rectification," on dating the *Huarochirí Manuscript*.

22. Durston, "Notes on the Authorship," 240n6.

23. Avila, *Tratado de los evangelios*, n.p.

24. Alan Durston, *Pastoral Quechua: The History of Christian Translation in Colonial Peru, 1550–1650*, 164–65.

25. When citing the *Huarochirí Manuscript* I use the section numbers of the 1991 Salomon and Urioste edition, which facilitate comparison of the translation and the original text.

26. Avila, *Tratado de los evangelios*, n.p.

27. On colonial Huarochirí see Karen Spalding, *Huarochirí: An Andean Society under Inca and Spanish Rule*; and Salomon, "Introductory Essay."

28. Cf. HM 244 and 484; also Willem F. H. Adelaar, "Spatial Reference and Speaker Orientation in Early Colonial Quechua," 135–48.

29. Frank Salomon, "Testimonios en triángulo: Personajes de la *Nueva Corónica* de Guaman Poma y el Manuscrito quechua de Huarochirí en el pleito sobre el cacicazgo principal de Mama."

30. Gerald Taylor, *Camac, camay y camasca y otros ensayos sobre Huarochirí y Yauyos*, 36n6.

31. Taylor, *Ritos y tradiciones*, 11.

32. Frank Salomon, "Nightmare Victory: The Meanings of Conversion among the Peruvian Indians (Huarochirí, 1608?)," 14–16.

33. Salomon "Nightmare Victory," 18.

34. Mills, *Idolatry and Its Enemies*, 262.

35. Salomon "Nightmare Victory," 10–11.

36. Taylor, *Camac, camay y camasca*, 35–48, 105–20. See Durston, "Notes on the Authorship," 234–36 for further discussion of the Quechua of the *Huarochirí Manuscript*.

37. Rodolfo Cerrón Palomino, "Diversidad y unificación léxica en el mundo andino," 205–35; Durston, *Pastoral Quechua*, ch. 4.

38. Itier, "Lengua general y comunicación escrita"; Alan Durston, "Native-Language Literacy in Colonial Peru: The Question of Mundane Quechua Writing Revisited."

39. César Itier has proposed that the lengua general did not originate as a standard of clerical creation but was instead a lingua franca that developed among certain sectors of the indigenous population during the second half of the sixteenth century as a result of socioeconomic and spatial dynamics set in motion by colonial rule: "What Was the *Lengua General* of Colonial Peru?" This is a complex issue that requires further research and discussion, but even if Choquecasa did learn a spoken lengua general from other Indians, he still must have acquired the specifically written forms he employed (e.g., orthography) from the clerical writings.

40. James Lockhart, "Three Experiences of Culture Contact: Nahua, Maya, and

Quechua," 46. In a couple of instances Choquecasa uses the Spanish *azul* for the color blue (HM 39, 101).

41. Archivo Histórico Arzobispal de Lima, Capítulos I:9. Causa de capítulos seguidos contra el doctor Francisco de Avila, cura de la doctrina de San Damián y anexos, ff. 92–92v, cf. 90v. The main anomaly in the Spanish of this petition is uncertainty in the use of the Spanish vowel system, specifically the o-u and e-i oppositions, a common trait among Andean nonnative speakers and writers of Spanish because both Quechua and Aymara have only three vowels. Issues with gender agreement are also a common problem.

42. Mills, *Idolatry and Its Enemies*, 246; John Charles, *Allies at Odds: The Andean Church and Its Indigenous Agents, 1583–1671*, 161.

43. José Carlos de la Puente Luna, *Los curacas hechiceros de Jauja: Batallas mágicas y legales en el Perú colonial*.

44. Cf. Acosta, "Francisco de Avila," 599.

45. In the *Huarochirí Manuscript* he is referred to as the late (huañoc) Don Juan Puyputacma, curaca of the Checa (HM 244), but he was alive as late as May 1608 (Frank Salomon and George Urioste, *The Huarochirí Manuscript: A Testament of Andean and Colonial Andean Religion*, 99n44); and cf. Durston, "Rectification."

46. Salomon, "Introductory Essay," 2. See pages 5–11 for an interpretive outline of the entire work.

47. Cf. Pablo Joseph de Arriaga, *La extirpación de la idolatría en el Pirú* (1621), and the Catholic Church's *Confessionario para los curas de indios*.

48. Salomon, "Introductory Essay."

49. Taylor, "Introducción a la edición de 1987," xxvi.

50. Avila, *Tratado y relación*, 208.

51. Choquecasa does not mention *khipus* (knotted cord records) as sources, even though they were in use in Huarochirí at his time of writing; see Frank Salomon, *The Cord Keepers: Khipus and Cultural Life in a Peruvian Village*, xviii, 117–20.

52. Frank Salomon, "Collquiri's Dam: The Colonial Re-Voicing of an Appeal to the Archaic," 265–93.

53. Rolena Adorno, "The Genesis of Felipe Guaman Poma de Ayala's *Nueva Corónica y buen gobierno*."

54. Tom Cummins, "Dibujado de mi mano: La relación artística entre Guaman Poma de Ayala y Martín de Murúa."

55. Arguedas, introduction, *Dioses y hombres de Huarochirí*, 9–10.

56. Rolena Adorno, *Guaman Poma: Writing and Resistance in Colonial Peru*.

57. Rolena Adorno, "Guaman Poma and His Illustrated Chronicle from Colonial Peru: From a Century of Scholarship to a New Era of Reading."

58. Arguedas, introduction, 9.

Part III

Forms of Knowledge

Genealogies, Maps,
and Archives

CHAPTER 8

Indigenous Genealogies

Lineage, History, and the Colonial Pact in Central Mexico and Peru

María Elena Martínez

Beginning in the early decades of the colonial period, Spain issued a series of policies that declared baptized native people Christian vassals who were required to pay tribute but also entitled to certain rights and privileges because of their acceptance of Christianity and Spanish rule. The colonial vassalage pact, which included upholding the rights of the descendants of pre-Hispanic rulers and nobles to retain their titles, keep their lands, and access political offices within their communities, helped turn genealogy into a crucial tool through which indigenous elites made political and economic claims under Spanish rule (see also Schwaller, chapter 2, and Schroeder, chapter 5). This chapter analyzes these and other functions of lineage and some of its representations in central Mexico and Peru, the principal seats of the early modern Spanish Empire. It focuses mainly on Nahua and Inca cultures and by no means intends to be exhaustive—to treat every town, region, and period. Rather, the primary objective is to provide an overview of some of the most important uses of genealogy in order to explore questions about the role of indigenous community leaders and intellectuals—the latter referring to individuals or groups who articulate the general feelings, experiences, and historical consciousness of their communities[1]—in producing narratives and images of the past, negotiating aspects of the vassalage pact, and altering the terms of colonial power more generally.

Lineage, Politics, and Law during the First Century of Spanish Rule

Genealogy had been important in numerous indigenous cultures long before the Spanish invasion. In both pre-Hispanic central Mexico and parts of Peru, for example, it was traditional to link political legitimacy with descent (see also Schroeder, chapter 5). Although the records for the two regions are vague in many respects, they suggest that these links were strengthened during the period of Mexica and Inca imperial expansion, respectively, under the rulers Itzcóatl (1426/1427–40) and Pachacuti Inca Yupanqui (1438–71).[2] Models for choosing local rulers in Mesoamerican and Andean communities continued to vary, in part because subjected communities defied imperial efforts to change their traditions. Nonetheless, by the time that the Europeans arrived in central Mexico and the central Andes, genealogy was prominent in Mexica (and more generally Nahua) and Inca notions of history, community, and political legitimacy.

Spanish colonialism did not erode the importance of indigenous genealogy and its association with political legitimacy, and lineage continued to be significant even in communities that were subject to tight administrative control. This continuity can be attributed to struggles by indigenous people to preserve their historical and cultural traditions but also crucial was the Spanish Crown's recognition of the descendants of pre-Hispanic rulers (called *caciques* in all of Spanish America and also *kurakas* in Peru) and nobles (*principales*), on whom Spaniards depended for the organization of labor and tribute collection. The recognition was part of the colonial relationship of vassalage or "pact" through which indigenous communities ostensibly accepted Christianity, Spanish authority, and in most cases also their tributary status in exchange for the right to retain their traditional lands and political leaders.[3]

Despite the political and economic costs for native communities, the pact with the Crown, frequently symbolized by the act of a Spanish official granting towns their coat of arms, offered tangible benefits to caciques and principales. It not only meant that they could keep their titles, landholdings, and tribute exemption status (nobles for the most part were not subject to taxes) and hold offices in native town government, but also and perhaps more important, that they could pass their privileges and rights to their descendants.

MARÍA ELENA MARTÍNEZ

Because these privileges and rights primarily (though not exclusively and not always) rested on bloodlines,[4] Spanish colonialism reinforced the importance of genealogy among indigenous elites. More concretely, lineage became an integral part of indigenous economic claims, political struggles, and historical narratives under the new imperial regime. For this reason, the practical and symbolic uses of genealogy quickly multiplied and native communities resorted to a variety of means to maintain genealogical information for their traditional ruling families.

In most towns, information about local dynasties was transmitted though oral history, which, despite the gradual incursion of alphabetic writing, continued to be of utmost importance for preserving the indigenous past. In this form of historical transmission, male elders (*viejos*) played a key role, at least in institutional settings, as both native and Spanish officials recognized them as the most reliable authorities on the community's social and political life. The legitimacy and credibility that colonial society granted to male elders meant that they were generally the ones selected to testify in legal proceedings involving disputes over local ruling and noble dynasties. It also meant that the formal construction of communal memory was a strongly gendered process.

In Mexico, genealogical information, textual and visual, also appeared in colonial codices, the earliest of which were relatively faithful to pre-Hispanic pictographic traditions. Such information appears, for example, in the *Mapa de Cuauhtinchan No. 2*, a "map" or cartographic history produced by indigenous artists about two decades after the fall of Tenochtitlan that contains information about the origins, migrations, myths, conquests, lineages, and territorial domains of the people of Cuauhtinchan, a town in the Valley of Puebla.[5] Other sixteenth-century Mesoamerican pictorial documents, particularly those produced in the Mixtec region, also reveal that in many communities land, genealogy, and political legitimacy were closely connected (see also Wake, chapter 9).[6]

In the Andes, no pictorial tradition existed prior to the sixteenth century, but that did not mean that Andean communities lacked visual forms of representing lineage. Indeed, some Spanish sources suggest the Incas knotted their hair (*ligaduras*) in particular ways to indicate the lineage group and province to which they belonged, which raises the intriguing possibility of a connection between the way genealogy was marked on the body and the system of *quipus* (knotted cords that conveyed meaning through texture, color, size, form, and arrangement) since both relied on knots to transmit information.[7] Representations of lineage in illustrated manuscripts (and illustrated manuscripts in general) were not common in the region until about 1571, when Viceroy Francisco de Toledo (1515–84) commissioned indigenous artists to produce portraits of the twelve *Sapa Incas* (sovereign rulers or emperors of the Incan Empire, or *Tahuantinsuyu*) and their wives (*coyas* or queens). The results were three canvases depicting Inca rulers in a single genealogical line that were based mainly on European artistic forms.[8] Now lost, these canvases would have been seen by contemporaries either in Peru before they were sent to Spain or in the king's royal palace in Madrid, the Alcázar. A number of Peruvianists have credited these three paintings with starting a tradition (evident in the illustrated manuscripts of Martín de Murúa and Guaman Poma de Ayala, and in El Inca Garcilaso de la Vega's histories of the Incas), of portraying Inca kings in a single line of succession that in Peru lasted until the middle of the nineteenth century.[9]

Besides appearing in colonial paintings and illustrations, indigenous genealogical information was also recorded in the written histories of towns and their ruling families, the production of which was encouraged early on by the Spanish government, partly to ascertain the status of caciques and principales. The accounts, usually called *relaciones geográficas*, were more common in Mexico, presumably because of the previous writing traditions.[10] They not only supplied historical and other knowledge to the vice-regal government, but also became important sources of information for indigenous and mestizo historians of the late sixteenth and early seventeenth centuries, most of whom wrote their own relaciones with extensive dynastic information in order to exalt the pre-Hispanic dynastic traditions to which they claimed to belong and thereby secure royal recognition of their status and privileges.[11]

That these histories and other written genres emphasized genealogy (sometimes indigenous noble blood, Spanish, or both) is partly indicative of the importance that lineage acquired as a source of political legitimation in the colonial legal system during the first century of Spanish rule. The second half of the sixteenth century was a key period in this process for it was then that the vice-regal government started to develop the criteria for cacique succession and the certification of *cacicazgos* (rulerships; also called *kuracazgos* in the Andes). The colonial legal system introduced Spanish notions of descent and succession for caciques and principales and generally helped to make indigenous lineage important for accessing certain colonial privileges and rights. The system tended to encourage rivalries within and between native communities, such that genealogy was often at the center of disputes between individuals or families competing for lands, titles, and political office.

MARÍA ELENA MARTÍNEZ

Given the social and legal significance of genealogy in Spanish colonial society, how did colonialism (its legal system and visual and textual forms of representing lineage in particular) transform indigenous conceptions and representations of descent as well as understandings of its link to history? The use of lineage by native political and cultural elites undoubtedly varied, but in many communities changes in the way it was conceived, represented, and connected to history were inevitable for at least two main reasons: not only did Europeans introduce new forms of thinking about lineage, time, and history (and visual traditions such as representing rulers in a single tree) but also the pre-Hispanic priesthood—a key player in the preservation of historical memory—was one of the main targets of Spanish campaigns to destroy the old religious order. Although attempts to eradicate pre-Hispanic religious beliefs by targeting priests (and in Mexico their sacred books) were not entirely successful in either New Spain or Peru, by the late sixteenth century these efforts had severely lessened the role played by the old official bearers of knowledge of the sacred and the past (two interrelated categories), and therefore affected how history was recalled.[12]

Changes to communal memory were also accelerated by imposing new political, economic, and spiritual regimes, and by introducing new forms of expression. The most significant of these forms was alphabetic writing, which gradually (if unevenly) led to the substitution of autochthonous systems of literacy, which in Mexico included images and glyphs, and quipus in Peru. Pre-Hispanic systems of literacy survived; nonetheless, by the early seventeenth century, both Mesoamerican pictorials and quipus were in decline, being replaced by alphabetic writing in indigenous languages and Castilian in the case of Mesoamerica, and almost totally in Castilian with a handful of indigenous-language documents in the case of the Andes[13] (see also Wake, chapter 9).

The introduction of European modes of writing mostly affected a relatively small group of indigenous intellectuals (artist-scribes, religious specialists, and quipucamayocs, or experts in making and reading quipus); but the effects of this change should not be underestimated. In the Andean case, the shift was perhaps a more dramatic transformation in modes of expression than in central Mexico because of the absence of a formal writing system and establishment of an entirely alien one. In other words, what was introduced was completely new, whereas there was more commensurability between Mesoamerican and European artistic styles and forms of recording knowledge.[14] On the other hand, the existence of hieroglyphic or pictographic writing systems in pre-Hispanic Mexico did not necessarily mean that the adoption of the Latin script was any less transformative, for as various scholars have argued, in Mesoamerica "paintings" were images as much as text and their decline implied transformations at the deepest layers of culture, a break with the rich ritual and performative dimensions of the codex tradition.[15] With the demise of the pre-Hispanic priesthood and of the traditional religious and calendrical codices, it was inevitable that indigenous historical memory and what it retained regarding older forms of tracing and representing descent would also be impacted.

In Mexico, the influence of Spanish law and culture was already reflected in some mid-sixteenth century codices, which, for example, began to depict hereditary rulers of a single community and depict succession in terms of a direct male line of descent or what Spaniards called *línea recta de varón* where no such traditions had existed.[16] This male-centered representation of descent and succession also characterizes Peruvian representations of Inca royal dynasties. Starting with the paintings of Inca rulers commissioned by Viceroy Toledo in 1572, images of Inca rulers placed them in a single straight bloodline, thus ignoring the possibilities that the Tahuantinsuyu had dual rulership and that political succession could sometimes be based on maternal bloodlines (see also Schroeder, chapter 5).[17] The style, which appeared more or less at the time that the colonial officials in New Spain and Peru were trying to establish the criteria for cacique (or kuraka) succession, followed the European visual and literary tradition of depicting the *translatio imperii*, the linear succession of empires, as a male dynastic sequence. Closely wedded to a conceptual model of history in which history was fundamentally the history of dynasties, this tradition made genealogy stand for the passage of historical time.[18]

Shaped in part by medieval historical and genealogical traditions, early modern Spanish notions and representations of political succession tended to privilege patrilineality and primogeniture, and thus had the potential to alter indigenous understandings (and depictions) of lineage. Depending on the region, these understandings might have placed considerable importance on maternal descent, allowed for the transmission of political offices and titles to, for example, brothers and uncles, or included more than one bloodline due to the existence of two or more recognized rulers. Spanish rule and law, which *in theory* did not recognize indigenous kinship systems, therefore threatened to homogenize Andean and Mesoamerican forms of succession, simplify native genealogies, and replace varied forms of transmitting

MARÍA ELENA MARTÍNEZ

inheritance and property with more of a patrilineal model, which in some places it did. The influence of Spanish law and notions of lineage can be detected in certain legal inheritance cases, some early colonial pictorial manuscripts and paintings, and in the dynastic histories produced by indigenous and mestizo writers in the late sixteenth and early seventeenth centuries.[19]

But despite the infiltration of Spanish models for determining and representing descent, it is clear that the meaning and function of indigenous genealogies continued to vary and in some cases were at least partly informed by much older traditions. Maternal descent, for example, was not effaced, at least not everywhere. In the Andes, paintings of coyas (wives of Inca rulers) and *ñustas* (Inca princesses) are probably linked to the importance that maternal lines acquired in colonial times to preserve Incan lineages (especially among mestizos descending from Inca royal bloodlines on the mother's side) and to sustain the rights and privileges associated with them; however, it is also likely that they built on older Andean kinship practices which, for example, recognized parallel (male and female) lines of descent and organized certain social, political, and religious activities accordingly.[20] The recognition of maternal descent in some of New Spain's indigenous communities, and in the memorials and *relaciones de méritos y servicios* (reports of merits and services) that some descendants of Mesoamerican rulers who wrote to the king to reclaim some of the property and privileges of their ancestors, perhaps too had pre-Hispanic antecedents (see also Schroeder, chapter 5).

What is also clear is that lineage became one of the key "devices of negotiation" of Spanish colonial culture, a sanctioned discursive tool through which different corporate groups displayed their virtues and loyalty in order to defend or advance their interests.[21] This use of genealogy was part of the indigenous appropriation of the language and symbols of the European aristocracy, a process that appeared not only in legal documents (petitions to the Crown, community charters, and cacicazgo titles) but also in a new artistic style that the art historian Luis Eduardo Wuffarden has described as "mestizo heraldry."[22] In both Mexico and Peru, the new style began to surface in the 1540s and 1550s, decades in which government officials implemented the first major indigenous resettlement and nucleation programs, and many towns received municipal and territorial recognition. The style included traditional indigenous themes and motifs but started to integrate Spanish ones as well, such as coats of arms, genealogical trees, individual and family portraits, Castile's imperial arms, and Christian iconography.

Key players in the emergence of this style were indigenous artists but also

Figure 8.1. Coat of arms from the primordial title of Totonicapán. In *Título de Totonicapán: texto, traducción y comentario*, Robert M. Carmack and James L. Mondloch, eds. (Mexico City: Universidad Nacional Autónoma de México, Instituto de Investigaciones Filológicas, Centro de Estudios Mayas, 1983), 40. Reproduced courtesy of © Universidad Nacional Autónoma de México, Instituto de Investigaciones Filológicas.

the legitimate descendants of the pre-Hispanic nobility. As towns were re-organized according to Spanish models and new cacique authorities were ap-pointed (because they collaborated with the Spaniards, or simply because of their royal or noble ancestry), these individuals reorganized to defend their status, usually by deploying indigenous symbols of rank and prestige, in-cluding the Andean *mascapaycha* (a red fringe or tassel made of wool that was worn by the Sapa Inca on his forehead to denote imperial authority),[23] as well as European ones, such as the European-style municipal coat of arms. These crests (many of which were produced internally in native communities and were included in historical manuscripts written in their own languages)

MARÍA ELENA MARTÍNEZ

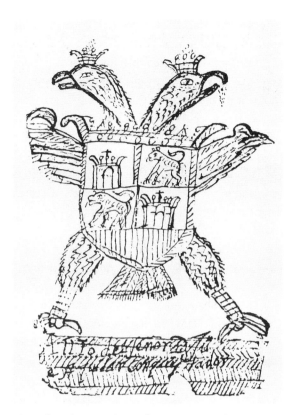

Figure 8.2. The coat of arms from the Lienzo de Tlaxcala. In *El Lienzo de Tlaxcala*, Mario de la Torre, ed., textos de Josefina García Quintana, Carlos Martínez Marín (Mexico City: Cartón y Papel de México, 1983), 57.

tended to symbolize corporate autonomy and political legitimacy; at times they also stood for the Spanish king, or rather, for the recognition and protection that royal patronage could offer communal lands.[24] They were thus part of the complex arsenal of imagery that indigenous artists and political leaders deployed, particularly in central New Spain, to convey the colonial pact.

For some scholars, the emergence of a new art style in New Spain and Peru together with the adoption of alphabetic writing indicate the radical transformation of indigenous cultures. These scholars view such developments as part of a larger process of acculturation, domination, and Christianization, which facilitated the introduction of European forms of belief, understanding, and learning that eventually transformed native mental structures.[25] Spanish colonialism undoubtedly led to profound social and ideological changes among many indigenous populations, but positing a linear and irreversible model of acculturation through European imagery, alphabetization, and Hispanic cultural concepts is more often than not reductive. It not only implies that all native cultures were affected in the same way by colonialism, but also fails to take into account that neither in Mexico nor Peru was there an absolute break with the past. More to the point, it disregards that in both regions the uses and functions of genealogy and memory were extremely complex, and that they were also preserved in rituals, myths, and especially in oral traditions.[26] Indigenous knowledge about lineage might also have survived in artistic mediums or activities in which women played an important role in encoding and preserving historical information, including textiles, storytelling, and dance.[27]

While scholars of Spanish America have not sufficiently studied the relationship of lineage, oral culture, and historical memory—not to mention the ways in which the appropriation of certain European genealogical images such as the tree might have shaped indigenous understandings of descent and the historical past—it is undeniable that within native cultures lineage could play numerous purposes, serve a variety of interests, and have multiple meanings. Lineage's malleability and its crucial role in both producing historical narratives and making political and economic claims became most apparent in the second half of the colonial period (which began around 1670) and in particular in the eighteenth century. At this time the concern with descent among Andean and Mesoamerican indigenous rulers and nobles reached new heights, and genealogies surfaced in a wider array of colonial written and illustrated genres. Furthermore, in both New Spain and Peru new iconographic programs surfaced that exalted, respectively, the Mexica and Inca past, which in both places involved turning genealogy into an instrument that helped construct indigenous memory, imagine imperial continuity, and reframe the vassalage pact.

Titles, Histories, and Royal Genealogies, 1670–c. 1810

Although indigenous written accounts declined in Mexico and Peru after about 1615, native people continued to produce other types of documents, including legal ones, which reveal the continued concern with genealogy and its connection to economic, political, and historical claims. This concern surged at the end of the seventeenth century, as the Spanish Crown issued several decrees validating the special status of the descendants of pre-

Figure 8.3. Illustration from the títulos primordiales of San Gregorio Atlapulco (a subject town of Xochimilco), compiled in the late seventeenth or early eighteenth century. The illustration, now in damaged condition, is of four pre-Hispanic figures (one is cut off except for his hand and staff) drawn in European style with their names and toponyms. In *La fundación de San Luis Tlaxialtemalco: según los títulos primordiales de San Gregorio Atlapulco, 1519–1606*, Juan Manuel Pérez Zevallos and Luis Reyes García, eds. (Mexico City: Comité Organizador del IV Centenario de la Fundación del Pueblo de San Luis Tlaxialtemalco, 1603–203/Instituto de Investigaciones Dr. José María Luis Mora/Gobierno del Distrito Federal/Delegación Xochimilco, 2003), 26–27.

Hispanic rulers and nobles, and the discourse of a colonial pact acquired a new life.[28]

In New Spain, the renewed indigenous concern with genealogy was manifested in a variety of legal documents, paintings, and in the *títulos primordiales* (primordial titles), a genre of community histories that revived the pictorial component of Mexican manuscripts (figure 8.3). Written mostly in indigenous languages and produced mainly by anonymous native artists, these documents appeared throughout central Mexico, and Mixtec, Zapotec, and Maya regions. Although the genre had antecedents in the sixteenth century, it began to spread in earnest in the second half of the seventeenth century as the combination of demographic increases, growing pressures on communal lands, and the Spanish Crown's program of *composiciones de tierras* (which required caciques to submit titles for their lands or those of their communities) provided a stimulus for the reconstruction of local histories (see also Wake, chapter 9).[29]

Even though they were similar to land titles and some were recognized as legal documents in territorial disputes, the títulos were not technically deeds and most appear to have been produced for internal purposes. In other words, they were fundamentally concerned with preserving certain information of a town's past (e.g., foundation, territorial boundaries, and succession of leaders) to ensure the social and political integrity of the community.[30] The manuscripts tended to include events that had occurred in the pre-Hispanic and early colonial periods. Thus, they usually incorporated images derived from indigenous and European traditions—including Mesoamerican place glyphs, Spanish coats of arms, and churches—that marked the conversion and colonization of American territories.

Although some aspects of the títulos primordiales vary depending on when and where they were produced, they generally share certain thematic and rhetorical characteristics with earlier indigenous legal and historical genres, including their emphasis on lineage. Because most titles sought to establish the noble and pre-Hispanic origins of the local ruling group, they often contain genealogical information, and some incorporate illustrations of genealogical trees. An example of a título with such information and a particularly prominent tree is the *Códice Techialoyan García Granados*, which was probably created sometime at the end of the seventeenth century or beginning of the eighteenth (figure 8.4). Part of a group of titles from central Mexico with their own pictorial style that scholars have labeled Techialoyans, it was drawn on the front and back of a long and relatively narrow strip (*tira*) of amate paper.[31] The codex does not provide any dates but includes extensive historical and genealogical information and references to several cities founded in the valleys of Toluca and Mexico in the late postclassic period, among them Azcapotzalco, Tenochtitlan, Tlatelolco, and Acolhuacán. It also contains numerous place glyphs drawn in the pre-Hispanic tradition, European-influenced illustrations (e.g., coats of arms, churches, lions, flags, and Christian crosses), notes in Náhuatl, and Latin characters.[32]

The most prominent image in the codex is the genealogical *nopal* (prickly pear tree or *tenochtli* in Nahuatl), which exemplifies the indigenous appropriation of a European symbol and its adaptation to the local context. An important symbol in fifteenth-century Mexica political and mystical notions of conquest, sacrificial death, and rebirth and common in pre-Hispanic and early colonial representations of New Spain's northern landscape,[33] the tenochtli became a visual means to represent political continuity between pre-Hispanic conquerors of the region and colonial caciques, the latter having descended from the "trunk."

The final or top branches of the genealogical nopal are followed by a series of images associated with Charles v and Christianity, including the coat of

MARÍA ELENA MARTÍNEZ

Figure 8.4. *Códice García Granados*. From *Códice Techialoyan Granados*, Xavier Noguez and María Teresa Jarquín Ortega, eds. (Toluca: El Colegio Mexiquense, 1992).

arms of the Spanish Hapsburgs (whose symbol was the bicephalus eagle), church towers, and a cross. These images symbolize the advent of a new political and religious order, and thus implicitly refer to the new imperial configuration or translatio imperii. The reverse side of the double-sided codex, or what remains of it, includes a second genealogical nopal and contains text in Nahuatl referring to lands that colonial cacique families claimed because their ancestors had conquered the region during the postclassic period.

Figure 8.5. Códice Techialoyan García Granados. Genealogical Nopal. From *Códice Techialoyan Granados*, Xavier Noguez and María Teresa Jarquín Ortega, eds. (Toluca: El Colegio Mexiquense, 1992).

Like other títulos primordiales, the *Códice Techialoyan García Granados* illustrates the continued importance of bloodlines in indigenous political and historical discourses. It also hints at the complex ways in which native local elites used imagery and text (and perhaps *images as text*) in colonial manuscripts to make the pre-Hispanic imperial past the point of departure of

MARÍA ELENA MARTÍNEZ

Figure 8.6. Detail of figure 8.5 Genealogical Nopal. From *Códice Techialoyan Granados*, Xavier Noguez and María Teresa Jarquín Ortega, eds. (Toluca: El Colegio Mexiquense, 1992).

their colonial claims, to affirm or reframe the terms of the colonial pact (by placing emphasis on the symbols of Spanish royal authority as well as on native dynastic continuity), and to legitimate their social rank.

Around the same time that títulos proliferated in Mexico, the descendants of the Inca nobility in Peru developed an iconographic project that relied on notions of blood, pre-Hispanic imperial imagery, and religion to symbolize the political and spiritual legitimacy of kurakas and rework the discourse of the pact. Although the images of the two regions differed in important ways, they nevertheless suggest that the colonial deployment and appropriation of images had entered a new phase, and that indigenous leaders and genealogies were at the center of it. The similar timing of the two iconographic programs also suggests that in both regions native communities and their intellectuals were responding to broad imperial, demographic, and socio-economic developments, including the composiciones de tierras program and growing struggles over lands and cacicazgos (see also Wake, chapter 9).

As a number of scholars of the Andes have argued, between 1680 and 1780 Peru experienced an Inca renaissance, a cultural affirmation of the pre-Hispanic imperial past that reached its apogee in the early decades of the

Figure 8.7. *Códice Techialoyan García Granados*. Hapsburg coats of arms and church towers. From *Códice Techialoyan Granados*, Xavier Noguez and María Teresa Jarquín Ortega, eds. (Toluca: El Colegio Mexiquense, 1992).

Figure 8.8. *Códice Techialoyan García Granados* (reverse side, second nopal). From *Códice Techialoyan Granados*, Xavier Noguez and María Teresa Jarquín Ortega, eds. (Toluca: El Colegio Mexiquense, 1992).

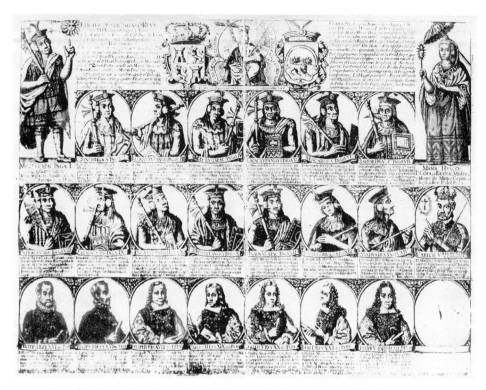

Figure 8.9. Engraving of Inca kings: "Efigies de los ingas y reyes del Perú," ca. 1725. Grabado ideado por el clérigo Alonso de la Cueva. Paradero desconocido. Photo courtesy of Natalia Majluf.

eighteenth century.[34] The movement, which included the use of Inca portraits, insignias, and sumptuary objects to adorn churches, private residencies, and government buildings, involved not only indigenous political leaders, artists, and intellectuals but also creole and mestizo ones, as well as Spanish religious authorities, including most notably the Jesuit Order. Images of Inca rulers and lineages were popular especially among the kurakas of Cuzco and the southern Andes, a development that was linked to the consolidation of a local tradition of painting in the former imperial capital known as the Cuzco School, and the prominence of its indigenous nobility. These images included a series of engravings and paintings that illustrated the merger of Inca and Spanish royal dynasties and incorporated Charles V and his successors as part of the line of rulers of Peru (figure 8.9).

Normally depicting rulers in a single line and historical sequence that

MARÍA ELENA MARTÍNEZ

Figure 8.10. Weddings of Captain Martín de Loyola and Beatriz Ñusta, and of Juan Henríquez de Borja and Ana María Clara Coya de Loyola, ca. 1675–1690. Iglesia de la Compañía, Cuzco (Bodas del capitán Martín de Loyola con Beatriz Ñusta y de Juan Henríquez de Borja con Ana María Clara Coya de Loyola, ca. 1675–1690. Iglesia de la Compañía de Jesús, Cuzco, Perú). Photo courtesy of Daniel Giannoni.

began with first Sapa Inca and ended with the Spanish king who was in power when the image was produced, these visual and stylized representations of Inca royal dynasties vividly conveyed the notion of a peaceful transfer of rule, the translatio imperii, and the idea that Spanish rule ushered in a new historical reality.[35] But by recognizing the Inca royal bloodline and alluding to the pact between two "nations" (Inca and Spanish), they also affirmed the political legitimacy of the descendants of pre-Hispanic rulers and nobles. According to Luis Eduardo Wuffarden, kurakas resorted to this type of image and to portraits of themselves with visual and textual references (such as mascaypachas) to their noble pedigrees as part of their efforts to generate new foundational images of their society. They aimed to replace depictions of subjected native Andeans with illustrations that invoked the imperial Inca tradition, as well as to stress their loyalty to the Crown and the Christian faith while simultaneously underplaying the idea of their subordination to the Spaniards.[36] At the same time that images of Inca royal dynasties circulated, individuals who claimed to descend from Inca kings continued to petition the Crown for recognition of their status and privileges.[37] Genealogy thus was simultaneously deployed in artistic representations and legal claims.

Despite their differences, eighteenth-century Andean depictions of Inca royal genealogies shared some characteristics and functions with Mexico's títulos primordiales. By illustrating dynasties from pre-Hispanic to colonial times, the Inca genealogical portraits emphasized notions of continuity rather than rupture, even as they recognized the advent of a new imperial order, the translatio imperii. Furthermore, these sets, which start with Manco Capac as the first "Inca monarch," reveal a conscious effort on the part of artists to add veracity or authenticity by making them seem archaic—much like the Techialoyans resorted to archaisms like the use of amate paper. Like the títulos, some of these Andean pictorial cycles and portraits of individual caciques claiming descent from Inca royal lines were used in legal proceedings to make economic and political claims.[38] Finally, both the Mexican títulos primordiales and the Inca pictorial sets emphasized conversion to Christianity as part of the colonial vassalage pact and thus tended to ground the claims of indigenous political elites not just in their noble descent but in their religious ancestry.

This dual use of genealogy—to stress both Christian and noble bloodlines—was not exclusive to caciques. In the Andes, the pact between Spain and Peru was most clearly represented in depictions of the marriage (arranged by Viceroy Toledo in 1572) of Beatriz Ñusta (aka Beatriz Clara Coya) and Captain Martín de Loyola (aka Captain Martín Garcia de Loyola), which were commissioned by the Jesuit Order in the seventeenth century. The bride, an Inca princess, was the niece of Túpac Amaru, whose death marked the end of the Inca royal succession through the masculine line; the groom was the nephew of St. Ignatius of Loyola, the founder of the Jesuit Order. The Jesuits commissioned paintings and murals of their marriage, as well as that of the couple's daughter Ana María Clara Coya de Loyola (aka Ana María Lorenza de Loyola) in 1611 to Juan Enríquez de Borja (grandson of San Francisco de Borja, a Jesuit saint) to claim a dual genealogy, one linking them to their founder and a prominent saint, the other to the royal Inca line.[39]

Members of the Order were also main sponsors of images of the baby Jesus wearing the mascaypacha and Inca clothing and displayed sculptures of him in that attire in religious celebrations. Through these carefully elaborated images of the Christ child and the marriages of Beatriz Clara Coya and her daughter, the Jesuits not only located themselves within a prestigious Chris-

　　　　　　　　MARÍA ELENA MARTÍNEZ

tian lineage but also appropriated Inca political genealogy.[40] Discourses of pre-Hispanic royal blood and political voluntarism (pacts) could thus be appropriated by indigenous and nonindigenous people alike to make specific historical and political claims.

In fact, representations of Inca royal genealogies were popular in part because they could be employed by various segments of the colonial population. Whereas kurakas resorted to them to claim their rights as descendants of Inca rulers, the Jesuits did so to emphasize the union of Inca royalty with Jesuit bloodlines and thereby attempt to enhance their prominence within Andean society. For some creole writers and mestizo elites, Inca royal portraits and genealogies served to grant their viceroyalty an important place within the history of Christian empires, and images of the marriages of Beatriz Clara Coya and Ana María Lorenza de Loyola helped them to stress the ties between Peruvian elites and the royal houses of Europe as well as to vindicate Peru's mestizo population.[41]

That is to say, representations of Inca dynasties were not inherently subversive as they could be used to promote the idea of a colonial pact and thus to legitimize colonialism. Yet Andean royal genealogies and other images of the pre-Hispanic imperial past had the potential to threaten Spanish rule because of the possibility that in addition to keeping the Inca past alive in historical memory, they could serve to imagine an alternative social order, ground political legitimacy more on pre-Hispanic royal blood than on Spanish recognition, and break the oftentimes tenuous pact between Spanish authorities and kurakas. Such was the official thinking, at least, after Túpac Amaru II's great rebellion of 1781. Whether Inca symbols of nobility and status were directly implicated in the rebellion or not, after the uprising Spanish officials placed part of the blame for the movement on kuraka claims of being descendants of Inca rulers.[42] As a result, the government lost little time in revoking kuraka privileges and banning Inca representation, imperial and otherwise, especially in Cuzco.[43]

Yet, not all images of Inca royal dynasties disappeared. Like the Nahua and Maya codices two centuries earlier, some survived because people hid them and they circulated in secret channels. Furthermore, the ban on Inca portraits, genealogies, and insignia did not end the cult to Inca nobility either among kurakas or creoles.[44] After 1780 Lima's creoles continued to employ Inca genealogies, albeit with considerable anxiety, in an effort to appropriate the Inca royal past and grant their lands an imperial pedigree. The appropriation of Inca history intensified during the political crisis that Napoleon's 1808 invasion of the Iberian Peninsula produced in Spain and Spanish America and during the independence wars (1810–24). In this period, Peruvian patriots deployed images of Inca monarchs as they mounted a concerted effort to create a classical past for the nascent country, condemn Spain's actions in the region, and cast the establishment of Spanish rule not as an imperial transfer but as an illegitimate removal of the Inca ruler.[45]

The importance of lineage among indigenous rulers and nobles of central Mexico and Peru did not begin with Spanish colonial rule. In preconquest times genealogy had been central to Mesoamerican and Andean myths of origin, practices of political succession, and patterns of establishing elite kinship ties. But by making nobility a requirement for certain political and economic rights in indigenous towns, colonial policies reinforced, and in the long term altered, native concerns with descent and history. These concerns and changes are evident in the writings of indigenous and mestizo historians as well as in legal petitions, written and illustrated manuscripts, and paintings, especially those produced starting in the second half of the seventeenth century. In a society in which political legitimation was based on fidelity to the Crown and the Catholic faith as well as on the worthiness of bloodlines, different written and artistic genres shared key rhetorical formulas and helped to produce certain (genealogical) narratives of the past.

Needless to say, these narratives were not uniform. The títulos primordiales, for example, did not all emphasize the same aspects of the past, rely on the same images, or arrange memories in the same manner. Their intended meaning, furthermore, differed depending on who produced them, when, and for what purposes. But in general, the títulos emphasized the pre-Hispanic bloodlines of caciques and principales, a strategy that was in consonance with the old regime's use of lineage to organize society and recognition of the "natural rights" of subjugated populations, but that also allowed indigenous communities to make the preconquest period crucial to constructions of the past and a basis for main sociopolitical demands.

The functions of Inca genealogies in legal petitions, histories, and paintings also varied. Images of Inca rulers and royal dynasties, for example, were used by kurakas, creole patriots, and Jesuits, among others, to make different historical claims. But here too, the widespread and multiple uses of pre-Hispanic genealogies highlight the ongoing and prominent role that lineage played in Spanish colonial society and its function as one of the key devices of negotiation that different individuals and social groups used to mold historical memory.

To be sure, there were similarities but also significant differences in the use of genealogy among the descendants of the Mexica and Inca, which raises a number of important questions. In terms of similarities, in both central New Spain and Peru lineage began to be used to determine cacique succession and reconstitute cacicazgos in the second half of the sixteenth century and thus had strong and early links to the law. Relaciones de méritos y servicios, claims to lands, and petitions for recognition of noble privileges were also often backed by both textual and visual evidence of noble descent. Furthermore, the decline of the pictographic tradition in Mexico and of quipus in Peru led to the loss of particular types of communication and knowledge, which probably affected the ways in which the past was remembered and facilitated the incorporation of Spanish genealogical traditions.

Yet, despite the imposition of Castilian laws privileging primogeniture and patrilineality, in both viceroyalties older patterns of determining local leaders and tracing descent continued to be practiced in some communities, especially those that were most removed from Spanish colonial influence.[46] That traditional forms of imagining and marking genealogy remain largely elusive in the historical sources is partly due to the gendered nature of constructing official memory (in terms of who testified, who painted, and who wrote), to the way that the law only sanctioned certain forms of framing the past and devalued cultural traditions in which women played a more prominent role, and perhaps also to indigenous people wanting to keep certain practices and knowledge hidden. Another commonality between the two regions is that, as of the late seventeenth century, the uses and representation of genealogy multiplied, a trend that was partly related to Spanish decrees confirming the political status of caciques and principales, the composiciones de tierras, and the more aggressive efforts by indigenous intellectuals to shape the historical narratives and foundational images of their societies.

In terms of the differences in the way lineage was used by native people or communities in central New Spain and Peru, in the former there was a pre-Hispanic tradition of representing genealogy pictographically, which continued throughout the sixteenth century (even if transformed by the gradual incorporation of European symbols, concepts, and alphabetic text). A similar tradition did not exist in the Andes. Another difference is the creation of títulos primordiales in Mexico, which probably resulted from the strong pre-Hispanic genre of "genealogical histories" in Mesoamerica and its survival during the sixteenth century. This genre, which revived in the late seventeenth century, apparently did not surface in Peru. For their part, Andeans generated documents and images with genealogical content that did not have Mexican equivalents, such as the iconography of royal genealogies that depict Incan rulers being succeeded by Castilian monarchs in one single line. Although dynastic portraits of Mexica rulers were produced and these too tended to depict the translatio imperii or voluntary transfer of power (or rather, Moctezuma's abdication of his crown to the Spanish king)[47] there appear to have been few (if any) attempts to depict Castile's monarchs as successors of the "Aztecs" and even fewer to include the wives of Mexica kings in royal representations. Further research is necessary to determine what these differences suggest in terms of the significance of the Mexica versus the Inca past in New Spain and Peru, respectively, the importance of parallel or maternal descent in the Andes, and the specific interests, political projects, and social conditions of the caciques and principales in each region during the eighteenth century.

What difference, moreover, did the strong presence and sociopolitical importance of the descendants of the Inca nobility in Cuzco and their physical separation from Lima's creole elite make in the reinvention of the pre-Hispanic imperial past, as opposed to the closer ties that the descendants of the Mexica established with the Spaniards and creoles in the capital city? Although the discourse of a pact was strong in both places, some scholars have argued that it was stronger in Peru.[48] If that was indeed the case, what explains the difference and was there a more concerted attempt by Andean indigenous political leaders and artists to emphasize that the pact involved religious but not political subjection? What effect might such attempts have had in the developments that led up the Túpac Amaru rebellion (which some colonial officials blamed on the prolific use of Inca imperial symbols and genealogies)? And what kind of emotional charge did genealogies and especially genealogical manuscripts carry in each region?

Whatever the differences between, and within, the two viceroyalties, it is undeniable that in both places the uses of indigenous lineage are testaments of cultural continuity and resistance as well as of cultural change, adaptation, and appropriation. Whether recorded in alphabetic or illustrated texts—be they written, painted, and even performed—genealogies could reflect the survival of pre-Hispanic notions of nobility and hierarchy as well as their complex relationship to Spanish legal, cultural, and pictorial approaches to

MARÍA ELENA MARTÍNEZ

lineage. Throughout the colonial period, genealogies were used by the descendants of pre-Hispanic rulers and nobles to affirm or negotiate the terms of the colonial pact, vindicate their political and spiritual legitimacy, reclaim lands, construct histories, deploy different symbols of power, and even imagine an alternative social order, one that turned the political hierarchies upside down. Indigenous artists and writers were integral to these efforts, producing a wide variety of manuscripts and images with genealogical content. To the extent that these texts and images were intended to promote certain communal visions of the past and political projects, the work of these different indigenous actors was unquestionably also intellectual labor—labor, in other words, meant to influence renditions of their history as well as its future course.

The ongoing and malleable uses of native lineage in Spanish colonial society ultimately points to the powerful role that genealogy played, along with the idea of conversion, in the simultaneous representation of the past and the political claims made in the present. Those uses also serve as reminders that the colonial discourse of a vassalage pact cannot be approached either as fixed or through the binary of domination of resistance but as an ongoing process of struggle over its meaning and content, one in which indigenous intellectuals played a central role.

Notes

I thank the participants in the panel "Discursos coloniales sobre raza y nación" at the 2010 Tepoztlán Institute for the Transnational History of the Americas for providing useful suggestions for this chapter. I also thank Ilona Katzew for her comments on early versions of this chapter.

1. Of course, no community is homogenous, so such intellectuals—who following Antonio Gramsci might be called "organic"—more often than not express the sentiments, thoughts, and visions of particular groups of people, even as they purport to speak for the collectivity as a whole, and their relationship to the dominant or governing class is not necessarily one of opposition.

2. Geoffrey Conrad and Arthur Demarest, *Religion and Empire: The Dynamics of Aztec and Inca Expansionism*; Enrique Florescano, *Memory, Myth, and Time in Mexico: From the Aztecs to Independence*; Richard F. Townsend, *The Aztecs*, 71–78, 80–114; J. Rounds, "Dynastic Succession and the Centralization of Power in Tenochtitlan"; and Irene Silverblatt, "Imperial Dilemmas, the Politics of Kinship, and Inca Reconstructions of History."

3. On the emergence and rhetoric of the pact in the aftermath of the Spanish conquest, see Juan Carlos Estenssoro Fuchs, "Construyendo la memoria: La figura del inca y el reino del Perú, de la conquista a Tupac Amaru II," 94–173, esp. 123.

4. María Elena Martínez, *Genealogical Fictions: Limpieza de Sangre, Religion, and Gender in Colonial Mexico*, 105–12.

5. On the genealogical markers and other components of the *Mapa de Cuauhtinchan No. 2*, see the excellent collection of articles in David Carrasco and Scott Sessions, *Cave, City, and Eagle's Nest: An Interpretive Journey through the Mapa De Cuauhtinchan N. 2*.

6. The scholarship on Mesoamerican codices is too abundant to cite here, but as a starting point, refer to the critical contributions of Elizabeth Hill Boone, which include *Stories in Red and Black: Pictorial Histories of the Aztecs and Mixtecs*; "Maps of Territory, History and Community in Aztec Mexico," 111–34; and "Aztec Pictorial Histories: Records without Words," 50–76.

7. Antonio de Herrera y Tordesillas, *Historia general de las Indias occidentales, ò, de los hechos de los castellanos en las islas y tierra firme del mar océano*, 3: 3. Given the importance of the bones or mummies of sacred ancestors (called *mallquis* in Quechua) in Andean cosmologies and social life it is also possible that they were part of the visual and ritual representation of lineage. I thank Alan Durston for sharing this observation with me.

8. The placement of rulers in single line was the standard way of depicting European kings during the medieval period, and in particular of visually representing the concept of *translatio imperii*, or transfer of rule from one emperor or empire to another. See Jacques Le Goff, *Medieval Civilization, 400–1500*, 131–94, esp. 171–72.

9. Catherine Julien, *Reading Inca History*, 45–46; Tom Cummins, "La fábula y el retrato: Imágenes tempranas del inca," 1–41, esp. 16–17 and 20–28; and Diana Fane, "Portraits of the Inca: Notes on an Influential European Engraving," 31.

10. Francisco de Solano, *Cuestionarios para la formación de las relaciones geográficas de Indias: Siglos XVI–XIX*; René Acuña, *Relaciones geográficas del siglo XVI*; and Barbara Mundy, *The Mapping of New Spain: Indigenous Cartography and the Maps of the Relaciones Geográficas*.

11. David A. Brading, *The First America: The Spanish Monarchy, Creole Patriots, and the Liberal State, 1492–1867*; Florescano, *Memory, Myth, and Time*, 120–31; Franklin Pease, *Las crónicas y los Andes*; and Frank Salomon, "Chronicles of the Impossible: Notes on Three Peruvian Indigenous Historians," 9–40.

12. Frances Karttunen, "Indigenous Writing as a Vehicle of Postconquest Continuity and Change in Mesoamerica," 421–47, esp. 423; Florescano, *Memory, Myth, and Time*, 36; Kenneth Mills, *Idolatry and Its Enemies: Colonial Andean Religion and Extirpation, 1640–1750*; and Gabriela Ramos and Henrique Urbano, *Catolicismo y extirpación de idolatrías: Charcas, Chile, México, Perú, Siglos XVI–XVIII*.

13. James Lockhart, *The Nahuas after the Conquest: A Social and Cultural History of the Indians of Central Mexico, Sixteenth through Eighteenth Centuries*, 330–35; Serge Gruzinski, *The Conquest of Mexico: The Incorporation of Indian Societies into the Western World, 16th–18th Centuries*, 47–53; John V. Murra, "Litigation over the Rights of 'Natural Lords' in Early Colonial Courts in the Andes," 55–62, esp. 55; Gary Urton, *Signs of the Inka Khipu: Binary Coding in the Andean Knotted-String Records*; and Frank Salomon, *The Cord Keepers: Khipus and Cultural Life in a Peruvian Village*.

14. Elizabeth H. Boone and Thomas B. F. Cummins, "Colonial Foundations: Points of Contact and Compatibility," in *The Arts in Latin America, 1492–1820*," 13–18.

15. Gruzinski, *The Conquest of Mexico*, 52–53. In distinguishing the Nahua graphic

system from European writing, Boone notes that the former never sought to convey speech, but rather to "preserve meaning visually" and in accordance with its own conventions. Thus, even though an oral discourse might accompany the "reading" of a visual text, it was the images themselves that encoded and structured knowledge without necessarily relying on a verbal narrative. Elizabeth H. Boone, "Pictorial Documents and Visual Thinking in Postconquest Mexico," 149–99, esp. 158; also see Elizabeth H. Boone, "Writing and Recording Knowledge," 3–26, esp. 17–20.

16. Refer, for example, to Mary Elizabeth Smith, "Why the Second Codex Selden Was Painted."

17. Cummins, "La fábula," 17; María Rostworowski de Diez Canseco, *History of the Inca Realm*, 177–78; R. Tom Zuidema, *The Ceque System of Cuzco: The Social Organization of the Capital of the Inca*; and Pierre Duviols, "La dinastía de los Incas: ¿monarquía o diarquía? Argumentos heurísticos a favor de una tesis estructuralista."

18. R. Howard Bloch, "Genealogy as a Medieval Mental Structure and Textual Form," 135–56. On the use of biological descent, and specifically the idea of generations, in historical discourse to connect lived time and universal time, see Paul Ricoeur, *Time and Narrative*, 3, esp. 104 and 109–12.

19. Susan Kellogg, *Law and the Transformation of Aztec Culture, 1500–1700*, 92–94; Charles Gibson, "The Aztec Aristocracy in Colonial Mexico"; Scarlett O'Phelan Godoy, *Kurakas sin sucesiones: Del cacique al alcalde de indios en Perú y Bolivia, 1750–1835*; and Enrique Florescano, "La reconstrucción histórica elaborada por la nobleza indígena y sus descendientes mestizos," 11–20.

20. See Irene Silverblatt, "Andean Women in the Inca Empire."

21. The term is from Jaime Cuadriello, "Moctezuma through the Centuries," 121.

22. Luis Eduardo Wuffarden, "La descendencia real y el 'renacimiento Inca' en el virreinato," 175–251, esp. 203; also see Gruzinski, *The Conquest of Mexico*, 21–23.

23. Gabriela Ramos, "Los símbolos de poder Inca durante el virreinato," 43–66; Estenssoro Fuchs, "Construyendo la memoria," 101.

24. On indigenous coats of arms as protective talismans, see Robert Haskett, "Paper Shields: The Ideology of Coats of Arms in Colonial Mexican Primordial Titles," 113.

25. Lockhart's *Nahuas after the Conquest* presents a three-stage model of gradual acculturation, culminating (circa mid-seventeenth century) with the merger of native and Spanish traditions in different structures of life compare with Gruzinski, *The Conquest of Mexico*, which also underscores processes of change wrought by colonialism but allows for older practices and ideas to resurface; also see Walter Mignolo, *The Darker Side of the Renaissance: Literacy, Territoriality, and Colonization*.

26. Florescano, *Memory, Myth, and Time*, 100–120.

27. On the religious, cultural, and historical significance of weaving patterns among the ancient Mixtecs, see Sharisse D. McCafferty and Geoffrey G. McCafferty, "Weaving Space: Textile Imagery and Landscape in the Mixtec Codices."

28. María Elena Martínez, *Genealogical Fictions: Limpieza de Sangre, Religion, and Gender in Colonial Mexico*, esp. ch. 4; and Wuffarden, "La descendencia," 229–32.

29. Recent contributions to the literature on the títulos primordiales include Stephanie Wood, "El problema de la historicidad de los títulos y los códices del grupo

Techialoyan," 167–207; and Stephanie Wood, *Transcending Conquest: Nahua Views of Spanish Colonial Mexico*; Enrique Florescano, "El canon memorioso forjado por los títulos primordiales"; Robert Haskett, *Visions of Paradise: Primordial Titles and Mesoamerican History in Cuernavaca*; and James Lockhart, "Views of Corporate Self and History in Some Valley of Mexico Towns: Late Seventeenth and Eighteenth Centuries," 367–93.

30. Robert Haskett, "El legendario don Toribio en los títulos primordiales de Cuernavaca"; Wood, "El problema de la historicidad," 137–65, esp. 168; and Wood, *Transcending Conquest*, 108.

31. The manuscript, which is part of the collection of the Biblioteca Nacional de Antropología e Historia in Mexico City, has been reproduced in facsimile form in Noguez and Hernández Rodríguez, *Códice Techialoyan García Granados*. Although the García Granados for the most part conforms to the graphic style characteristic of the Techialoyan group, it is considered unique within the genre because of its content (which includes information on the main lineages of noble families in government in several central Mexican cities) and use of pictorial space (which thanks to the length allows for the inclusion of a great deal of information). For more on the codex and other Techialoyans, see María Teresa Jarquín Ortega, "El códice Techialoyan García Granados y las congregaciones en el altiplano central de México," in *De Tlacuilos y escribanos*, 49–58, esp. 52–53; Donald Robertson and Martha Barton Robertson, "Techialoyan Manuscripts and Paintings, with a Catalog"; Donald Robertson, *Mexican Manuscript Painting of the Early Colonial Period*, 265–80; and Woodrow Borah, "Yet Another Look at the Techialoyan Codices," 209–22.

32. An extensive description and analysis of the García Granados is well beyond the scope of this essay and other scholars have already provided excellent detailed discussions of its content. See, in particular, the facsimile, descriptions, and articles in *Códice Techialoyan García Granados*.

33. Gutierre Tibón, "El corazón de la luna"; and Solange Alberro, *El águila y la cruz: orígenes religiosos de la conciencia criolla*, 69–73.

34. Wuffarden, "La descendencia," 176.

35. Estenssoro Fuchs, "Construyendo la memoria," 163; also see Diana Fane, "Portraits of the Inca," 36; and Wuffarden, "La descendencia," 232–44.

36. Wuffarden, "La descendencia," 205–22.

37. Archivo General de Indias, Lima 472, which includes many such petitions and supporting documents from the first half of the eighteenth century. One petition, for example, is by Don Juan de Bustamante Carlos Inca, who claimed to descend from Manco Inca and proceeds to chart his royal blood across eighteen generations and by "línea recta de varón."

38. Wuffarden, "La descendencia," 212–24.

39. See the images in Estenssoro Fuchs, *Los Incas, Reyes del Perú*, 190–91 and 198–200.

40. Estenssoro Fuchs, "Construyendo la memoria," 141; also refer to Marie Timberlake, "The Painted Colonial Image: Jesuit and Andean Fabrication of History in Matrimonio de García de Loyola con Ñusta Beatriz"; and Dana Leibsohn and Barbara Mundy, "Vistas: Spanish American Visual Culture, 1520–1820."

41. Wuffarden, "La descendencia," 200–201.

MARÍA ELENA MARTÍNEZ

42. On the complex ideologies and platforms of the movement, see Charles Walker, *Smoldering Ashes: Cuzco and the Creation of Republican Peru, 1780–1840*; Scarlett O'Phelan Godoy, *La gran rebelión en los Andes: De Túpac Amaru a Túpac Catari*; Ward Stavig, *The World of Túpac Amaru: Conflict, Community and Identity in Colonial Peru*; and Ward Stavig and Ella Schmidt, *The Tupac Amaru and Catarista Rebellions: An Anthology of Sources*. An earlier case in which Spaniards treated claims to royal Incan ancestry as potentially subversive revolved around Alonso Arenas Florencia Inca, who in 1666 was named corregidor of Ibarra, a town that was part of the Audiencia de Quito. Although he received his post in large part because of his royal Incan ancestry, his fondness for touting his genealogical links to Huayna Capac and Huascar (through the use of genealogical trees, among other things) aroused suspicions and he was imprisoned for allegedly being at the center of a neo-Inca political movement. The case is described in detail in Carlos Espinosa Fernández de Córdoba, "El retorno del Inca"; and Carlos Espinosa Fernández de Córdoba, "The Fabrication of Andean Particularism."

43. The suppression of Inca royal symbols and assault on the status and privileges of kurakas that began in 1783 is discussed in Natalia Majluf, "De la rebelión al museo: genealogías y retratos de los Incas, 1781–1900," 253–319; Wuffarden, "La descendencia," 205, 254; O'Phelan, *Kuracas sin sucesiones*, 35–39; and David Garrett, *Shadows of Empire: The Indian Nobility of Cusco, 1750–1825*, 38–39.

44. Wuffarden, "La descendencia," 256.

45. Majluf, "De la rebelión al museo," 257–60.

46. For a discussion of how pre-Hispanic matrilineal principles of kinship determination and land rights among the Chibcha of the Sabana de Bogotá might have coexisted with Spanish patrilineal inheritance ones during the colonial period, see Juan A. Villamarín and Judith E. Villamarín, "Kinship and Inheritance among the Sabana de Bogotá Chibcha at the Time of Spanish Conquest." And for a recent contribution to the study of indigenous South American communities under Iberian colonialism that includes an analysis of the survival and adaptation of Guaraní kinship notions and networks, see Guillermo Wilde, *Religión y poder en las misiones de guaraníes*.

47. Cuadriello, "Moctezuma through the Centuries," 125–27; and Giovanni Francesco Gemelli Carreri, *Viaje a la Nueva España*, 24–55.

48. François-Xavier Guerra, "Modernidad e independencies: ensayos sobre las revoluciones Hispánicas," 55–83.

CHAPTER 9

The Dawning Places

Celestially Defined Land Maps, *Títulos Primordiales*, and Indigenous Statements of Territorial Possession in Early Colonial Mexico

Eleanor Wake

In memory of Luis Reyes García

These were the dawning places. . . . And this is where our grandfathers, our fathers had their sowing, their dawning . . . And here is the dawning and showing of the sun, moon, and stars . . . [they] were overjoyed when they saw the daybringer. It came up first. It looked brilliant when it came up, since it was ahead of the sun. And that became their citadel, since they were there when the sun, moon, and stars appeared, when it dawned and cleared on the face of the earth, over everything under the sky.

Popol Vuh: The Definitive Edition of The Mayan Book of The Dawn of Life and .
The Glories of Gods and Kings, translated by Dennis Tedlock, 180–82

In 1699 the indigenous leaders of San Antonio Zoyatzingo submitted the *títulos primordiales* of their pueblo as evidence against a Spanish rancher who had appropriated some of Zoyatzingo's land.[1] In five Nahuatl documents, translated into Spanish by a court scribe, the títulos's authors attempted to convince the authorities that under colonial law Zoyatzingo's lands were inalienable: in recognition of their antiquity they were protected by at least two sixteenth-century *mercedes* (land grants) and a formal act of *posesión*.[2] The authors added: "We went to acknowledge the boundaries of the land that they [the founders] established, in accordance with and in the ancient way in which, in pre-Christian times, those of this pueblo possessed [them]. . . ."[3] The "ancient way" consisted of a boundary tour commencing "toward the east, where the sun rises, in this way the *selorio* is found/met, where the sun sets, the west and it meets with Mercury, in this way [the land] is demarcated by the four directions on the 8th day of the month of August 1537,"[4] and "toward Mercury, toward the west, in this way it was done by those who measure the land."[5]

At first reading, Zoyatzingo's boundary definitions might seem esoteric. Yet boundary tours of a "celestial" nature, adhering to almost identical sequential formulas, were included in the Nahuatl texts of at least eight other central Mexican títulos.[6] This chapter argues that references to celestially defined territory in the texts of the títulos primordiales have not only iconic, but also ideological parallels to a group of Mexican mercedes land maps that appeared beginning in the sixteenth century. Despite their resemblance to European signs, the suns, moons, stars, and planets named in the texts or depicted on the maps refer to an indigenous system of reckoning geography that emphasized the antiquity and inalienability of indigenous land. I first examine the boundary descriptions in the títulos primordiales in light of the symbolic and cosmological meaning of their celestial references, and the temporal dimension such references imply. Next I consider possible European sources for the depictions of celestial bodies in the maps, then situate these signs in the context of indigenous cosmology and astronomy. I examine the significance of the geographical distribution of the maps and the historical context of intensified threats to land and indigenous culture in the period in which most of the maps were produced, with attention to the changes in Crown policies and in the legal options available to the Indians in the sixteenth and seventeenth centuries. Finally, I outline the correlations of purpose and ideology between the celestially defined mercedes maps and the títulos primordiales.

The Boundary Descriptions in the Títulos

Each of the boundary descriptions in the títulos explains a counterclockwise route starting where the sun rises and covering four directional zones, although only those toward east and west appear as named determinants — that is, in the Nahuatl originals movement toward north and south is understood. The tour is made over the course of a full day and night, from dawn to dawn. The selorio is met at a point between east and west, and night commences proper at the place of sunset where a star appears; from there the tour turns (south) and continues onward to meet the dawn. Seven of the

TABLE 9.1

Reported dates of celestially defined boundary tours mentioning Mercury.
Nahuatl Títulos from the Chalco, Toluca, and Xochimilco areas

Celestial boundary tour	Date	Notes
Atlapulco	August 1556 [1537]	
Atlauhtla	August 1556 [1537]	Boundaries established 1556
Los Reyes	August 1556 [1537]	Land measured out
Ocoyoacac	August 1556	
Tenango Tepopula	August 2, 1556 [1537]	Boundaries (re-)established
Xocopetlalpan	August 1537	
Zoyatzingo	August 8, 1537	Order to measure land 1556

Source: AGN; López Caballero, Los títulos, 2003.

eight cited versions specify Mercury as the evening star, a point to which I will return.[7]

The títulos's celestially defined boundary tours are paralleled in other indigenous, alphabetical texts describing first foundings, which were equated with cosmic genesis.[8] As the people of Zoyatzingo emphasized, celestially defined indigenous territory speaks of antiquity of occupancy from the dawning, or colonial redawning, of a community's historical time, and thus to the inalienable right of possession. Colonial law, promulgated by the Crown in 1530 and reiterated in 1563 and 1591,[9] also protected community and inherited Indian lands held in this way. Antiquity and inalienability were therefore the key concepts the títulos's celestially defined boundary tours sought to impress on their readers.

But in this group of títulos the specificity of the celestially defined boundary tours in terms of the presence of Mercury in the west suggests more than just conceptual or symbolic statements of possession. Mercury is the evening star for an average of thirty-eight days out of its 115.9-day synodic cycle, with fluctuations on either side of up to ten days. However, due to the sun's glare it is visible less than half of that period.[10] These boundary tours, then, were defined within an actual and specific temporality: they took place when Mercury was visible in the west after sunset.[11]

As table 9.1 shows, two of the seven celestially defined boundary tours described in these títulos are dated August 1537, while five give August 1556. However, four of those dated 1556 have that year written out in full, but it is immediately followed by "1537" in numerals. The títulos's repetition of dates is probably due to procedures surrounding colonial endorsements of indigenous landholdings taking place in these areas around these same years.[12] Indeed, Zoyatzingo's títulos state that in 1556 "orders came from Spain" for its boundaries to be formally measured.[13] We can surmise that the year 1537 corresponds to the first viceregal land concessions made on the basis of antiquity of possession, while 1556 saw the formal measurement and verification of the boundaries under the Spanish colonial system[14]: that is, on the basis of four cardinal directions, or "the four winds" as some court scribes translated the variations on the Nahuatl *nauhcampa* ("toward the four directions"). I will return to the distinction between European cardinal directions and native directions later.

From a native perspective, however, both dates were critically important and almost certainly conceived of as sacred, for together they endorsed the pueblos' landholdings as inalienable under both the ancient and the new ways. In this sense, they were also understood to be inseparable in historical time, as is strongly hinted in the Nahuatl original of the títulos from Los Reyes where "y tlapuhuali 1537" followed the year 1556.[15] The scribe translated this as "que se quentan 1537" (which are counted [as] 1537 [years]).[16]

Here, the títulos's noting the presence of Mercury in the west is striking: Mercury was evening star on August 1, 6, and 16, 1537, albeit barely visible. Additionally, it was evening star, and this time visible, on August 1, 2 and 6, 1556.[17] Although none of the dates for August 1537 coincides with Zoyatzingo's August 8 sighting of Mercury (here we might speculate on problems with specific date correlations), for a star of such restricted visibility during most of its cycle, the correspondence with even a weak appearance during the first two weeks of August in both years is intriguing. It seems that the (literally) landmark events taking place on those dates were registered using a system based directly on astronomical observation. That is, as in the great traditions of cosmic genesis, territorial space was also conceived of in terms of celestial time.[18]

Celestially Defined Mapping

I will argue below that celestial boundary references in the títulos primordiales are related to a subgroup of approximately two hundred land maps belonging to the mercedes corpus of the Mexican National Archive (AGN). Unlike their corpus partners, these maps carry graphic representations of the

Figure 9.1. Zolipa, Misantla, Veracruz, 1573 (AGN No. 1535). Spanish request for a farm. © Archivo General de la Nación, Fondo Hermanos Mayo, concentrados sobre 363.

sun and (most commonly) a crescent moon, or two suns, placed in vertical, horizontal, or diagonal opposition, and usually with human faces (see figures 9.1–9.10).[19] The maps often show stars, particularly Polaris, the North Star, and either the Southern Cross (Crux) or, most frequently, its principal star *alpha Crucis* (hereafter, Acrux) (see figures 9.1, 9.3–9.9).[20] On some, other stars are also included on the eastern or western margins, often accompanying a sun (see figures 9.6, 9.11). Where single stars exist, most are carefully drawn with six to eight points (see figures 9.1, 9.3, 9.4, 9.6, 9.7); a few are elaborated further as if to emphasize radiance or an encoded importance (see figure 9.9). Other representations are limited to simply sketched asterisks of European origin, usually with eight points (see figures 9.5, 9.8).[21]

Mercedes maps were prepared in the thousands throughout the colonial period for use in legal proceedings relating to requests for land grants, or to resolve land claims, invasions, boundary disputes, and similar problems. In the first two centuries they were mainly the work of indigenous cartogra-

ELEANOR WAKE

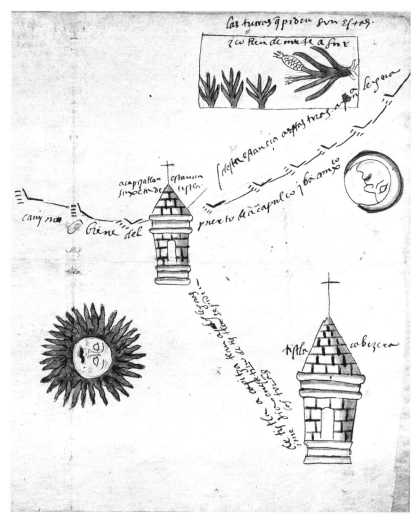

Figure 9.2. Tiztla, Guerrero, 1580 (AGN No. 1882). Spanish request for land within boundaries of Tiztla and Mochitlan. © Archivo General de la Nación, Fondo Hermanos Mayo, concentrados sobre 363.

phers. In general, nonindigenous participation in mapmaking during that period seems to have been restricted to adding alphabetical glosses,[22] and, where required, signing off the map as good and true. Thus despite European graphic and cultural intrusions, the maps studied here display to a greater or lesser degree the iconic and structural conventions of the native pictorial tradition to which indigenous cartography belongs.

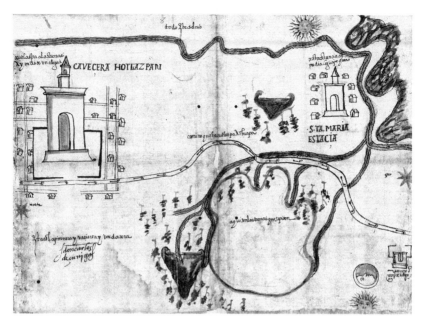

Figure 9.3. Otlaspa and Sta. María Estancia, Tula, Hidalgo, 1580 (AGN No. 1931). Spanish request for land within boundaries of Otlaspa and Chiapa. © Archivo General de la Nación, Fondo Hermanos Mayo, concentrados sobre 363.

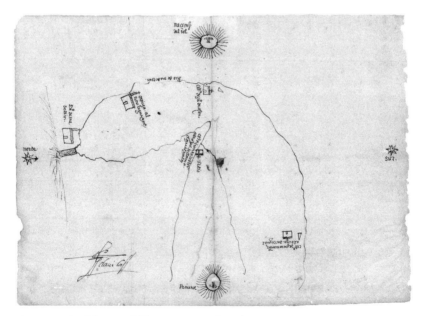

Figure 9.4. Ospicha y Medellín, Veracruz, 1581-B (AGN No. 0557). © Archivo General de la Nación, Fondo Hermanos Mayo, concentrados sobre 363.

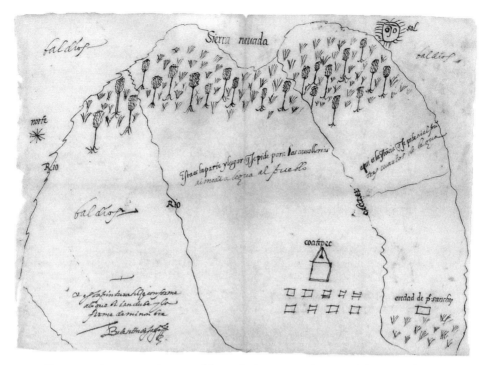

Figure 9.5. Coatepec, Sultepec, México, 1589 (AGN No. 1672). Spanish request for land within boundaries of Coatepec and Cuitlapilco. © Archivo General de la Nación, Fondo Hermanos Mayo, concentrados sobre 363.

Early Pictorial Dialogues

At first it might seem that the only purpose of the celestial signs on the maps was to orientate the viewer. North and south are indicated by Polaris and Crux, respectively; the sun rises in the east and sets in the west. And while the real moon is visible just above the western horizon around sunset only during the first days of its waxing,[23] its ideological associations with the night nevertheless make it an appropriate sign for west. Given the strong European graphic influence evident in the signs themselves, it could be argued that the mapmakers were simply copying contemporary European cartographical conventions.

However, a much higher number of Indian maps within the larger mercedes corpus employ exclusively alphabetical glosses to mark the cardinal directions. Given that the maps were intended for European viewing, this is perhaps to be expected. Yet almost all the celestially defined maps also carry

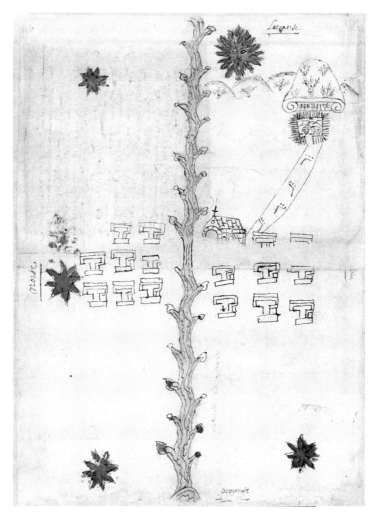

Figure 9.6. Tepenene, Yanhuitlan, Oaxaca, 1600 (AGN No. 1812). Request for land within boundaries of Tepenene. © Archivo General de la Nación, Fondo Hermanos Mayo, concentrados sobre 363.

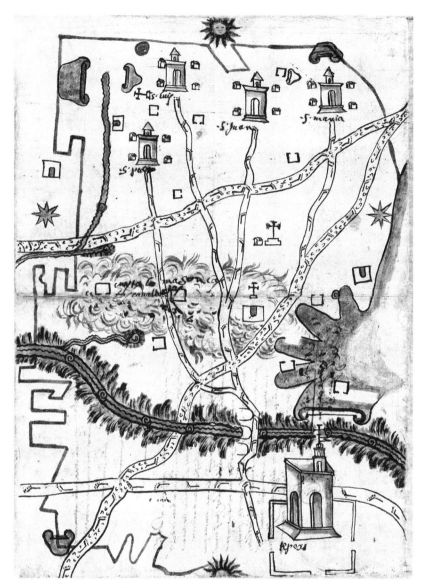

Figure 9.7. Tepexi del Río, Hidalgo, 1601 (AGN No. 2016). Request from *gobernador* and *alcalde* of Tepexi for land within boundaries of the pueblo. © Archivo General de la Nación, Fondo Hermanos Mayo, concentrados sobre 363.

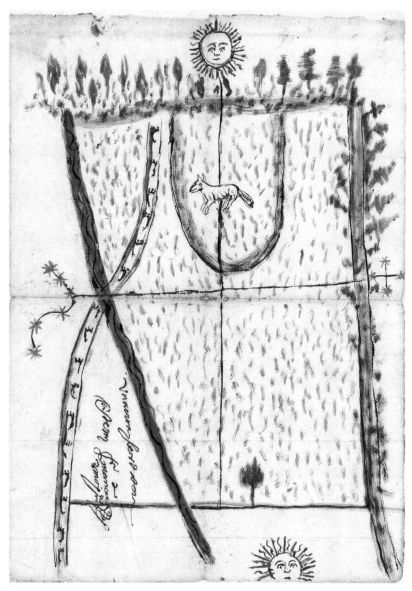

Figure 9.8. Amecameca, México, 1610 (AGN No. 1548). Spanish request for land for cultivation of wheat and maize on pastureland within boundaries of the pueblo. © Archivo General de la Nación, Fondo Hermanos Mayo, concentrados sobre 363.

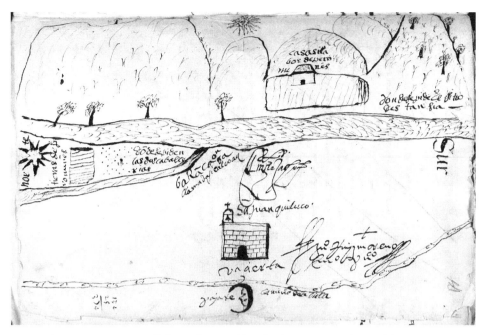

Figure 9.9. San Juan Quilulco, Izúcar, Puebla, 1611 (AGN No. 2025). Spanish request for land within boundaries of Quilulco. © Archivo General de la Nación, Fondo Hermanos Mayo, concentrados sobre 363.

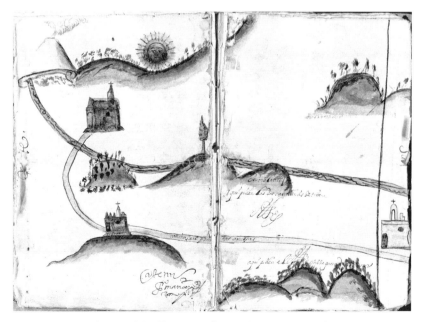

Figure 9.10. Tepetlispac, Chimalhuacan, México, 1611 (AGN No. 2287). Indian request for pasture and community land within boundaries of Tepetlispac and Chimalhuacan. © Archivo General de la Nación, Fondo Hermanos Mayo, concentrados sobre 363.

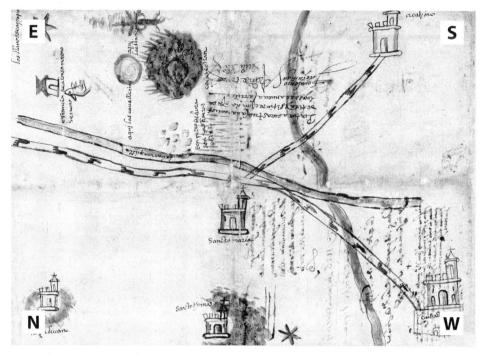

Figure 9.11. Map of Acatzingo and villages, Puebla, 1590 (AGN No. 2089).
Request for land within boundaries of Acatzingo. © Archivo General de la Nación,
Fondo Hermanos Mayo, concentrados sobre 363.

glosses (see figures 9.1, 9.3–9.6, 9.9), an unnecessary clarification if the celestial signs would have been understood as cardinal directions on their own. Conversely, an equally good number of indigenous maps offer no indication of the cardinal directions whatsoever. This has been explained in terms of a community's perception of itself as the whole rather than a small part of a whole,[24] but it also suggests a system of geographical orientation possibly based on elements internal to the map or the landscape.[25] These maps thus explain an Indian vision and ordering of geography that was unlikely to have been comprehensible to European eyes, in matters of orientation or anything else.

Because colonial indigenous mapping was a pictorial genre it could offer alternative readings that depended on the cultural background or expectations of both author and viewer.[26] Moreover, contemporary European cartographical conventions did not employ symmetrically arranged representations of celestial bodies to mark the four cardinal directions.[27] Even the

ELEANOR WAKE

navigational aid Polaris, and the then recently discovered Southern Cross were omitted from sea charts.[28] Orientational conventions at the time most of the celestially defined maps were produced (see table 9.2) were mainly confined to directional wind heads at a map's corners or around its margins, or to wind or compass "roses" marking the points where the rhumb lines met. Single wind compasses might carry an arrowhead or a fleur-de-lis indicating north. And while the seven planets of the geocentric universe (the Moon, Mercury, Venus, the Sun, Mars, Jupiter, and Saturn) sometimes appeared in the margins of some medieval and Renaissance maps,[29] these had nothing to do with cartographical orientation. Whoever added the glosses intended the signs to be read as orientational rather than as astrological figures, when, in fact, they were neither.

All in all, influence from European orientational conventions on the celestially defined mercedes maps seems minimal. Only one example depicts wind heads, at north and south, with the sun and moon at east and west.[30] Another carries a trumpet-blowing, winged cherub at north.[31] The earliest celestially defined map (1554) includes a star at north and south and a profiled face at east and west—perhaps protowind heads, but equally reminiscent of suns or moons.[32] Two sister maps of Ospicha y Medellín, Veracruz, dated 1581 (see figure 9.4),[33] which include animated suns and north and south stars, each attach an arrowhead to the North Star, although these point south, which might indicate some confusion as to the sign's intended usage.[34]

European cartographical conventions thus are unlikely as a direct source for the celestially defined maps. While it is possible that celestial signs may have been native in concept,[35] they might also have been copied from other European prototypes such as maps depicting the planets, or book illustrations and engravings that included a sun and/or moon over a landscape or in a background.[36] A more widely disseminated source comes in astrological or cosmological charts or diagrams, and the almanacs or astrological publications known as the *Repertorios de los tiempos*, distributed throughout New Spain's intellectual circles between the sixteenth and eighteenth centuries.[37] Indian access to and interest in them is evident from several surviving native-authored manuscripts on European astrology, in both alphabetized Nahuatl and pictorial form, such as the *Codex Mexicanus*.[38] In general, *Repertorio* drawings of celestial bodies are strikingly similar to those on the maps.

In addition, the astrological texts and drawings linked planetary movement to prediction: they determined specific moments in time in accordance with the positions of celestial bodies in the sky. Without asserting a connec-

TABLE 9.2

Chronological distribution of celestially defined maps from the
AGN *Mercedes* Collection

1554	•
1570–1574	••• (3)
1575–1579	••••••••••••••••• (19)
1580–1584	•••••••••••••••••••••••• (25)
1585–1589	•••••••••••••••••• (20)
1590–1594	••• (43)
1595–1599	••••••••••••••• (15)
1600–1604	••••••••••• (11)
1605–1609	•••••••••••• (12)
1610–1614	••••••••••••••••• (17)
1615–1619	•••••••••••• (12)
1620–1624	•• (2)
1625–1629	
1630–1634	•• (2)
1635–1639	•
1640–1644	
1645–1649	
1650–1654	•• (2)
1655–1659	••• (3)
1660–1664	• [earlier]
1665–1669	
1686	•
1714	•
1730	• [early 17th c?]
1734	• [earlier]
1743	•
1746	• [earlier]
1750	• [poss. earlier]
1752	• [lienzo, earlier]
1785	•

• = 1 map

tion between European astrological practices per se, but certainly recalling the títulos's celestially defined system of recording boundary tours, I will show below that the arrangements of many of the celestial signs also give the mercedes maps a certain temporal dimension. In this context, the celestial bodies cease to be cartographical signs, representing instead the real thing in both space and time.

The widespread use of native cartographers has been attributed to the limited geographical knowledge—not to mention cartographical training—of Spanish colonial officials, who were frequently reassigned to different areas.[39] Nevertheless, the colonial body had recognized early on that the Indians' pictorial texts (the *pinturas*, or paintings) contained historical and other information. From the 1530s on, codices and maps were presented in the courts by indigenous litigants. Their contents were often read out by a native specialist, translated by a court interpreter, and used as evidence.[40] While this did not ensure that the judicial tide ran with the Indians, it was a means by which indigenous practices and customs could enter the colonial legal system, and indigenous perspectives be put forward.[41] After 1590 the pinturas were formally dropped in favor of "written" evidence.[42] However, this shift to written documentation did not stifle the indigenous context. From 1585 through to the mid-seventeenth century, indigenous litigants self-consciously embedded key cultural symbols into legal narratives with the aim of influencing judges' decisions in respect of the special rights of the Indians.[43] In addition, the mainly native-produced mercedes maps remained a principal requirement for all types of land proceedings. These maps could also have been inscribed with cultural symbols in the form of celestial signs to remind colonial officialdom that the Indians had specifically designated land rights too.

The Maps in the Context of Indigenous Cosmology and Astronomy

The native peoples did not share the Western concept of four external, essentially abstract, cardinal directions. In indigenous cosmology the terrestrial plane was square or rectangular. It was divided into four quarters with a defined center, but the divisions were diagonally organized and can be defined as topological,[44] or cosmological,[45] as opposed to strictly orientational. A number of the celestially defined maps continued to adhere to this structure even though their corners seemingly designate the four fixed Western directions. The native quarters or quadrants might also be described as astronomically defined, for they probably originated through observation of the positions of the rising and setting sun on the horizon at the summer and winter solstices; they are still understood in this way by some traditional groups today.[46] Thus, the perceived movement of the sun on the eastern and western horizons over the solar year, and its east-west daily path across the sky served as the fundament of Mesoamerican spatial orientation.

The preconquest *Codex Fejérváry* 1 illustrates the predominance of the east-west determinant well for it is these quadrants alone that link up with the center,[47] as if north and south were mere cosmic appendages. North and south might thus be better explained as "moments" between east and west, or if spatially determined, "up" and "down,"[48] possibly appealing in this way to the further dimension of zenith and nadir.[49] In Otomi cosmology, the terrestrial plane is conceived as tilted upward from east to west.[50] Thus a counterclockwise circumambulation of terrestrial space would be understood to take in north as an upward movement, and south as downward. Until recently, the Zoque peoples of Chimalapa, Tehuantepec, Oaxaca, from which area a number of celestially defined maps originate, also understood that on its daily route between the eastern and western regions, the sun divided up space into two further regions, one to the north and the other to the south. Unlike the east and west regions, which were moveable, north and south were seen as fixed and lacking any specific orientation points with which to form an axis. The paths of the sun and the moon across the sky thus defined and opposed the north and south regions.[51]

The perceived spatial fixedness of the north and south regions echoes the perceived nonmovement of celestial bodies around the poles. Gilberto Rendón Ortiz observes that in indigenous belief the fixed positions of the pole stars defined them as immortal and separate from the common destiny of other stars,[52] a distinction which in many ways accounts for the Mesoamerican preoccupation with the moveable and ultimately destructible solar regions of east and west, as exemplified in creation narratives. But the native world considered the pole stars important in other ways. Polaris was used universally by travelers to find their way,[53] while among modern-day indigenous groups that still retain much of their ancient cultural heritage, the Southern Cross remains an integral part of their cosmological organization.[54] Also relevant here, in respect of the written boundary tours, are names used by still-traditional, Nahuatl-speaking groups: north is associated with wind (*ehecatl*) that is cold; south is likened to *yoallan* (literally "night place").[55]

The Nahuatl terms for "east" (*tonatiuh yquizayanpa*) and "west" (*tonatiuh yca-*

ELEANOR WAKE

laquianpa) are instructive for they translate literally as "where the sun rises" and "where the sun sinks,"[56] thus encompassing the whole extension of the eastern and western horizons between the solstitial points at any moment across the solar year. Where the four directions are sometimes alternatively named (tlapcopa [east]; mictlampa [north]; cihuatlampa [west]; uitzlampa [south]), the Nahuatl pa ("toward," "to," "from")[57] maintains the—for us—apparent vagueness of the system. With or without Spanish loanwords, this idiosyncrasy persisted well into the colonial era.[58]

Most of the celestially defined maps depict suns or sun and moon; that is, graphically they give precedence to the east-west determinant. Many of these signs are comparable in size to the main features of the map and therefore, in native pictorial terms, carry the same level of importance: they are integral to the mapmakers' vision of the geography represented, in ways that also ask us to look at them as real celestial bodies over real geographical horizons.

For example, setting suns sit on the maps' western edges or on specially drawn-in horizons, fall upside-down toward them, or sink beneath them, providing direct textual readings of "where the sun sinks" (see figure 9.12, and figures 9.3, 9.4, 9.7, 9.8). And while a human face within a crescent moon may be European in graphic origin, by astronomical definition two-thirds of the moons on the maps are nevertheless "Mexican" for they hang U-shaped—like their pulque-cup avatars—in parallel to the western cartographical horizons (i.e., the margins), just as the real moon appears viewed from Mexico at the start of its waxing (see figure 9.13). The position of the crescent moon vis-à-vis the setting sun in figure 9.3, too, is astronomically correct for its horns are always directly angled on the perpendicular away from the point of sunset.[59] The same may be true for figure 9.2 and other examples where a Mexican moon is included instead of a setting sun. Thus, the maps appear to reflect an astronomical input of some sophistication.

Astronomical observation for the computation of time also focused on the movement of the sun. A number of maps depict suns rising or setting over prominent local topographical features, an iconic detail strongly reminiscent of the native system of horizon calendars whereby the perceived movement of the sun between the solstices over the physical irregularities of a skyline served to compute time.[60] On the 1611 map of Tepetlispac, Chimalhuacan, México (figure 9.10), for example, the sun rises at a point over the Popocatepetl Ridge, the most important horizon calendar of the valley of Mexico.[61] At Coatepec, Sultepec, México, and San Juan Quilulco, Izúcar, Puebla (figures 9.5, 9.9), the sun again appears directly over one of several naturally defined

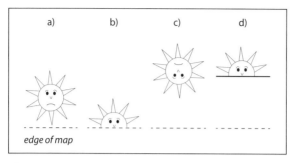

Figure 9.12. Cartographical modes of expressing "where the sun sinks," or the western horizon.

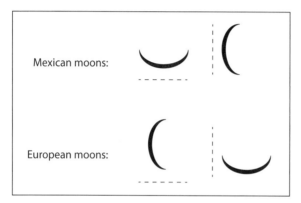

Figure 9.13. The relationship of crescent moons to the cartographical horizon.

peaks, while in a 1603 map from Tula, Hidalgo,[62] sections of mountain sky-lines were inserted for its rising and setting. Those mountains were probably not part of the geography of the map, but if the suns were exclusively orientational, why include the mountains at all?

While solar and lunar signs mark east and west on the maps, they do not always stand symmetrically in opposition one to the other or in relation to points marked as north and south, as might be expected if they were registering the European cardinal points exclusively. Examples might be figure 9.10 and its noticeably off-center sun, or figure 9.8, from Amecameca, México, where, despite lines linking the cardinal points, the sun still does not set at cardinal west. The 1580 example from Otlaspa and Sta. María, Tula, Hidalgo (see figure 9.3) marks north and south with stars at the center of the left and right margins, while rising and setting suns, and the rising moon, lie at top

ELEANOR WAKE

and bottom toward the map's south side. The arrangement suggests that the map represents Otlaspa when the sun is in the south (that is, when it rises and sets south of the east-west axis between the autumn equinox and winter solstice), possibly with a newly waxing moon on the western horizon—again, at a real moment in celestial time. A 1588 map from neighboring Tepexi[63] places the rising sun slightly to the north, although it shows it sinking below the horizon at a point still further north. At Coatepec, Sultepec (see figure 9.5) the sun rises to the south over the Sierra Nevada.

As with east and west, strange emplacements also occur with signs for north and south, which leads us to another possible interpretation of their meaning. Occasionally, suns or sun and moon lie centrally on opposing margins while the north-south axis shifts eastward or westward, as in figures 9.5 and 9.7.[64] Rather than indicate geographical orientation, the celestial signs for north and south here might denote irregular extensions of landholdings in a specific direction (in figures 9.5 and 9.7, west), *as viewed or measured from the center of the map, or the geographical siting of the pueblo.* This may also be true of the southerly or northerly placed solar and lunar signs. If such a reading is correct, then the graphic manipulation of celestial signs can add dimensional information to the maps' geography.

A final example comes in the 1590 map of Acatzingo and villages, Puebla (see figure 9.11; my glosses). Based on the geography of the area depicted, the asterisks at top left and bottom center correspond to cardinal east and west, respectively. The axis of the map therefore lies on a diagonal, where north and south appear to be marked by the villages of Nopaluca and Acatzingo, perhaps "toward Nopaluca" and "toward Acatzingo." The map might serve to orient the viewer correctly, although it excludes Tepeaca (a mainly Spanish-occupied town) from the focus of its business: a request for a land grant within Acatzingo's boundaries. The signs represent the cardinal points only circumstantially, for they are *internal* to the map's geography. What is clearer is that they depict a celestially defined vision of Acatzingo's threatened ancestral territory.

Despite the pre-Hispanic observation of and cultural ascription to the pole stars noted above, it might still be argued that their representation on colonial maps derives from European influence. As I propose below, this is true only at an indirect and nongraphic level. On the celestially defined maps, the pole stars constitute a conceptualized mode of native signage, prompted by colonial circumstance rather than colonial imposition or native acculturation.[65]

Although astronomically fixed in their positions over the north and south horizons, on some maps Polaris and Acrux also appear directly behind or over a particular architectural structure or a hill,[66] or between two mountain ridges as the sun (or a large star) appears over a peak to the east.[67] Thus, while certainly serving to orientate the viewer, on these maps these stars are also shown to be intrinsic to local geography.

Two of the five maps depicting the constellation of Crux present a Latin cross,[68] undoubtedly drawn from Euro-Christian interpretations of its aspect as the cross of Christ. But in figure 9.8, a relatively late map from Amecameca, and in maps from Quahuitlan, Guerrero, 1589,[69] and Temoxtitlan, Cholula, Puebla 1730 (see table 9.2),[70] the symmetrically cruciform cluster of four stars argues for native astronomical observation and description: today's Quiché Maya still include the constellation within a series of cross-like asterisms that they refer to as "daggers."[71]

In addition to Crux, the Amecameca map (see figure 9.8) depicts a near-complete Little Dipper.[72] Both constellations appear as linked chains of asterisk-stars, strongly reminiscent of the native asterisms on ff. 282r–v of the mid-sixteenth century *Códice Matritense del Palacio Real*.[73] The mapmaker and whoever signed off the map seem to have been unconcerned that its orientation may have been unclear to a European viewer. It lacks helpful glosses and it is debatable if any among New Spain's land officials would have been able to recognize either constellation or what it was supposed to represent on the map.

On the 1573 map from Zolipa, Misantla, Veracruz (see figure 9.1), the stars glossed as "north" and "south" at upper left and lower right seem to indicate that the centrally placed sun is rising in the northeast but setting in the southwest, an astronomical impossibility. This arrangement also raises problems from the perspective of the map's orientation. But on that map, did the glossator in fact err in identifying these stars as the pole stars, when they were intended to record other stars accompanying the rising and setting sun?

The Maps in a Geographical and Historical Context

Both pre-Hispanic and colonial developments contributed to the geographical pattern of the celestially defined maps' production. Their distribution over a wide area (see map 9.1) highlights the Spanish-dominated centers of Mexico, Toluca, Puebla, Izúcar, and Tehuantepec, where the pressure placed on surrounding indigenous lands is well documented.[74] Similar pressure existed further afield, as the distribution also suggests. The main reason be-

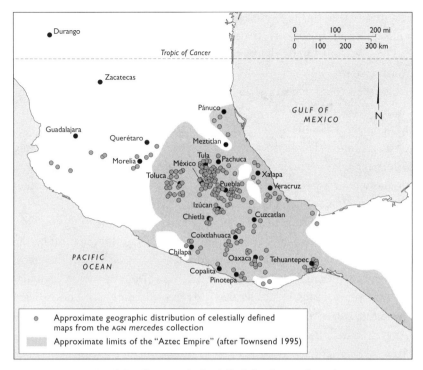

Map 9.1. Geographical distribution of celestially defined maps from the
AGN *mercedes* collection.

hind the preparation of the celestially defined maps reflects this: approximately two-thirds corresponded to requests for land grants within one or more Indian pueblos' boundaries, mostly made by Spaniards.[75] All the maps concern *indigenous* landholdings, with an emphasis on direct or potential threats to existing boundaries.[76] Two lacunae in the central area correspond to today's states of Tlaxcala and Morelos.[77] Only a handful of mercedes maps exist for the state of Tlaxcala (none for the city of Tlaxcala), probably because of its special status as a Crown protectorate and the low numbers of Spaniards settling there at the time the celestially defined maps were being produced.[78] Few maps were produced in Morelos, because most of the area fell under Cortés's own holdings.[79] Yet other gaps are apparent, most noticeably for Meztitlan, the area east of the states of Puebla and México (which includes Tlaxcala), southeastern Guerrero, and part of the coastal strip west of Tehuantepec. These correspond rather precisely to the small pockets of successful resistance to the Aztec Triple Alliance. In other words, the maps' distribution closely corresponds to the geographical extension of the Aztec

Empire and land that it expropriated and/or redistributed through conquest and subjection. In the early years of the colonial regime some of this land had been returned to its rightful owners[80] and thus fell under the category of inalienable.

Like their geographical distribution, the period when the maps were produced is significant. With one example from 1554, the celestially defined maps appear from the second half of the sixteenth through the late eighteenth century, although from 1620 onward they are incidental or their dating is questionable (see table 9.2).[81] Production surged in 1575, and most were produced between 1575 and 1620, with an increase in 1580–84 and another peak between 1590 and 1594.

While the threat to autochthonous landholdings was ongoing throughout the sixteenth century, certain events and program that intensified the pressure on indigenous lands seem to correlate to the patterns of the maps' production. At the end of the 1560s, New Spain's viceroy recommended that the ever-complaining Indians be given less access to the courts and the legal apparatus, and a *Sala de Crimen* was established in 1569 to rule over disputes between Spaniards and Indians in a radius of five leagues from Mexico City.[82] From 1570 onward, due to his need for additional income, Phillip II's change in colonial policies was noted in Indian Mexico, as elsewhere.[83] In 1575, precisely at the point the maps start to appear in good numbers, the king declared fiscal bankruptcy,[84] forewarning further pressure on Mexico's indigenous population still occupying what were technically Crown possessions.

The *Relaciones geográficas* project (1579–82) might be considered a warning of things to come and a source of indigenous reaction. Not only did it coincide with the great epidemic of 1576–80/81 (epidemics always being propitious for the acquisition of abandoned or uncultivated land), but its questionnaire, with its enquiries regarding geopolitical and religious organization of indigenous communities, reads in parts like a preliminary investigation for the second *congregaciones* program or as a land survey to boost the economic interests of colonists.[85] The potential heralded by the *Relaciones geográficas* was probably noted with alarm when, in 1581, although ultimately discouraged by his viceroy, Phillip started to consider the sale of pasturelands reserved for Indian communal use.[86] In 1582, the viceroy was ordered to make an inventory of all uncultivated lands in the province of México.[87]

Direct threats to indigenous land came in the second main congregaciones program of 1595–1606 (initiated in a few localized pueblos between 1591 and 1592).[88] The consequences were far-reaching, and included the beginning

ELEANOR WAKE

of an irrevocable breakdown of traditional Indian social, cultural, and economic structures. In addition, the years 1591 to 1620 correspond to the first round of *composiciones*, a land legalization program designed to replenish the royal coffers.[89] Although the Indians were excluded from *composición* until 1707, for them the outcome was still negative for the Spaniards were now able to legalize the lands they had invaded, usurped, or acquired by other fraudulent means at an earlier date.[90] Exclusion from *composición* also meant that the Indians were unable to obtain legal titles to their own lands, which continued to be considered Crown concessions.

As we have seen, the promotion of written documentation in the 1580s also registers the first moves to discourage the use of native pictorials as a formal element of the colonial legal system. Their presentation in the courts was all but discontinued after 1590. In 1591, the *Juzgado General de Naturales* (General Indian Court) was created to deal specifically with Indian affairs. It too barred court interpreters from presenting codices and other pictorial manuscripts on behalf of their litigants.[91] Thus, by 1591, the Indians had not only been denied their traditional means of negotiation with the colonial legal system, but were also technically excluded from the system itself. At this point we see a spike in the production of the celestially defined maps: of the forty-three prepared between 1590 and 1594, more than half are concentrated in 1590–91. Neither the congregaciones nor the composiciones can be implicated here: as noted above the 1591 congregaciones were not widespread,[92] while the order to "compose" was not signed until November of the same year.[93]

The need to protect their land and their exclusion from the means of doing so are two key factors to emerge from this period, combined with a third: the general assault on indigenous culture that royal and colonial directives had instigated. Two elements still operated in the Indians' favor, however. The 1530 law regarding the antiquity and inalienability of indigenous inherited lands was promulgated for a third time precisely in 1591,[94] while the mercedes maps, exempt from classification as "native" pinturas, could still provide a platform from which to invoke that law within the Spanish judicial system.

Correlations with the Títulos Primordiales

The temptation to separate the celestially defined maps from the títulos primordiales, either across time or as two different genres of colonial native expression (pictorial versus alphabetical; cartographical versus historical), is misguided. Chronology, shared purpose, and ideological projections hint at a close overlapping of the two.

The títulos's origins remain unclear. They start to appear around the mid-seventeenth century,[95] although some scholars believe that their preparation—as prototypes that may later have been rewritten in an updated form—may correspond to the last decades of the sixteenth century or the first half of the seventeenth.[96]

It has been suggested that the 1581 Crown initiative to sell off communal Indian pasturelands was the precipitating factor behind the títulos's production, but also the further series of composiciones which, from 1629, lasted through most of the seventeenth century, again opening the way to false claims. Thus, the títulos's unsolicited presentation was a "precautionary measure" to avoid Indian land being "composed" by Spaniards.[97] Clearly, if the títulos were at least conceived in the late sixteenth century, the 1582 survey of uncultivated lands would impact here too. The first round of composiciones (1591–1620) must have added fuel to the fire. In addition, as Margarita Menegus Bornemann has convincingly argued, the títulos's almost consistent references to early sixteenth-century land endorsements suggest a reminder of the "political pact" made between Carlos V and the native peoples: as understood by them, in return for religious conversion and tribute, the king recognized and protected their land possessions (see also Martínez, chapter 8). Philip II's policies were seen to break the pact.[98] As I propose below, the Crown's side of the pact is encoded in the celestially defined maps. In short, did the títulos start to be written in-house at the same time as the first maps were being produced? And, after 1620, under the realization that, politically and culturally, the written word carried more weight than the pictorial, did the títulos continue to press the case where the maps had failed?

While this chronology and the shared purpose of land defense may be suggestive, in another area the relationship between the títulos primordiales and the celestially defined maps is clear: the títulos often incorporate drawings and maps which, implicitly or explicitly, reproduce celestially defined boundary tours. In short, the títulos included celestially defined "maps." Three examples must suffice here.

The title page of the ostensibly mid-sixteenth-century títulos of Xi[uh]calco, Xochimilco, México (see figure 9.14)[99] places a sun and a circular moon bearing a crescent and a star (Mercury? Venus?) at either side of the head of the pueblo's Christian patron-founder, San Miguel. He stands on a rock, between a tree and the toponym of Xiucalco, evidently a representa-

Figure 9.14. Title page of the *Títulos* of San Miguel Xi[uh]calco, Xochimilco (AGN CDTT, Caja 1, Exp. 5). © Archivo General de la Nación, Fondo Hermanos Mayo, concentrados sobre 363.

tion of community lands. Although the patron saint and local landmarks seem to draw from Spanish heraldic traditions,[100] the celestial signs above play heavily on both celestially defined descriptions of boundaries and celestially defined maps. Heavenly protection comes from San Miguel, but over and above him the signs of the "ancient way" also make their encoded statement. Beneath the ensemble is drawn the coat of arms of Castile and León, symbol of the town's colonial political protection.[101] Xi[uh]calco's domains are, thus, encased protectively between the symbols of their antiquity and its recognition by the Crown of Spain.

The village of San Lorenzo Chiamilpa, in the area of Cuernavaca, Morelos, presented its territorial symbols as a coat of arms proper lying within a protective shield.[102] It shows two quadrupeds (possibly sheep or cattle where lions rampant once posed) and the toponym of Chiamilpa,[103] which doubles as the gridiron on which Chiamilpa's patron saint met martyrdom. Above, a sun-face, a Mexican moon, and a series of asterisk-stars preside. Around the shield sprays of vegetation mingle with more stars to the south, one group of which may represent Orion's belt.

A final example comes in a full-page image from Cuernavaca's own extensive títulos,[104] described by Haskett as a sacred landscape, "the visual counterpart of the primordial titles themselves."[105] Yet it is also a terrestrial map that invokes celestial precepts. A sun-face, with a scattering of stars, and a Mexican moon-face flank a central curved mountain, the glyph par excellence to designate the ancestral place.[106] Immediately beneath, the gloss "Cuernavaca" appears as if to denote the site of the urban center in relation to the whole. In accordance with the placement of the sun and moon, an eagle on a cactus, the toponym of Tenochitlan, lies to its north. Although possibly an allusion to Cuauhnahuac's prior subjection to the Aztec Triple Alliance,[107] it is nevertheless geographically correct ("toward Tenochtitlan"?). Thus, the Latin cross surmounting the coat of arms of Castile and León, with a large star to one side, corresponds to the south. This map is the visual rendering of Cuernavaca's "dawning (or redawning) place," as it was recorded by those who knew the ancient way.

The Cartographical Statement

From their sources, arrangement, and internal nuances, it seems clear that the celestial signs on the mercedes maps were not primarily orientational in purpose, even doubtfully so, at the level of the four, fixed cardinal directions and other European cartographical conventions. For the indigenous mapmakers, they were not cartographical signs but actual celestial bodies on real horizons. In this sense, for both parties, the signs are better qualified as directional.

More important with respect to the mapmakers' intentions is how the signs reflect the celestially defined mode of recording ancestral boundaries later/ also narrated in the títulos primordiales. That some maps may inscribe dates or refer to specific events in time, or the organization of space, as determined by the positioning of those bodies on an internal horizon is also a distinct possibility. The predominance of the traditional east-west directional determinant (that is, E-n-W-s) is to be emphasized, however, especially in its apparent complimentary opposition to the N-S-e-w of colonial directives. If the celestial signs for north and south are related to any European source it is to these directives, for the inclusion of Polaris and/or Crux—as "north" and "south"—seems to serve as a graphic extension that acknowledges the *colonial* act of measurement of the same territorial boundaries, this time to the four cardinal directions, or four winds. Thus, echoing the mixed texts (Nahuatl with Spanish loanwords: *oriede*, *puniyede*, *mercurio*, and the mysterious *selorio*) of the títulos, the signs read as a hybridized formula that narrates, in an iconic nutshell, the legitimating acts of both eras with regard to the ancestral and the inalienable.

Here we might query why, with one exception, wind heads were not written into the maps to give a direct reading of Spanish instructions. Direct references to "wind" do not occur in the Nahuatl originals of the títulos's celestially defined boundary descriptions either; court translators introduced the phrase into those texts, at a time well past the main period of production of the celestially defined maps.[108] Cartographical wind heads would have been read as orientational, which neither the celestial signs nor the Spanish directives were understood to be. In native perception, both were exclusively directional in the context of the topology of the geographical areas and their defined horizons or boundary limits. Likewise, we might also qualify somewhat differently the single clear example of a map displaying wind heads. Placed at north and south, with sun and moon presiding over east and west, they did indeed express the intended reading. In this sense, the map was not an exception, but it was open to misreading.

The interpretation offered is given more weight by the geographical evidence that the distribution of the maps yields. That the areas of their production are almost all confined, first, within the limits of the Aztec Empire, where confiscated ancestral lands were in some measure returned to their rightful possessors after the Spanish arrival, and second, to similarly classed landholdings lying uncomfortably close to the main Spanish-occupied centers, cannot be coincidental. The equation antiquity + illegal encroachment = map is well expressed in the distribution.

The maps were produced almost exclusively over the fifty-year period that witnessed a series of major changes in Crown and colonial policies, changes that not only increased the already-escalating threat to indigenous inherited lands but also denied their possessors the traditional means to defend them. Both visually and textually, the celestially defined maps and the títulos primordiales are too close to each other to suggest that they are not ideologically connected, or do not pertain to the same genre of literary purpose.

In conclusion, the intention of the celestially defined maps was the same as that of the títulos. With some possible exceptions (nothing can be cut-and-dried in the interpretation of indigenous graphic expression), I read the celestial signs as an attempt—one that, predictably, would fail at every level—to defend indigenous lands from ever-increasing Crown and colonial ambition by introducing a cartographical formula into the land distribution system and its courts. This stated that Crown dispositions regarding autochthonous landholdings, including the reiterated orders of 1530, were still in force. The celestial signs complemented the other information contained in the mercedes maps by defining the land depicted on them as indigenous, ancestral, and therefore inalienable.

Notes

1. AGN, Tierras 1665, Exp. 5; Paula López Caballero, Los Títulos primordiales del centro de México, 251–52. Zoyatzingo was a small dependence of Tenango-Tepopula in the Chalco region of the modern state of México. Usually written in native languages, with some Spanish loanwords, the Mexican títulos primordiales (hereafter títulos) are primarily concerned with defending indigenous ancestral lands. They recount the histories of pre-Hispanic territorial foundings and/or colonial refoundings and describe land boundaries. For monographs focusing on títulos, see Robert Haskett, Visions of Paradise: Primordial Titles and Mesoamerican History in Cuernavaca; López Caballero, Los títulos primordiales; and Robert Haskett and Stephanie Wood, "Primordial Titles Revisited," include a comprehensive listing of known títulos and related works.

2. The grants were technically Crown concessions, without full rights of possession. See Hans J. Prem, Milpa y hacienda: Tenencia de la tierra indígena y española en la cuenca del Alto Atoyac, Puebla, México (1520–1650), 72 and nn40, 90.

3. AGN, Tierras 1665, Exp. 5, ff. 183r–v; López Caballero, Los títulos, 254.

4. AGN, Tierras 1665, Exp. 5, f. 177v; translation Nahuatl-Spanish: Ignacio Silva. El selorio, or celorio, also appears in other Nahuatl títulos (see n8), always falling sequen-

ELEANOR WAKE

tially between east and west—that is, on the basis of a counterclockwise circumambulation, to the north. Although a loanword, none of the scribes attempted a direct translation, suggesting it was alien to them too, although the translator of the Atlauhtla *Títulos* (AGN Tierras 2674, Exp. 1, f. 17v; López Caballero, *Los títulos*, 347) replaced it with "*el Norte donde biene el frío*" (the north from where the cold comes). Ignacio Silva's translation understands *el selorio* as a corruption of *el solar*, a plot of land for construction or cultivation. Ethelia Ruiz (personal communication, July 2011) suggests a derivation from the Spanish verb *celar*, "to enclose" in order to safeguard; thus, "place of enclosure" (of the boundaries). A further possibility comes in a corruption of *celleru*, sometimes *celoriu* (Asturian, "granary"), from the Latin *cellarius*. In native Tlaxcala, the grain store was always located to the north, the coolest side of the house (Nazario Sánchez, personal communication, March 2012). In this sense, community territory may have been perceived as a macrocosmos of the nuclear domestic unit.

5. AGN, Tierras 1665, Exp. 5, f. 178v; translation Nahuatl-Spanish: Ignacio Silva.

6. Other títulos in their original indigenous languages may also contain celestially defined boundary tours that were omitted or rephrased by court translators. Eight alphabetized examples are sufficient to point to an established convention in the central highlands.

7. In the títulos from Santo Tomás Ajusco, unnamed stars in the west and/or south are recorded: "I order that the boundary starts where the sun rises . . . and we will go to where the cold comes from, where it is called Tzictecomatitlan. In this way we will turn toward where the sun sets, we will see the place where the star comes out, we will go to where it is called Tlatlatilollan . . . we will go where it is called Tlecuilco, next to it, we will go to where the star comes out, we will go to where the sun rises . . . (títulos of Santo Tomás Ajusco, Lafragua ms., f. 13v; translation Nahuatl-Spanish: Ignacio Silva). S/*Celorio* is not used. "[W]here the cold comes from" is north (Marcelo Díaz de Salas and Luis Reyes García, "Testimonio de la fundación de Santo Tomás Ajusco," 200, n24; Joaquín Galarza and Carlos López Avila, *Tlacotenco Tonantzin Santa Ana: Tradiciones: Toponimia, técnicas, fiestas, canciones, versos y danzas*, 40, 191). No Nahuatl reference to south is used but the direction can be understood in context, unless the second star lies toward the east. The 1710 colonial translator, believed to have been a native Nahuatl speaker (Stephanie Wood, "The Ajusco Town Founding Document: Affinities with Documents of the Sixteenth Century," 333–48, esp. 343), qualified the second-referred star as "*la estrella del sur*" (the star of the south) (AGN, Tierras 2676, Exp. 4, f. 5v; López Caballero, *Los títulos primordiales*, 195).

8. See, for example, the Mayan *Popol vuh* (opening citation), where "daybringer" is the great star that rises before the dawn, probably Venus; and the *Memorial de Sololá*, 81–83. In the Tarascan *Codex Plancarte*, 56, the founder-ancestor of San Juan Carapan, Tzintzuntzan, symbolically embodied the defining properties of territory and settlement, including the sun, moon, and a star. Amos Megged, *Social Memory in Ancient and Colonial Mesoamerica*, 224, equates territorial foundings with cosmic genesis.

9. See Emma Pérez-Rocha, *La tierra y el hombre en la villa de Tacuba*, 49; Enrique Florescano, *Origen y desarrollo de los problemas agrarios de México, 1500–1821*, 40; and Francisco González de Cossío, *Historia de la tenencia y explotación del campo desde la época precortesiana hasta las leyes de 6 de enero de 1915*, 304–5.

10. Anthony Aveni, *Skywatchers of Ancient Mexico*, 87; personal communication, June 2011.

11. The títulos's reference to Mercury, rather than the more conspicuous and conventional Venus (which also orbits the sun), is unusual. However, the two were unlikely to be confused at the level of astronomical identification (Aveni, personal communication, August 2011).

12. We can perhaps assume that Zoyatzingo's landholdings were measured in August 1556. Year dates are taken from the Nahuatl texts, for the court translators often transcribed them incorrectly. López Caballero, *Los títulos*, footnotes some discrepancies. While the consistency of the dates is notable, it is possible that the seven pueblos were using a shared source.

13. AGN, Tierras 1665, Exp. 5, f. 173r.

14. Precise boundaries were measured from 1540 (Florescano, *Origen y desarrollo*, 41).

15. AGN, Tierras 3032, 2a parte, Exp. 7, f. 267.

16. AGN, Tierras 3032, 2a parte, Exp. 7, f. 286r.

17. Aveni, personal communication, August 2011.

18. Prominent in the southern sky on February 4, 1531, when the leader of Ajusco ordered reduced boundaries to be demarcated, were Sirius (southeast) and Formalhaut (southwest) after sunset, and Antares (southeast) and Spica (southwest) before dawn. Two of these may account for the stars recorded in Ajusco's celestial boundary tour. I am doubly indebted to Anthony Aveni for checking all these possible celestial appearances.

19. See http://www.agn.gob.mx/mapilu/index1.htm. The number of maps in this subgroup is approximate; some are damaged where the celestial signs usually appear, while others are not reproduced online. Celestially defined maps can also be found among the 1579–82 *Relaciones geográficas* (approximately seventeen examples). These are excluded from the present study although arguably they carry the same proposed reading (see nn79,104 below). Also excluded are examples housed in Mexican agrarian archives and in non-Mexican repositories. Given its size, the AGN mercedes collection is considered representative of this subgroup.

20. Both Polaris and Crux can be seen from central and southern Mexico although visibility can be low or intermittent; see Aveni, *Skywatchers of Ancient Mexico*, 36–37; and Gilberto Rendón Ortiz, "Un drama cosmogónico en el cielo prehispánico"; http://en.wikipedia.org/wiki/Crux; http://www.skyscript.co.uk/crux.html.

21. Half of the maps in the study depict only suns or sun and moon; a quarter also include stars, while the remainder carry stars only.

22. Barbara Mundy, *The Mapping of New Spain: Indigenous Cartography and the Maps of the Relaciones Geográficas*, 210; and Mercedes Montes de Oca, "Las glosas y las imágenes en la cartografía colonial del centro de México: ¿Dos recorridos que se oponen?," 133.

23. See Aveni, *Skywatchers of Ancient Mexico*, 67–71; and Anthony Aveni, *Conversing with the Planets: How Science and Myth Invented the Cosmos*, 21–24.

24. Mundy, *The Mapping of New Spain*, 176–77.

25. See Adam T. Sellen, "Estrategias de orientación en el valle de Tenancingo"; Eleanor Wake, "Actualización del texto de la geografía sagrada: El caso de *altepetl* Cuauhtinchan" and *Framing the Sacred: The Indian Churches of Early Colonial Mexico*, 130–37.

26. See Gordon Brotherston, *Book of the Fourth World: Reading the Native Americas through Their Literature*, 50–73.

27. An exception might be the medieval T-O maps, but these were not widely distributed in Europe, much less in Mexico.

28. Pre-1500 Catalan examples favored an eight-pointed North Star, however; see Tony Campbell, "Portolan Charts from the Late Thirteenth Century to 1500," 371–463, esp. 395.

29. Helga-María Miram and Victoria R. Bricker, "Relating Time to Space: The Maya Calendar Compasses," 393–402, esp. 393–95.

30. San Simón Malinalco, México, 1578; and AGN 2539.

31. Tecualoya y Tenancingo, México, 1580; and AGN 1960.

32. San Gerónimo Coyoacan, DF, 1554; and AGN 2440.

33. AGN 0556, 0557.

34. These two examples are European in style, but include an irregular arrangement of architectural structures, a native convention that asks for a map to be read from its center.

35. In concept, the celestial signs may have been drawn from the native pictorial tradition (Sellen, "Estrategias de orientación," 190). The title page of the preconquest *Codex Fejérváry* hints at the semianthropomorphism of certain celestial bodies. The U-shaped sign above its eyes inscribes the *Fejérváry* "monster" as lunar. Full anthropomorphism comes in representations of native deities, often identified with stars and planets.

36. See, for example, Santiago Sebastián, "Los libros de emblemas: Uso y difusión en Iberoamérica," 56–82.

37. Susan Spitler, *Nahua Intellectual Responses to the Spanish: The Incorporation of European Ideas into the Central Mexican Calendar*, 78–79, 230.

38. See Alfredo López Austin, "Un repertorio de los tiempos en idioma Náhuatl"; Spitler, *Nahua Intellectual Responses to the Spanish*, 78–79, 208–37; and Soren Wichmann and Ilona Heijnen, "Un manuscrito en náhuatl sobre astrología europea," 106–24 (n.d.: 8). *Codex Mexicanus*'s chapter on the lunar phases includes several images of a crescent moon with a human face, probably drawn from its source *Repertorio*. See Spitler, *Nahua Intellectual Responses to the Spanish*, 187–92, 209–14.

39. Mundy, *The Mapping of New Spain*, 34; and Thelma D. Sullivan, *Documentos tlaxcaltecas del siglo XVI en lengua Náhuatl*, 21.

40. See Gordon Brotherston et. al, *Footprints through Time: Mexican Pictorial Manuscripts at the Lilly Library*, 11–12; María de los Angeles Romero Frizzi, "The Power of the Law: The Construction of Colonial Power in an Indigenous Region," 107–35, esp. 118; and Ethelia Ruiz Medrano, "Códices y justicia: Los caminos de la dominación," "El espejo y su reflejo: Títulos primordiales de los pueblos indios utilizados por españoles en Tlaxcala, siglo XVIII," 167–202, esp. 169–70, and *Mexico's Indigenous Communities: Their Lands and Histories, 1500–2010*, 11–12, 24, 31–46.

41. Ethelia Ruiz Medrano, *Mexico's Indigenous Communities*, 30.

42. Ethelia Ruiz Medrano, "El espejo y su reflejo," 171, and *Mexico's Indigenous Communities*, 68.

43. Susan Kellogg, *Law and the Transformation of Aztec Culture 1500–1700*, 70–77.

44. Sellen, "Estrategias de orientación," 189.

45. Johanna Broda, "The Sacred Landscape of Aztec Calendar Festivals: Myth, Nature, and Society," 74–120, esp. 132.

46. Aveni, *Skywatchers of Ancient Mexico*, 44.

47. Gordon Brotherston, "Mesoamerican Description of Space II: Signes for Direction," 45, and *Book of the Fourth World: Reading the Native Americas through Their Literature*, 96–97; and Anthony Aveni, "Concepts of Positional Astronomy Employed in Ancient Mesoamerican Architecture," 140.

48. Brotherston, "Mesoamerican Description of Space II," 55, 59, *Book of the Fourth World*, 87 and n7; Aveni, *Skywatchers of Ancient Mexico*, 149–50.

49. Brotherston, *Book of the Fourth World*, 87; Aveni, *Skywatchers of Ancient Mexico*, 45.

50. Andrés Medina, *En las cuatro esquinas, en el centro: Etnografía de la cosmovisión Mesoamericana*, 292, after Jacques Galinier.

51. Leopoldo Trejo, "Los espacios de la selva: Territorialidad zoque 'chima' de San Miguel Chimalapa," 249–71, esp. 250–52.

52. Gilberto Rendón Ortiz, "Un drama cosmogónico," 5.

53. Aveni, *Skywatchers of Ancient Mexico*, 38.

54. See, for example, Aveni, *Skywatchers of Ancient Mexico*, 41; J. A. Remington, "Current Astronomical Practices among the Maya," 75–88; and Vincent Stanzione, *Rituals of Sacrifice: Walking the Face of the Earth on the Sacred Path of the Sun: A Journey through the Tz'utujil Maya World of Santiago Atitlán*, 246–47.

55. Galarza and López Avila, *Tlacotenco Tonantzin Santa Ana*, 39–40, 191.

56. Galarza and López Avila, *Tlacotenco Tonantzin Santa Ana*, 39–40; and Rémi Siméon, *Diccionario*, 717.

57. Siméon, *Diccionario*, 113, 275, 368, 636, 759.

58. See Arthur J. O. Anderson et al., *Beyond the Codices: The Nahuatl View of Colonial Mexico*; James Lockhart, *The Nahuas after the Conquest: A Social and Cultural History of the Indians of Central Mexico, Sixteenth through Eighteenth Centuries*, 263–318; Susan Kellogg and Mathew Restall, *Dead Giveaways: Indigenous Testaments of Colonial Mesoamerica and the Andes*; and Caterina Pizzigoni, *Testaments of Toluca*. In wills, north and south were usually defined through reference to a nearby place lying in the corresponding direction, for example, "toward Toluca." Pizzigoni, *Testaments of Toluca*, 22, 54, n1.

59. Aveni, personal communication, August 2011.

60. See Aveni, "Concepts of Positional Astronomy," *Skywatchers of Ancient Mexico*, 61–67; Broda, "The Sacred Landscape," "Archaeoastronomical Knowledge, Calendrics and Sacred Geography in Mesoamerica," 253–95, and "Lenguaje visual del paisaje ritual de la cuenca de México," 129–61; and Broda et al., *Arqueastronomía y etnoastronomía en Mesoamérica* and *La montaña en el paisaje ritual*.

61. Broda, "Lenguaje visual," 135.

62. AGN 0604.

63. AGN 1907.

64. Other examples are Zapotitlan, Tehuacan, Puebla, 1609 (AGN 2479) and Tepexoxuma, Puebla, 1633 (AGN 2030).

65. The 1579–82 *Relaciones geográficas* questionnaire asked for the elevation of Polaris over the horizon (Question 6), and a map showing the northerly or southerly ori-

entation of towns (Question 10); see René Acuña, *Relaciones geográficas del siglo XVI*; and Mundy, *The Mapping of New Spain*, 227–30. This might suggest that native cartographers were influenced by the questions or encouraged to start including the pole stars. However, most respondents failed to reply to Question 6, and only seven known maps of the *Relaciones* series carry such representations at north and south.

66. Tlacolula and villages, Oaxaca, 1576 (AGN 1969); Iztaquimaxtitlan, Puebla, 1580 (AGN 1909).

67. Tacáscuaro, Michoacán, 1576 (AGN 2069).

68. Ixtlahuaca, México, 1584 (AGN 1705); Toluca, México, 1589 (AGN 1959).

69. AGN 2155.

70. AGN 0709.

71. Remington, "Current Astronomical Practices," 87. In modern-day Santa Ana Tlacotenco, Milpa Alta, México, the same cluster is perceived; see Galarza and López Avila, *Tlacotenco Tonantzin Santa Ana*, 39–40.

72. The drawing depicts six stars instead of seven.

73. The codex employs near-traditional, star-eye glyphs, also linked by lines. The similarities between the map's representation of the Little Dipper and the codex's native asterism named *citlalxonecuilli* ("twisted-foot star") are interesting, although on both codex and map identification with the Big Dipper might also be the case; see Aveni, *Skywatchers of Ancient Mexico*, 32–37; and personal communication, August 2011.

74. See Charles Gibson, *Los aztecas bajo el dominio español 1519–1810*, 278–79, on Mexico; Peter Gerhard, *Geografía histórica de la Nueva España 1519–1821*, 166, 341, on Izúcar and Toluca; Hildeberto Martínez, *Codiciaban la tierra: El despojo agrario en los señoríos de Tecamachalco y Quecholac (Puebla, 1520–1650)*, 71–73, on Puebla; and Ronald Spores, "Differential Response to Colonial Control among the Mixtecs and Zapotecs of Oaxaca," 30–46, esp. 42, on Tehuantepec.

75. The statistics approximated here are based on AGN summaries of accompanying documentation where petitioners are usually defined as Indian or Spaniard, but not consistently so.

76. A much larger number of mercedes maps also focused on the main issues outlined here. However, that so many of the celestially defined examples concern Spanish requests for land lying inside Indian boundaries is seen as significant.

77. Olintepec, Anenecuilco y Quautla, 1605 (AGN 2482).

78. See Gerhard, *Geografía histórica*, 335.

79. Mundy, *The Mapping of New Spain*, 245. Quautla Amilpas was an exception; see Gerhard, *Geografía histórica*, 93.

80. Margarita Menegus Bornemann, "Los títulos primordiales de los Pueblos de Indios," 137–61, and *Del señorío indígena a la república de indios, el caso de Toluca 1500–1600*, 60; Gibson, *Los aztecas*, 271; but see also Martínez, *Codiciaban la tierra*, 75–84, on "tierras de nadie."

81. The maps are dated from the written documents they accompany. Stylistically, however, a few of the later examples correspond to an earlier date, or are later copies of the same. Two undated examples are excluded from table 2; one of these appears to be from the late sixteenth or early seventeenth century.

82. Ruiz Medrano, *Mexico's Indigenous Communities*, 61.

83. Ruiz Medrano, *Mexico's Indigenous Communities*, 61.

84. Ruiz Medrano, *Mexico's Indigenous Communities*, 61.

85. See, e.g., the questions concerning distances between native towns and their indoctrination centers, and between native and Spanish towns; appropriateness of the land for the cultivation of Spanish food crops; potential mining and quarrying areas.

86. Ruiz Medrano, "El espejo y su reflejo," 173, and *Mexico's Indigenous Communities*, 100–101.

87. Menegus Bornemann, *Del señorío indígena a la república de indios*, 209. Francisco de Solano, *Cedulario de tierras: Compilación de legislación agraria colonial (1497–1820)*, 259, reproduces a general order to all provinces, signed November 1581.

88. Ruiz Medrano, *Mexico's Indigenous Communities*, 9, 92, and n9.

89. See Solano, *Cedulario de tierras*, 269–75.

90. Gibson, *Los aztecas*, 295; Martínez, *Codiciaban la tierra*, 158–59; Marcelo Ramírez Ruiz, "Territorialidad, pintura y paisaje del pueblo de indios," 168–227, esp. 187; and Ruiz Medrano, "El espejo y su reflejo," 173–76, and *Mexico's Indigenous Communities*, 102.

91. Ruiz Medrano, *Mexico's Indigenous Communities*, 67–68.

92. Ruiz Medrano, *Mexico's Indigenous Communities*, 9.

93. See Solano, *Cedulario de tierras*, 269–75.

94. Pérez-Rocha, *La tierra*, 49.

95. Ruiz Medrano, "El espejo y su reflejo," 173–76, and *Mexico's Indigenous Communities*, 100–105.

96. See, for example, Stephanie Wood, "The Social vs. Legal Context of Nahuatl Títulos," 201–31, esp. 205n8; Amos Megged, "El 'Relato de Memoria' de los axoxpanecas (Posclásico Tardío a 1610 DC)," 114–15, 119, 128–29, and nn38–39; and Amos Megged, *Social Memory*, 262–65, 271.

97. Ruiz Medrano, "El espejo y su reflejo," 173–74, 176, and *Mexico's Indigenous Communities*, 100–101, 103, 105.

98. Menegus Bornemann, *Del señorío indígena a la república de indios*, 219–25.

99. AGN, CDTT, Caja 1, Exp. 5, nf.

100. See Robert Haskett, "Paper Shields: The Ideology of Coats of Arms in Colonial Mexican Primordial Titles," 104–5.

101. Haskett, "Paper Shields," 105.

102. AGN, Hospital de Jesús, Leg. 79, Exp. 4.

103. Juan Dubernard Chauveau, *Códices de Cuernavaca y unos títulos de sus pueblos*, 292.

104. CLCP, f. 14r., reproduced in Haskett, *Visions of Paradise*.

105. Haskett, *Visions of Paradise*, 253.

106. From the Nahuatl *coliu* (to lean over), thence *coliuhqui* (curved) and *colli* (ancestor), Siméon, *Diccionario*, 123, and [al]*tepetl* (literally [water]-mountain), a common term for a polity and/or its territory, Siméon, *Diccionario*, 21.

107. See, among others, Haskett, *Visions of Paradise*, 69–84.

108. The imported Spanish term *a/por los cuatro vientos* (as opposed to *a/por las cuatro direcciones*) starts to appear frequently in colonial documentation of the second half of the sixteenth century. When it became part of the jargon of colonial land directives is not clear.

ELEANOR WAKE

CHAPTER 10

Making Indigenous Archives

The Quilcaycamayoc of Colonial Cuzco

Kathryn Burns

In 1936 a Parisian press brought out a "new chronicle" that had been submitted for publication in Spain over three centuries earlier. King Philip III, the intended audience for this twelve-hundred-page critique of Spanish colonialism, probably never saw it. But the *Nueva corónica y buen gobierno* has since circulated widely. Its Andean author, Felipe Guaman Poma de Ayala, has become emblematic of the native intermediary and of those critical colonial locations Mary Louise Pratt calls "contact zones": "social spaces where cultures meet, clash, and grapple with each other, often in contexts of highly asymmetrical relations of power"[1] (see also Durston, chapter 7).

Yet Guaman Poma was hardly the only Andean to master alphabetic writing. He depicts another native Andean seated at a table, rosary before him, writing in Spanish (figure 10.1). Guaman Poma labels this man a notary or *escribano*. He would seem to be the indigenous equivalent of the ubiquitous Spanish notaries who made most of the colonial paper trail now available in Andean archives.[2] But Guaman Poma also labels this figure in Quechua as a *quilcaycamayoc*, or "paper-keeper," suggesting a parallel with the *quipucamayoc* or Andean keeper of records on knotted cords (*quipus*).[3]

Who is this intriguing figure? He is all but absent from the scholarly literature. Andean notaries nevertheless deserve our attention, I argue, for

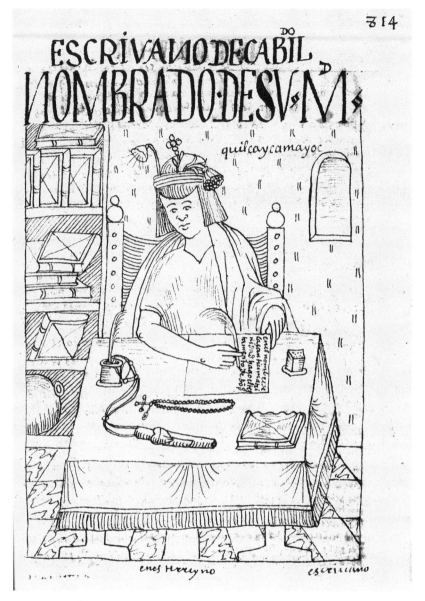

Figure 10.1. Felipe Guaman Poma de Ayala depicts an Andean notary, identified as both *escribano de cabildo* and *quilcaycamayoc*. Photograph supplied by The Royal Library, Copenhagen, Denmark, from manuscript GKS 2232 40.

fragments of the Spanish-language records they kept are still in the colonial record. This material, though sparse, suggests the productivity of the notary/quilcaycamayoc within a distinctively Andean "lettered city."[4] The contact zone of Spanish and Andean forms of expression opened up a range of possibilities to him as camayoc—a specialist in, or guardian of, archives. He was in a position to work both for *and* against his community's interests. The challenge for us is to flesh out our understanding of him as a historical actor rather than an emblem of the contact zone.

Competing Dreams of Andean Literacy

It is worth noting first that Spaniards and other Europeans came to trust the written word only after a lengthy historical process. Before the Norman Conquest in 1066, for example, the English relied primarily on memory to keep track of important things. Michael T. Clanchy argues that by the early 1300s a major cultural shift had occurred.[5] Influenced by growing medieval bureaucracies of various kinds, the English had come to trust writing more; they wanted written records. Clanchy emphasizes that this was a gradual historical process: "Documents did not immediately inspire trust. . . . People had to be persuaded—and it was difficult to do—that documentary proof was a sufficient improvement on existing methods to merit the extra expense and mastery of novel techniques which it demanded."[6] Reaching a comfort level with writing took the English some two-and-a-half centuries.[7]

When Andean peoples were invaded in the 1530s, they did not have the luxury of time. Faced with a sudden onslaught of Spaniards and new technologies, they had to make an almost instantaneous adjustment to the power of written documents or risk losing their most valuable possessions. And adjust they did, although I doubt the feelings they initially developed toward Spaniards' writings were those of trust. Consider Guaman Poma's account of the dramatic initial events at Cajamarca. The Inca Atahualpa and his companions were astonished that the Spaniards seemed not to sleep at all, had an immense appetite for silver and gold, and "spoke day and night with their papers" ("de día y noche hablauan cada uno con sus papeles, *quilca*").[8] I imagine Guaman Poma reproduces bits of oral traditions here, and this passage reflects quite well early modern European reading technique: people often read things aloud rather than silently.[9] Andeans, for their part, expected *huacas*—shrines and other sites of the sacred and powerful—to speak (see also Durston, chapter 7).[10] Thus when Atahualpa was handed the Dominican friar

Vicente's breviary in the famous scene that Guaman Poma recounts, he expected it to speak to him of the things the friar had told him it said. But when he leafed through the book, he did not get the response he expected: "¿Qué, cómo no me lo dize? ¡Ni me habla a mí el dicho libro!" ("Why won't it tell me? The book won't speak to me!")[11] Guaman Poma's account of this fatal misreading captures the enormous power of words on paper, quilca, and the high stakes for Andeans of coming rapidly to terms with Castilian literacy.[12]

Andeans immediately sought to master the skills and power of alphabetic writing for themselves. And the way to acquire those skills, in Peru as in Mesoamerica, was through the Church (see also Charles, chapter 3). Spanish missionaries relied heavily on native assistants from the start, which meant educating them to speak, read, and write competent Spanish.[13] By the mid-1500s, a fast-growing corps of lettered Andeans was working alongside Peru's missionaries. Fiscales accompanied and assisted priests in their day-to-day work of parish administration; sacristanes helped to maintain order in the church itself; and cantores led choral music, and so forth (see also Yannakakis, chapter 4).[14] The most prestigious post was that of fiscal. As John Charles has found, its occupants were often (though not necessarily) nobles, and in addition to acting as parish disciplinarians, they were charged with maintaining their parishes' Spanish-language archives: records of births, deaths, marriages, and confessions.[15] The earliest Andean makers of alphabetic archives were thus the Church's lettered assistants—a group who seems to have attained considerable autonomy and power by the 1560s and 1570s.[16] They were among the linguistic pioneers of written, Andean Spanish.[17]

Just how indigenous authorities began to use Spanish literacy outside the parish structure is a process that has yet to be studied. Unlike the Nahua of central Mexico—who, according to James Lockhart, "adapted to the post of notary quickly, successfully, and permanently" within two to three decades after the Spanish invasion—Andeans do not seem to have created a flourishing native-language notarial culture.[18] By mid-century, however, Andean leaders (kurakas and principales) were becoming adept at the use of legal petitions to defend their communities' resources before Spanish judges. Much of this advocacy probably happened by means of what Armando Petrucci calls "delegated writing": writing done not by Andean leaders themselves, but by intermediaries (such as the fiscales) at their behest.[19] At the same time, Andean leaders continued using the venerable record-keeping system of the quipu as they pressed their claims, adducing quipu-based evidence (which judges accepted).[20]

KATHRYN BURNS

Guaman Poma, himself a missionary's assistant during the 1560s and 1570s, vigorously advocated the spread of Spanish literacy beyond the parish realm. He did not press for the demise of the quipu—to the contrary, he wanted the use of quipus to continue—but he clearly believed that new tools were needed for new times.[21] Writing could be used by Spaniards in numerous ways against Andeans: for example, to spread falsehoods about them, and thwart the Crown's efforts to protect them. Indigenous authorities thus had to learn to write in Spanish themselves. All indigenous leaders, Guaman Poma insists, must learn—especially the art of composing legal petitions.[22] This knowledge could be dangerous: Guaman Poma cites examples of kurakas and principales who were harassed, even killed, for mounting a written defense of their communities.[23] Yet the overall sense one gets from Guaman Poma's passionate appeal to Philip III is that he *does* trust writing, as long as it is in Andeans' hands. He dreams of a day when all Andeans, men and women, boys and girls, will know how to write, and there will be native Andean saints as well as "jurists, lawyers, doctors, teachers, Indian men and women as well as Spanish men and women, to serve God our father and his Majesty."[24]

By the early 1600s, however, when Guaman Poma was advocating his vision of a fully literate society complete with Andean saints and letrados, other plans for Andean literacy had recently been laid by Peru's fifth viceroy, Francisco de Toledo (see also Ramos, chapter 1). This dogged administrator undertook thorough reforms during his long term of office (1569–81). He is best known for mandating reducción as part of his extensive ordinances concerning Indians: a program of forced resettlement of indigenous communities into Castilian-style towns.[25] But Toledo ordered many other things as well as he sought to impose the power of the Spanish state on native communities. His literacy program included schools for Andean children "so that children, especially the sons of chiefs, their principales, and other rich Indians, are taught to read and write and speak the Spanish language as His Majesty commands." To this end, he continued:

> a bilingual and capable Indian shall be found, of which there are a great number everywhere, to serve as teacher in the said school . . . and the priest shall name one who seems to him most capable and sufficient . . . and the children who are in school shall not reside there past the age of thirteen or fourteen years, so that they may go on to help their parents, and those who are sons of chiefs may stay longer and the poor ones less time.[26]

Exactly what were these literate children supposed to help their parents do? Toledo does not spell out what he intends here, but the ordinances in their entirety make it clear that, unlike Guaman Poma, he did not want children helping their parents to compose legal petitions. Toledo wanted *less* Andean litigiousness, not more: he aimed to curtail the voluminous petitioning that he regarded as a scourge ruining indigenous communities. And whatever amount of written petitioning there was he wanted to channel as much as possible through Spanish, not Andean, hands. Hence his efforts to limit the numbers of Spanish lawyers, *procuradores*, and other legal agents; to have specially designated Spanish judges (*jueces de naturales*) rather than far-away high courts (*audiencias*) decide indigenous cases; and so forth.[27]

Toledo's intentions are more clearly spelled out in a different portion of the ordinances regarding the offices he creates for administering the towns formed through forced resettlement. Here he seems to have accepted that he cannot simply legislate kurakas out of existence—but he can erect new, Spanish-style authorities to compete with and marginalize them. He thus decrees a set of local officials modeled on Spanish municipal ones. Just like Spanish officials, these men are to gather on New Year's Day each year to elect their replacements for the following year. Toledo specifies that there should be "two mayors (*alcaldes*) and four councilmen (*regidores*) and one constable (*alguacil*) and a notary or quipocamayo, and the latter shall serve for life as long as he is capable of doing so."[28] (Note that only one of them is supposed to serve for more than a year: the notary). The alcaldes were to exercise jurisdiction over local disputes, both civil and criminal, as long as large stakes were not involved. Any criminal suit that might merit the death penalty or other serious physical harm was to be sent to the corregidor, as well as any civil suit involving more than thirty pesos, allegations against caciques, or disputes between pueblos over land or labor. But the local pueblo authorities might decide many kinds of cases, including local-level disputes over land (*pleitos de chacras*).

Writing was not supposed to figure prominently in this scheme of pueblo-administered justice, however. In fact, Toledo specifically limited the amount of written records that Andean mayors and notaries could generate in their judicial role: "they shall not write, because they are to [administer justice] summarily."[29] (Summary justice meant cases were decided on the basis of oral arguments rather than written petitions.[30]) Still, the Toledan ordinances do single out one judicial occasion for making written records: that of criminal cases serious enough to merit forwarding to the corregidor. In such cases, people might have to be arrested and evidence taken from witnesses while their memories were still fresh. Thus pueblo authorities were ordered to do as follows: "they shall arrest the delinquents," who might be Spaniards or other non-Indians, "and when testimony has been taken they shall send everything to the said Magistrate so that he may punish them."[31] This is a most interesting deviation from Toledo's overall plan to rein in indigenous legal writing, and I will return to it below. First, let's note the one place in the Toledan ordinances where we find what we might call, tweaking Foucault's well-worn words a bit, an incitement to Andean writing: in the realm of *testamentos*, as people sought to manage death.

When it came to the form of the last will and testament, Toledo was an enthusiastic advocate of Andean writing, and his ordinances become positively prolix. Several pages are devoted to the subject, including specific instructions for a well-made will.[32] Dying well clearly mattered greatly to early modern Spaniards.[33] If we did not know this already, Toledo's orders alone would be enough to make us suspect it. He was particularly concerned about orderly inheritance, since according to him, "when an Indian man or woman dies and leaves property, those who are present take it for themselves, or those who arrive first, which leaves their children in poverty, if they left any, and nothing with which to do good works for their souls or settle their wills."[34] (As usual he could only think in terms of Castilian family and inheritance patterns; all else was "disorder.") And to be sure nothing was left to chance, he provided a detailed template for a will.

Toledo's template is much the same as the ones provided in Spanish notarial manuals.[35] Standard sections are laid out: first come masses and pious donations ("clausula de entierro y misas"); next, debts and assets ("clausula de deudas y bienes que dejan"); and so forth. But Toledo introduces changes that make this a template for a distinctively Andean will. For example, in listing assets, the indigenous testator is to be specific, "and if it is livestock, which shepherds keep it, and in which pastures, and who has the quipu of it."[36] Here Toledo implicitly acknowledges the continuing local-level practice of recording things on quipus. A dual recordation system does not seem to bother him as long as the proper order of things is maintained and a Spanish will is produced.[37] Even death could be annexed to his grand plan for reducción—for colonizing memory in written records, and thereby consolidating a new property regime in the Andes.

So Toledo's plan for Andean literacy aimed to limit Andean judicial writing—that is, making petitions and pleitos—while fomenting Andean extra-judicial writing, especially the production of wills. Clearly he was out to create Andean subjects who were both Christians and subalterns, who knew and obeyed the rules but did not contest them. He also wanted their access to writing channeled through reliable hands. Hence his orders for an ambidextrous new kind of pueblo authority, the "escribano o quipucamayo." As we might expect, drawing up wills was one of the main duties listed in the job description Toledo provided for this particular official. But he had other responsibilities for making and archiving written records about his pueblo. In the following passage we have Toledo's detailed orders about making an indigenous archive:

> First, each [notary] shall reside permanently in his pueblo to witness all the orders that all the mayors and councilmen may make in council meetings [cabildo] and otherwise . . . [NB: like Spanish council notaries]. Also, [the notary] shall be obliged to go expeditiously to draw up any wills, property lists, witness testimony, or other things pertinent to his office which he may be requested to do, whether in the community chest [caja de comunidad] or in any other business that needs to be written down for whatever purposes pursuant to the common good; because all the rest that the Indians customarily record on quipus, shall be reduced to writing by the hand of the said notary, so that it may be more accurate and durable, especially their absences from catechism and mass [faltas de doctrina] and the comings and goings of priests and their absences, and the same with respect to the magistrates and their lieutenants and other particular things that they commonly register on the said quipus, so that if they are asked to account for these things or it is in their interest to do so, [the account] shall be clearer, and better given, and the said notary shall make and write it without excuses, on penalty of losing the said office.[38]

This remarkable passage makes this particular indigenous official—the one with a lifetime job of maintaining his community's archives—a linchpin in Toledo's overall endeavor to "reduce" what he considered inferior Andean patterns and technologies to superior Spanish ones. It is hardly surprising that the viceroy considered quipus in need of translation ("que se reduzca a escritura"); he implies they are less accurate. But this passage seems to charge the indigenous notary with keeping written tabs on parishioners' church absences and priests' comings and goings, as well as those of corregidores. His role as outlined by Toledo makes him a kind of moral policeman.[39] Whether he wants to or not, he must do it "without excuses," so that if he is later asked to show a written account, he can do so. And his capacity to display his pueblo's business in writing could conceivably be used both for and against pueblo interests: whenever outsiders intervened ("cuando se les pidiere cuenta de ello") or whenever the pueblo wanted to make its case outside its borders ("o les convenga").

This word-portrait of an indigenous notary evokes Karen Spalding's acute depiction of Andean kurakas as a double-edged sword, capable of both hurting and protecting their communities because of the special powers entrusted to them.[40] If the notary did the job Toledo wanted him to, then he was integrally involved in disciplining Andean village life into more Castilian patterns.[41] But if he did the work Guaman Poma wanted Andean writers to do, then he protected his community from Spaniards' demands, using his quills and legal templates as defensive weapons. Whatever the case, we can only start to weave hypotheses if we can find some archival traces of these men. As we know, prescription was one thing in the colonial Andes; follow-through was another. To the extent that Toledo's orders were carried out, what kind of people were Andean notaries, and what did they do with writing?

Here Guaman Poma's illustrated manuscript from the early 1600s is once again useful. His escribano de cabildo is also labeled a "quilcaycamayoc," a keeper of papers (see figure 10.1). He appears to have an archive behind him: several books sitting on a bookshelf, and an earthen jar on the lowest shelf—perhaps a container for storing quipus.[42] If notaries did all that Toledo had instructed them to do, they would indeed have had such archives: translated, "reduced" quipus; actas del cabildo (council meeting records); the account books of their cajas de comunidad (community chests), and of course wills. And this notary is in the process of adding to it: he is shown writing the words "En el nombre de la Santícima Trinidad hago el testamento de don Pedro. . . ." He is in the process of making out a will. This visual clue links this drawing to a previous one, of indigenous boys being taught—some rather against their will—to write in Spanish (figure 10.2). The child in the front row is also writing notarial language, the two most-used words in the whole notarial repertoire: "Sepan cuantos . . ." ("Be it known to all . . ."). If schooling worked the way Toledo wanted, training mostly children from the indigenous elite, then indigenous notaries might well have been Andean nobles.

Other sources also suggest the existence of indigenous notaries by the early 1600s. One, the "Memorial de Charcas"—signed in 1582 by twenty-four kurakas of the Aymara "naciones" of Charka and Qaraqara and directed to royal authorities—requests exemption from tribute for those holding eccle-

Figure 10.2. Felipe Guaman Poma de Ayala depicts a choirmaster and schoolmaster teaching indigenous pupils, one of whom writes "*Sepan quantos*" ("Be it known to all"). Photograph supplied by The Royal Library, Copenhagen, Denmark, from manuscript GKS 2232 40.

siastical and other offices at the parish or pueblo level. The kurakas include in their list of offices those that Toledo had mandated just seven years earlier, in 1575. Intriguingly, their list starts with parish assistants, and seems to align the notary with them ("sacristanes, campaneros, fiscal y escribano del cabildo,") before proceeding to the newer, more secular indigenous authorities ("y a los alcaldes y regidores y alguacil mayor . . .").[43] Whether or not any newly mandated Toledan authorities had been installed in their communities by 1582 is not clear from this particular source.[44] Still, it seems to hint at the proximity of the escribanos de cabildo and the preexisting fiscales. In theory, both of these men kept important community archives. Perhaps in many places they were the same man.

Clearer evidence of an indigenous notariate appears in the confessional manual by Juan Pérez Bocanegra, published in Lima in 1631. Pérez Bocanegra had served for many years both as parish priest in Andahuaylillas ("Antahuaylla la chica"), near Cuzco, and as linguistic examiner in Quechua and Aymara for his diocese. Like many others before and after him, he was concerned by the linguistic chasm that separated his fellow priests from their parishioners. He thus provides detailed instructions on how to confess Indians effectively: how to tell when they are lying (liars, according to him, swallow their saliva a lot, jiggle their knees, cough, and look from side to side); how to recognize their most common errors; and what specific questions to ask them (see also Yannakakis, chapter 4). Among the questions he provides is a list of fourteen "that should be asked of Indian notaries." These focus from the start (and throughout) on making wills: "1. Have you ever made a false testament? Did you do it because you were ordered to by the Priest, or the Corregidor, or the Curaca, the husband or wife of the sick person, or someone else? What did they give you in order to induce you to falsify it?"[45] Again, the notary appears heavily involved in parish business; this is, after all, a confessional manual. Pérez Bocanegra's exclusive focus on will making makes it appear to be the indigenous notary's main duty.

These published sources from the early 1600s raise at least as many questions as they answer. Indigenous Andean notaries do seem to have existed in some places (like Andahuaylillas, just south of Cuzco), but firmly within the parish orbit, their duties perhaps merging with those of indigenous fiscales. We are left to wonder how much of a cabildo structure Andean pueblos actually created for themselves in the wake of Toledo's reducciones. Did these indigenous authorities—including the notary—exist in any significant numbers? And did the indigenous notary's pen produce more than parishioners' testaments?

Making Colonial Archives: The Escribanos de Cabildo

Thanks to sources from the Archivo Regional del Cuzco, we can answer at least some of the questions I have posed. They indicate that by the late 1500s, escribanos de cabildo not only existed in substantial numbers but also produced a variety of documents. Take the case of Pedro Quispe of Cuzco. In a couple of loose notebooks or *registros* that once belonged to a much more extensive volume, he kept the notarized records of indigenous parishioners' business, signing himself, "I, Pedro Quispe, notary public and of the cabildo for His Majesty in the parish of Our Lady of Purificación of the Hospital for Natives"[46] (figure 10.3). The fragmentary record that remains of his work consists largely of wills, codicils, death certificates, and *inventarios* (property lists). Clearly Quispe spent a lot of time in the Hospital de Naturales around priests and sick and dying patients. But he also made other kinds of records. Take, for example, a sale entered into by a woman named Isabel Tocto Coca, whose 1586 contract indicates that she needed to settle a debt of thirty-eight pesos left by her deceased first husband Antón Aymara. The contract is by Spanish standards unusually explicit about the motive: "because she could hardly afford to pay because she had no money and even less [did she have] movable assets of any kind of which she was not in great need, she considered it the best remedy to sell a straw hut [*buhio*] which the said Anton Aymara her husband left in the said parish."[47]

A few years later, the notary Pedro Quispe had acquired another job. He worked alongside Cuzco's *juez de naturales*, a Spanish judge elected annually by the city council to hear the suits brought before him by indigenous *cuzqueños* (people of Cuzco).[48] The Archivo Regional del Cuzco contains a partial record by Quispe of the kind of summary justice that Toledo had wanted judges to administer in indigenous cases. This material, all of it in excellent Spanish, gives us a remarkably textured look at day-to-day frictions in urban indigenous life. For example, on June 10, 1595, Juan Tupia, a regidor in the Cuzco parish of Belén, lodged a complaint against Don Gerónimo Chanca Topa for drunkenly resisting Tupia's orders to make him contribute labor to the local church. Pedro Quispe recorded Tupia's account of Don Gerónimo's conduct as follows: "he resisted and mistreated [Tupia], joined by some *montañeses* who were his kinsmen, and they tore his shirt, and thus he displayed it before

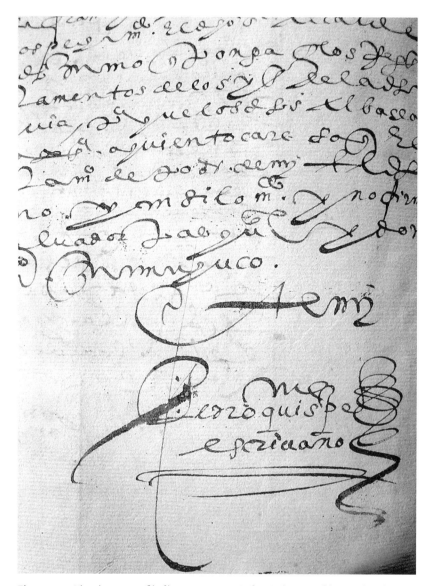

Figure 10.3. The signature of indigenous notary Pedro Quispe. Archivo Regional de Cusco, Protocolos notariales, Pedro de la Carrera Ron, protocolo 4 (1586–96). Photograph by Kathryn Burns.

the judge and asked him to order [Don Gerónimo] punished."[49] This is the only time I have seen the term "montañés" in a colonial document. According to the Inca Garcilaso, it was used in sixteenth-century Cuzco to signify "mestizo," but he considered it an insult, and the term seems to have disappeared from local usage.[50] We cannot be sure whether this was Tupia's term or Quispe's. But this is definitely not legalese. Thus Quispe provides us some remarkable glimpses, not only of local dilemmas and frictions, but also of cuzqueños' terms for those involved in them.

Nor was Pedro Quispe alone. The names of other escribanos de cabildo turn up in the Cuzco archives, too. Usually their work is mentioned in connection with someone's will, but not always. In 1702, for example, an indigenous widow named doña Leonor María petitioned to have fresh titles made for her house, indicating that the original sales contract had been stolen by robbers, and that it had been drawn up by her parish notary, don Bartolomé Roque Ynga, "who was the escribano de cabildo of the said parish [of the Hospital de Naturales]."[51] Two years later, a different local widow, doña María Asa Ñusta of the parish of San Sebastián, had her parish notary, don Nicolás Quispe Amaro, draw up a sales contract for her.[52] Cuzco's escribanos de cabildo thus do seem to have merged with the local parish hierarchy that existed prior to Toledo's reforms (and may well have maintained the archives that were once in fiscales' hands). John Charles argues that the Toledan cabildo structure—of alcaldes, regidores, alguaciles mayores, and notary— "gave religious officialdom its definitive form, especially in the more populated indigenous settlements."[53]

However, this is the city, where we might expect a paper trail to form sooner or later. What about the countryside, where most Andeans lived? By the 1590s, a fairly dense network of escribanos de cabildo had been established in the pueblos of the Cuzco region. This much is indicated in the records of the *residencia* (official inspection) that began late in November 1596 when a new corregidor arrived in Cuzco.[54] Don Gabriel Paniagua de Loaysa ordered that all those living in the region receive notice of the residencia so they might testify of any officials' malfeasance under his predecessor, don Antonio de Osorio. A handful of indigenous messengers subsequently fanned out across the region to notify the authorities in each pueblo to announce the edict of the residencia and send back notarized word that they had done so. This created a fascinating paper trail of more than three dozen notarized certificates. About half the signatures of the escribanos de cabildo are preceded by the honorific "don," which suggests they were noblemen.

KATHRYN BURNS

No two of these certificates are exactly alike, yet all display excellent Spanish. Many also give the names of several other pueblo authorities. In Quiquijana, for example, notary don Domingo Luis certified on November 24, 1596, that he had given formal notice of the edict "to don Diego Tasmi and don Alonso Yunga Guaman alcaldes ordinarios and to the other regidores of this said pueblo and they responded and said that they heard and obeyed and complied with it . . . before witnesses Miguel Naca Yapa and Francisco Yuto cantores of the church of this aforementioned pueblo."[55] The central place of the Church in community life figures saliently in other certificates as well. In Chinchero, notary don Cristóbal de Betanzos certified that "all the Indians obeyed and understood [the edict] in the cemetery of the church and Alonso Cusiguaman the Indian crier [yndio pregonero] announced [it] before the alcalde don Agustín Turo Manya [and] the witnesses were don Cristóbal Conde and don Pedro Jaime and don Diego Caqui."[56] Only two certificates were signed by interim notaries (escribanos nombrados). Two decades after Toledo's ordinances, then, a remarkably complete network of pueblo officials had come into existence in the Cuzco region, including escribanos de cabildo capable of producing Spanish documents.[57]

Other fragments of pueblo writing also turn up in the Archivo Regional del Cuzco. Let's return to the passage in Toledo's ordinances that I cited earlier as being somewhat against the grain of his overall effort to limit Andean litigiousness. Toledo required pueblo authorities to take matters into their own hands in serious criminal cases: they had to arrest and depose witnesses before forwarding the prisoners and paperwork to higher authorities. Some bits of this kind of writing do turn up among the lawsuits in the Cuzco archive. In 1638, for example, the indigenous alcalde of Guarocondo, don Francisco Guamantica, deposed witnesses to a fight that had broken out in someone's house one Sunday when Baltazar Bayon, a "mestizo dressed like an Indian" (mestizo en hábitos de indio), could not cover his gambling losses and allegedly attacked the man who had won. Papers transferring jurisdiction to the corregidor of Cuzco were drawn up, signed by both the alcalde Guamantica and don Diego Ñaupa Conchoy, the escribano de cabildo.[58] All is recorded in perfect Spanish and obeys conventional procedures.

But there are other varieties of rural Andean writing that do not derive from Toledan orders and expectations. Pueblos might keep books of their land records, libros de repartición de tierras, and these were probably also in the hands of the escribanos de cabildo. Perhaps these were mandated during the late sixteenth-century land sales known as composiciones de tierras (see also

Wake, chapter 9).[59] In any case, their overall purpose seems to have been more about meeting communities' needs than about meeting outsiders' expectations. This comes through in a late seventeenth-century petition from the kurakas of Anta to recover their book from the authorities in Cuzco after it was requisitioned and kept for more than a year and a half. The book had been taken away in connection with a lawsuit over tribute, even though, as the petitioning kurakas pointed out, the book did not contain tribute data at all. They protested their need for it to settle local land conflicts: "Every day lawsuits arise over the said lands, involving Indians as well as others who extend claims further than they have a right to, and . . . by the aforesaid book we can recognize the boundaries and markers [mojones] that each should observe."[60] The kurakas' request was eventually honored. When the book was returned to them in September 1697, the (Spanish) notary who certified its devolution described it as comprising 203 folios, the first nineteen and last thirteen of which were "torn and rotted" with age.[61]

Finally, there are petitions for justice. These never stopped, though Toledo and other Spanish authorities did their best to discourage them and to channel justice through summary proceedings and Spanish hands. Pueblo authorities kept bringing petitions to both ecclesiastical and secular judges, working through official Spanish go-betweens when necessary. Take, for example, an unusual cover letter from Cuzco's archives dated November 23, 1650. It came from a kuraka of Oropesa named don Diego Gualpanina. We cannot be certain this document was actually written by Gualpanina's own hand, since writing, including signatures, often happened through literate underlings. But there is a good chance Gualpanina penned it himself. Writing to the protector de naturales in Cuzco, don Pedro de Olivera, whom he addresses as his "Amo y Señor," Gualpanina asks him to do something about a local hacendado named Francisco de Alarcón, who has been holding an elderly Indian laborer against his will.[62] And Olivera did what he was requested to do: he filed a lawsuit before Cuzco's corregidor. We do not know how the case ends, as the record is incomplete, but Francisco de Alarcón was detained in the Cuzco jail and interrogated as a result of Gualpanina's written denunciation.[63]

In conclusion, then, Guaman Poma's "quilcaycamayoc" did exist in significant numbers by the 1590s, at least in the Cuzco region. While not the sole handler of his community's written business, he maintained its archives, probably merging municipal and ecclesiastical records in one repository. Many of these Andean notaries seem to have been nobles. In any case, to go

KATHRYN BURNS

by the available fragments, these men were bilingual, probably quipu-literate cultural intermediaries who by the late sixteenth century had brought the forms of Spanish colonial rule to the pueblo level, at least in the southern Andean highlands.

This certainly obliges us to rethink the exclusivity of what Angel Rama called la ciudad letrada. With its privileged relationship to the written word, this figurative city-within-a-city—"a myriad of administrators, educators, professionals, notaries, religious personnel, and other wielders of pen and paper"—wielded great influence. Rama stressed "the letrados' drastic exclusivity and strict concentration in urban centers."[64] He included among his examples the creole luminaries Sor Juana Inés de la Cruz and Carlos Sigüenza y Góngora. But Rama's construct, useful as it is, overdraws the cities' isolation from their hinterlands and neglects the extent to which transculturation was a two-way street. The figure of the escribano de cabildo reminds us that native writers were part of the lettered city. Their work went on in rural towns and villages as well as in urban parishes. And Toledo's very designation of the native notary—as "escribano de cabildo o quipucamayo"—indicates the transculturated nature of their activities.

Whose interests did these Andean notaries serve? Their job was designed to secure Spanish domination, enabling Spanish authorities to "see like a state" and check up on Andean communities' numbers and productive capacity, as well as their observance of basic rites of Christianity.[65] Yet it simultaneously prepared them to defend their communities in writing. At present we know so little about these men that we should neither imagine them as linchpins of indigenous resistance nor damn them as agents of their communities' subjugation to Spanish control; they could have acted as both, or neither. No doubt much depended on their relationship to their communities' kurakas and other authorities (and these relations surely varied from place to place, as well as over time).[66] If we keep these escribanos de cabildo in mind as we page through the extant colonial archive, we are likely to learn more.

The figure of the escribano de cabildo also raises several questions for us that may not be easy to answer but are still worth asking. How did Spanish forms change when they were put in indigenous notaries' hands and became, to some extent, a medium for transmitting quipu-based knowledge? If Guaman Poma's obra maestra can be seen as a kind of "textual contact zone," as Galen Brokaw suggests, "in which the metatextual principles of khipu and alphabetic literacies vie for position," can something similar be seen in the more quotidian writing of Andean notaries?[67] Gradual incorporation of Spanish loanwords into Mesoamerican notaries' native-language records has been a focal point of analysis for James Lockhart and others, who use it to gauge overall "rapprochement" between native and Spanish culture.[68] Andean notarial records are different: they are already in Spanish. Yet as José Luis Rivarola has shown, Andean Spanish also changed across time and space as its users grew more familiar with the language and honed their capabilities. Indigenous notarial writing, to the extent that we can locate it, will give us important insight into this process.

As for quipus, their use has lasted far longer in the Andes than was once supposed. Frank Salomon's ethnographic work in the pueblos of Tupicocha and Rapaz demonstrates the quipu's remarkable versatility as a means of certifying authority.[69] But this is hardly a precolonial survival. Rather, quipu use has always changed to suit communities' changing needs. Mercedarian friar Martín de Murúa witnessed this in the 1590s in the parish where he had taught *doctrina*:

> I saw an Indian, an elderly curaca, who had on one of those long cords the entire Roman calendar and all the saints' days and festivals, and he gave me to understand how and by what means he knew it, and that he had asked a very inquisitive friar of my order a few years ago to read him the calendar and explain it to him, and that as the friar read it to him he put it on his quipu, and it was an amazing thing to see the way in which the old man understood it as though it were in paper and ink.[70]

As quipus were yoked to new purposes beyond doctrinal ones, and people began to want (or require) written, notarized records, how did this change quipu use?[71] How, in other words, did these varieties of literacy inflect each other? How were alphabetic and quipu archives related?

Above all, it seems important not to hold these archives too separate— and to imagine one as present and the other as lost. Unfortunately, due to the Spanish Empire's archival politics and those of its successor republic, the records that Andean pueblo notaries made were not gathered together and preserved, except in fragments that occasionally turn up or receive mention. But the escribanos de cabildo were not the only Andeans who wrote. So did many indigenous parish assistants. Kurakas wrote, too, and had others write for them when they did not manage the technology themselves. And don Diego Gualpanina's cover letter indicates that when we are reading the words of a Spanish lawsuit filed by a Spanish official like the protector de naturales, we may be reading words more or less ventriloquized by an Andean authority like don Diego Gualpanina. Spanish and Andean archives may not be as separate as we might think. One may actually bleed through the other more than we suppose. For if Guaman Poma's dream of a fully literate Andean society was not realized, neither was Toledo's vision of docile Andeans who did not talk or write back.

Notes

1. Mary Louise Pratt, "Arts of the Contact Zone."

2. On notaries, see James Lockhart, *Spanish Peru: A Colonial Society*, 68–76; Tamar Herzog, *Mediación, archivos y ejercicio: Los escribanos de Quito (siglo XVII)*; and Kathryn Burns, *Into the Archive: Writing and Power in Colonial Peru*.

3. This contemporary Cuzco usage is confirmed by the Spanish Jesuit Diego González Holguín (1552–1618), whose *Vocabulario de la lengua general de todo el Perú llamada lengua Qqichua o del Inca*, 301, defines "Quellca" as "Papel carta, o escriptura," and "Quellcaycamayok" as "El escriuano de officio, o el gran escriuidor."

4. Angel Rama, *La ciudad letrada*, available in English as *The Lettered City*.

5. Michael T. Clanchy, *From Memory to Written Record: England 1066–1307*, 185–96.

6. Clanchy, *From Memory to Written Record*, 294.

7. This trust was not unmitigated; to the contrary, as I show in "Notaries, Truth, and Consequences," early modern Europeans might be quite suspicious of official writing and the mediations and conventions that produced it.

8. Felipe Guaman Poma de Ayala, *El primer nueva corónica y buen gobierno*, 2: 353.

9. Paul Saenger, "Silent Reading: Its Impact on Late Medieval Script and Society," and *Space between Words: The Origins of Silent Reading*.

10. Gonzalo Lamana, *Domination without Dominance: Inca-Spanish Encounters in Early Colonial Peru*, 57–59.

11. Guaman Poma, *El primer nueva corónica*, 2: 357. Unless otherwise noted, all translations are mine.

12. As Lamana points out in *Domination*, 58, "painting" (*quilca, quillca, quellca*) was the closest Quechua term to "book"; and by Guaman Poma's day it seems also to have meant "paper."

13. On indigenous education, see Juan Carlos Estenssoro Fuchs, *Del paganismo a la santidad: La incorporación de los indios del Perú al catolicismo, 1532–1750*; and Monique Alaperrine-Bouyer, *La educación de las elites indígenas en el Perú colonial*. A byproduct of this transcultural learning process was "pastoral Quechua," as Alan Durston aptly calls it (*Pastoral Quechua: The History of Christian Translation in Colonial Peru*).

14. Alan Durston, *Pastoral Quechua, 1550–1650*, 76–81, 273–75, 282–84; and Guaman Poma, *El primer nueva corónica*, 2: 624–36.

15. John Charles, "Indios Ladinos: Colonial Andean Testimony and Ecclesiastical Institutions (1583–1650)," 124: "Chief among their obligations was to assist parish priests

in keeping account of native births, marriages, and deaths (for the purpose of administering to parishioners the appropriate sacramental rites), and informing local clergy of any surviving native religious practices, including ceremonial dance [taki] and ritual drunkenness."

16. Charles, "Indios Ladinos," discusses Toledo's efforts to abolish the office of fiscal, a quest that ultimately proved unsuccessful.

17. José Luis Rivarola, Español andino: Textos bilingües de los siglos XVI y XVII.

18. James Lockhart, The Nahuas after the Conquest: A Social and Cultural History of the Indians of Central Mexico, Sixteenth through Eighteenth Centuries, 40–41. Tom Cummins has argued that the cultural distance between Andean and Spanish literacies proved too great for the quipucamayoc to bridge; see "Representation in the Sixteenth Century and the Colonial Image of the Inca," in Writing without Words: Alternative Literacies in Mesoamerica and the Andes, 194–95.

19. Armando Petrucci, Prima lezione di paleografia, 25.

20. Carmen Beatriz Loza, "Du bon usage des quipus face à l'administration coloniale espagnole (1500–1600)."

21. See, for example, Guaman Poma, El primer nueva corónica, 2: 746–47, regarding indigenous regidores: "tenga libro qvipo, cv[en]ta." As Charles notes in "Indios Ladinos," though some clerics opposed it, quipu use had worked its way into parish practice by Guaman Poma's day, with native assistants helping parishioners make quipus for catechism and confession (114–15).

22. Guaman Poma, El primer nueva corónica, 2: 718–19: "que sepa hazer una petición, enterrogatorio y pleyto."

23. El primer nueva corónica, 2: 542, regarding priests' persecution of "un prencipal" who was literate and stood up to the local Spanish authorities; see also 2: 458–63 regarding Don Cristóbal de León, segunda persona.

24. El primer nueva corónica, 3: 729: "letrados, lesenciados, dotores, maystros, yndios, yndias como españoles, españolas para serbir a Dios nuestro señor y a su Magestad." For more on this point, see Rocío Quispe-Agnoli, La fe andina en la escritura: resistencia e identidad en la obra de Guaman Poma de Ayala.

25. For an important revisionary study of Toledan reducciones, see Jeremy Ravi Mumford, Vertical Empire: The Struggle for Andean Space in the Sixteenth Century.

26. Guillermo Lohmann Villena and María Justina Sarabia Viejo, Francisco de Toledo: Disposiciones gubernativas para el virreinato del Perú, 2: 251.

27. Peru's "Indian justice" system has yet to be studied in depth; see Woodrow Borah, "Juzgado general de Indios del Perú o Juzgado particular de Indios de El Cercado de Lim"; and on the General Indian Court of Mexico, see Woodrow Borah, Justice by Insurance: The General Indian Court of Colonial Mexico and the Legal Aides of the Half-Real.

28. Lohmann Villena and Sarabia Viejo, Francisco de Toledo, 2: 218. For additional historical context, see Waldemar Espinoza Soriano, "El alcalde mayor indígena en el virreinato del Perú."

29. Lohmann Villena and Sarabia Viejo, Francisco de Toledo, 2: 222.

30. See Joaquín Escriche, Diccionario razonado de legislación civil, penal, comcercial y forense, 359, regarding the juicio sumario: "Aquel en que se conoce brevemente de la causa, des-

preciando las largas solemnidades del derecho, y atendiendo solamente á la verdad del hecho."

31. Lohmann Villena and Sarabia Viejo, *Francisco de Toledo*, 2: 224. Just in case, a subsequent ordinance elaborates: "si algún español agraviare a algún indio, mestizo, mulato o negro . . . permito que le prendan y lleven preso ante el Corregidor con información del agravio que hubiere hecho" (2: 229).

32. Lohmann Villena and Sarabia Viejo, *Francisco de Toledo*, 2: 229–32. For a slightly earlier Mesoamerican template, made by a Franciscan friar in 1569, see Sarah Cline, "Fray Alonso de Molina's Model Testament and Antecedents to Indigenous Wills in Spanish America," 1–33.

33. See Carlos M. N. Eire, *From Madrid to Purgatory: The Art and Craft of Dying in Sixteenth-Century Spain*; and Gabriela Ramos, *Death and Conversion in the Andes: Lima and Cuzco, 1532–1670*.

34. Lohmann Villena and Sarabia Viejo, *Francisco de Toledo*, 2: 229.

35. On the Spanish notarial literature that circulated extensively in Spanish America, see Jorge Luján Muñoz, "La literatura notarial en España e Hispanoamérica"; and Kathryn Burns, "Notaries, Truth, and Consequences." Juan de la Ripia wrote a manual dedicated exclusively to the subject of correct preparation of wills, *Practica de testamentos y modos de subceder*.

36. Lohmann Villena and Sarabia Viejo, *Francisco de Toledo*, 2: 230.

37. See Guaman Poma's counterproposal, *El primer nueva corónica*, 2: 478, modeled on the 1612 will of Don Cristóbal de León. Guaman Poma underscores the need to keep priests from making off with the property of the deceased—not other Indians.

38. Lohmann Villena and Sarabia Viejo, *Francisco de Toledo*, 2: 237–38. I am grateful to Ari Zighelboim for his insight into this passage. In earlier editions of Toledo's ordinances, both Thomas Ballesteros and Roberto Levillier put the native notary's quipu-translating project in his "hands" ("mano" rather than "mando"); I have followed them in my translation.

39. Toledo outlines a job description similar to that of the Andean parish fiscal, an office he tried unsuccessfully to abolish. See Charles, "Indios Ladinos," 127: "Typically, each parish employed one or two fiscales who were named by the bishop for an indefinite period. . . . They tended the newborn and sick in their spiritual needs, kept guard against heterodox religious practices and illicit cohabitations, and maintained a sacramental register for all native parishioners."

40. Karen Spalding, *Huarochirí: An Andean Society under Inca and Spanish Rule*, especially 209–38.

41. Perhaps they engaged in some malpractice as well: Lockhart, in *The Nahuas after the Conquest*, 218, mentions Nahua notaries of Culhuacán who manipulated the wills of members of their community in order to profit from the property they left. Such manipulations by Spaniards and creoles in various parts of Spanish America seem to have been common enough, to go by the frequency with which they were denounced and legislated against.

42. Archaeologists have found quipus stored inside such ceramic containers. I thank Gary Urton for helping me "read" this possibility in Guaman Poma's drawing.

43. Tristan Platt, Thérèse Bouysse-Cassagne, and Olivia Harris, *Qaraqara-Charka: Mallku, Inka y Rey en la provincia de Charcas (siglos XV–XVII): Historia antropológica de una confederación aymara*, 834.

44. Indeed, another source in the same collection indicates that when corregidor Miguel Ruiz de Bustillo passed through the pueblo of Macha in 1613 to audit its community chest (caja de comunidad), he found no archives to inspect; according to him, the kurakas had seized everything and done what they wanted with it. He responded by installing a local principal, don Sebastián Paria, as escribano de cabildo; Platt, Bouysse-Cassagne, and Harris, *Qaraqara-Charka*, 785–86. My thanks to Tristan Platt for providing me these references.

45. Juan Pérez Bocanegra, *Ritual formulario e institucion de curas, para administrar a los naturales de este reyno, los santos sacramentos del baptismo, confirmacion, eucaristia y viatico, penitencia, extremauncion, y matrimonio, con advertencias muy necessarias*, 277–78: "As hecho algun testamento falso? hizistelo por que te lo mandò el Padre (278) ò el Corregidor, ó el Curaca, el marido, ó la muger del enfermo, ó otra persona? que te dieron porque lo hiziesses falsamente?"

46. "Yo Pedro quispe escrivano pu[blico] y de cavildo por Su Mag[esta]d en la perroquia de nuestra s[eñor]a de purificacion del [H]ospital de los Naturales," in Archivo Regional de Cusco, Protocolos Notariales (hereafter ARC-PN), Pedro de la Carrera Ron, protocolo 4 (1586–96), unbound notebook marked with a strip of paper that says Pedro Quispe, 1586–87, fol. 652v., death certificate of "Jhoan ninamanco yndio pechero en la dha parroquia . . . jueves a las doze del dia [20 febrero 1586]."

47. ARC-PN, Pedro de la Carrera Ron, protocolo 4 (1586–96), unbound notebook of Pedro Quispe, 1586–87, fols. 650v–51: "visto el poco remedio que tenia de poderle pagar porque dineros no los tenia ni menos bienes muebles ni de otro genero de que no tenga grande necesidad entendio ser el mas comodo remedio vender un buhio de paxa que el dho anton aimara su marido dexo en la dha parroquia."

48. ARC-PN, Corregimiento, Causas Ordinarias, Leg. 2 (1587–1602), Exp. 46 (1595), Cuaderno 25. This too is a fragment of what was once a more extensive record; it begins on fol. 167 and ends on fol. 190, and contains documents from June and part of July 1595.

49. "Se resistió y le maltrató juntamente con unos montañeses sobrinos suyos y le rompieron la camiseta y así lo manifestó ante el dicho juez y pidió a su merced le mande castigar."

50. Inca Garcilaso de la Vega, *Comentarios Reales de los Incas*, 2: 627–28.

51. ARC-PN, Cabildo, Justicia Ordinaria, Causas Civiles, Leg. 14 (1700–1704), Exp. 423 (1702), cuaderno 17. Don Bartolomé also appears in a 1654 lawsuit (ARC-PN, Corregimiento, Causas Criminales, Leg. 77 (1582) Leg. 1693), suing other indigenous nobles for trying to usurp his lands. A member of the city's proud Inca nobility, he seems to confirm for Cuzco's native notariate the pattern that Lockhart and others have seen among Mesoamerican notaries: they were often local nobles. See, for example, Lockhart, *The Nahuas after the Conquest*, 41.

52. ARC-PN, Cabildo, Justicia Ordinaria, Causas Civiles, Leg. 14 (1700 Leg. 1704), Exp. 431 (1704), Cuaderno 25.

53. He draws on parish records from the early 1600s from the Hospital de Naturales, which "show that cabildo officials were the exclusive indigenous authorities of the parish" (Charles, "Indios Ladinos," 177). Thus the old parish hierarchy—of native fiscales et al.—was successfully displaced, at least in large urban centers like Cuzco. This was part of a larger agenda: "Toledo's reforms of the evangelization program (and those of his successors) obeyed a two-part strategy. First, he granted to corregidores and cabildo members religious duties that were previously associated with the retinue of the missionary priest. Then he moved to strip clergymen and parish assistants of any civil powers they had acquired as exclusive mediators of colonial government in native villages"; see Charles, "Indios Ladinos," 172.

54. ARC-PN, Miguel de Contreras, Leg. 5 (1596 Leg.1597), consists entirely of the record of this residencia.

55. ARC-PN, Miguel de Contreras, Leg. 5 (1596–97), fol. 46.

56. ARC-PN, Miguel de Contreras, Leg. 5 (1596–97), fol. 95.

57. José Luis Rivarola, *Español andino: Textos bilingües de los siglos XVI y XVII*, 41–44, publishes two similar certificates from Jauja (1591); both are by indigenous escribanos nombrados who write a Quechua-inflected Spanish (as do the Cuzco escribanos nombrados to a lesser degree). These temporary notaries may have been local parish officials; they are lettered but less familiar with the norms of written Spanish legalese.

58. ARC-PN, Cabildo, Justicia Ordinaria, Causas Civiles [Pedimentos], Leg. 112 (1571–1732). See also a 1654 lawsuit concerning a stolen horse (ARC, Corregimiento, Causas Criminales, Leg. 77 [1582–1693], Expediente dated April 20, 1654): documentation was remitted to Cuzco's corregidor from Maras, where several indigenous witnesses were sworn in and deposed by the alcalde ordinario don Francisco Mayllac. In this case depositions were taken without a notary, "a falta de escribano." Yet all is scrupulously correct; the proper forms are followed and the Spanish is flawless.

59. *Composiciones*, as Spalding explains (*Huarochirí*, 181), "were periodically ordered to throw lands defined as vacant onto the market," beginning in the late sixteenth century and continuing in the seventeenth century and early eighteenth century (see 181–83). ARC-PN, Corregimiento, Causas Criminales, Leg. 77 (1582–1693), Exp. July 1658: the record of a conflict over land rights between Alonso de Vargas Valdes and the indigenous community of Pantipata mentions the *libro de repartición de tierras* of Pantipata made by Lic. Alonso Maldonado de Torres, *oidor* (fol. 20); during the 1590s, this Spanish official carried out composiciones in the Cuzco region.

60. Cabildo, Justicia Ordinaria, Causas Civiles, Leg. 13 (1695–99), Exp. 391 (1697).

61. A comparable book is in the Archivo General de la Nación in Lima: see Derecho Indígena, L. 39, C. 807 (1671–1713), "Libro donde se asientan los contratos de arrendamientos que de sus tierras hacían los indios del pueblo de Surco," a leather-bound volume maintained by don Esteban Callha, escribano de cabildo. More commonly, pueblo authorities referred to their "títulos"—bundles of documents that comprised their claim to specific pieces of land. These documents were not written by community members themselves, but contained contracts, viceregal *amparos*, and other records that could be adduced before colonial judges to bolster land rights.

62. On this official Spanish "protector of natives," see Diana Bonnett, *El protector de*

naturales en la Audiencia de Quito, siglos XVII y XVIII; Bernard Lavallé, "Presión colonial y reivindicación indígena en Cajamarca (1785–1820) según el Archivo del 'Protector de Naturales.'"

63. ARC-PN, Corregimiento, Causas Criminales, Leg. 77 (1582–1693), expediente with cover letter dated November 23, 1650, preceding an incomplete lawsuit that consists of 7 fols.

64. Rama, *The Lettered City*, 23.

65. James C. Scott, *Seeing Like a State: How Certain Schemes to Improve the Human Condition Have Failed*.

66. Though Toledo wanted to keep caciques out of indigenous cabildos, they might nevertheless find their way in, and even dominate cabildos, during the late 1500s and the 1600s: see, for example, Jacques Poloni-Simard's detailed study of the Cuenca region, *El mosaico indígena: Movilidad, estratificación social y mestizaje en el corregimiento de Cuenca (Ecuador) del siglo XVI al XVIII*, 323–29. This cacical dominance began to be questioned in the 1700s, however, as cabildos gained importance and autonomy; see Poloni-Simard, *El mosaico indígena*, 475–81.

67. Galen Brokaw, "Khipu Numeracy and Alphabetic Literacy in the Andes: Felipe Guaman Poma De Ayala's *Nueva Corónica Y Buen Gobierno*," 300; see also Rocío Quispe-Agnoli, "Cuando Occidente y los Andes se encuentran: qellcay, escritura alfabética y tokhapu en el siglo XVI."

68. Lockhart, *The Nahuas after the Conquest*, 430.

69. See Frank Salomon, *The Cord Keepers: Khipus and Cultural Life in a Peruvian Village*, especially 126–27. Salomon observes that "[c]entral Huarochirí . . . is one of the three areas known to have preserved into modern times a political-civic khipu complex (as compared to herding and confessional khipus, which exist elsewhere)" (267). See also his book with Mercedes Niño-Murcia, *The Lettered Mountain*.

70. Martín de Murúa, *Códice Murúa: Historia y genealogía de los reyes incas del Perú del padre mercedario fray Martín de Murúa: Códice Galvin*, fol. 77v. Murúa goes on to compare preconquest quipus explicitly to notarial archives: "antiguamente tenian grandes montones destas cuentas a manera de Registros como los tienen los escrivanos y alli tenian sus archivos." For more on colonial cronistas' accounts, see Carlos Sempat Assadourian, "String Registries: Native Accounting and Memory According to the Colonial Sources," 119–50.

71. See Thomas A. Abercrombie, *Pathways of Memory and Power: Ethnography and History among an Andean People*, 213–314.

KATHRYN BURNS

Conclusion

Tristan Platt

The preceding chapters have offered ten perspectives on native American writing and plural literacies under Spanish rule. They illustrate the complexity and variety of colonial situations in different parts of the viceroyalties of Peru and New Spain. They draw on a wealth of new materials emerging from the archives. The theoretical implications are complex, but important for our understanding of national as well as colonial and even pre-Hispanic American societies. In conclusion, I offer an overview of some of the themes treated, adopting a perspective from the great urban-industrial hub of the early colonial Andes: Potosí, whose mines lay in the lands of the Aymara-speaking federation of Qaraqara, in the old Inka province of Charcas.[1]

The book interweaves analyses of the two viceroyalties, and the comparison is intriguing. Why were so many more native languages written down, and so much more extensively, in Mexico than in Peru? Why did so much linguistic variety disappear from colonial Peru, while persisting in Mexico? Regional situations differed, and Mexico was spared a viceroy like Francisco de Toledo, whose efforts to curb indian litigiousness may have screened out some Amerindian language texts that would otherwise have been filed by notaries.[2] But Gabriela Ramos underlines one key factor: the almost total opacity to Europeans of Andean *khipu* literacy in comparison with Mexican pictographs.[3] In Peru, some late sixteenth-century *khipukamayu* kept their khipus together with paper account books in their community chest, to register the delivery of tributes and laborers; but as the ink-written accounts were dependent on the khipu strings, they could not be audited by the Spanish, although in the 1570s some judges simply accepted the khipus, and had them and their keepers admitted as evidence.

Let us take the example of a late sixteenth-century scribe and khipukamayu from Macha, the pre-Hispanic capital of the Qaraqara federation. Don Andrés Tanquiri, head of one of the five *ayllus* of the Lower Moiety of Macha, was paid his salary from the town community chest. In 1584, he was closely involved in collecting and dispatching the Spanish tribute. He kept the basic quantitative data on his cords, and probably only transferred his information to paper and Arabic/Roman numerals for clearing the accounts with the Spanish *corregidor* of the province. His accounting expertise with both systems of literacy and numeracy was recognized by other senior authorities of Macha, as well as by the corregidor, when he was elected deputy lord (*segunda persona*) of Macha (Lower Moiety) by twelve Macha authorities (ten ayllu and two *moiety*) in 1584.

But the idea of the community chest as central archive was not always successful. When the corregidor came to oversee the accounts of another Macha community, this time of the Upper Moiety, he found no scribe, and "no sign of any papers, nor of the books set up for the good government of the community": all had been taken to their houses by the indian authorities, and "they have done whatever they wanted with them." This made it difficult for the corregidor to check and balance the books. His solution was to name a new indian scribe, ordering him to set out the legal cases as succinctly as possible before passing them on to the corregidor or to the indian *alcalde mayor* (lord mayor); he was also to draw up wills and testaments for the indians of the town.[4]

Andean customary procedure may have been for each khipukamayu to keep his own knotted cord accounts with him at all times, unless placed in a local group or state archive.[5] But in this case the scribes had also taken home the papers and books. They could then administer the Spanish tributes at their leisure from a "home archive," transferring to the books the demographic and fiscal data knotted into their khipus. After all, they alone knew all the details of the construction and coding of their khipus. But the corregidor complained because he couldn't exercise vigilance over a plural home-based graphic system.

This may suggest why, increasingly, colonial officials preferred representations to be made in Spanish in order to be able to audit more easily accounts and declarations which would otherwise be made in an Amerindian language, using an information technology that the Europeans were unable to fathom.[6] The use of interpreters could partially solve the linguistic problem, but not the audit problem, because the graphic system was not understood. This made it more difficult for an Andean *lingua franca* (such as Quechua) to play a role like the long-lived Nahuatl shadow régime who administered the Mixe language groups of Oaxaca, as described in fascinating detail by Yanna Yannakakis.

The impressive annals of Tlaxcala by don Juan Buenaventura and his group, described by Camilla Townsend, may be contrasted in the northern Andes with the Cañari, who also sided with the Spanish but soon found *their* language submerged beneath local Quechua.[7] This leads us to another explanatory factor proposed for the difference between Peru and Mexico: the greater degree of centralized control imposed by the Incas than in Mexico, where there were several rival cities since pre-Hispanic times. In the southern Andes, however, this view from Cusco may underestimate the Inka policy of adjusting their policies to each new province, sometimes resorting to blitzkrieg, but at others constructing hegemony through negotiation, and then renegotiating relations as the empire expanded.

Let us take an example. According to the dynastic tradition presented in 1638 by don Fernando Ayra de Ariutu, Mallku (Condor Chief) of the Qaraqara federation in whose territory lay the mining city of Potosí, his ancestor Tata Ayra Kanchi, lord of Macha and Chaquí, had sent an ambassador to Cusco in the mid-fifteenth century who "gave" Inka Pachakuti the idea of organizing the empire into "Four Parts" (the Tawantinsuyu). In reward for this gift of a principle of social, political, and (possibly) calendrical organization, the Inca gave Ayra Kanchi a woven map, probably a treaty document in the form of a fine textile with symbolic territorial designs.[8] Later, his people received from Inca Wayna Qhapaq the name of "Dawn" ("Caracara"; before, they had been known as the "White Charka," or *hanco charka*), suggesting they were to be recognized as the harbingers of the Inca Sun. We are reminded of the maps of "dawning places" made in Mexico, sometimes to accompany the *títulos primordiales*, whose pre-Hispanic astronomical coordinates are described here by Eleanor Wake.

This is an example of an Inka *pact of reciprocity* as a political and aesthetic exchange. In the silver-mining regions of the south, therefore, the idea of the pact was already present and ready to be updated in 1538, when Hernando

Pizarro and Gonzalo Pizarro invaded the Inka provinces of Collao and Charcas, accompanied by Inka Paullu and five thousand Pukina speakers from Hatun Qulla (Lake Titicaca), who were hereditary enemies of the Aymara. Wayna Qhapaq's silver mine in Porco was then formally transferred to King Charles v by the Aymara lords of Charcas. Only by reference to this revised pact can we make sense of their actions during the following decades.

Faced with the later destabilization of the pact, especially by Viceroy Toledo in the 1570s, the Charcas lords again insisted on Inka precedent in their famous *Memorial of 1582*.[9] Transformed into a "vassalage pact" with the king of Spain, the previous Inka treaty made plausible the ideology of a *translatio imperii*, whose forms and significance are studied here by María Elena Martínez.

It has been argued that khipus were a state-sponsored and centralized semasiography intelligible throughout the empire, and this may well be true of Inca policy and practice. However, Inka regional khipus were articulated with local traditions, especially among Aymara speakers who had developed their own "chinu literacy" (chinu means knot in Aymara). The idiosyncrasies and opacity of khipu construction meant that the Inca's fiscal khipus preserved in Chucuito were investigated in 1567 by Spanish inspectors using interpreters to produce Spanish-language *visitas*, rather than through any Andean equivalent of the *Codex Mendoza*. Today, our formal and typological understanding of numerical khipu continues to grow; but historical khipu are only intelligible through contemporary transcriptions made by Spanish notaries through interpreters translating the declarations made by Andean cord keepers.[10] And these lack the musical and poetic enhancement with which such histories were traditionally performed by a different group of experts, the singers, poets, and musicians.

But to all these considerations must be added the higher levels of colonial violence in Peru (especially in the south Andean *mita* catchment area). Peru differed from Mexico in what Assadourian calls its higher "coefficient of exploitation," which in Peru made tributary and labor prestations such oppressive institutions.[11] In Mexico, colonial policies such as the formation of indian towns (*congregaciones*) had first been implemented when Lascasian ideas were still powerful, and before the need for silver had overwhelmed the Royal Conscience. In Peru, on the other hand, Viceroy Toledo (1569–81) forced many Andean rural societies into poverty and desperation. After defending the king's title in America by having Sarmiento conflate the quipo histories of different Inka panacas to prove the Inka were "tyrants," Toledo travelled to Potosí at the end of 1572 to implement the new system of silver refining by amalgamation. But he also set labor obligations and a head tax on the basis of a fixed census in a context of demographic decline—something that the Inka would never have contemplated. The level of tribute paid by the indians of Peru was higher than in Mexico. And labor assignations in Mexico were light in comparison with the Potosí mita, reorganized by Viceroy Toledo in 1573 on the basis of Inka precedent: a fourteen-thousand-strong labor force, but now assigned to the silver mines instead of the maize plantations of Cochabamba as under Wayna Qhapaq.[12] Most of the laborers' subsistence and reproduction costs were covered by their rural communities, by their wives' retail activities in the marketplace, and by additional waged and/or unregulated labor during their so-called periods of "rest."

The Potosí mita was a colossal institution that required Toledo to negotiate with the south Andean Mallku and fiscal authorities over a vast area from Cusco to Porco. In the case of the Qaraqara, the Mallku resident in Macha had lost their southern province (Chaquí, where Porco and Potosí lay) following the formation of the colonial *corregimientos* of Chayanta and Porco according to García de Castro's *Ordenanzas* of 1565. They therefore bargained with Toledo, offering to help set up and deliver the mita in exchange for the restoration of their lost jurisdiction. The deal was accepted. These *caciques* then became "Mita Captains," but their legitimacy as educated exemplars of Spanish culture was undermined when they were expected to force their tributaries to fulfill the demands of the Spanish miners' state, although this did not save them from paying the penalty if there were not enough mitayos. In 1622 we hear an Aymara echo of Guaman Poma's lament from the alphabetically literate Lupaqa lord from Lake Titicaca, don Diego Chambilla, who wrote in a letter in Spanish to his steward in Potosí: "there is no remedy nor justice for the caciques, there is only justice for torments: all this province has been completely destroyed and finished."[13] After being tortured and having their arms broken by the corregidor of Chucuito in a vain attempt to oblige them to deliver more mita laborers, some Lupaqa caciques thought of taking refuge among the lowland Chuncho indians of the Amazon headwaters. And indeed, we know of mitayos who left with their captains to take refuge in the tropical yungas, sometimes joining Amazonian gold-mining groups with whom they shared rituals and fiestas.

The combination in the Andes of an opaque alternative literacy that could not be audited by Spaniards, together with greater fiscal pressures and systemic violence, created a society with higher levels of fear, secrecy, and suspicion than in New Spain. Spanish became the written medium generally preferred by the authorities because that way they could control the indians better, and indians generally preferred Spanish because that way they could defend themselves more effectively, since their own graphic system was practically denied (and would continue to be so until recently, in spite of some early efforts at recognition). Consequently, south Andeans wrote relatively few paper-and-ink texts in Quechua,[14] little in Aymara, and nothing in Pukina, the third of the three Andean *lenguas generales*. Most of their literate energies went into the production of alphabetic documents in Spanish that could be used in case of litigation.

The size and cosmopolitan nature of Potosí demanded the use of lenguas generales, but Thérèse Bouysse-Casagne has been able to document the precise distribution of these languages between each rural parish of La Paz and La Plata, together with Uruquilla spoken by the water folk—the Uru-Chipaya—of the lakes, rivers, and saltpans.[15] Two or three languages were sometimes spoken in the same parish. The priest Alonso de Barzana, author of a lost Pukina grammar, puts at forty the number of Pukina-speaking towns, including Arica, Arequipa, and the Pacific Coast, similar to the number of Aymara-speaking towns; and Pukina was also spoken in the valley parishes reaching down toward the Andean pie-de-monte (Créqui-Montfort proposed a relation between Pukina and Arawak which has still to be substantiated).[16] It has further been argued that Pukina was the dominant language of the pre-Inca state of Tiwanaku, as Aymara was of Wari, and Cunza of San Pedro de Atacama.[17]

Although we have few remnants of this language, the recovery of stray words in precise, generally ritual contexts has intrigued specialists in pursuit of the submerged "continent of Pukina."[18] In seventeenth-century Potosí, the Franciscan Bernardino de Cárdenas reported that a Pukina solar deity, Capac Iqui (Supreme Ancestor), was revered by miners as the divine patron of the Rich Mountain. In Oruro, miners transformed into jaguar priests using the hallucinogen *khuru* (possibly a wild tobacco), which probably occurred also in Potosí. And at the end of the sixteenth century we hear of an early extirpation carried out by a secular priest in the 1570s, who found a "witch" (*hechicero*) with the Pukina name Iquisi as "door-keeper" (*pongocamayo*) to the adit at the mines of Porco, a silver mountain that was the cult center of the triple lightning divinity. This pagan priest was the officiant at ceremonies of confession and purification, perhaps involving the hallucinogen *achuma* (San Pedro cactus).[19] So can we say that these shamanic miners and priests were themselves examples of a Pukina-language intellectual tradition?

TRISTAN PLATT

The term "intellectual" reflects a European attitude to *knowing* with a different genealogy from that of its Amerindian counterparts. Emerging in late Latin to refer to persons possessed of a mental clarity reflecting the divine light (Tertullian), it was opposed by theologians to other forms of knowing founded on sensation, imagination, or the will. In the Middle Ages, intellect became the "mind's eye," with Neoplatonic and Christian resonances.[20] One imperfect bridge or translation constructed in the Andes was through the solar-sacrificial resonances of both Christian and Andean religious traditions, which met in the symbolism of the Host.

This deep-seated European distinction between contemplative (theoretical) and practical ways of knowing is not so evident in the Amerindian tradition. Other imaginative and practical forms of knowing lay outside the disembodied remit of European intellectuals, such as shamanic practices and visions, the steamy ritual techniques of midwifery and childbirth, and other forms of incorporated skills, observation, and craft: weaving and metallurgy, as well as agriculture, herding, and mining were all framed by embodied performance, ritual, and ceremonial. These ways of knowing could be extended, seamlessly, to the practices of inscription (*quillqa*-writing), painting, and quipoliteracy. The term "intellectual" circumscribes Amerindian ways of knowing under Spanish rule in a peculiarly European way; indeed, the search for intellectuals may itself be part of a specifically European intellectual project.

How do these studies flesh out the "intellectual" of the book's title? The word is here taken generally as equivalent to different kinds of indian *letrado*, scholars, poets, fiscals, sacristans, scribes, and caciques, in different positions of political, cultural, and linguistic mediation or intracommunal reflection. The letrado no longer appears as mainly an urban creole or mestizo phenomenon, as in Angel Rama's *Lettered City* or Gonzalez Echeverría's *Myth and Archive* (a change of focus that forms the point of departure for Kathryn Burns's perceptive intervention). No less than markets, representational aesthetics, Arabic numerals, tonal harmonies, or prestigious items of Spanish fashion, alphabetic technologies were sought by indians for self-defense and modernization, both in Mexican cities and in the Andean colonial centers of Lima, Cusco, Quito, and Potosí, as well as in the countryside and rural towns. Translation, interpretation, and education here come to the fore, but in Peru they had to traverse the exceptionally conflictive, violent, and ambiguous spaces of Andean colonial society.

As a tool of agency in a context of graphic pluralism, alphabetic writing flourished among indians long before nineteenth-century citizens imported enlightened forms of writing and liberal education as part of a new civilizing mission.[21] Early forms of alphabetic literacy were quickly adopted in post-conquest Mexico and Peru, and they were *appropriated* as well as learned. In 1588 Bartolomé Álvarez, parish priest of the indian town of Andamarca in the Altiplanic province of Carangas, expostulated against the sale in local markets of King Alfonso the Wise's *Siete Partidas*, and other mediaeval and early modern legal texts, which local indians were buying to hone their skills of litigation. A knowledgeable but angry priest, Álvarez concluded that the only way of combatting indian litigiousness and secrecy would be to call in the Inquisition.[22]

But the editors also refer to the different Gramscian sense of "intellectual" to guide our framing of the book. The application of Gramsci's ideas to a colonial situation throws up some interesting lines of discussion. The editors do not use Gramsci's distinction between "organic intellectuals" who husband new political and economic relations into being by organizing rational forms of cultural legitimacy (hegemony), and "traditional intellectuals" persisting from previous periods whose legitimacy is in the throes of being dislodged, superceded, or incorporated. Could this distinction be usefully applied to the colonial situations that face us?

The best candidates for the role of "organic intellectuals" in the late sixteenth to mid-seventeenth centuries were probably the Jesuits, whose counter-reformation project aimed to create a new hegemony in America for an emergent order of Catholic and (in some cases) ecumenical modernity.[23] Their preference for persuasion, their careful attention to language and translation, and even a degree of tolerance of traditional Amerindian religious beliefs and practices, were all part of an effort to organize a new legitimacy on the basis of consent as well as force. They opposed the repressive methods of the Inquisition in Mexico and particularly the extirpation campaigns in Peru, which tried to impose forced conversion with zero tolerance at brutal cost.[24]

In this sense, the new indian and mestizo *letrados* and/or regional caciques educated in Lima and Cusco (many but not all, as Ramos shows, from the Jesuit Colegios) were "traditional intellectuals," who nevertheless positioned themselves or were recruited within a new order whose emergence they were able to facilitate, while also constructing, preserving, or refounding their pre-Colombian genealogies (as in the remarkable case of the two Alva brothers of Texcoco analyzed by John Schwaller). This ambiguity was a consequence of the colonial system in which they were caught, whether as indians or as mestizos.

In colonial Peru, as John Charles shows, many Jesuits distanced themselves from the vicious methods of the extirpators of idolatries, while some of their indian alumni behaved like local big men, using their literacy to legitimate political roles as regional caciques and noble governors. Here they clashed with Spanish colonial administrators, as well as with extirpating secular priests. In the case of don Juan Chupica from Ihuari (Checras), his interest in being an exemplar to his indians was secondary to the local political career for which he believed his education had prepared him.

In Potosí, cases of *apparent* exemplars are to be found in caciques' *Probanzas* and *Relaciones de méritos y servicios*, although these need controlling by reference to denunciations of their caciques by their indian tributaries, documents that only sometimes survive. But the two-facedness of our seventeenth-century Mallku of Qaraqara is revealed by one such denunciation.[25] Within his own rural community, don Fernando Ayra de Ariutu was accused of running a tyrannical regime, combined with luxury and sensual delights: he ate his food adorned with gold, had two unmarried women living with him (probably a persistence of pre-Hispanic cacical polygyny), as well as twenty indians specialized in bringing him honey from the lowlands, and a bevy of eight girls who accompanied him to the valleys to sing and sleep with him. He accumulated land and pastures, flocks of llamas and herds of cows, and ordered his dependent indians to look after them, or be punished, keeping the proceeds for himself. He threatened to cut out the tongues of the wives of the indians who denounced him if the women complained. He ceded community lands to his compadre, a Spanish miner who wanted to build a silver refinery. And yet don Fernando also preached to his indians from the pulpit in "his" church (he had financed its construction), and in the city of Potosí he rubbed shoulders with eminent Spaniards, authorities and churchmen who were prepared to vouch for him. For his *Probanza* he mobilized the collective memories of other Mallku as witnesses to bear out his dynastic traditions; versions were compared at special meetings (*juntas*) of Aymara traditional intellectuals. As alcaldes mayores, these were also important indian letrados charged with resolving disputes within their jurisdictions; but the first words of praise by Spanish corregidores in their cover letters to Madrid always concerned the Mallku's success in paying the tribute and delivering the miners.

Another exemplar in the 1580s was don Fernando Ayawiri, the Charka

Mallku of the Aymara-speaking triple alliance of Charka, Qaraqara, and Sura, whose lands stretched eastward and down from the mines and pastures of the Silver Sierra to the valley of Cochabamba and the Pilcomayo River. Aya-wiri was named alcalde mayor of the indians of Potosí. He claimed to have led his indians every Sunday to hear the Jesuits preach, helping to reduce coca consumption and ritual drunkenness. In the 1580s, don Fernando sent his son to the Jesuit college in Potosí where he learned Latin grammar and mixed with Spanish boys.[26] In 1590, don Fernando Ayawiri was also the first to present himself before don Juan Lopez de Cepeda, president of the Char-cas Audiencia in La Plata, who had summoned the caciques and indians to the Jesuit college of Potosí, asking them to contribute a "free gift" (*servicio gra-cioso*) to help King Philip II with his projected new invasion of the "Lutheran English." Don Fernando's loyal curriculum was notably different from that of the rebellious Pakasa, in the province of Collao around La Paz and Lake Titicaca, who, some years before, had sent letters to Arica (which were inter-cepted) inviting Sir Francis Drake to come up to the Altiplano to free them from the Spanish, and addressing the English corsair and his crew as "Very Magnificent Lutheran Lords."[27]

These cases show well-informed Aymara caciques intervening politically on opposite sides in the European religious wars of the last third of the six-teenth century, thereby giving an international projection to long-durational regional rivalries between the provinces of Collao and Charcas. Under the Inka, the Collao had been characterized by resistance and rebellion, while the Charcas confederations were able to negotiate the pact. Now each offered loyalty and support to a different European state.

But while the Pakasa letters were intercepted, don Fernando Ayawiri re-tained his position as loyal subject of the king. Even Toledo expressed respect for his advice and judgment.[28] On retiring in 1592, because of illness, to his emblazoned house in the Charka capital of Sakaka, he could pride himself on having done his duty as facilitator of Christian hegemony, but also as a loyal, high-ranking indian authority and diplomat, who became a middle-ranking colonial administrator: a "traditional intellectual" incorporated into the Jesuit hegemonic project, rather than himself an organizer of hegemony. No denunciation has yet been found that might show him to have been as two-faced as don Fernando Ayra de Ariutu.

Finally, Susan Schroeder argues for the importance of women in the lin-eages collected among the Mexica by Chimalpahin. Women also figure in Aymara caciques' genealogies, although these too respected the Spanish patrilineal bias. Far from the cities, as we have seen, Aymara lords continued to practice polygyny, although only one wife was considered legitimate and the offspring of concubines could be disqualified from succession disputes as bastards. But one Aymara lady, doña Ursula Ayra Kanchi, was a key figure who transmitted to her energetic son, don Fernando Ayra de Ariutu, the lordship of the house (*casa*) originally founded by her great-great-grandfather, Tata Ayra Kanchi, in the mid-fifteenth century. This house was refounded by doña Ursula in the last years of Philip II's reign through her Christian marriage in c. 1595 to don Fernando Chinchi II, the parallel descendent of Lukalarama, Tata Ayra Kanchi's ambassador to Inka Yupanki (Pachakuti). Doña Ursula also took the epithet "White Flower that Blossoms," another gift to her ancestor by Pachakuti; for "the lordship and government of the province of Qaraqara belongs to her by direct line."

This marriage took place during the period of the early *composiciones* implemented by royal command between 1591 and 1620 in both the Andes and Mexico, which threatened indian lands and lineages, and in Mexico provoked the production of the first *títulos primordiales* to demonstrate the inalienability of ancestral territories.[29] In Peru, they generated probanzas in which Aymara lords tried to reclaim their threatened status and privileges through the presentation of genealogies. By claiming the old jurisdiction of the Qaraqara, doña Ursula was claiming authority over the lands and indians of the two colonial provinces, Chayanta and Porco, into which her ancestral jurisdiction had been divided, and implicitly confirming the priceless service to the Spanish monarchy signified by the cession to Charles V of the two silver mountains themselves.[30] She also claimed the honors and privileges given by Pachakuti to her ancestor, including the memory of the textile map that expressed the ancient treaty, as described in the 1638 *Probanza* of her son, don Fernando Ayra de Ariutu.

Don Fernando also attached to his petition to the king our only copy of the *encomienda* document of Gonzalo Pizarro (1540) in which, thirty years before its colonial subdivision, the "province of Caracara" of "20,000 indians" was itemized by capitals (*cabeceras*), towns, hamlets, and population. This was the documentary proof of the justice of don Fernando's claim to keep his wider jurisdiction, and in 1673 he had a copy made of all the papers in Potosí. But by then the two colonial provinces were well established, and the details of the process through which the parallel jurisdiction of the "Province of Qaraqara" was finally extinguished (probably following the revised tributary order introduced by the duke of La Palata) are still unknown.

"Drawing on his experience of Italy," Nigel Greaves writes, "Gramsci understood that a measure of the success of bourgeois revolutions is the extent to which its organic intellectuals succeed in absorbing into its *visione mentale* (world view) the organic intellectuals of the declining feudal class."[31] At first glance, this suggests parallels with colonial America: surely this is, *mutatis mutandis*, exactly what many of the papers in this book are about. But was there really a rising class, in support of which these organic intellectuals—the Jesuits and other orders—were trying to absorb declining indigenous intellectuals into a new structure of hegemony? Or were the Jesuits acting in a vacuum by trying to create hegemony for a Christian religion and state whose colonial nature simultaneously opposed any endogenous class transformation? The systemic violence of the colonial order supported wealthy mining and merchant guilds closely linked with Seville and Cadiz through trans-Atlantic trade, and trade was intense within the viceroyalties. But following the revolutionary moment between 1809 and 1825, a creole-mestizo citizenry took control over the postcolonial state.

One wonders what would have happened if Tupaq Amaru had defeated the Spanish in the 1780s. No doubt he would have encouraged the further growth of American commerce, in which he was immersed; but how would he have negotiated terms with a North Atlantic mercantilism which, with European capital and the industrial and political revolutions of Britain, the United States, and France behind it, would soon have come knocking at his doors? Long before such a question could be posed, however, the Jesuits had taken refuge in the missions, and were then expelled from America for their efforts to continue their project on the margins of a new Bourbon effort to make the colonies profitable.

How then did the pact survive? Europeans and creoles have long considered the discovery of America a unique and epoch-making event, marking a rupture in the histories of the Old World and the New. But the reemergence of the Inka utopia in the eighteenth- and nineteenth-century Andes, shown by Martínez to be expressed in the linear positioning of Spanish kings continuously with their Inka predecessors in contemporary royal genealogies and works of art,[32] may contribute to explaining the widespread south Andean myth of the Chullpa. This "pre-social" lunar humanity was shriveled into mummies with the rising of the Inka Sun (except for the Uru-Chipaya and the Chunchos, who dived into the waters of the rivers and lakes).[33] Here mythohistorical rupture is provided, not by the arrival of the Spanish, but by the dawning of the Inca's solar state, an event more profoundly memorable, even, than the arrival of the Spanish. This myth, which may be a republican reinvention or transformation of distant memories, suggests that the Inca "dawn" inaugurated the state and the "pact of reciprocity," which—however downtrodden by the systemic violence of colonialism—was common to both Inka and Hapsburg states. It therefore echoes the dynastic tradition presented by don Fernando Ayra de Ariutu. No equivalent rupture could be attributed to the Spanish conquest because the solar state *had already dawned*: so Spanish rule was incorporated into the same continuous mythohistoric period through the ideology of the translatio imperii. But once colonial violence was institutionalized, and the Jesuits were no longer calling the tune in the Andean parishes, the fulfillment of the pact became more and more one-sided and disconnected from the realities of colonial (and especially post-colonial) marginalization and abuse.

As the Andean noble lineages' power waned, before and after the failure of Tupaq Amaru's insurrection, they abandoned their communities and merged with the creole-mestizo urban elites. But new rural leaders were rising from the peasant ranks to defend the tributary pact. Nicolas Katari and Dámaso Katari, brothers of Tomás Katari of Macha (now administratively dependent on the colonial capital of Chayanta), assumed the roles of attorneys (*apoderados*) who represented their communities against creole and Spanish abuses by laying siege to La Plata (today's Sucre), with the hope of presenting it as a new gift of vassalage to Tupaq Amaru.[34]

The Inka Utopia resurfaced briefly during the Wars of Independence, and again during the Bolivian Federal War of 1899, when indian apoderados reappeared, some proposing the restoration of the Inka and the cult of the Sun. In the 1920s, a new movement of indian intellectuals, the caciques apoderados, arose to defend the colonial land grants, or *repartimientos*,[35] providing further evidence of the persistence of the old legal literacy that Frank Salomon and Mercedes Niño-Murcia have uncovered for Tupicocha, Perú, in *The Lettered Mountain*.

In 1970–71, I found flourishing among the rural ayllus of the old Province of Chayanta, not only the Chullpa myth but also tributary indians. In Macha the Upper Moiety authority, or *kuraka*, don Agustín Carbajal, had denounced in 1963 the control of local MNR[36] peasant unions by abusive mestizos living in Macha. A monolingual Quechua speaker who nevertheless employed legal Spanish in written communications, he showed me a document typewritten in Spanish and signed with the fingerprints of his accompanying authorities. These were latter-day intellectuals, some of whom—such as don Agustín—

had been members of the *caciques apoderados* movement in the 1930s. They remembered their ownership of the town tambo with its two kitchen-gardens (one for each moiety), and until 1973 continued to defend the pact by sending postillions by turn to staff it, even though they were no longer required to do so by law. Like other Andean groups, their colonial titles and boundary inspections were stored in a moiety archive in the care of the kuraka, who with his sons continued to collect and issue receipts for the semestral tribute paid in ceremonial councils, or *cabildos* (though the MNR state was no longer very interested). Bank notes placed by each tributary on open-air tributary tables were sprinkled with libations under the ritual name of "butterflies" (*pillpintu*), and held from blowing away in the wind by stone paper weights called "Inkas." Clearly, these twentieth-century intellectuals and tributaries were still choosing to prolong the memory of an Inka hegemony, which until now no regime has been able to eradicate completely.[37]

Notes

1. I follow the orthography used by Tristan Platt, Thérèse Bouysse-Cassagne, and Olivia Harris, *Qaraqara-Charka: Mallku, Inka y Rey en la provincia de Charcas (siglos XV–XVII): Historia antropológica de una confederación aymara*. Here Charcas (both Inka province and Spanish Audiencia), together with some other conventional spellings, is contrasted with Charka (Aymara federation), Qaraqara (for Caracara), Inka, Mallku, Wayna Qhapaq, and so on.

2. In a survey of early colonial Quechua "mundane" literacy, Alan Durston attributes the contrast with Mexico to the comparative underdevelopment of Peruvian cabildos and scribes, and the stronger persistence of nonalphabetic alternatives in the Andes. See Durston, "Native-Language Literacy in Colonial Peru: The Question of Mundane Quechua Writing Revisited." César Itier has published examples of early colonial Quechua letter writing; see "Lengua general y comunicación escrita: Cinco cartas en quechua de Cotahuasi—1616."

3. Cf. Joanne Rappaport and Tom Cummins, who attribute to the processes of translation and writing in colonial Peru the exclusion of any "Andean representational form from becoming part of the documentary record, as they did in . . . the Viceroyalty of New Spain"; see "Literacy and Power in Colonial Latin America," 89–109.

4. I use indian (without capitalization) as a generic category meaning "native inhabitant of the Indies" (following Columbus's great mistake), rather than as a state, legal, or racial classification. The Amerindian people of the New World had many ethnic and group names among themselves, which were expressed in Spanish as, for example, "indians of Macha" (not "Indians of Macha"), equivalent to today's *macha runa* (Que means "Macha people"). In the colonial period, we only find "Indian" in some legal phrases, such as "Republic of Indians." In the early Bolivian Republic "indigenous"

(*indígena*, without capitalization) appears already in the 1830s as a liberal-republican euphemism for colonial "indian," though "indian" (indios) later returns to predominate until the 1990s. "Indian" (capitalized) is a more recent ethnolegal classification (but cf. Partido Indio de Bolivia), which has become generalized on the basis of the U.S. legal term "American Indian" (now imposed by spelling checks regardless of historical or anthropological considerations).

5. For pre-Hispanic khipu archives see Gary Urton, "Khipu Archives: Duplicate Accounts and Identity Labels in the Inka Knotted String Cords," 319–52.

6. Local-level quipos for counting herds survived. For a recent benchmark study of archaeological khipu, see Gary Urton and Carrie J. Brezine, "Khipu Typologies." It now appears that khipu were not logographic, that is, they did not represent the phonemes of spoken language.

7. See Rosaleen Howard-Malverde, "'Why Do They Steal Our Phonemes?': Inventing the Survival of the Cañari Language (Ecuador)," 123–45.

8. According to don Juan Chocata, lord of Chuquicota in Carangas Province, the textile had been made of cumbe cloth: "*un mapa tejido en ropa de cumbe que los indios llaman Carpatira.*" It seems that Pachakuti's gift to Ayra Kanchi was notorious among neighboring Aymara federations. Polo Ondegardo was also aware of several other "painted" territorial maps in the southern Andes; see Mercedes del Río, *Etnicidad, territorialidad y colonialismo en los Andes: Tradición y cambio entre los soras de los siglos XVI y XVII*; and Platt, Bouysse-Cassagne, and Harris, *Qaraqara-Charka*, 74, 743–44.

9. Platt, Bouysse-Cassagne, and Harris, *Qaraqara-Charka*, document 20.

10. For khipu in colonial written sources, see Carlos Sempat Assadourian, "String Registries: Native Accounting and Memory According to the Colonial Sources." For the notarial distinction between khipukamayu declarations and witness testimonies, see Platt, Bouysse-Cassagne, and Harris, *Qaraqara-Charka*, document 6, 399n196.

11. Carlos Sempat Assadourian, "La despoblación indígena en Perú y Nueva España durante el siglo XVI y la formación de la economía colonial."

12. Nathan Wachtel, "The Mitimas of the Cochabamba Valley: The Colonization Policy of Huayna Capac," 199–235.

13. Ximena Medinaceli and Marcela Inch, *Pleitos y riqueza: Los caciques andinos en Potosí del siglo XVII: Transcripción y estudios del expediente de don Diego Chambilla contra los bienes de su administrador*, f. 230v.

14. The *Huarochirí Manuscript* is an exception; the idea of its attribution to the noble indian convert don Cristobal Choquecasa is consolidated here by Alan Durston.

15. Uchumataqu, language of the Urus of Lake Titicaca, is distinguished from Chipaya, language of the Urus or Chipaya of Lake Coipasa in Western Carangas (Bolivia). Neither should be confused with Pukina, although some Urus call their language "Puquina." See Willem F. H. Adelaar and Peter Muysken, *The Languages of the Andes*, 362–75.

16. Thérèse Bouysse-Cassagne, "Apuntes para la historia de los puquina-hablantes."

17. See Rodolfo Cerrón-Palomino, "El origen centro-andino del aimara"; and "Contactos y desplazamientos lingüísticos en los Andes centro-sureños: el puquina, el aimara y el quechua." It is tempting to hypothesize that the Aymara chinu tradition was brought south from Wari by speakers of Aymara around 1000 A.D., since we know

there was an important Middle Horizon khipu tradition in Wari. See Urton and Brezine, "Khipu Typologies."

18. Bouysse-Cassagne, "Apuntes para la historia." For the Pukina vocabulary of the Callahuaya "secret language," see Pieter Muysken, "Callahuaya," in Sarah G. Thomason, *Contact Languages: A Wider Perspective*, 427.

19. Platt, Bouyse-Cassagne, and Harris, *Qaraqara-Charka*, Documents 1 and 2, with Presentation to part I. Confession was practiced in the Andes before the Spanish invasion; Iquisi was punished by being made slave of the hospital (186).

20. See *Oxford English Dictionary*, "intellect" 1. a. . . . Intellect generally excludes, and is sometimes distinguished from, sensation, imagination, and will"; "intellectual, adj. and n. ." OED Online. September 2013. Oxford University Press. Accessed October 9, 2013. http://www.oed.com/view/Entry/97387?redirectedFrom=intellectual. 1398: J Trevisa. tr. Bartholomaeus Anglicus *De Proprietatibus Rerum* (BL Add. 27944) (1975) I. iii. iii. 93, "As þe y3e is in þe body so is þe intellect, vndirstondinge, in þe soule." Cf. 1773: Ld. Monboddo, *Orig. & Progress of Lang.* (1774) I. i. iv. 45: "The faculty by which it [the mind] operates singly, and without participation of the body, I call *intellect*."

21. Frank Salomon and Mercedes Niño-Murcia, *The Lettered Mountain*.

22. Bartolomé de Álvarez, *De las costumbres y conversión de los indios del Perú: Memorial a Felipe II* (1588).

23. Laura Laurencich-Minelli, *Exsul Immeritus Blas Valera Populo Suo e Historia et Rudimenta Linguae Piruanorum*.

24. Not all Jesuits were tolerant, however; see Pablo Josef de Arriaga, *The Extirpation of Idolatry in Peru*, on the use made of the Company of Jesus by the archbishop of Lima, Bartolomé Lobo Guerrero, to advance the campaign against Andean religion.

25. Platt, Bouysse-Cassagne, and Harris, *Qaraqara-Charka*, document 16, appendix.

26. In their "Memorial" to the King of 1582, don Fernando and other Charcas Mallku asked for the Jesuit College in Lima to be transferred to Cusco "because of the distance, and besides because the said City of the Kings is a land of sickness for natives of the highlands, we who are accustomed to cold lands." The caciques may have acted in conjunction with Diego de Torres Rubio, who was one of the witnesses of the *Probanza* presented in 1598 by the son of don Fernando, don Juan Ayawiri. Torres Rubio said he had known don Juan since 1588, when the latter was sixteen; see Platt, Bouysse-Cassagne, and Harris, *Qaraqara-Charka*, 845, 875–78.

27. See Ramírez del Águila, *Noticias políticas de Indias*.

28. Platt, Bouysse-Cassagne, and Harris, *Qaraqara-Charka*, 910–11.

29. See Margarita Menegus Bornemann, "Los títulos primordiales de los pueblos de indios."

30. See Tristan Platt and Pablo Quisbert, "Tras las huellas del silencio: Potosí, los inka y el virrey Toledo."

31. Nigel M. Greaves, *Intellectuals and the Historical Construction of Knowledge and Identity: A Reappraisal of Gramsci's Ideas on Leadership*.

32. Teresa Gisbert, *Iconografía y mitos indígenas en el arte*; and Natalia Majluf, *Los incas, reyes del Perú*.

33. The Chunchos variant of the myth comes from Quispecanchis, near Cusco; see

Pablo Sendón, "Los límites de la humanidad: El mito de los ch'ullpa en Marcapata (Quispecanchi), Perú."

34. Sergio Serulnikov, *Subverting Colonial Authority: Challenges to Spanish Rule in Eighteenth-Century Southern Andes*.

35. Laura Gotkowitz, *A Revolution for Our Rights: Indigenous Struggles for Land and Justice in Bolivia, 1880–1952*.

36. MNR is the Movimiento Nacionalista Revolucionario.

37. See Alberto Flores Galindo, *In Search of an Inca: Identity and Utopia in the Andes*. Tribute was still being paid by some groups when I passed through Macha in 2009; the money was going to the peasant unions controlled by Evo Morales's "Movement to Socialism" (MAS).

Bibliography

Abercrombie, Thomas A. *Pathways of Memory and Power: Ethnography and History among an Andean People*. Madison: University of Wisconsin Press, 1997.

Acosta, Antonio. "Francisco De Avila, Cusco 1573 (?)—Lima 1647." In *Ritos y tradiciones de Huarochirí*. Edited by Gerald Taylor. Lima: Instituto de Estudios Peruanos; Instituto Francés de Estudios Andinos, 1987.

Acosta, José de. *"De procuranda indorum salute o predicación del evangelio en las Indias."* In *Obras del P. José De Acosta*. Edited by S. J. Francisco Mateos. Biblioteca de Autores Españoles. Madrid: Atlas, 1954 [1588].

Acuña, René, ed. *Relaciones geográficas del siglo XVI*. Mexico City: Universidad Nacional Autónoma de México, Instituto de Investigaciones Antropológicas, 1982–1986.

Adelaar, Willem F. H. "Spatial Reference and Speaker Orientation in Early Colonial Quechua." In *Creating Context in Andean Cultures*. Edited by Rosaleen Howard-Malverde. New York: Oxford University Press, 1997.

Adelaar, Willem F. H., and Peter Muysken. *The Languages of the Andes*. Cambridge: Cambridge University Press, 2004.

Adorno, Rolena. *Guaman Poma: Writing and Resistance in Colonial Peru*. Austin: University of Texas Press, 1986.

Adorno, Rolena. "Images of Indios Ladinos in Early Colonial Peru." In *Transatlantic Encounters: Europeans and Andeans in the Sixteenth Century*. Edited by Rolena Adorno and Kenneth Andrien. Berkeley: University of California Press, 1991.

Adorno, Rolena. "The Genesis of Felipe Guaman Poma de Ayala's *Nueva Corónica y Buen Gobierno.*" *Colonial Latin American Review* 2, no. 1–2 (1993): 53–92.

Adorno, Rolena. "Guaman Poma and His Illustrated Chronicle from Colonial Peru: From a Century of Scholarship to a New Era of Reading." (2001). Accessed September 18, 2013. http://www2.kb.dk/elib/mss/poma/presentation/pres-en.htm.

Adorno, Rolena. "Arms, Letters, and the Native Historian in Early Colonial Mexico," *1492–1992: Re/Discovering Colonial Writing.* Edited by René Jara and Nicholas Spadaccini. Minneapolis: The Prisma Institute, 1989.

Alaperrine-Bouyer, Monique. "Saber y poder: La cuestión de la educación de las elites indígenas." In *Incas e indios cristianos: Elites indígenas e identidades cristianas en los Andes coloniales.* Edited by Jean-Jacques Decoster. Cuzco: Centro de Estudios Regionales Andinos Bartolomé de las Casas, 2002.

Alaperrine-Bouyer, Monique. *La educación de las elites indígenas en el Perú colonial.* Lima: Instituto Francés de Estudios Andinos, Instituto Riva Agüero, Instituto de Estudios Peruanos, 2007.

Alberro, Solange. *El águila y la cruz: Orígenes religiosos de la conciencia criolla, México, siglos* XVI–XVII. Mexico City: Fondo de Cultura Económica, 1999.

Albó, Xavier. "Jesuitas y culturas indígenas Perú 1568–1606: Su actitud, métodos y criterios de aculturación." *América Indígena* 26, no. 3–4 (1966): 249–308, 95–446.

Albó, Xavier. *El futuro de los idiomas oprimidos en los Andes.* Lima: Centro de Investigación de Lingüística Aplicada, 1977.

Alcina Franch, José. *Calendario y religión entre los zapotecos.* Mexico City: Universidad Nacional Autónoma de México, 1993.

Alva Ixtlilxochitl, Fernando de. *Obras históricas.* Edited by Edmundo O'Gorman. 2 vols. Mexico City: Universidad Nacional Autónoma de México, 1975–77.

Alvarado Tezozomoc, Fernando. *Crónica mexicayotl.* 2nd ed. Mexico City: Universidad Nacional Autónoma de México, 1992.

Álvarez, Bartolomé de. *De las costumbres y conversión de los indios del Perú: Memorial a Felipe* II *(1588).* Madrid: Polifemo, 1998 [1588].

Amado González, Donato. "El alférez real de los incas: resistencia, cambios y continuidad de la identidad indígena." In *Incas e indios cristianos: Elites indígenas e identidades cristianas en los Andes coloniales.* Edited by Jean-Jacques Decoster. Cuzco: CBC-IFEA, 2002.

Anderson, Arthur J. O., Frances Berdan, and James Lockhart. *Beyond the Codices: The Nahuatl View of Colonial Mexico.* UCLA Latin American Studies 27. Los Angeles: University of California Press, 1976.

Arguedas, José María, and Pierre Duviols, eds. *Dioses y hombres de Huarochirí: Edición bilingüe; Narración quechua recogida por Francisco de Avila [1598?].* Lima: Museo Nacional de Historia, Instituto de Estudios Peruanos, 1966.

Arriaga, Pablo Josef. *The Extirpation of Idolatry in Peru.* Translated by L. Clark Keating. Lexington: University of Kentucky Press, 1968.

Arriaga, Pablo Josef. "La Extirpación de la idolatría del Pirú." In *Crónicas peruanas de interés indígena*. Edited by Francisco Esteve Barba. Madrid: Biblioteca de Autores Españoles, 1968 [1621].

Assadourian, Carlos Sempat. "Los señores étnicos y los corregidores de indios en la conformación del Estado colonial," *Anuario de Estudios Americanos* (Sevilla) 44 (1987): 325–427.

Assadourian, Carlos Sempat. "La despoblación indígena en Perú y Nueva España durante el siglo XVI y la formación de la economía colonial." *Historia Mexicana* 38, no. 3 (1989): 419–53.

Assadourian, Carlos Sempat. *Transiciones hacia el sistema colonial andino*. Lima: IEP/El Colegio de México, 1994.

Assadourian, Carlos Sempat. "String Registries: Native Accounting and Memory According to the Colonial Sources." In *Narrative Threads: Accounting and Recounting in Andean Khipu*. Edited by Jeffrey Quilter and Gary Urton. Austin: University of Texas Press, 2002.

Asselbergs, Florine. *Conquered Conquistadors: The Lienzo of Quauhquechollan; A Nahua Vision of the Conquest of Guatemala*. Boulder: University Press of Colorado, 2005.

Aveni, Anthony, ed. *Archaeoastronomy in Pre-Columbian America*. Austin: University of Texas Press, 1975.

Aveni, Anthony. "Concepts of Positional Astronomy Employed in Ancient Meso-american Architecture." In *Native American Astronomy*, edited by Anthony Aveni. Austin: University of Texas Press, 1979.

Aveni, Anthony, ed. *Archaeoastronomy in the New World: American Primitive Astronomy*. Cambridge: Cambridge University Press, 1982.

Aveni, Anthony. *Skywatchers of Ancient Mexico*. Austin: University of Texas Press, 2001.

Aveni, Anthony. *Conversing with the Planets: How Science and Myth Invented the Cosmos*. Boulder: University Press of Colorado, 2002.

Ávila, Francisco de. *Tratado de los evangelios que nuestra madre la Iglesia nos propone en todo el año*. 2 vols. Lima: Pedro de Cabrera, 1647.

Barlow, Robert. "Anales de Tula, Hidalgo, 1361–1521." *Tlalocan* 3, no. 1 (1949): 2–13.

Barros van Hövell tot Westerflier, Alonso. "Cien años de guerras mixes: Territoria-lidades prehispánicas, expansión burocrática y zapotequización en el istmo de Tehuantepec durante el siglo XVI." *Historia Mexicana* 57, no. 2 (2007): 325–403.

Benton, Lauren. *Law and Colonial Cultures: Legal Regimes in World History, 1400–1900*. Cambridge: Cambridge University Press, 2002.

Berdan, Frances. *The Essential Codex Mendoza*. Berkeley: University of California Press, 1997.

Bertonio, Ludovico. *Libro de la vida y milagros de Nuestro Señor Jesucristo en dos lenguas, aymara y romance*. Juli: Francisco del Canto, 1612.

Bertonio, Ludovico. *Vocabulario de la lengua aymara*. Juli: Francisco del Canto, 1612.

Bierhorst, John. Transcriber and translator, *Ballads of the Lords of New Spain: The Codex Romances de los Señores de la Nueva España*. Austin: University of Texas Press, 2009.

Bloch, R. Howard. "Genealogy as a Medieval Mental Structure and Textual Form."

In *La littérature historiographique des origines à 1500*. Vol. 11/1 of *Grudriss Der Romanischen Literaturen Des Mittelalters*. Edited by Hans Ulrich Gumbrecht. Heidelberg: Carl Winter Universittsverlag, 1986.

Bonnett, Diana. *El protector de naturales en la audiencia de Quito, siglos XVII y XVIII*. Quito: FLACSO, Editorial Abya Yala, 1992.

Boone, Elizabeth H. "Writing and Recording Knowledge." In *Writing without Words: Alternative Literacies in Mesoamerica and the Andes*. Edited by Elizabeth H. Boone and Walter D. Mignolo. Durham, NC: Duke University Press, 1994.

Boone, Elizabeth H. "Aztec Pictorial Histories: Records without Words." In *Writing without Words: Alternative Literacies in Mesoamerica and the Andes*. Edited by Elizabeth H. Boone and Walter Mignolo. Durham, NC: Duke University Press, 1994.

Boone, Elizabeth H. "Maps of Territory, History and Community in Aztec Mexico." In *Cartographic Encounters: Perspectives on Native American Mapmaking and Map Use*. Edited by Malcolm Lewis. Chicago: University of Chicago Press, 1998.

Boone, Elizabeth H. "Pictorial Documents and Visual Thinking in Postconquest Mexico." In *Native Traditions in the Postconquest World*. Edited by Elizabeth H. Boone and Thomas B. F. Cummins. Washington, DC: Dumbarton Oaks, 1998.

Boone, Elizabeth H. *Stories in Red and Black: Pictorial Histories of the Aztecs and Mixtecs*. Austin: University of Texas Press, 2000.

Boone, Elizabeth H. "In Tlamatinime: The Wise Men and Women of Aztec Mexico." In *Painted Books and Indigenous Knowledge: Manuscript Studies in Honor of Mary Elizabeth Smith*. Edited by Elizabeth H. Boone. New Orleans: Middle American Research Institute, Tulane University, 2005.

Boone, Elizabeth H. *Cycles of Time and Meaning in the Mexican Books of Fate*. Austin: University of Texas Press, 2007.

Boone, Elizabeth H., and Walter Mignolo, eds. *Writing without Words: Alternative Literacies in Mesoamerica and the Andes*. Durham, NC: Duke University Press, 1994.

Boone, Elizabeth H., and Thomas B. F. Cummins, eds. *Native Traditions in the Postconquest World: A Symposium at Dumbarton Oaks, 2nd through 4th October 1992*. Washington, DC: Dumbarton Oaks, 1998.

Boone, Elizabeth H., and Thomas B. F. Cummins. "Colonial Foundations: Points of Contact and Compatibility." In *The Arts in Latin America, 1492–1820*. Edited by Joseph J. Rishel and Suzanne L. Stratton. Philadelphia: Philadelphia Museum of Art, 2006.

Boone, Elizabeth H., and Gary Urton, eds. *Their Way of Writing: Scripts, Signs, and Pictography in Pre-Columbian America*. Washington, DC: Dumbarton Oaks, 2011.

Borah, Woodrow. "Juzgado general de indios del Perú o Juzgado particular de indios de el Cercado de Lima." *Revista Chilena de Historia del Derecho* 6 (1970): 129–42.

Borah, Woodrow. *Justice by Insurance: The General Indian Court of Colonial Mexico and the Legal Aides of the Half-Real*. Berkeley: University of California Press, 1983.

Borah, Woodrow. "Yet Another Look at the Techialoyan Codices." In *Land and Politics in the Valley of Mexico: A Two Thousand Year Perspective*. Edited by Herbert R. Harvey. Albuquerque: University of New Mexico Press, 1991.

Bouysse-Cassagne, Thérèse. "Apuntes para la historia de los puquina-hablantes." *Boletín de Arqueología* PUCP 14 (2010): 283–307.

Boyd-Bowman, Peter. *Indice geobiográfico de cuarenta mil pobladores españoles de América en el siglo* XVI, *1493–1519*. Bogotá: Instituto Caro y Cuervo, 1964.

Brading, David A. *The First America: The Spanish Monarchy, Creole Patriots, and the Liberal State, 1492–1867*. Cambridge: Cambridge University Press, 1991.

Brito Guadarrama, Baltazar. *Lienzo de Ajusco: Títulos primordiales*. Mexico City: GDF, 2006.

Broda, Johanna. "The Sacred Landscape of Aztec Calendar Festivals: Myth, Nature, and Society." In *To Change Place: Aztec Ceremonial Landscapes*. Edited by David Carrasco. Boulder: University Press of Colorado, 1991.

Broda, Johanna. "Archaeoastronomical Knowledge, Calendrics and Sacred Geography in Mesoamerica." In *Astronomies and Cultures*. Edited by Clive Ruggles and Nicholas Saunders. Boulder: University Press of Colorado, 1993.

Broda, Johanna. "Lenguaje visual del paisaje ritual de la cuenca de México." In *Códices y documentos sobre México: Segundo simposio*. Edited by Salvador Rueda Smithers, Constanza Vega Sosa, and Rodrigo Martínez Baracs. Mexico City: INAH-CONACULTA, 1997.

Broda, Johanna. "Mesoamerican Astronomy and the Ritual Calendar." In *Science across Cultures: The History of Non-Western Science. Vol. 1: The History of Non-Western Astronomy*. Edited by Helaine Selin. Dordrecht: Kluwer Academic Publications, 2000.

Broda, Johanna, Stanislaw Iwaniszewski, and Lucrecia Maupomé, eds. *Arqueoastronomía y etnoastronomía en Mesoamérica*. Mexico City: IIH/UNAM, 1991.

Broda, Johanna, Stanislaw Iwaniszewski, and Arturo Montero, eds. *La montaña en el paisaje ritual*. Mexico City: CONACULTA/INAH, 2001.

Broggio, Paolo. *Evangelizzare il mondo: Le missioni della Compagnia di Gesù tra Europa e America (Secoli* XVI–XVII). Rome: Carocci Editore, 2004.

Brokaw, Galen. "Khipu Numeracy and Alphabetic Literacy in the Andes: Felipe Guaman Poma de Ayala's *Nueva Corónica y Buen Gobierno.*" *Colonial Latin American Review* 11, no. 2 (2002): 275–303.

Brokaw, Galen. *A History of the Khipu*. Cambridge: Cambridge University Press, 2010.

Brotherson, Gordon. "Mesoamerican Description of Space II: Signs for Direction." *Ibero-Amerikanisches Archiv (Neue Folge)* 2, no. 1 (1976): 39–62.

Brotherson, Gordon. *Image of the New World*. London: Thames and Hudson, 1979.

Brotherson, Gordon. "Astronomical Norms in Mesoamerican Ritual and Time-Reckoning." In *Archaeoastronomy in the New World: American Primitive Astronomy*. Edited by Anthony Aveni. Cambridge: Cambridge University Press, 1982.

Brotherson, Gordon. *Book of the Fourth World: Reading the Native Americas through Their Literature*. Cambridge: Cambridge University Press, 1992.

Brotherson, Gordon. *Painted Books from Mexico: Codices in UK Collections and the World They Represent*. London: British Museum Press, 1995.

Brotherson, Gordon. *Feather Crown: The Eighteen Feasts of the Mexica Year*. British Museum Research Paper. London: The British Museum, 2005.

Brotherson, Gordon, Galen Brokaw, Aaron Dziubinsnkyj, Millie Gimmel, and Mark Morris, eds. *Footprints through Time: Mexican Pictorial Manuscripts at the Lilly Library.* Bloomington: Lilly Library, Indiana University, 1997.

Bruhns, Karen Olsen, and Karen E. Stothert, eds. *Women in Ancient America.* Norman: University of Oklahoma Press, 1999.

Burga, Manuel. *Nacimiento de una utopía: Muerte y resurrección de los incas.* 2nd ed. Lima: Universidad Nacional de San Marcos, Universidad de Guadalajara, [1988] 2005.

Burgoa, Francisco de. *Palestra historial de virtudes y ejemplares apostólicos fundada del celo de insignes heroes de la sagrada Orden de Predicadores en este Nuevo Mundo de la America en las Indias Occidentales.* 3rd ed. Mexico City: Editorial Porrúa, [1670] 1989.

Burgoa, Francisco de. *Geográfica descripción: De la parte septentrional del polo ártico de la América y nueva iglesia de las Indias Occidentales, y sitio astronómico de esta provincia de predicadores de Antequera, Valle de Oaxaca.* 3rd ed. 2 vols. Mexico City: Editorial Porrúa, [1674] 1989.

Burkhart, Louise. *The Slippery Earth: Nahua-Christian Moral Dialogue in Sixteenth-Century Mexico.* Tucson: University of Arizona Press, 1989.

Burkhart, Louise. *Holy Wednesday: A Nahua Drama from Early Colonial Mexico.* Philadelphia: University of Pennsylvania Press, 1996.

Burns, Kathryn. "Notaries, Truth, and Consequences." *The American Historical Review* 110, no. 2 (2005): 350–79.

Burns, Kathryn. "Andean Women in Religion: Beatas, 'Decency' and the Defence of Honour in Colonial Cuzco." In *Gender, Race, and Religion in the Colonization of the Americas.* Edited by Nora E. Jaffary. Aldershot, UK: Ashgate, 2007.

Burns, Kathryn. *Into the Archive: Writing and Power in Colonial Peru.* Durham, NC: Duke University Press, 2010.

Calancha, Antonio de la. *Corónica moralizada del orden de San Agustín.* 6 vols. Lima: Ignacio Prado Pastor, 1974.

Calvo, Thomas. *Vencer la derrota: Vivir en la sierra zapoteca de México (1674–1707).* Zamora, Michoacán: El Colegio de Michoacán, Centro de Estudios Mexicanos y Centroamericanos, CIESAS, Universidad Autónoma Benito Juárez de Oaxaca, 2010.

Campbell, Tony. "Portolan Charts from the Late Thirteenth Century to 1500." In *The History of Cartography.* Edited by J. B. Harley and David Woodward. Chicago: University of Chicago Press, 1987.

Canedo Gómez, Lino. *La educación de los marginados durante la época colonial: Escuelas y colegios para indios y mestizos en la Nueva España.* Mexico City: Porrúa, 1982.

Cárdenas Ayaipoma, Mario. "El colegio de caciques y el sometimiento ideológico de los residuos de la nobleza aborigen." *Revista del Archivo General de la Nación* 4/5 (1975–76): 5–24.

Cárdenas Ayaipoma, Mario. "El pueblo de Santiago: Un ghetto en Lima virreinal." *Boletín del Instituto Francés de Estudios Andinos* 9, no. 3 (1980): 19–48.

Carmagnani, Marcello. *El regreso de los dioses: El proceso de reconstitución de la identidad étnica en Oaxaca, siglos XVII y XVIII.* Mexico City: Fondo de Cultura Económica, 1988.

Carochi, Horacio. *Grammar of the Mexican Language: With an Explanation of Its Adverbs.* Translated by James Lockhart. Palo Alto, CA: Stanford University Press, [1645] 2001.

Carrasco, David, and Scott Sessions, eds. *Cave, City, and Eagle's Nest: An Interpretive Journey through the Mapa De Cuauhtinchan N. 2.* Albuquerque: University of New Mexico Press, 2007.

Carrasco, Pedro. "Royal Marriages in Ancient Mexico." In *Explorations in Ethnohistory.* Edited by Herbert R. Harvey. Albuquerque: Universtiy of New Mexico Press, 1984.

Catholic Church. *Confessionario para los curas de indios.* Lima: Antonio Ricardo, 1585.

Cerrón Palomino, Rodolfo. "Diversidad y unificación léxica en el mundo andino." In *El quechua en debate: Ideología, normalización y enseñanza.* Edited by Juan Carlos Godenzzi. Cuzco: Centro de Estudios Regionales Andinos Bartolomé de las Casas, 1992.

Cerrón Palomino, Rodolfo. *Lingüística quechua.* Cuzco: Centro de Estudios Rurales Andinos Bartolomé de las Casas, 1987.

Cerrón Palomino, Rodolfo. "El origen centro-andino del aimara." *Boletín de Arqueología PUCP* 4 (2000): 131–42.

Cerrón Palomino, Rodolfo. *Castellano andino: Aspectos sociolingüísticos, pedagógicos y gramaticales.* Lima: Pontificia Universidad Católica del Perú, Cooperación Técnica Alemana, 2003.

Cerrón Palomino, Rodolfo. "Contactos y desplazamientos lingüísticos en los Andes centro-sureños: El puquina, el aimara y el quechua." *Boletín de Arqueología PUCP* 14 (2010): 255–82.

Chance, John K. *Conquest of the Sierra: Spaniards and Indians in Colonial Oaxaca.* Norman: University of Oklahoma Press, 1989.

Chance, John K., and William B. Taylor. "Cofradías and Cargos: An Historical Perspective of the Mesoamerican Civil-Religious Hierarchy." *American Ethnologist* 12, no. 1 (1984): 1–26.

Charles, John. "Indios Ladinos: Colonial Andean Testimony and Ecclesiastical Institutions (1583–1650)." PhD diss., Yale University, 2003.

Charles, John. "Unreliable Confessions: Khipus in the Colonial Parish." *The Americas* 64, no. 1 (2007): 11–33.

Charles, John. "'More Ladino than Necessary': Indigenous Litigants and the Language Policy Debate in Mid-Colonial Peru." *Colonial Latin American Review* 16, no. 1 (2007): 23–47.

Charles, John. *Allies at Odds: The Andean Church and Its Indigenous Agents, 1583–1671.* Albuquerque: University of New Mexico Press, 2010.

Charney, Paul. *Indian Society in the Valley of Lima, Peru, 1532–1824.* Lanham, MD: University Press of America, 2001.

Chavero, Alfredo. "Anónimo Mexicano." *Anales del Museo Nacional de México* 7 (1903): 115–32.

Chimalpahin, Domingo. *Las ocho relaciones y el memorial de Cohuacan.* 2 vols. Edited by Rafael Tena. Mexico City: Cien de México, 1998.

Chimalpahin, Domingo de San Antón Muñón Quauhtlehuanitzin. *Codex Chimalpa-hin: Society and Politics in Mexico Tenochtitlan, Tlatelolco, Texcoco, Culhuacan, and Other Nahua Altepetl in Central Mexico.* 2 vols. Edited by Arthur J. O. Anderson and Susan Schroeder. Norman: University of Oklahoma Press, 1997.

Chimalpahin, Domingo de San Antón Muñón Quauhtlehuanitzin. *Annals of His Time.* Edited by James Lockhart, Susan Schroeder, and Doris Namala. Palo Alto, CA: Stanford University Press, 2006.

Chipman, Donald E. *Moctezuma's Children: Aztec Royalty under Spanish Rule, 1520–1700.* Austin: University of Texas Press, 2005.

Chocano Mena, Magdalena. *La fortaleza docta: Elite letrada y dominación social en México colonial (siglos XVI–XVII).* Barcelona: Bellaterra, 2000.

Clanchy, Michael T. *From Memory to Written Record: England 1066–1307.* 2nd ed. Oxford: Blackwell, 1993.

Cline, Sarah. "Fray Alonso de Molina's Model Testament and Antecedents to Indige-nous Wills in Spanish America." In *Dead Giveaways: Indigenous Testaments of Colonial Mesoamerica and the Andes.* Edited by Susan Kellogg and Matthew Restall. Salt Lake City: University of Utah Press, 1998.

Codex. "Codex Plancarte." In *Tres códices michoacanos.* Edited by José Corona Núñez. Morelia, Mexico: Universidad Michoacana de San Nicolás de Hidalgo, 1986.

Codex. "Codex Matritense del Palacio Real." In *Primeros Memoriales* by fray Bernardino de Sahagún. Norman: University of Oklahoma Press, 1993.

"Colegio de caciques: libro de la fundación del colegio de los hijos de caciques." *Inca* 1, no. 4 (1923): 779–883.

Conrad, Geoffrey, and Arthur Demarest. *Religion and Empire: The Dynamics of Aztec and Inca Expansionism.* Cambridge: Cambridge University Press, 1984.

Cook, Noble David, ed. *Padrón de los indios de Lima en 1613, por Miguel de Contreras.* Lima: Universidad Nacional Mayor de San Marcos, Seminario de Historia Rural Andina, 1968.

Córdoba, Juan de. *Vocabulario en lengua zapoteca.* Mexico City: En casa de P. Balli, 1578.

Cornejo, Miguel. "Pachacamac y el canal de Guatca." *Boletín del Instituto Francés de Es-tudios Andinos* 33, no. 3 (2004): 783–814.

Cuadriello, Jaime. "Moctezuma through the Centuries." In *Race and Classification: The Case of Mexican America.* Edited by Susan Deans-Smith and Ilona Katzew. Palo Alto, CA: Stanford University Press, 2009.

Cummins, Tom. "'Let Me See! Writing Is for Them': Colonial Andean Images and Objects 'como es costumbre tener los caciques señores.'" In *Native Traditions in the Post-Conquest World.* Edited by Elizabeth H. Boone and Tom Cummins. Washing-ton, DC: Dumbarton Oaks, 1998.

Cummins, Tom. *Toasts with the Inca: Andean Abstraction and Colonial Images on Quero Ves-sels.* Ann Arbor: University of Michigan Press, 2002.

Cummins, Tom. "Queros, Aquillas, Uncus, and Chulpas: The Composition of Inka Artistic Expression and Power." In *Variations in the Expression of Inka Power: A Sympo-sium at Dumbarton Oaks, 18 and 19 October 1997.* Edited by Richard L. Burger, Craig

Morris, and Ramiro Matos Mendieta. Washington, DC: Dumbarton Oaks Research Library and Collection, 2007.

Cummins, Tom. "Representation in the Sixteenth Century and the Colonial Image of the Inca." In *Writing without Words: Alternative Literacies in Mesoamerica and the Andes*. Edited by Elizabeth H. Boone and Walter Mignolo. Durham, NC: Duke University Press, 1994.

Cummins, Tom. "From Lies to Truth: Colonial Ekphrasis and the Act of Cross Cultural Translation." In *Reframing the Renaissance: Visual Culture in Europe and Latin America, 1450–1650*. Edited by Claire Farago. New Haven, CT: Yale University Press, 1995.

Cummins, Tom. "La fábula y el retrato: Imágenes tempranas del inca." In *Los incas, reyes del Perú*. Edited by Natalia Majluf. Lima: Banco de Crédito, 2005.

Cummins, Tom. "Dibujado de mi mano: La relación artística entre Guaman Poma de Ayala y Martín de Murúa." Talk given at Museo Chileno de Arte Precolombino (Santiago, Chile), 2011.

Cushner, Nicholas. *Lords of the Land: Sugar, Wine, and Jesuit Estates of Coastal Peru, 1600–1767*. Albany: University of New York Press, 1980.

De la Puente Brunke, José. "'Los vasallos se desentrañan por su rey': notas sobre quejas de curacas en el Perú del siglo XVII." *Anuario de Estudios Americanos* 55, no. 2 (1998): 459–73.

De la Puente Luna, José Carlos. *Los curacas hechiceros de Jauja: Batallas mágicas y legales en el Perú colonial*. Lima: Pontificia Universidad Católica del Perú, 2007.

Dean, Carolyn. *Inka Bodies and the Body of Christ: Corpus Christi in Colonial Cuzco*. Durham, NC: Duke University Press, 1999.

Dean, Carolyn, and Dana Leibsohn. "Hybridity and Its Discontents: Considering Visual Culture in Colonial Spanish America." *Colonial Latin American Review* 12, no. 1 (2003): 5–35.

Díaz de Salas, Marcelo, and Luis Reyes García. "Testimonio de la fundación de Santo Tomás Ajusco." *Tlalocan* 6, no. 3 (1970): 193–212.

Díaz Rementería, Carlos J. *El cacique en el virreinato del Perú*. Seville: Universidad de Sevilla, 1977.

Diel, Lori Boornazian. *The Tira de Tepechpan: Negotiating Place under Aztec and Spanish Rule*. Austin: University of Texas Press, 2008.

Diez de San Miguel, Garci. *Visita hecha a la provincia de Chucuito*. Lima: Casa de la Cultura, [1567] 1964.

Douglas, Eduardo de Jesus. "Pictorial History in the 'Quinatzin Map' of About 1542." *The Art Bulletin* 85, no. 2 (2003): 281–309.

Douglas, Eduardo de Jesus. *In the Palace of Nezahualcoyotl: Painting Manuscripts, Writing the Pre-Hispanic Past in Early Colonial Period Tetzcoco, Mexico*. Austin: University of Texas Press, 2010.

Dubernard Chauveau, Juan. *Códices de Cuernavaca y unos títulos de sus pueblos*. Mexico City: Porrúa, 1991.

Dueñas, Alcira. "Ethnic Power and Identity Formation in Mid-Colonial Andean Writing." *Colonial Latin American Review* 3 (2009): 407–33.

Dueñas, Alcira. *Indians and Mestizos in the "Lettered City": Reshaping Justice, Social Hierarchy, and Political Culture in Colonial Peru*. Boulder: University Press of Colorado, 2010.

Durston, Alan. *Pastoral Quechua: The History of Christian Translation in Colonial Peru, 1550–1650*. Notre Dame, IN: University of Notre Dame Press, 2007.

Durston, Alan. "Notes on the Authorship of the Huarochirí Manuscript." *Colonial Latin American Review* 16, no. 2 (2007): 227–41.

Durston, Alan. "Native-Language Literacy in Colonial Peru: The Question of Mundane Quechua Writing Revisited." *Hispanic American Historical Review* 88, no. 1 (2008): 41–70.

Durston, Alan. "Rectification of 'Notes on the Authorship of the Huarochirí Manuscript.'" *Colonial Latin American Review* 20, no. 2 (2011): 249–50.

Duviols, Pierre. *La destrucción de las religiones andinas (conquista y colonia)*. Translated by Albor Maruenda. Mexico City: Universidad Nacional Autónoma de México, 1977.

Duviols, Pierre. "La dinastía de los incas: ¿Monarquía o diarquía? Argumentos heurísticos a favor de una tesis estructuralista." *Journal de la Société des Américanistes* 56 (1979): 67–85.

Duviols, Pierre. "Introducción." In *Relación de antigüedades destos reynos del Piru*. Edited by Pierre Duviols. Cuzco: Centro de Estudios Regionales Andinos Bartolomé de Las Casas, Instituto Francés de Estudios Andinos, 1993.

Egaña, Antonio de, ed. *Monumenta Peruana*. 8 vols. Rome: Monumenta Historica Societatis Iesu, 1954–86.

Egido, Teófanes, Javier Burrieza Sánchez, and Manuel Revuelta González, eds. *Los Jesuitas en España y en el mundo hispánico*. Madrid: Marcial Pons, 2004.

Eguiguren, Luis Antonio. *Diccionario histórico-cronológico de la Real y Pontificia Universidad de San Marcos y sus colegios*. 3 vols. Lima: Imprenta Torres Aguirre, 1940–51.

Eire, Carlos M. N. *From Madrid to Purgatory: The Art and Craft of Dying in Sixteenth-Century Spain*. New York: Cambridge University Press, 1995.

Escriche, Joaquín. *Diccionario razonado de legislación civil, penal, comercial y forense*. Mexico City: Universidad Nacional Autónoma de México, 1993.

Espinosa Fernández de Córdova, Carlos. "The Fabrication of Andean Particularism." *Boletín del Instituto Francés de Estudios Andinos* 18, no. 2 (1989): 269–98.

Espinosa Fernández de Córdova, Carlos. "El retorno del Inca: Los movimientos neoincas en el contexto de la intercultura barroca." *Procesos* 18 (2002): 3–30.

Espinoza Soriano, Waldemar. "El alcalde mayor indígena en el virreinato del Perú." *Anuario de Estudios Americanos* 17 (1960): 183–300.

Estenssoro Fuchs, Juan Carlos. *Del paganismo a la santidad: La incorporación de los indios del Perú al catolicismo, 1532–1750*. Lima: Institut Français d'Études Andines, Pontificia Universidad Católica del Perú, 2003.

Estenssoro Fuchs, Juan Carlos. "Construyendo la memoria: La figura del inca y el reino del Perú, de la conquista a Tupac Amaru II." In *Los incas, reyes del Perú*. Edited by Natalia Majluf. Lima: Banco de Crédito, 2005.

Fane, Diana. "Portraits of the Inca: Notes on an Influential European Engraving." *Source* 29, no. 3 (2010): 31–39.

Farriss, Nancy M. *Maya Society under Colonial Rule: The Collective Enterprise of Survival.* Princeton, NJ: Princeton University Press, 1984.

Feierman, Steven. *Peasant Intellectuals: Anthropology and History in Tanzania.* Madison: University of Wisconsin Press, 1990.

Flores Galindo, Alberto. *In Search of an Inka: Identity and Utopia in the Andes.* Cambridge: Cambridge University Press, 2010.

Florescano, Enrique. *Origen y desarrollo de los problemas agrarios en México, 1500–1821.* Mexico City: ERA, 1976.

Florescano, Enrique. "La reconstrucción histórica elaborada por la nobleza indígena y sus descendientes mestizos." In *La memoria y el olvido: Segundo simposio de historia de las mentalidades.* Mexico City: Instituto Nacional de Antropología e Historia, 1985.

Florescano, Enrique. *Memory, Myth, and Time in Mexico: From the Aztecs to Independence.* Translated by Albert G. Bork. Austin: University of Texas Press, 1994.

Florescano, Enrique. "El canon memorioso forjado por los títulos primordiales." *Colonial Latin American Review* 11, no. 2 (2002): 183–230.

Galarza, Joaquín, and Carlos López Avila. *Tlacotenco Tonantzin Santa Ana: Tradiciones: Toponimia, técnicas, fiestas, canciones, versos y danzas.* Mexico City and Paris: CIESAS/ Musée de l'Homme, 1995.

Galdo Gutiérrez, Virgilio. *La educación de los curacas: Una forma de dominación colonial.* Huamanga: Universidad Nacional de San Cristóbal de Huamanga, 1982.

García Martínez, Bernardo. *Los Pueblos de la Sierra: El poder y el espacio entre los indios del norte de Puebla hasta 1700.* Mexico City: El Colegio de México, 1987.

García Martínez, Bernardo. "Jurisdicción y propiedad: Una distinción fundamental en la historia de los pueblos indios del México colonial." *Revista Europea de Estudios Latinoamericanos y del Caribe* 53 (1992): 47–60.

García, Pablo. "Saldos del criollismo: El *Teatro de virtudes políticas* de Carlos de Sigüenza y Góngora a la luz de la historiografía de Fernando de Alva Ixtlilxóchitl." *Colonial Latin American Review* 18, no. 2 (2009): 219–35.

Garcilaso de la Vega, Inca. *Comentarios reales de los incas.* 2 vols. Edited by Carlos Araníbar. Lima: Fondo de Cultura Económica, 1991 [1609].

Garibay, Angel María. *Historia de la literatura nahuatl.* 2 vols. Mexico City: Editorial Porrúa, 1971.

Garrett, David. *Shadows of Empire: The Indian Nobility of Cusco, 1750–1825.* Cambridge: Cambridge University Press, 2005.

Gemelli Carreri, Giovanni Francesco. *Viaje a la Nueva España.* Translated by Francisca Perujo. Mexico City: Universidad Nacional Autónoma de México, 1983.

Gerhard, Peter. *Geografía histórica de la Nueva España 1519–1821.* Translated by Stella Mastrangelo. Mexico City: UNAM, 1986.

Gibson, Charles. *Tlaxcala in the Sixteenth Century.* New Haven, CT: Yale University Press, 1952.

Gibson, Charles. "The Aztec Aristocracy in Colonial Mexico." *Comparative Studies in Society and History* 2, no. 2 (1960): 169–96.

Gibson, Charles. *The Aztecs under Spanish Rule: A History of the Indians of the Valley of Mexico, 1519–1810*. Palo Alto, CA: Stanford University Press, 1964.

Gibson, Charles. *Los aztecas bajo el dominio español, 1519–1810*. Mexico City: Siglo XXI, 1986.

Gibson, Charles, and John B. Glass. "A Census of Middle American Prose Manuscripts in the Native Historical Tradition." In *Guide to Ethnohistorical Sources*. Edited by Howard Cline. Austin: University of Texas Press, 1972–75.

Gillespie, Susan D. *The Aztec Kings: The Construction of Rulership in Mexica History*. Tucson: University of Arizona Press, 1989.

Gisbert, Teresa. *Iconografía y mitos indígenas en el arte*. La Paz: Gisbert, 1980.

Gonzalbo Aizpuru, Pilar. *Historia de la educación en la época colonial: El mundo indígena*. Mexico City: El Colegio de México, Centro de Estudios Históricos, 1990.

González de Cossío, Francisco. *Historia de la tenencia y explotación del campo desde la época precortesiana hasta las leyes de 6 de enero de 1915*, vol. 1. Mexico City: Talleres Gráficos de la Nación, 1957.

González Holguín, Diego. *Vocabulario de la lengua general de todo el Perú llamada lengua qquichua o del Inca*. Lima: Universidad Nacional Mayor de San Marcos, [1608] 1952.

Gotkowitz, Laura. *A Revolution for Our Rights: Indigenous Struggles for Land and Justice in Bolivia, 1880–1952*. Durham, NC: Duke University Press, 2007.

Gramsci, Antonio. *Selections from the Prison Notebooks*. New York: International Publishers, 1971.

Greaves, Nigel M. "Intellectuals and the Historical Construction of Knowledge and Identity: A Reappraisal of Gramsci's Ideas on Leadership," 2009. Accessed September 18, 2013. http://clogic.eserver.org/2008/Greaves.pdf.

Griffiths, Nicholas. *The Cross and the Serpent: Religious Repression and Resurgence in Colonial Peru*. Norman: University of Oklahoma Press, 1996.

Gruzinski, Serge. "Colonial Indian Maps in Sixteenth-Century Mexico: An Essay in Mixed Cartography." *RES: Anthropology and Aesthetics* 13 (1987): 46–61.

Gruzinski, Serge. *The Conquest of Mexico: The Incorporation of Indian Societies into the Western World, 16th–18th Centuries*. Translated by Eileen Corrigan. Cambridge: Polity Press, 1993.

Guerra, François-Xavier. *Modernidad e independencias: Ensayos sobre las revoluciones hispánicas*. Madrid: MAPFRE, 1992.

Guibovich, Pedro. "La educación en el Perú colonial: Fuentes e historiografía." *Histórica* 17, no. 2 (1993): 271–96.

Gutiérrez Arbulú, Laura, and Javier Flores Espinoza. "Dos documentos sobre los jesuitas en Huarochirí." *Boletín del Instituto Riva-Agüero* 19 (1992): 201–16.

Hanks, William F. *Converting Words: Maya in the Age of the Cross*. Berkeley: University of California Press, 2010.

Hartmann, Roswith. "El texto quechua de Huarochirí: Una evaluación crítica de las ediciones a disposición." *Histórica* 5, no. 2 (1981): 180–85.

Haskett, Robert. *Indigenous Rulers: An Ethnohistory of Town Government in Colonial Cuernavaca*. Albuquerque: University of New Mexico Press, 1991.

Haskett, Robert. "Visions of Municipal Glory Undimmed: The Nahuatl Town Histories of Colonial Cuernavaca." *Colonial Latin American Review* 1, no. 1 (1992): 1–36.

Haskett, Robert. "Paper Shields: The Ideology of Coats of Arms in Colonial Mexican Primordial Titles." *Ethnohistory* 43, no. 1 (1996): 99–126.

Haskett, Robert. "El legendario don Toribio en los títulos primordiales de Cuernavaca." In *De tlacuilos y escribanos: Estudios sobre documentos indígenas coloniales del centro de México*. Edited by Xavier Noguez and Stephanie Wood. Zamora, Michoacán: El Colegio de Michoacán, El Colegio Mexiquense, 1998.

Haskett, Robert. *Visions of Paradise: Primordial Titles and Mesoamerican History in Cuernavaca*. Norman: University of Oklahoma Press, 2005.

Haskett, Robert. "Primordial Titles." In *Sources and Methods for the Study of Postconquest Mesoamerican Ethnohistory*. Edited by James Lockhart, Lisa Sousa, and Stephanie Wood. Eugene: Wired Humanities Project, University of Oregon, 2007. Accessed September 18, 2013. http://whp.uoregon.edu/Lockhart/HaskettTitulos.pdf.

Haskett, Robert, and Stephanie Wood. "Primordial Titles Revisited, with a New Census and Bibliography," unpublished ms.

Heath, Shirley Bryce. *Telling Tongues: Language Policy in Mexico, Colony to Nation*. New York: Teachers College Press, 1972.

Herrera y Tordesillas, Antonio de. *Historia general de las Indias Occidentales, ò, de los hechos de los castellanos en las islas y tierra firme del mar océano*. Antwerp: J. B. Verdussen, [1601–15] 1728.

Herzog, Tamar. *Mediación, archivos y ejercicio: Los escribanos de Quito (siglo XVII)*. Frankfurt: Vittorio Klostermann, 1996.

Herzog, Tamar. *Upholding Justice: Society, State, and the Penal System in Quito (1650–1750)*. Ann Arbor: University of Michigan Press, 2004.

Hill, Robert M. "Land, Family, and Community in Highland Guatemala: Seventeenth-Century Cakchiquel Maya Testaments." In *Dead Giveaways: Indigenous Testaments of Mesoamerica and the Andes*. Edited by Susan Kellogg and Matthew Restall. Salt Lake City: University of Utah Press, 1998.

Houston, Stephen D. "All Things Must Change: Maya Writing over Time and Space." In *Their Way of Writing: Scripts, Signs, and Pictography in Pre-Columbian America*. Edited by Elizabeth H. Boone and Gary Urton. Washington, DC: Dumbarton Oaks, 2011.

Howard-Malverde, Rosaleen. "'Why Do They Steal Our Phonemes?' Inventing the Survival of the Cañari Language (Ecuador)." In *Linguistics and Archaeology in the Americas*. Edited by Eithne B. Carlin and Simon van de Kerke. Leiden: Brill, 2010.

Icaza, Francisco A. de. *Diccionario de conquistadores de Nueva España*. 2 vols. Madrid: Adelantado de Segovia, 1923.

Irvine, Judith, and Susan Gal. "Language Ideology and Linguistic Differentiation." In *Regimes of Language: Ideologies, Polities, and Identities*. Edited by Paul V. Kroskrity. Santa Fe, NM: School of American Research, 2000.

Itier, César. "Lengua general y comunicación escrita: Cinco cartas en quechua de Cotahuasi—1616." *Revista Andina* 9, no. 1 (1991): 65–107.

Itier, César. "What Was the '*Lengua General*' of Colonial Peru?" In *History and Lan-*

guage in the Andes. Edited by Paul Heggarty and Adrian Pearce. London: Palgrave-Macmillan, 2011.

Jarquín Ortega, María Teresa. "El códice Techialoyan García Granados y las congregaciones en el altiplano central de México." In *De tlacuilos y escribanos: Estudios sobre documentos indígenas coloniales del centro de México.* Edited by Xavier Noguez and Stephanie Wood. Zamora, Michoacán: El Colegio de Michoacán, El Colegio Mexiquense, 1998.

Joyce, Rosemary A. *Gender and Power in Prehispanic Mesoamerica.* Austin: University of Texas Press, 2000.

Julien, Catherine. "La organización parroquial del Cuzco y la ciudad incaica." *Tawantinsuyu* 5 (1998): 82–96.

Julien, Catherine. *Reading Inca History.* Iowa City: University of Iowa Press, 2009.

Kagan, Richard. *Lawsuits and Litigants in Castile, 1500–1700.* Chapel Hill: University of North Carolina Press, 1981.

Karttunen, Frances. *Between Worlds: Interpreters, Guides, and Survivors.* New Brunswick, NJ: Rutgers University Press, 1994.

Karttunen, Frances. "From Court Yard to the Seat of Government: The Career of Antonio Valeriano, Nahua Colleague of Bernardino De Sahagún." *Amerindia* 19/20 (1995): 113–20.

Karttunen, Frances. "Indigenous Writing as a Vehicle of Postconquest Continuity and Change in Mesoamerica." In *Native Traditions in the Postconquest World.* Edited by Elizabeth H. Boone and Thomas B. F. Cummins. Washington, DC: Dumbarton Oaks, 1998.

Kellogg, Susan. *Law and the Transformation of Aztec Culture, 1500–1700.* Norman: University of Oklahoma Press, 1995.

Kellogg, Susan, and Matthew Restall, eds. *Dead Giveaways: Indigenous Testaments of Colonial Mesoamerica and the Andes.* Salt Lake City: University of Utah Press, 1998.

Kobayashi, José María. *La educación como conquista: Empresa franciscana en México.* Mexico City: El Colegio de México, 1974.

Konetzke, Richard, ed. *Colección de documentos para la historia de la formación social de Hispanoamérica, 1493–1810.* 2 vols. Madrid: Consejo Superior de Investigaciones Científicas, 1953.

Kranz, Travis Barton. "Visual Persuasion: Sixteenth-Century Tlaxcalan Pictorials in Response to the Conquest of Mexico." In *The Conquest All over Again: Nahuas and Zapotecs Thinking, Writing, and Painting Spanish Colonialism.* Edited by Susan Schroeder. Eastbourne, UK: Sussex Academic Press, 2010.

Krug, Frances. "The Nahuatl Annals of the Tlaxcala-Puebla Region." UCLA, n.d.

Krug, Frances, and Camilla Townsend. "The Tlaxcala-Puebla Family of Annals." In *Sources and Methods for the Study of Post-Conquest Mesoamerican Ethnohistory.* Edited by James Lockhart, Lisa Sousa, and Stephanie Wood, University of Oregon, Eugene, 2007.

Lamana, Gonzalo. *Domination without Dominance: Inca-Spanish Encounters in Early Colonial Peru.* Durham, NC: Duke University Press, 2008.

Laurencich-Minelli, Laura, ed. *Exsul Immeritus Blas Valera Populo Suo e Historia et Rudimenta Linguae Piruanorum.* Bologna: Lexis, Biblioteca di Scienze umane 16; Cooperativa Libraria Universitaria Editrice Bologna (CLUEB), 2007.

Lavallé, Bernard. "Presión colonial y reivindicación indígena en Cajamarca (1785–1820)." *Allpanchis* 35–36 (1990): 105–37.

Le Goff, Jacques. *Medieval Civilization, 400–1500.* Oxford: Blackwell, 1990.

Leibsohn, Dana. "Primers for Memory: Cartographic Histories and Nahua Identity." In *Writing without Words: Alternative Literacies in Mesoamerica and the Andes.* Edited by Elizabeth H. Boone and Walter Mignolo. Durham, NC: Duke University Press, 1994.

Leibsohn, Dana. "Colony and Cartography: Shifting Signs on Indigenous Maps of New Spain." In *Reframing the Renaissance: Visual Culture in Europe and Latin America, 1450–1650.* Edited by Claire Farago. New Haven, CT: Yale University Press, 1995.

Leibsohn, Dana, and Barbara Mundy. "Vistas: Spanish American Visual Culture, 1520–1820." 2005. Accessed September 18, 2013. http://www.smith.edu/vistas/index.html.

León Pinelo, Diego de. *Mandó que se imprimiesse este escrito el Excelent.mo señor Conde de Alva de Aliste, y de Villaflor, grande de Castilla, virrey destos Reynos del Peru, en la iunta, que se ha formado, por cedula de Su Magestad, de 21 de setiembre de 1660 Años.* Lima: n.p., 1661.

León Portilla, Miguel, and Earl Shorris, eds. *In the Language of Kings: An Anthology of Mesoamerican Literature.* New York: W. W. Norton, 2001.

Liss, Peggy K. "Jesuit Contributions to the Ideology of Spanish Empire in Mexico: Part I. The Spanish Imperial Ideology and the Establishment of the Jesuits within Mexican Society." *The Americas* 29, no. 3 (1973): 314–33.

Liss, Peggy K. *Isabel the Queen: Life and Times.* Rev. ed. Philadelphia: University of Pennsylvania Press, 2004.

Lockhart, James. *Spanish Peru: A Colonial Society.* Madison: University of Wisconsin Press, 1968.

Lockhart, James. "Views of Corporate Self and History in Some Valley of Mexico Towns: Late Seventeenth and Eighteenth Centuries." In *The Inca and Aztec States 1400–1800: Anthropology and History,* edited by George Collier, Renato Rosaldo, and John Wirth. New York: Academic Press, 1982.

Lockhart, James. "Views of Corporate Self and History in Some Valley of Mexico Towns, Seventeenth and Eighteenth Centuries." In *Nahuas and Spaniards: Postconquest Central Mexican History and Philology.* Edited by James Lockhart. Los Angeles: UCLA Latin American Center Publications, 1991.

Lockhart, James. "Three Experiences of Culture Contact: Nahua, Maya, and Quechua." In *Native Traditions in the Postconquest World.* Edited by Elizabeth H. Boone and Thomas B. F. Cummins. Washington, DC: Dumbarton Oaks, 1998.

Lockhart, James. *The Nahuas after the Conquest: A Social and Cultural History of the Indians of Central Mexico, Sixteenth through Eighteenth Centuries.* Palo Alto, CA: Stanford University Press, 1992.

Lockhart, James, Frances Berdan, and Arthur J. O. Anderson, eds. and trans. *The Tlaxcalan Actas: A Compendium of the Records of the Cabildo of Tlaxcala, 1545–1627*. Salt Lake City: University of Utah Press, 1986.

Lohmann Villena, Guillermo, and María Justina Sarabia Viejo, eds. *Francisco de Toledo: Disposiciones gubernativas para el virreinato del Perú*. 2 vols. Seville: Escuela de Estudios Hispanomericanos, Consejo Superior de Investigaciones Científicas, 1986–89.

Lopes Don, Patricia. "The 1539 Inquisition and Trial of Don Carlos of Texcoco." *Hispanic American Historical Review* 88, no. 4 (2008): 573–606.

López Austin, Alfredo. "Un repertorio de los tiempos en idioma náhuatl." *Anales de Antropología* 10 (1973): 285–96.

López Austin, Alfredo. "Sahagún's Work and the Medicine of the Ancient Nahuas: Possibilities for Study." In *Sixteenth-Century Mexico: The Work of Sahagún*. Edited by Munro S. Edmonson. Albuquerque: University of New Mexico Press, 1974.

López Caballero, Paula, ed. *Los títulos primordiales del centro de México*. Mexico City: CONACULTA, 2003.

Lowry, Lyn B. "Forging an Indian Nation: Urban Indians under Spanish Colonial Control (Lima, Peru, 1535–1765)." PhD diss., University of California, 1991.

Loza, Carmen Beatriz. "Du bon usage des *quipus* face à l'administration coloniale espagnole (1500–1600)." *Population* 1–2 (1998): 139–60.

Luján Muñoz, Jorge. "La literatura notarial en España e Hispanoamérica." *Anuario de Estudios Americanos* 38 (1981): 101–16.

MacCormack, Sabine. "Grammar and Virtue: The Formulation of a Cultural and Missionary Program by the Jesuits in Early Colonial Peru." In *The Jesuits: Cultures, Sciences, and the Arts, 1540–1773*. Edited by John O'Malley, Gauvin Alexander Baily, Steven J. Harris, and T. Frank Kennedy. Toronto: University of Toronto, 2006.

MacCormack, Sabine. *On the Wings of Time: Rome, the Incas, Spain and Peru*. Princeton, NJ: Princeton University Press, 2007.

Macera, Pablo. "Noticias sobre la enseñanza elemental en el Perú durante el siglo XVIII." *Revista Histórica* 29 (1967): 327–76.

Majluf, Natalia. "De la rebelión al museo: genealogías y retratos de los incas, 1781–1900." In *Los incas, reyes del Perú*. Edited by Natalia Majluf. Lima: Banco de Crédito del Perú, 2005.

Majluf, Natalia, ed. *Los incas, reyes del Perú*. Arte y Tesoros del Perú. Lima: Banco de Crédito del Perú, 2005.

Mannheim, Bruce. *The Language of the Inka since European Invasion*. Austin: University of Texas Press, 1991.

Mannheim, Bruce. "The Inka Language in the Colonial World." *Colonial Latin American Review* 1, nos. 1–2 (1992): 77–108.

Martín, Luis. "The Peruvian Indian through Jesuit Eyes: The Case of José de Acosta and Pablo José de Arriaga." In *The Jesuit Tradition in Education and Missions: A 450-Year Perspective*. Edited by Christopher Capple. Scranton, PA: University of Scranton Press, 1993.

Martínez Baracs, Andrea. *Un gobierno de indios: Tlaxcala, 1519–1750*. Mexico City: Fondo de Cultura Económica, 2008.

Martínez, Henrico. *Reportorio de los tiempos e historia natural de Nueva España*. Mexico City: Secretaría de Educación Pública, [1606] 1948.

Martínez, Hildeberto. *Codiciaban la tierra: El despojo agrario en los señoríos de Tecamachalco y Quecholac (Puebla, 1520–1650)*. Mexico City: CIESAS, 1994.

Martínez, María Elena. *Genealogical Fictions: Limpieza de Sangre, Religion, and Gender in Colonial Mexico*. Palo Alto, CA: Stanford University Press, 2008.

Matthew, Laura, Matthew Restall, and Michel Oudijk, eds. *Indian Conquistadors: Indigenous Allies in the Conquest of Mesoamerica*. Norman: University of Oklahoma Press, 2007.

McCafferty, Sharisse D., and Geoffrey G. McCafferty. "Weaving Space: Textile Imagery and Landscape in the Mixtec Codices." In *Space and Spatial Analysis in Archaeology*. Edited by Elizabeth Robertson, Jeffrey D. Seibert, Deepika C. Fernandez, and Marc U. Zender. Calgary: University of Calgary Press, 2006.

Medina, Andrés. *En las cuatro esquinas, en el centro: Etnografía de la cosmovisión Mesoamericana*. Mexico City: IIA-UNAM, 2003.

Medinaceli, Ximena, and Marcela Inch, eds. *Pleitos y riqueza: Los caciques andinos en Potosí del siglo XVII; Transcripción y estudios del expediente de don Diego Chambilla contra los bienes de su administrador*. Sucre: Archivo y Biblioteca Nacionales de Bolivia, Fundación Cultural del Banco Central de Bolivia, Instituto de Estudios Bolivianos, 2010.

Megged, Amos. "El 'Relato de Memoria' de los axoxpanecas (Posclásico Tardío a 1610 DC)." *Relaciones: Estudios de Historia y Sociedad* 31, no. 122 (2010): 107–62.

Megged, Amos. *Social Memory in Ancient and Colonial Mesoamerica*. Cambridge: Cambridge University Press, 2010.

Meiklejohn, Norman. *La Iglesia y los lupaqas de Chucuito durante la colonia*. Cuzco: Centro de Estudios Regionales Andinos Bartolomé de las Casas, 1988.

"Memorial de Sololá [c. 1604]." In *Anales de los cakchiqueles*. Edited by Adrián Recinos. Mexico City: Fondo de Cultura Económica, 1980.

Menegus Bornemann, Margarita. "Los títulos primordiales de los Pueblos de Indios." In *Dos décadas de investigación en historia económica en América Latina: Homenaje a Carlos Sempat Assadourian*. Edited by M. Menegus. Mexico City: El Colegio de México, 1999.

Menegus Bornemann, Margarita. *Del señorío indígena a la república de indios, el caso de Toluca 1500–1600*. Mexico City: Consejo Nacional para la Cultura y las Artes, 1994.

Mignolo, Walter. *The Darker Side of the Renaissance: Literacy, Territoriality, and Colonization*. Ann Arbor: University of Michigan Press, 1995.

Mills, Kenneth. "The Limits of Religious Coercion in Mid-Colonial Peru." *Past and Present* 145 (1994): 84–121.

Mills, Kenneth. *An Evil Lost to View? An Investigation of Post-Evangelisation Andean Religion in Mid-Colonial Peru*, vol. 18. Liverpool: Institute of Latin American Studies, University of Liverpool, 1994.

Mills, Kenneth. "Bad Christians in Colonial Peru." *Colonial Latin American Review* 5, no. 2 (1996): 183–218.

Mills, Kenneth. *Idolatry and Its Enemies: Colonial Andean Religion and Extirpation, 1640–1750.* Princeton, NJ: Princeton University Press, 1997.

Mills, Kenneth. "The Naturalization of Andean Christianities." In *The Cambridge History of Christianity.* Edited by R. Po-Chia Hsia. Cambridge: Cambridge University Press, 2007.

Miram, Helga-María, and Victoria R. Bricker. "Relating Time to Space: The Maya Calendar Compasses." In *Eighth Palenque Round Table, 1993.* Edited by Martha J. Macri and Jan McHargue. San Francisco: Pre-Columbian Art Research Institute, 1996.

Montes de Oca, Mercedes. "Las glosas y las imágenes en la cartografía colonial del centro de México: ¿Dos recorridos que se oponen?" In *Cartografía de tradición indígena: Mapas de mercedes de tierras siglos XVI y XVII.* Edited by Mercedes Montes de Oca, Dominique Raby, Reyes Equiguas, and Adam T. Sellen. Mexico City: UNAM/AGN, 2003.

Morales, Francisco. *Ethnic and Social Background of the Franciscan Friars in Seventeenth Century Mexico.* Washington, DC: Academy of American Franciscan History, 1973.

Mumford, Jeremy Ravi. "Vertical Empire: The Struggle for Andean Space in the Sixteenth Century." PhD diss., Yale University, 2003.

Mundy, Barbara. *The Mapping of New Spain: Indigenous Cartography and the Maps of the Relaciones Geográficas.* Chicago: University of Chicago Press, 1996.

Muñoz Camargo, Diego. *Historia de Tlaxcala.* Edited by Luis Reyes García. Tlaxcala: Gobierno del Estado de Tlaxcala; CIESAS; Universidad Autónoma de Tlaxcala, 1998.

Murra, John V. *Formaciones económicas y políticas del mundo andino.* Lima: Instituto de Estudios Peruanos, 1975.

Murra, John V. "Litigation over the Rights of 'Natural Lords' in Early Colonial Courts in the Andes." In *Native Traditions in the Postconquest World.* Edited by Elizabeth H. Boone and Thomas B. F. Cummins. Washington, DC: Dumbarton Oaks, 1998.

Murúa, Martín de. *Códice Murúa: Historia y genealogía de los reyes Incas del Perú del padre mercedario fray Martín de Murúa; Códice Galvin.* Edited by Juan Ossio. Madrid: Testimonio Compañía Editorial, S.A., 2004.

Muysken, Pieter. "Callahuaya." In *Contact Languages: A Wider Perspective.* Edited by Sarah G. Thomason. Amsterdam: J. Benjamins, 1997.

O'Gorman, Edmundo, ed. *Guía de las actas del cabildo de la ciudad de México, siglo XVI.* Mexico City: Fondo de Cultura Económica, 1970.

Olaechea Labayen, Juan B. "La política selectiva de los jesuitas en los colegios de hijos de caciques." *Estudios de Deusto* 21, no. 48–49 (1973): 405–27.

O'Malley, John. *The First Jesuits.* Cambridge, MA: Harvard University Press, 1993.

O'Phelan Gody, Scarlett. *Kurakas sin sucesiones: Del cacique al alcalde de Indios en Perú y Bolivia, 1750–1835.* Cuzco: Centro de Estudios Regionales Andinos Bartolomé de Las Casas, 1997.

O'Phelan Gody, Scarlett. *La Gran Rebelión de los Andes: De Túpac Amaru a Túpac Catari.* Archivos de Historia Andina. Cuzco: Centro de Estudios Regionales Andinos Bartolomé de Las Casas, 1995.

Osowski, Edward W. "Indigenous Centurions and Triumphal Arches: Negotiation in Eighteenth-Century Mexico City." In *Negotiation within Domination: New Spain's Indian Pueblos Confront the Spanish State.* Edited by Ethelia Ruiz-Medrano and Susan Kellogg. Boulder: University Press of Colorado, 2010.

Oudijk, Michel. *Historiography of the Benizaa: The Postclassic and Early Colonial Periods (1000–1600 A.D.).* Leiden: University of Leiden, 2000.

Oudijk, Michel, and Matthew Restall. "Mesoamerican Conquistadors in the Sixteenth Century." In *Indian Conquistadors: Indigenous Allies in the Conquest of Mesoamerica.* Edited by Laura Matthew and Michel Oudijk. Norman: University of Oklahoma Press, 2007.

Owensby, Brian P. *Empire of Law and Indian Justice in Colonial Mexico.* Palo Alto, CA: Stanford University Press, 2008.

Pärssinen, Martti, and Jukka Kiviharju. *Textos andinos: Corpus de textos khipu incaicos y coloniales.* Madrid: Instituto Iberoamericano de Finlandia y Departamento de Filología Española de la Universidad Complutense de Madrid, 2004.

Pease, Franklin. *Las crónicas y los Andes.* Lima: Fondo de Cultura Económica, 1995.

Pérez Bocanegra, Juan. *Ritual formulario e institucion de curas, para administrar a los naturales de este reyno, los santos sacramentos del baptismo, confirmacion, eucaristia y viatico, penitencia, extremauncion, y matrimonio, con advertencias muy necessarias.* Lima: Geronimo de Contreras, 1631.

Pérez-Rocha, Emma. *La tierra y el hombre en la villa de Tacuba.* Mexico City: UNAM, 1992.

Petrucci, Armando. *Prima lezione di paleografia.* Rome: Laterza, 2002.

Pizzigoni, Caterina, ed. and trans. *Testaments of Toluca.* Palo Alto, CA: Stanford University Press, 2007.

Platt, Tristan, Thérèse Bouysse-Cassagne, and Olivia Harris, eds. *Qaraqara-Charka: Mallku, Inka y Rey en la provincia de Charcas (siglos XV–XVII): Historia antropológica de una confederación aymara.* La Paz: Plural Editores, 2006.

Platt, Tristan, and Pablo Quisbert. "Tras las huellas del silencio: Potosí, los inka y el virrey Toledo." In *Mina y metalurgia en los Andes del sur.* Edited by Pablo José Cruz and Jean Vacher. Lima: Instituto Francés de Estudios Andinos, Institut de Recherche pour le Développement, 2008.

Polia Meconi, Mario, ed. *La cosmovisión religiosa andina en los documentos inéditos del archivo romano de la Compañía de Jesús (1581–1752).* Lima: Pontificia Universidad Católica del Perú, 1999.

Poloni-Simard, Jacques. *El mosaico indígena: Movilidad, estratificación social y mestizaje en el corregimiento de Cuenca (Ecuador) del siglo XVI al XVIII.* Quito: Instituto Francés de Estudios Andinos, Abya Yala, 2006.

Poma, Felipe Guaman. *El primer nueva corónica y buen gobierno.* Edited by John V. Murra and Rolena Adorno. 3 vols. Mexico City: Siglo XXI, 1980.

Pratt, Mary Louise. "Arts of the Contact Zone." *Profession* 91 (1991): 33–40.

Prem, Hans J. *Milpa y hacienda: Tenencia de la tierra indígena y española en la cuenca del Alto Atoyac, Puebla, México (1520–1650).* Mexico City: CIESAS; Gobierno del Estado de Puebla; Fondo de Cultura Económica, 1988.

Quispe-Agnoli, Rocío. "Cuando Occidente y los Andes se encuentran: Qellcay, escritura alfabética y tokhapu en el siglo XVI." *Colonial Latin American Review* 14, no. 2 (2005): 263–98.

Quispe-Agnoli, Rocío. *La fe andina en la escritura: Resistencia e identidad en la obra de Guaman Poma de Ayala.* Lima: Universidad Nacional Mayor de San Marcos, 2006.

Rama, Angel. *La ciudad letrada.* Hanover, NH: Ediciones del Norte, 1984.

Rama, Angel. *The Lettered City.* Translated by John Charles Chasteen. Durham, NC: Duke University Press, 1996.

Ramírez Ruiz, Marcelo. "Territorialidad, pintura y paisaje del pueblo de indios." In *Territorialidad y paisaje en el altepetl del siglo XVI.* Edited by Fernández Christlieb and Angel Julián García Zambrano. Mexico City: Fondo de Cultura Económica-Instituto de Geografía, UNAM, 2006.

Ramos, Gabriela. "Los símbolos de poder inca durante el virreinato." In *Los incas, reyes del Perú.* Edited by Natalia Majluf. Lima: Banco de Crédito, 2005.

Ramos, Gabriela. *Death and Conversion in the Andes: Lima and Cuzco, 1532–1670.* Notre Dame, IN: University of Notre Dame Press, 2010.

Ramos, Gabriela. "Language and Society in Early Colonial Peru." In *History and Languages in the Andes.* Edited by Paul Heggarty and Adrian Pearce. London: Palgrave Macmillan, 2011.

Ramos, Gabriela. " 'Mi Tierra': Indigenous Urban Indians and Their Hometowns in the Colonial Andes." In *City Indians in Spain's American Empire: Urban Indigenous Society in Colonial Mesoamerica and Andean South America, 1600–1830.* Edited by Dana Velasco Murillo, Margarita Ochoa, and Mark Lentz. Brighton, UK: Sussex Academic Press, 2012.

Ramos, Gabriela, and Henrique Urbano, eds. *Catolicismo y extirpación de idolatrías: Charcas, Chile, México, Perú, siglos XVI–XVIII.* Cuzco: Centro de Estudios Regionales Andinos Bartolomé de Las Casas, 1993.

Rappaport, Joanne. *Cumbe Reborn: An Andean Ethnography of History.* Chicago: University of Chicago Press, 1993.

Rappaport, Joanne. "Between Sovereignty and Culture: Who Is an Indigenous Intellectual in Colombia?" *International Review of Social History* 49 (2004): 111–32.

Rappaport, Joanne, and Thomas B. F. Cummins. "Literacy and Power in Colonial Latin America." In *The Social Construction of the Past: Representation as Power.* Edited by Angela Gilliam and George Bond. London: Routledge, 1994.

Rappaport, Joanne, and Thomas B. F. Cummins. *Beyond the Lettered City: Indigenous Literacies in the Andes.* Durham, NC: Duke University Press, 2012.

Rémi, Siméon. *Diccionario de la lengua nahuatl o mexicana.* Mexico City: Siglo Veintiuno, [1885] 1997.

Remington, J. A. "Current Astronomical Practices among the Maya." In *Native American Astronomy.* Edited by Anthony Aveni. Austin: University of Texas Press, 1977.

Rendón Ortiz, Gilberto. "Un drama cosmogónico en el cielo prehispánico." *Odisea, Revista personal de revistas* 1, no. 1 (2008).

Restall, Matthew. *Life and Death in a Maya Community: The Ixil Testaments of the 1760s.* Lancaster, PA: Latyrinthos, 1995.

Restall, Matthew. "Heirs to the Hieroglyphs: Indigenous Writing in Colonial Mesoamerica." *The Americas* 54 (1997): 239–67.

Restall, Matthew. *The Maya World: Yucatec Culture and Society, 1550–1850.* Palo Alto, CA: Stanford University Press, 1997.

Restall, Matthew. "Interculturation and the Indigenous Testament in Colonial Yucatan." In *Dead Giveaways: Indigenous Testaments of Mesoamerica and the Andes.* Edited by Susan Kellogg and Matthew Restall. Salt Lake City: University of Utah Press, 1998.

Restall, Matthew, Lisa Sousa, and Kevin Terraciano, eds. *Mesoamerican Voices: Native-Language Writings from Colonial Mexico, Oaxaca, Yucatan, and Guatemala.* Cambridge: Cambridge University Press, 2005.

Reyes García, Luis. *La escritura pictográfica en Tlaxcala: Dos mil años de experiencia mesoamericana.* Tlaxcala: Universidad Autónoma de Tlaxcala, 1993.

Reyes García, Luis, ed. *¿Cómo te confundes? ¿Acaso no somos conquistados? Anales de Juan Bautista.* Mexico City: CIESAS, 2001.

Ricard, Robert. *The Spiritual Conquest of Mexico.* Berkeley: University of California Press, 1966.

Ricoeur, Paul. *Time and Narrative.* 3 vols. Translated by Kathleen McLaughlin and David Pellauer. Chicago: University of Chicago Press, 1985.

Río, Mercedes del. *Etnicidad, territorialidad y colonialismo en los Andes: Tradición y cambio entre los soras de los siglos XVI y XVII.* La Paz: Instituto de Estudios Bolivianos, Instituto Francés de Estudios Andinos, 2006.

Ripia, Juan de la. *Practica de testamentos y modos de subceder.* Cuenca: Antonio Núñez Enríquez, 1676.

Rivarola, José Luis. *Español andino: Textos bilingües de los siglos XVI y XVII.* Frankfurt and Madrid: Vervuert/Iberoamericana, 2000.

Robertson, Donald. *Mexican Manuscript Painting of the Early Colonial Period.* Norman: University of Oklahoma Press, 1994.

Robertson, Donald, and Martha Barton Robertson. "Techialoyan Manuscripts and Paintings, with a Catalog." In *Handbook of Middle American Indians.* Edited by Robert Wauchope. Austin: University of Texas Press, 1975.

Romero Frizzi, María de los Angeles. "The Power of the Law: The Construction of Colonial Power in an Indigenous Region." In *Negotiation within Domination: New Spain's Indian Pueblos Confront the Spanish State.* Edited by Ethelia Ruiz Medrano and Susan Kellogg. Boulder: University Press of Colorado, 2010.

Rostworowski de Diez Canseco, María. *Señoríos indígenas de Lima y Canta.* Lima: Instituto de Estudios Peruanos, 1978.

Rostworowski de Diez Canseco, María. *Estructuras andinas del poder: Ideología religiosa y política.* Lima: Instituto de Estudios Peruanos, 1983.

Rostworowski de Diez Canseco, María. *El señorío de Pachacamac: El informe de Rodrigo Cantos de Andrade de 1573*. Lima: Instituto de Estudios Peruanos/Banco Central de Reserva del Perú, 1999.

Rostworowski de Diez Canseco, María. *History of the Inca Realm*. Translated by Harry B. Iceland. Cambridge: Cambridge University Press, 1999.

Rounds, J. "Dynastic Succession and the Centralization of Power in Tenochtitlan." In *The Inca and Aztec States 1400–1800: Anthropology and History*. Edited by George A. Collier, Renato Rosaldo, and John Wirth. New York: Academic Press, 1982.

Rowe, John H. "El movimiento nacional inca del siglo XVIII." *Revista Universitaria* 43, no. 107 (1954): 17–47.

Roys, Ralph Loveland. *The Maya Katun Prophecies of the Books of Chilam Balam*. Series I. Washington, DC: Carnegie Institution, 1954.

Roys, Ralph Loveland. *Ritual of the Bacabs: A Book of Maya Incantations*. Norman: University of Oklahoma Press, 1965.

Roys, Ralph Loveland, ed. *The Book of Chilam Balam of Chumayel: Civilization of the American Indian*. Norman: University of Oklahoma Press, 1967.

Ruiz de Alarcón, Hernando. *Treatise on the Heathen Superstitions That Today Live among the Indians Native to This New Spain*. Norman: University of Oklahoma Press, [1626] 1984.

Ruiz Medrano, Ethelia. "Códices y justicia: Los caminos de la dominación." *Arqueología Mexicana* 7, no. 38 (1999): 44–50.

Ruiz Medrano, Ethelia. "El espejo y su reflejo: Títulos primordiales de los pueblos Indios utilizados por españoles en Tlaxcala, siglo XVIII." In *Indios, mestizos y españoles: Interculturalidad historiográfica en la Nueva España*. Edited by Danna Levin and Federico Navarrete. Mexico City: UAM/IIH-UNAM, 2007.

Ruiz Medrano, Ethelia. *Mexico's Indigenous Communities: Their Lands and Histories, 1500–2010*. Boulder: University Press of Colorado, 2010.

Ruiz Medrano, Ethelia, and Susan Kellogg, eds. *Negotiation within Domination: New Spain's Indian Pueblos Confront the Spanish State*. Boulder: University Press of Colorado, 2010.

Saenger, Paul. "Silent Reading: Its Impact on Late Medieval Script and Society." *Viator* 13 (1982): 367–414.

Saenger, Paul. *Space between Words: The Origins of Silent Reading*. Palo Alto, CA: Stanford University Press, 1997.

Sahagún, Bernardino de. *Florentine Codex: General History of the Things of New Spain*. 12 vols. Translated by Arthur J. O. Anderson and Charles E. Dibble. Santa Fe, NM: School of American Research and University of Utah, 1975.

Salomon, Frank. "Chronicles of the Impossible: Notes on Three Peruvian Indigenous Historians." In *From Oral to Written Expression: Native Andean Chronicles of the Early Colonial Period*. Edited by Rolena Adorno. Syracuse, NY: Maxwell School of Citizenship and Public Affairs, 1982.

Salomon, Frank. *Nightmare Victory: The Meanings of Conversion among the Peruvian Indians*

(*Huarochirí, 1608?*). 1992 Lecture Series, Working Papers No. 7. College Park: Department of Spanish and Portuguese, University of Maryland, 1990.

Salomon, Frank. "Collquiri's Dam: The Colonial Re-Voicing of an Appeal to the Archaic." In *Native Traditions in the Post-Conquest World*. Edited by Elizabeth H. Boone and Tom Cummins. Washington, DC: Dumbarton Oaks, 1998.

Salomon, Frank. "How an Andean 'Writing without Words' Works." *Current Anthropology* 42, no. 1 (2001): 1–27.

Salomon, Frank. "Testimonios en triángulo: Personajes de la *Nueva Corónica* de Guaman Poma y el Manuscrito quechua de Huarochirí en el pleito sobre el cacicazgo principal de Mama." *Chungara, Revista de Antropología Chilena* 35, no. 2 (2003): 253–68.

Salomon, Frank. *The Cord Keepers: Khipus and Cultural Life in a Peruvian Village*. Durham, NC: Duke University Press, 2004.

Salomon, Frank, and Sabine Hyland, eds. "Graphic Pluralism: Native American Systems of Inscription and the Colonial Situation." *Ethnohistory* 57, no. 1 (2010).

Salomon, Frank, and George Urioste, eds. *The Huarochirí Manuscript: A Testament of Andean and Colonial Andean Religion*. Austin: University of Texas Press, 1991.

Salomon, Frank, and Mercedes Niño-Murcia. *The Lettered Mountain: A Peruvian Village's Way with Writing*. Durham, NC: Duke University Press, 2012.

Sarmiento de Gamboa, Pedro. *Historia Indica*. Edited by Carmelo Sáenz de Santa María. Biblioteca de Autores Españoles. Vol. 135. Madrid: Atlas, [1572] 1960.

Sarmiento de Gamboa, Pedro. *The History of the Incas*. Translated by Brian Bauer and Vania Smith. Austin: University of Texas Press, 2007.

Schrader-Kniffki, Martina, and Yanna Yannakakis. "Sins and Crimes: Zapotec-Spanish Translation from Catholic Evangelization to Colonial Law (Oaxaca, New Spain)." In *Missionary Linguistics V/Lingüística Misionera V: Translation Theories and Practices*. Edited by Klaus Zimmerman, Martina Schrader-Kniffki, and Otto Zwartjes. Amsterdam: J. Benjamins, 2014.

Schroeder, Susan. *Chimalpahin and the Kingdoms of Chalco*. Tucson: University of Arizona Press, 1991.

Schroeder, Susan. "The Noblewomen of Chalco." *Estudios de Cultura Náhuatl* 22 (1992): 45–86.

Schroeder, Susan. "The First American Valentine: Nahua Courtship and Other Aspects of Family Structuring in Mesoamerica." *Journal of Family History* 23, no. 4 (1998): 341–54.

Schroeder, Susan. "Chimalpahin, Don Carlos María de Bustamante and *The Conquest of Mexico* as Cause for Mexican Nationalism." *Estudios de Cultura Náhuatl* 39 (2008): 288–89.

Schroeder, Susan, ed. "Chimalpahin Rewrites the Conquest: Yet Another Epic History?" In *The Conquest All over Again: Nahuas and Zapotecs Thinking, Writing, and Painting Spanish Colonialism*. Eastbourne, UK: Sussex Academic Press, 2010.

Schroeder, Susan. "The Truth about the Crónica Mexicayotl." *Colonial Latin American Review* 20, no. 2 (2011): 233–47.

Schroeder, Susan, Stephanie Wood, and Robert Haskett, eds. *Indian Women in Early Mexico*. Norman: University of Oklahoma Press, 1997.

Schroeder, Susan, Anne J. Cruz, Cristián Roa-de-la-Carrera, and David E. Tavárez, eds. *Chimalpahin's Conquest: A Nahua Historian's Rewriting of Francisco López de Gómara's La Conquista de México*. Palo Alto, CA: Stanford University Press, 2010.

Schwaller, John F. "Don Bartolomé de Alva, Nahuatl Scholar of the Seventeenth Century." In *Bartolomé de Alva: Guide to Confessions Large and Small*, edited by Barry Sell and John F. Schwaller. Norman: University of Oklahoma Press, 1999.

Schwaller, Robert, ed. "A Language of Empire, a Quotidian Tongue: The Uses of Nahuatl in Colonial New Spain." Special Issue. *Ethnohistory* 59, no. 4 (fall 2012).

Scott, James C. *Seeing Like a State: How Certain Schemes to Improve the Human Condition Have Failed*. New Haven, CT: Yale University Press, 1998.

Sebastián, Santiago. "Los libros de emblemas: Uso y difusión en Iberoamérica." In *Juegos de ingenio y agudeza: La pintura emblemática en la Nueva España*. Mexico City: Patronato del Museo Nacional de Arte-CONACULTA, 1994.

Sell, Barry, Louise Burkhart, and Elizabeth R. Wright, eds. *Nahuatl Theater*. 3 vols. Norman: University of Oklahoma Press, 2008.

Sellen, Adam T. "Estrategias de orientación en el valle de Tenancingo." In *Cartografía de tradición indígena: Mapas de mercedes de tierras siglos XVI y XVII*. Edited by Mercedes Montes de Oca, Dominique Raby, Salvador Reyes Equiguas, and Adam T. Sellen. Mexico City: UNAM/AGN, 2003.

Sendón, Pablo. "Los límites de la humanidad: El mito de los ch'ullpa en Marcapata (Quispecanchi), Perú." *Journal de la Société des Américanistes* 96, no. 2 (2010).

Serulnikov, Sergio. *Subverting Colonial Authority: Challenges to Spanish Rule in Eighteenth-Century Southern Andes*. Durham, NC: Duke University Press, 2003.

Silverblatt, Irene. "Imperial Dilemmas, the Politics of Kinship, and Inca Reconstructions of History." *Comparative Studies in Society and History* 30, no. 1 (1988): 83–102.

Smith, Mary Elizabeth. "Why the Second Codex Selden Was Painted." In *Caciques and Their People: A Volume in Honor of Ronald Spores*. Anthropological Papers No. 89. Edited by Joyce Marcus and Judith Francis Zeitlin. Ann Arbor, MI: Museum of Anthropology, 1994.

Solá, Miguel. *Historia del arte hispano-americano: Arquitectura, escultura, pintura y artes menores en la América española durante los siglos XVI, XVII y XVIII*. Colección Labor. Barcelona: Editorial Labor, 1935.

Solano, Francisco de. *Cedulario de tierras: Compilación de legislación agraria colonial (1497–1820)*. Mexico City: UNAM, 1984.

Solano, Francisco de, ed. *Cuestionarios para la formación de las Relaciones Geográficas de Indias: Siglos XVI–XIX*. Madrid: Consejo Superior de Investigaciones Científicas, Centro de Estudios Históricos, Departamento de Historia de América, 1988.

Sousa, Lisa. "The Devil and Deviance in Native Criminal Narratives from Early Mexico." *Americas* 59, no. 2 (October 2002): 161–79.

Spalding, Karen. *Huarochirí: An Andean Society under Inca and Spanish Rule*. Palo Alto, CA: Stanford University Press, 1984.

Spalding, Karen. "La otra cara de la reciprocidad." In *Incas e indios cristianos: Elites indígenas e identidades cristianas en los Andes Coloniales.* Edited by Jean-Jacques Decoster. Cuzco: Centro de Estudios Regionales Andinos Bartolomé de las Casas, 2002.

Spitler, Susan. "Nahua Intellectual Responses to the Spanish: The Incorporation of European Ideas into the Central Mexican Calendar." PhD diss., Tulane University, 2005.

Spores, Ronald. "Differential Response to Colonial Control among the Mixtecs and Zapotecs of Oaxaca." In *Native Resistance and the Pax Colonial in New Spain.* Edited by Susan Schroeder. Lincoln: University of Nebraska Press, 1998.

Stanzione, Vincent. *Rituals of Sacrifice: Walking the Face of the Earth on the Sacred Path of the Sun; A Journey through the Tz'utujil Maya World of Santiago Atitlán.* Albuquerque: University of New Mexico Press, 2003.

Stavig, Ward. *The World of Tupac Amaru: Conflict, Community and Identity in Colonial Peru.* Lincoln: University of Nebraska Press, 1999.

Stavig, Ward, and Ella Schmidt, eds. *The Tupac Amaru and Catarista Rebellions: An Anthology of Sources.* Indianapolis: Hackett Publishing Company, 2008.

Sullivan, Thelma D. *Documentos tlaxcaltecas del siglo XVI en lengua náhuatl.* Mexico City: UNAM/IAA, 1987.

Tavárez, David E. "La idolatría letrada: Un análisis comparativo de textos clandestinos rituales y devocionales en comunidades nahuas y zapotecas, 1613–1654." *Historia Mexicana* 49 (1999): 197–252.

Tavárez, David E. *The Invisible War: Indigenous Devotions, Discipline, and Dissent in Colonial Mexico.* Palo Alto, CA: Stanford University Press, 2011.

Taylor, Gerald, ed. *Ritos y tradiciones de Huarochirí: Manuscrito quechua de comienzos del siglo XVII.* Lima: Instituto de Estudios Peruanos/Instituto Francés de Estudios Andinos, 1987.

Taylor, Gerald, ed. *Ritos y tradiciones de Huarochirí.* 2nd ed. Lima: Instituto Francés de Estudios Andinos, Banco Central de Reserva del Perú, Universidad Particular Ricardo Palma, 1999.

Taylor, Gerald. "Camac, camay y camasca en el manuscrito quechua de Huarochirí." In *Camac, camay y camasca y otros ensayos sobre Huarochirí y Yauyos.* Lima: Instituto Francés de Estudios Andinos, 2000.

Taylor, William B. *Magistrates of the Sacred: Priests and Parishioners in Eighteenth-Century Mexico.* Palo Alto, CA: Stanford University Press, 1996.

Tedlock, Dennis, trans. *Popol Vuh: The Definitive Edition of the Mayan Book of the Dawn of Life and the Glories of Gods and Kings.* New York: Simon and Schuster, 1985.

Tedlock, Dennis. *2000 Years of Mayan Literature.* Berkeley: University of California Press, 2011.

Terraciano, Kevin. "Native Expressions of Piety in Mixtec Testaments." In *Dead Giveaways: Indigenous Testaments of Mesoamerica and the Andes.* Edited by Susan Kellogg and Matthew Restall. Salt Lake City: University of Utah Press, 1998.

Terraciano, Kevin. "Crime and Culture in Colonial Mexico: The Case of the Mixtec Murder Note." *Ethnohistory* 45, no. 4 (1998): 709–45.

Terraciano, Kevin. *The Mixtecs of Colonial Oaxaca: Ñudzahui History, Sixteenth through Eighteenth Centuries*. Palo Alto, CA: Stanford University Press, 2001.

Thomason, Sarah G. *Contact Languages: A Wider Perspective*. Amsterdam: J. Benjamins, 1997.

Tibón, Gutierre. "El corazón de la luna." *Artes de México* 59 (2002): 46–50.

Timberlake, Marie. "The Painted Colonial Image: Jesuit and Andean Fabrication of History in Matrimonio de García de Loyola and Ñusta Beatriz." *Journal of Medieval and Early Modern Studies* 29, no. 3 (1999): 563–98.

Torre Villar, Enrique de la. "Estudio crítico en torno de los catecismos y cartillas como instrumentos de evangelización." In *Doctrina Christiana*. Mexico City: Centro de Estudios Históricos fray Bernardino de Sahagún, 1981.

Torre Villar, Ernesto de la. *Las congregaciones de los pueblos de indios: Fase terminal*. Mexico City: UNAM, 1995.

Torres Saldamando, Enrique, Pablo Patrón, and Nicanor Boloña, eds. *Libro primero de cabildos de Lima*. 3 vols. Paris: Paul Dupont, 1888.

Tovar, Virginia, and Juan Martín González. *El arte del barroco*. Madrid: Taurus, 1990.

Townsend, Camilla. "'What in the World Have You Done to Me, My Lover': Sex, Servitude and Politics among the Pre-Conquest Nahuas as Seen in the *Cantares Mexicanos*." *Americas* 62, no. 3 (2006): 349–89.

Townsend, Camilla. *Malintzin's Choices: An Indian Woman in the Conquest of Mexico*. Albuquerque: University of New Mexico Press, 2006.

Townsend, Camilla. "Glimpsing Native American Historiography: The Cellular Principle in Sixteenth-Century Nahuatl Annals." *Ethnohistory* 56, no. 4 (2009): 625–50.

Townsend, Camilla. *Here in This Year: Seventeenth-Century Nahuatl Annals of the Tlaxcala-Puebla Valley*. Palo Alto, CA: Stanford University Press, 2010.

Townsend, Camilla. "Don Juan Buenaventura Zapata y Mendoza and the Notion of a Nahua Identity." In *The Conquest All over Again: Nahuas and Zapotecs Thinking, Writing, and Painting Spanish Colonialism*. Eastbourne, UK: Sussex Academic Press, 2010.

Townsend, Richard F. *The Aztecs*. London: Thames and Hudson, 2000.

Trejo, Leopoldo. "Los espacios de la selva: Territorialidad zoque 'chima' de San Miguel Chimalapa." In *Diálogos con el territorio: Simbolizaciones sobre el espacio en las culturas indígenas de México*. Edited by Alicia Barabas. Mexico City: INAH, 2003.

Urton, Gary. *Signs of the Inka Khipu: Binary Coding in the Andean Knotted-String Records*. Austin: University of Texas Press, 2003.

Urton, Gary. "Khipu Archives: Duplicate Accounts and Identity Labels in the Inka Knotted String Cords." *Latin American Antiquity* 16, no. 2 (2005): 147–67.

Urton, Gary, and Carrie J. Brezine. "Khipu Typologies." In *Their Way of Writing: Scripts, Signs, and Pictographies in Pre-Columbian America*, edited by Elizabeth H. Boone. Washington, DC: Dumbarton Oaks, 2011.

Urton, Gary, and Jeffrey Quilter, eds. *Narrative Threads: Accounting and Recounting in Andean Khipu*. Austin: University of Texas Press, 2002.

Valero de García Lascuráin, Ana Rita. *Solares y conquistadores: Orígenes de la propiedad en la ciudad de México*. Mexico City: INAH, 1991.

Van Deusen, Nancy. *Between the Sacred and the Worldly: The Institutional and Cultural Practice of Recogimiento in Colonial Lima.* Palo Alto, CA: Stanford University Press, 2001.

Van Deusen, Nancy. "Circuits of Knowledge among Women in Early Seventeenth-Century Lima." In *Gender, Race and Religion in the Colonization of the Americas.* Edited by Nora E. Jaffary. Aldershot, UK: Ashgate, 2007.

Vargas Ugarte, Rubén, ed. *Concilios Limenses (1551–1772).* 3 vols. Lima, 1951.

Vargas Ugarte, Rubén, ed. *Historia de la Compañía de Jesús en el Perú.* 4 vols. Burgos, Spain: Imprenta de Aldecoa, 1963–65.

Velazco, Salvador. "La imaginación historiográfica de Fernando de Alva Ixtlilxochitl." *Colonial Latin American Review* 7, no. 1 (1998).

Viesca Treviño, Carlos. "Los médicos indígenas ante la medicina europea." In *Historia general de la medicina en México.* Edited by F. Martínez Cortés. Mexico City: UNAM, 1984.

Viesca Treviño, Carlos. *Medicina prehispánica de México: El conocimiento médico de los nahuas.* Mexico City: Panorama Editorial, 1986.

Villamarín, Juan A., and Judith E. Villamarín. "Kinship and Inheritance among the Sabana de Bogotá Chibcha at the Time of Spanish Conquest." *Ethnology* 14, no. 2 (1975): 173–79.

Villanueva Urteaga, Horacio. "La Compañía de Jesús en el Cuzco." *Revista Universitaria* 97 (1949): 271–99.

Voigt, Lisa. "Peregrine Peregrinations: Rewriting Travel and Discovery in Mestizo Chronicles of New Spain." *Revista de Estudios Hispánicos* 40, no. 1 (2006): 3–24.

Wachtel, Nathan. "The Mitimas of the Cochabamba Valley: The Colonization Policy of Huayna Capac." In *The Inka and Aztec States, 1400–1800: Anthropology and History.* Edited by George Collier, Renato Rosaldo, and John Wirth. New York: Academic Press, 1982.

Wake, Eleanor. "Actualización del texto de la geografía sagrada: El caso de *altepetl* Cuauhtinchan." In *Cultural Change in 16th Century Mexico.* Vienna: University of Vienna, 2002.

Wake, Eleanor. "Desde el centro de la iglesia a los cuatro vientos: A Tentative Reading of Two Glyphs from the Drawings of the Primordial Titles of Central Mexico." Presentation at 53rd *International Congress of Americanists*, Mexico City, 2009.

Wake, Eleanor. *Framing the Sacred: The Indian Churches of Early Colonial Mexico.* Norman: University of Oklahoma Press, 2010.

Walker, Charles. *Smoldering Ashes: Cuzco and the Creation of Republican Peru, 1780–1840.* Durham, NC: Duke University Press, 1999.

Wichmann, Soren, and Ilona Heijnen. "Un manuscrito en náhuatl sobre astrología europea." In *XV Congreso Internacional de AHILA: Crisis y Problemas en el Mundo Atlántico.* Edited by Raymond Buve, Neeske Ruitenbeek, and Marianne Wiesebron. Leiden: University of Leiden, 2008.

Wood, Stephanie. "The Cosmic Conquest: Late-Colonial Views of the Sword and Cross in Central Mexican Títulos." *Ethnohistory* 38, no. 2 (1991): 176–95.

Wood, Stephanie. "The Ajusco Town Founding Document: Affinities with Documents of the Sixteenth Century." In *Códices y documentos sobre México: Segundo simposio*. Edited by Salvador Rueda Smithers, Constanza Vega Sosa, and Rodrigo Martínez Baracs. Mexico City: INAH-CONACULTA, 1997.

Wood, Stephanie. "El problema de la historicidad de los títulos y los códices del grupo Techialoyan." In *De tlacuilos y escribanos: Estudios sobre documentos indígenas coloniales del centro de México*. Edited by Xavier Noguez and Stephanie Wood. Zamora: El Colegio de Michoacán/El Colegio Mexiquense, 1998.

Wood, Stephanie. "Testaments and Títulos: Conflict and Coincidence of Cacique and Community Interests." In *Dead Giveaways: Indigenous Testaments of Colonial Mesoamerica and the Andes*. Edited by Susan Kellogg and Matthew Restall. Salt Lake City: University of Utah Press, 1998.

Wood, Stephanie. "The Social vs. Legal Context of Nahuatl Títulos." In *Native Traditions in the Postconquest World*. Edited by Elizabeth H. Boone and Thomas B. F. Cummins. Washington, DC: Dumbarton Oaks, 1998.

Wood, Stephanie. *Transcending Conquest: Nahua Views of Spanish Colonial Mexico*. Norman: University of Oklahoma Press, 2003.

Wuffarden, Luis Eduardo. "La descendencia real y el 'renacimiento inca' en el virreinato." In *Los incas, reyes del Perú*. Edited by Natalia Majluf. Lima: Banco de Crédito, 2005.

Yannakakis, Yanna. "The 'Indios Conquistadores' of Oaxaca's Sierra Norte: From Indian Conquerors to Local Indians." In *Indian Conquistadors: Indigenous Allies in the Conquest of Mesoamerica*. Edited by Laura Matthew and Michel Oudijk. Norman: University of Oklahoma Press, 2007.

Yannakakis, Yanna. *The Art of Being In-Between: Native Intermediaries, Indian Identity, and Local Rule in Colonial Oaxaca*. Durham, NC: Duke University Press, 2008.

Yannakakis, Yanna. "Costumbre: A Language of Negotiation in Eighteenth-Century Oaxaca." In *Negotiation within Domination: New Spain's Indian Pueblos Confront the Spanish State*, edited by Ethelia Ruiz Medrano and Susan Kellogg. Boulder: University Press of Colorado, 2010.

Yoneda, Keiko. *Los mapas de Cuauhtinchan y la historia cartográfica prehispánica*. Mexico City: Fondo de Cultura Económica, 1991.

Yoneda, Keiko. *Mapa de Cuauhtinchan, Núm. 2*. Mexico City: CIESAS/Miguel Angel Porrúa, 2005.

Zapata y Mendoza, don Juan Buenaventura. *Historia chronológica de la noble ciudad de Tlaxcala*. Edited by Luis Reyes García and Andrea Martínez Baracs. Tlaxcala: Universidad Autónoma de Tlaxcala, 1995.

Zuidema, R. Tom. *The Ceque System of Cuzco: The Social Organization of the Capital of the Inca*. Leiden: E. J. Brill, 1964.

Contributors

ELIZABETH HILL BOONE holds the Martha and Donald Robertson Chair of Latin American Art at Tulane University. She is the author of many articles and books about Mesoamerican art and pictographic writing, including most recently Elizabeth Hill Boone and Gary Urton, editors, *Their Way of Writing: Scripts, Signs, and Pictographies in Pre-Columbian America* (2011).

KATHRYN BURNS is Professor of History at the University of North Carolina, Chapel Hill. She is the author of *Colonial Habits: Convents and the Spiritual Economy of Cuzco, Peru* (Duke University Press, 1999); and *Into the Archive: Writing and Power in Colonial Peru* (Duke University Press, 2010).

JOHN CHARLES is Associate Professor in the Department of Spanish and Portuguese at Tulane University. He is the author of numerous articles on the Andean Church, and the book *Allies at Odds: The Andean Church and Its Indigenous Agents, 1583–1671* (2010).

ALAN DURSTON is Associate Professor in the History Department at York University in Toronto. He is the author of articles and book chapters on the history of language in the Andes, and of the book *Pastoral Quechua: The History of Christian Translation in Colonial Peru, 1550–1650* (2007).

MARÍA ELENA MARTÍNEZ is Associate Professor of Latin American History and American Studies and Ethnicity at the University of Southern California. Martínez's publications include a number of articles on space, religion, gender, and race in New Spain as well as the book *Genealogical Fictions: Limpieza de Sangre, Religion, and Gender in Colonial Mexico* (2008).

TRISTAN PLATT is Professor of History and Anthropology at the University of St. Andrews. His recent publications include (editor), "Número especial en memoria del Dr. John V Murra," *Chungará Revista de Antropología Chilena* 42, no. 1 (2010); and "'From the Island's Point of View': Warfare and Transformation in an Andean Vertical Archipelago," *Journal de la Société des Américanistes* 95, no. 2 (2010).

GABRIELA RAMOS is University Lecturer in Latin American History and Fellow and College Lecturer at Newnham College at the University of Cambridge, UK. She is the author of many articles and books on the colonial Andes, including most recently *Death and Conversion in the Andes: Lima and Cuzco, 1532–1670* (2010).

SUSAN SCHROEDER is France Vinton Scholes Professor of Colonial Latin American History, emerita, at Tulane University. She is the editor and translator with Arthur J. O. Anderson of the *Codex Chimalpahin* and the general editor and translator of the series *Chimalpahin*, as well as the author of numerous works about native intellectuals, religion, resistance, women, and most recently indigenous perspectives of the Spanish conquest of Mexico, including *Chimalpahin's Conquest* (2010).

JOHN F. SCHWALLER is Professor of History at the University at Albany (formerly SUNY Albany). His works include studies of the Catholic Church in sixteenth-century Mexico and the use of Nahuatl, the Aztec language, in the evangelization of Mexico. His most recent book is *The History of the Catholic Church in Latin America* (2011).

CAMILLA TOWNSEND is Professor of History at Rutgers University. She is the author of several books, most recently *Malintzin's Choices: An Indian Woman in the Conquest of Mexico* (2006); and *Here in This Year: Seventeenth-Century Nahuatl Annals of the Tlaxcala-Puebla Valley* (2010).

ELEANOR WAKE (1948–2013) was Lecturer in Latin American Cultural Studies, and Associate Research Fellow, Department of Iberian and Latin American Studies, Birkbeck College, University of London. Her recent publications include "The Serpent Road: Iconic Encoding and the Historical Narrative of *Mapa de Cuauhtinchan No. 2*," in David Carrasco and Scott Sessions, editors, *Cave, City and Eagle's Nest: An Interpretative Journey through the Mapa de Cuauhtinchan No. 2* (2007); and *Framing the Sacred: The Indian Churches of Early Colonial Mexico* (2010).

YANNA YANNAKAKIS is Associate Professor of History at Emory University. Her recent publications include *The Art of Being In-Between: Native Intermediaries, Indian Identity, and Local Rule in Colonial Oaxaca* (Duke University Press, 2008); and "Allies or Servants? The Journey of Indian Conquistadors in the Lienzo of Analco," *Ethnohistory* 58, no. 4 (fall 2011).

Index

Page numbers followed by *f* indicate a figure; those with t indicate a table.

caciques (hereditary elites), 24, 56n4, 260n66; alliances with priests of, 92; as cultural intermediaries, 61–63, 72; recognition by the Crown of, 174–75; succession system of, 176–77

caciques apoderados movement, 274

Cajonos Rebellion, 81–82

Calancha, Antonio de la, 3

Calderón de la Barca, Pedro, 51

Callha, Esteban, 259n61

Camacguacho, Gabriel, 71

Canchoguaman, Gerónimo, 156, 160

Canger, Una, 99n5

Capilla de San Josef (Mexico City), 108, 118

Capuy, Martín, 36n15

Carbajal, Agustín, 273

Cardenas, Margarita de, 102n31

Carhuachin Pariasca, Cristóbal, 73

Carhua Mango, Felipe, 73–74

Carlos V, Holy Roman Emperor, King of Spain. See Charles V

Carochi, Horacio, 51–52, 54

Casa de Santa Cruz (Lima), 65, 71, 76n19

casas de recogimiento, 32–33, 38n33

Castillo, Cristóbal del, 108

Castillo Ecaxoxouhqui, Josef del, 114

Castro, García de, 265

Catholic Church. See religious practices; names of specific orders, e.g., Jesuits

celestially defined maps. See mapmaking

Celis, Joseph de, 90–97

Cerrón-Palomino, Rodolfo, 159

Chalchiuhnenetzin, Queen, 115, 128n45, 129n47

Chambilla, Diego, 265

Chanca Topa, Gerónimo, 248–50

Chance, John, 101n20

Charles, John, 240, 250, 259n53, 269

Charles V, Holy Roman Emperor, King of Spain, 124, 184–85, 190, 226

Chaucaguaman, Martín, 37n26

Chaupiñamca, 161–62

Chavero, Alfredo, 148n14

Chaves, Nicolás de, 100n15

Chavín Palpa, Francisco, 71

Chicomoztoc Aztlan, 109

Chilcuetzin Matlaltzin, Queen, 116

Chimallaxotzin, 111, 127n19

Chimalman, 110–11, 127n16

Chimalpahin Quauhtlehuanitzin, Domingo de San Antón Muñón, xiii, 6, 13, 46, 47, 107–10, 136; accounts of women by, 109–25, 126n6; Nahua audience of, 108; oeuvre of, 109; royal ancestry of, 120–21, 124, 127n24; sources of, 108–9, 125n1

Chimalpilli the younger, King, 123

Chimbo Quipe, Inés, 38n33

Chinantec, 83

Chinchi, Fernando, 271

Chipaya, 275n15

Chocata, Juan, 275n8

Choquecasa, Cristóbal, 13–14, 151–66; anti-idolatry work of, 152; on huacas, 156–62, 166n3; as Huarochirí Manuscript author, 153–56, 165–66, 167n12, 275n14; language use by, 159–60; lineage of, 156, 165; spelling variants of, 166n1

Christianity. See religious practices

Chuircho, Juan Enriquez, 15n9

Chumpica, Juan, 269

Chupica, Antonio, 63, 65–70; education of, 65–66; legal disputes of, 67–68, 70, 77n31; religious duties of, 66–67, 77n30

Clanchy, Michael T., 239

Coanachoch, 41

Coatepec, Sultepec (México) map, 209f, 219–20, 221

Codex Fejérváry, 218

Codex Mendoza, 5, 264

Codex Mexicanus, 215

Codex Xolotl, 45

Códice Matritense del Palacio Real, 221–22, 235n73

Códice Techialoyan García Granados, 184–89, 200n35

Cohuazacatzin, King, 123

Colegio de Príncipe (Lima), 61–74; building of, 65, 75n4; enrollment at, 62, 73, 75n9, 76n19; legal disputes of graduates of, 68–74; native elite support for, 65–66; tuition at, 75n11

Colegio de San Francisco de Borja (Cuzco), 61, 71

Colegio de San Francisco Tlaltelolco (Mexico), 8

colegios (schools), 8–10, 31, 61. See also education

commensuration, 88–97, 103n47

and, 9–10, 49–52, 54–55, 85; Jesuit education and, 60–63, 74; nurturing approaches to, 65

Eve, 110

extirpation of idolatries, 50–51, 65, 268–69, 276n24; Avila's role in, 152, 153–54, 160; Jews and, 119–20; prosecutions in, 66–67, 71–73, 77n30; punishments in, 67, 73–74, 120; in Villa Alta (Oaxaca), 81–82

Feierman, Steven, 2

Ferdinand II, King of Aragón, 124, 130n105

Feria, Pedro de, 85, 101n29

fiscal de la idolatría, 66–67

fiscales (indigenous priest's assistants), 91, 135, 240. *See also* notaries/notarial writing

Florentine Codex (Sahagún et al.), 8

Flores Caja Malqui, Rodrigo, 69–70

Franciscans, 108, 118. *See also* religious practices

Galvin codex (Murúa), 164

Gamarra, Francisco, 73

Garcilaso de la Vega, Inca, 176, 250

Garibay, Angel María, 51

gender, 12; of Conquest-era intellectuals, xi; education and, 37n26; in genealogical lines of succession, 12, 178–79, 201n46, 270–71; in oral history transmission practices, 175; of precolonial sages, ix

genealogies, 12, 173–97, 268–69; Christian imagery in, 192–93; European linear style of, 198n6, 272; female lineage in, 12, 178–79, 201n46, 270–71; heraldry styles in, 179–82; Incan imagery in, 187–95, 200n37, 201n42; male lines in, 178–79, 270–71; *nopal* (prickly pear) images in, 184, 185–89f, 200n31; oral histories of, 175; in pictographic script, 175–76, 198n15; of the preconquest era, 174; *quipus/khipus* records of, 175–76; of royal Mexicas, 110–12, 196; social and political significance of, 174–81, 192, 194–97; in *títulos primordiales* of indigenous rulers, 182–90, 192, 194–95, 200n31; transformation under Spanish rule of, 174–82, 199n25; in written *relaciones geográficas*, 176

General History of the Things of New Spain (Sahagún), ix, 3

General Interpreters, 11, 26–29; official status of, 99n2; sociopolitical significance of, 34–35, 36n19, 80–88, 100nn13–14

Germana, Queen of Aragón, 124

godcarriers, 110–11, 127n16

Gómez, Josef, 118

Gómez de León, Juan, 37n27

Gonzalbo Aizpuru, Pilar, 37n26

González Echeverría, Roberto, 267

González Holguín, Diego, 64, 255n3

Gramsci, Antonio, 1–2, 197n1, 268, 272

Grande, Juan, 42, 43, 56n5

Greaves, Nigel, 272

Gualpanina, Diego, 252, 254–55

Guaman Poma de Ayala, Felipe, 7, 14, 151, 164–66, 176, 265; apprenticeship with Murúa of, 164; family background of, 165; on *quilcaycamayocs*, 237, 238f, 245, 246f, 252–53; on Spanish-language literacy, 241–42, 255, 256n23; on Spanish record-keeping practices, 239–40; travels of, 165

Guamantica Francisco, 251

Guaraní, 64

Guide to Confession Large and Small (B. de Alva), 49–52

Gutiérrez de Melo, Lucas, 37n24

Guzmán Rupay Chagua, Rodrigo de, 69, 73

Hanks, William, 88

Haskett, Robert, 228

healing knowledge, 3–4, 15n10

heraldry, 179–82, 228

Historia chichimeca (Alva Ixtlilxochitl), 45

Historia de los señores chichimecos (Alva Ixtlilxo-chitl), 45

histories/historians: in Chimalpahin's work on the Nahua, 107–25; in Choquecasa's *Huarochirí Manuscript*, 6–7, 13–14, 151–66, 275n14; European chronological style of, 43, 47, 58n24; genealogies and, 177, 196; government records and, xi, 13–14; of Guaman Poma de Ayala, 7, 14, 151, 164–66; of the Lienzo de Tlaxcala, 133–35, 181f; oral performance traditions of, 136, 148n12, 175, 198n15; of

knowledge, 3–8. *See also* ideological knowledge; pragmatic knowledge

Krug, Frances, 148n13, 148n14

kurakas (hereditary elites), 24–26, 174–75, 193, 240, 245, 254–55

landholding: antiquity of possession and, 205; celestially defined boundaries in *títulos primordiales* and, 202–5, 259n61; *composiciones de tierras* program and, 225, 226, 251–52, 259n59; *congregaciones* programs and, 224–25, 236n85; of indigenous common lands, 224–25, 226; law of 1530 on, 204, 225, 230; local-level disputes over, 242; *mercedes* maps and, 205–17, 221, 225, 228–30, 232n19; Spanish pressure on, 222–25, 226, 230, 235nn75–76; surveys of uncultivated lands and, 226. *See also* mapmaking

language policies, 5–6, 10–11. *See also* court interpreters; education; notaries/notarial writing; translation of written works; writing

legal agents, 97–98

legal system, 7–8, 79; criminal cases in, 86; designated Spanish positions in, 242; indigenous use of, 62–63, 68–74, 77n31, 258n51, 268; local-level disputes in, 242–45, 252; mapmaking and, 202–5, 217; *memorias* in, 92–97; multilingual functionaries of, 82–83, 240–41; recordkeeping in, 242–45; *Sala de Crimen* in, 224; Toledo's limitations on access to, 224, 242–44, 248, 252, 255, 261; translator networks in, 79–98; women's use of, 118. *See also* notaries/notarial writing

Leibsohn, Dana, 6

León Pinelo, Diego de, 72

letrados (as term), 2, 14n3

Lettered City (Rama), 267

The Lettered Mountain (Salomon and Niño-Murcia), 273

Levillier, Roberto, 257n38

libraries, ix–xi, 108

Lienzo de Tlaxcala, 133–35, 181*f*

ligaduras (hair knots), 175

Lima (Peru), 21–22, 24–30; census of 1613 of, 25–26; as colonial administrative center, 23–24, 34–35; Incan genealogies in, 193–94; traditional indigenous authority in, 24–25

lineage. *See* genealogies

literacy skills, x–xi, 2, 4–8, 261–74; of Andean interpreters, 27–28; of Andean *quilcaycamayocs*, 240–42, 245, 246*f*, 255, 256n18, 256n23; of indigenous pictographic script, xi, 5–7; Toledo's program in, 241–42, 257nn38–39. *See also* education; indigenous languages; Spanish language; writing

litigation. *See* legal system

Little Dipper, 222, 235nn72–73

Llocllayhuancupa, 157–58, 160

Lobo Guerrero, Bartolomé, 65, 71

Lockhart, James, 16n21, 159, 199n25, 240, 254, 257n41, 258n51

Lope de Vega Carpio, Félix Arturo, 51

López, María, 118

Lopez de Cepeda, Juan, 270

López de Gómara, Francisco, 117

Loyola, Martín de, 191*f*, 192

lunar signs, 206, 217–21, 228, 232n21, 233n38

Macas, Luis, 73–74

Mais, Pedro, 67

Maíz, Pedro, 26–27

Maldonado de Torres, Alonso, 259n59

Malinalxoch, 116–17

Malintzin, 117–18, 129n62

Mallku, 265, 269

Manco Capac, 192

Mannheim, Bruce, 167n12

Manual breve y conpendioso para enpezar a aprender Lengua Zapoteca y administrar en case de necesidad (Martínez), 89–90

Mapa de Cuauhtinchan, 175

Mapa Quinatzin, 45

Mapa Tlotzin, 45

mapmaking, 202–30, 263; celestial boundaries in *títulos primordiales* and, 202–5, 225–28, 230, 231n4, 231nn6–8; chronology of, 216*t*, 224–25, 230, 235n81; cosmological symbols in, 203, 209–17, 228–30, 231nn7–8, 232n11, 232nn18–21, 233n35; directional wind heads and

mapmaking (*continued*)
  compasses in, 215, 229, 236n108; European cardinal directions in, 205, 209, 214–15, 217, 229; geographical context of, 222–24, 229–30, 235nn75–76; indigenous geographic orientation in, 214–17; *mercedes* corpus of, 205–17, 225, 228–30, 232n19; pictorial traditions in, 207, 225; solar and lunar images in, 206, 217–21, 220*f*, 228, 232n21, 233n38
maps, 12–13; of the Andes, xvi; of Mexico, xv; of Villa Alta, Oaxaca, 80, 84
Marcos, Juan, 87
Margarita of Austria, Queen of Spain, 112
marriage alliances, 28
marriage images, 191*f*, 192–93
Martínez, Alonso, 89–90
Martínez, María Elena, 12, 264
Martínez Baracs, Andrea, 148n14
Matlalchihuatzin, 112
Maya, 10
Mayta Carrasco, Domingo, 38n33
McCormack, Sabine, 72–73
medicinal knowledge, 3–4, 15n10
"Memorial de Charcas," 245–47
memorias, 92–97
Méndez de Luna, Nicolás, 150n37
Mendoza, Antonio de, 5, 123, 130n102
Mendoza, Juan de, 70, 135
Mendoza, Magdalena de, 135
Mendoza Tlaltecatzin, Jacobo de, 47
Menegus Bornemann, Margarita, 226
mercedes maps, 203, 205–17, 225, 228–30, 232n19; chronological distribution of, 216t, 224–25, 230, 233n38; cosmological symbols in, 203, 209–22, 228–30; geographical distribution of, 222–24, 229–30, 235nn75–76. *See also* mapmaking
Mercury, 204–5, 231n7, 232n11
Mexicas: genealogy practices of, 174; original name of, 126n13; royal genealogy of, 110–12, 196
Mexico and Mesoamerica, xiii, 9–10; ancient calendar of, 108; Aztec tribute system in, 5; court interpreters in, 11, 44, 48, 56, 79–98; decentralized municipalities of, 10, 23, 34, 263, 264; extirpation movement in, 81–82, 120; genealogy customs of, 173–90, 192, 194–97; indige-

nous histories of, 6, 13, 39, 43, 45–48, 53–54; indigenous languages of, 261–62; libraries of, 108; map of, xi; Nahuatl as *lingua franca* in, 84–87; preconquest Triple Alliance in, 40, 84, 223–24, 228; royal lines of, 110–12, 120–25, 126n9, 130n100; *títulos primordiales* of indigenous nobles in, 182–90, 192, 194–95, 200n31; urban centers of, 22–23; Zapata's histories of, 132–47. *See also* Nahua/Nahuatl
Miccacalcatl Tlaltetecuintzin, King, 123
Mignolo, Walter, 5
Mills, Kenneth, 158
Mira de Améscuq, Antonio, 51
missionaries. *See* evangelization
Mixe people: iconic reputation of, 87, 102n38; language use of, 83, 85–88, 98, 102n39; pictorial genealogies of, 175
Miztliyauhtzin, Queen, 116
Moquihuixtli, King, 115, 123
Morales, Evo, 277n37
Moteuczoma, Francisca de, 121, 122*f*
Moteuczoma, Isabel de, 121–22
Moteuczoma Xocoyotl, Emperor, 112, 113*f*, 122*f*; daughters of, 119, 121, 128n45; wives of, 121–22
Movement to Socialism (MAS), 277n37
Movimiento Nacionalista Revolucionario (MNR), 273–74
municipal councils, 9
Muñoz Camargo, Diego, 46, 47, 138, 149n17
Murúa, Martín de, 164, 176, 254, 260n70
musical instruments, 136, 148n10
Myth and Archive (González Echeverría), 267

Nahua/Nahuatl: alphabetic annals of, 135, 148n7; Alva's translations into, 49–55, 59n40; Carochi's language scholarship of, 51–52, 54; ceremonial weeping of, 142, 149n29; Chimalpahin's histories of, 107–25; court interpreter use of, 83–88, 98; directional terms in, 218–19; genealogy practices of, 173–82; histories and historians of, 6, 13, 39, 43, 45–48, 53–54, 126n6; as indigenous *lingua franca*, 84–87, 101n24, 263; intermarriages with Spanish of, 42; literature and theater of, 51; mapmaking practices of, 202–30;

noble sources (*tlatoque*) of, 136, 137–40, 144–47; notarial writing of, 240, 257n41; pictorial manuscripts in, 108–9, 198n15; political structure of, 133–34; religious practices of, 50–51, 58n34; royal women of, 110–12, 120–25, 126n9, 130n100; Spanish acquisition of, 85–86; *títulos primordiales* in, 203, 231n6; women's histories and, 109–25, 126n6; yearly accounts of, 134–35, 136, 148n13; Zapata's histories of, 132–47

Nahuas after the Conquest (Lockhart), 199n25

Napoleon, 193–94

Ñaupa Conchoy, Diego, 251, 259n57

Navas Pereleda, Francisco de, 42, 44

networks of knowledge, xiii, 27, 28, 36n19, 79–98. *See also* court interpreters; notaries/notarial writing

New Spain. *See* Mexico

Nezahualcoyotl, King, 39–42, 45, 53, 55; in Alva Ixtlilxochitl's histories, 47–48; in indigenous ballads, 59n41

Nezahualcoyotzin, King, 112, 113*f*

Nezahualpilli, King, 39–42, 55, 114; in Alva Ixtlilxochitl's histories, 47–48; daughters of, 128n42

Niño-Murcia, Mercedes, 273

nopal (prickly pear) images, 184, 185–89*f*

North Star. *See* Polaris

notaries/notarial writing, 24, 27–28, 30, 66, 237; court interpretation roles of, 86; creation of archives by, 248–55, 261–65; educational role of, 37n26; *memorias* produced by, 92–97; as *mestizo* position, 30, 37n27; of Nahua, 240; native language usage in, 81; official government responsibilities of, 242–47, 258n51, 262–63; official use of Spanish in, 5–6, 10–11, 29, 34–35, 240–45, 246*f*, 255, 263, 265–66; parish duties of, 240, 247–48, 250, 255n15, 257n37, 259n53; in pueblos, 250–55, 258n44; by *quilcaycamayocs*, 237–55, 261–65; *quipus/khipus* records of, 6, 29, 240–41, 243–44, 254, 256n21, 257n42, 260nn69–70, 261–66; of tribute records, 5–6, 262; of wills, 243–44, 250, 257n35, 257n41

Noticias de los pobladores (Alva Ixtlilxochitl), 45

Nueva corónica y buen gobierno (Guaman Poma), 237

Ñusta, Beatriz Clara Coya, 191*f*, 192–93

Oaxaca, 79–82

O'Gorman, Edmundo, 43

Ojeda Quauhcececuitzin, Juan de, 124

older sister roles, 111, 115–18

Olivera, Pedro de, 252

oral histories, 136, 148n12, 175, 198n15

Ordenanzas of 1565 (Castro), 265

Ordinances of Nezahualcoyotl, 45

organic intellectuals, 268–69

Osorio, Antonio de, 250

Ospicha y Medellín (Veracruz) map, 208*f*, 215

Otlaspa and Sta. María Estancia, Tula (Hidalgo) map, 208*f*, 220–21

Oudijk, Michel, 99n5

Pachacuti Inca Yupanqui, 174, 263, 271, 275n8

Pacheco de Silva, Francisco, 85, 90, 95, 101n29

Páez, Juan, 114

Paniagua de Loaysa, Gabriel, 250

Paredes, Petronila de, 136

Paria, Sebastián, 258n44

Pariacaca, 161–62

Pas, Francisco de, 92–95

Paullu, Inka, 264

Pérez Bocanegra, Juan, 247

Pérez Pereleda, Juan de, 41*f*, 42, 49, 57n7

Peru. *See* the Andes

Petrucci, Armando, 240

Philip II, King of Spain, 64, 85, 224, 226, 271

Philip III, King of Spain, 61, 112, 237, 241

Philip IV, King of Spain, 72

pictographic texts, ix, xi, 5–7, 10, 15nn12–13, 217; of genealogical information, 175–76, 198n15; of historical sources, 108–9; in micropatriotic boosterism, 12; Spanish attitudes toward, 6–7, 225. *See also* mapmaking

pipiltin (noble offspring), 133–35, 147

Pizarro, Francisco, 23, 29

Pizarro, Gonzalo, 264, 271

Pizarro, Hernando, 263–64

Plata, Juan de la, 67
Plaza, Juan de la, 63–64
Polaris (North Star), 206, 209, 215, 218, 221–22, 229, 232n20
pole stars, 206, 209, 215, 218, 221–22
Poloni-Simard, Jacques, 260n66
Poole, Stafford, 126n11
Popocatzin, King, 123
Popol vuh, 202, 231n8
Potosí mita, 261, 263–74; indigenous agency in, 269–74; *lenguas generales* in, 266; Toledo's tribute system in, 264–65; tributes paid in, 271, 277n37
pragmatic knowledge, xi, 1–2, 3–8, 267; local administrative records-keeping in, 5–8, 16n21; local transmission of, 9–11
preconquest era: Aztec Triple Alliance of, 40, 84, 223–24, 228; books and libraries of, ix–x; calendar of, 108; community leadership in, x–xi, 56n1; ethnic polities of, 10; founding stories of, 109–12, 126n11, 126n13, 154, 161–62, 204, 230n1, 272–73, 276n33; gender-neutral sages of, ix; genealogy practices of, 174; geographic distinctions in, xiii; poet-kings of Texcoco of, 39–42; record-keeping methods in, ix, xi, 5–7, 10, 12, 13, 15nn12–13, 22–23, 29, 108–9, 175–76; religious practices of, 6, 50–51, 58n34, 126n13; sages of, ix–xi, 3–4. *See also* the Andes; Mexico and Mesoamerica
Primer nueva corónica y buen gobierno (Guaman Poma), 14, 164–66
principales (authorities), 174–75, 240
Probanzas, 269
Pukina, 266
Puyputacma, Juan, 160, 169n45

Quahuitlan (Guerrero) map, 222
Quauhtemoc, King, 113f, 117, 122–23
Quauhtlehuanitzin, King, 116
Quechua, 9–11, 30, 263, 266; alphabetization of, 64; Avila's preaching in, 155; *Huarochirí Manuscript* in, 151–66; indigenous education in, 63–64; *quilcaycamayocs* and, 237–55; standardized *lengua general* of, 10–11, 28, 159, 168n39
Quetzalmaçatzin, King, 123
quilcaycamayocs (indigenous notaries), 6,

237–55, 255n3; creation of archives by, 248–55, 261–65; cultural mediation and agency of, 245, 252–55, 267–74; education of, 240, 245, 246f; legal responsibilities of, 242–48, 258n51; parish duties of, 240, 247–48, 250, 255n15, 257n37, 259n53; Spanish literacy of, 240–42, 245, 246f, 256n18, 256n23
quipucamayocs (cord keepers), 5, 22–23, 35n1, 177, 262
quipus/khipus (knotted cord records), xi, 5, 22–23, 36n22, 169n51, 257n42, 261–64; as alternative literacy, 261–66; for counting, 275n6; of genealogies, 175–76; in notarial records, 6, 29, 240–41, 243–44, 254, 256n21, 260nn69–70; Spanish attitudes toward, 5–6, 23, 263, 265–66
Quispe, Pedro, 248–50
Quispe Amaro, Nicolás, 250
Quispe Condor, Pedro, 69
Quispe Ninavilca, Sebastián, 69

race, 24, 34–35
Rama, Angel, 253, 267
Ramos, Gabriela, 9, 11, 261–62
Ramos, Joseph, 81–85, 91, 97–98, 100n6, 100nn13–15
Rappaport, Joanne, 274n3
Real Audiencia, 11, 26–27. *See also* General Interpreters
record keeping. *See* notaries/notarial writing
regidores (councilmen), 242, 250
Relaciónes (Alva Ixtlilxochitl), 45, 232n19
Relaciones de méritos y servicios, 269
relaciónes de parte y de oficio, 44, 57n16
Relaciones geográficas, 176, 224, 234n65
Relación sucinta (Alva Ixtlilxochitl), 45
religious practices: of *casas de recogimiento*, 32–33, 38n33; of indigenous peoples, 63, 65, 155; Jesuit education in, 63–65; of nuns and beatas, 119, 120; of ordination, 49, 58n27, 64, 65; of preconquest era, 6, 50–51, 58n34, 126n13; race and gender factors in, 33, 37n32; translated pastoral guides for, 49–52, 54–55, 85, 88–97, 101n29, 247. *See also* education; evangelization; extirpation of idolatries
Rendón Ortiz, Gilberto, 218

theoretical knowledge. *See* ideological
knowledge
Título de Totonicapán, 180f
títulos primordiales (primordial titles):
boundaries maps in, 202–5, 225–28,
230, 231n4, 231nn6–8, 259n61; lineage
in, 182–90, 192, 194–95, 200n31; origins
of, 226
Tiztla (Guerrero) map, 207f
Tlacocihuatzin, Queen, 121
Tlapalizquixotzin, Queen, 121, 122f
Tlaquilxochtzin, 111
tlatoque (noble rulers), 136, 137–40, 144–47
Tlaxcala: alliance with Spanish of, 136–37;
cabildos of, 133–35; Muñoz Camargo's
histories of, 138, 149n17; Spanish land
grants in, 222–25; Spanish repression in,
144–47, 150nn37–38, 150n46; Zapata's
histories of, 132–47. *See also* Zapata y
Mendoza, Juan Buenaventura
Tliltecatzin Yaotequihua, King, 116
Toçancoztli, King, 122
Tocto Coca, Isabel, 248
Toledo, Francisco de, 5, 11, 176, 192, 264,
270; administrative reforms of, 26; on
indigenous authorities, 245–47; limitations on indigenous litigation by, 224,
242–44, 248, 252, 255, 261; literacy program of, 241–42, 245, 246f, 257nn38–
39; on *quilcaycamayoc* responsibilities,
242–48, 259n53; *reducción* (land settlement) reforms by, 156, 241, 242; silver
mining system of, 264–65; tribute policies of, 265
Toltecatl, 123
Torres Rubio, Diego de, 64, 276n26
Totonicapán *título primordial*, 180f
Townsend, Camilla, 13, 46–47, 263
Toyaotzin, Juan Bautista, 114, 123
traditional intellectuals, 268–69
translatio imperii, 198n6, 264
translation of written works: by Bartolomé
de Alva, 49–53; commensuration process and, 88–97, 103n47; for Jesuit education, 64, 77n31; of pastoral guides,
49–52, 54–55, 85, 88–97, 101n29, 247.
See also court interpreters
Tratado de los evangelios (Avila), 155, 167n14
Tratado y relación (Avila), 153–54

tribute system, 271, 277n37; indigenous
forms of record keeping of, 5–6, 262;
violence and oppression of, 264–65
Triple Alliance, 40, 84, 223–24, 228
Túpac Amaru, 192
Túpac Amaru II, 193, 272–73
Tupia, Juan, 248–59
Tziuhtecatl, King, 116
Tziuhtlacauqui Yaopol Tzompahua, King,
116

Uchumataqu, 275n15
urban centers: administrative roles in,
25–27; of the Andes, 21–35; archives of,
248–50; *la ciudad letrada* of, 253; libraries
of, 108; of the preconquest era, 21–24;
transformed political landscape in,
23–30; of the Valley of Mexico, 40. *See
also* names of specific places, e.g., Cuzco
Uruquilla, 266

Valeriano, Antonio de, the younger, 123
Valley of Mexico, 40
Vargas, Juan de, 102n31
Vargas, Nicolás, 102n31
Vargas, Pablo de, 90–94
Vargas, Ramón de, 86, 102n31
Vargas Valdez, Alonso de, 259n59
vassalage pacts, 173, 174–75, 192, 197, 264
Vázquez, Antonio, 72
Vázquez, Juan, 65
Vera, Fernando de, 71
Verdugo Ixtlilxochitl, Francisca Cristina,
41f, 42
Verdugo Quetzalmamalintzin, Francisco,
41f, 42
Villa Alta, Oaxaca, 79–80, 98; court inter-
preters of, 81–83, 85–86, 100n6; demo-
graphic recovery in, 81–83; indigenous
language writing in, 81; languages of,
83–84; notarial documentation of, 99n5
Villagómez, Pedro de, 63, 67, 70–71
Vocabulario en Lengua Zapoteca (Córdoba), 89

Wake, Eleanor, 12–13, 263
Wars of Independence, 194, 273
Wayna Qhapaq, Inca, 263–64, 265
ways of knowing, 267. *See also* ideological
knowledge; pragmatic knowledge